The Curse

The Curse
THE COLORFUL & CHAOTIC HISTORY OF THE LA CLIPPERS

Mick Minas

Copyright © 2016 Mick Minas
All rights reserved.

ISBN: 1539148750
ISBN 13: 9781539148753
Library of Congress Control Number: 2016916899
CreateSpace Independent Publishing Platform
North Charleston, South Carolina

Dedicated to
Jae, Nash and Isaiah.

"I'm not a superstitious person and I don't believe in jinxes.
Bad things just happen.
Unfortunately, they happened to us every year."

Elgin Baylor

Contents

Foreword · xiii
Author's Note · xv

Prologue	The Start of Your Ending · · · · · · · · · · · · · · · · · ·	1
Chapter 1	An Unconventional Birth · · · · · · · · · · · · · · · · · ·	5
Chapter 2	The Homecoming ·	29
Chapter 3	The Don ·	55
Chapter 4	To Live and Die in LA ·	69
Chapter 5	If at First You Don't Succeed · · · · · · · · · · · · · · · ·	94
Chapter 6	Thank God for the 1973 Philadelphia 76ers · · · · · · · · ·	118
Chapter 7	If I Have to Play for the Clippers, Let's Just Forget the Whole Thing · · · · · · · · · · · · ·	157
Chapter 8	One Riot, Two Playoff Wins and Three Head Coaches ·	183
Chapter 9	The Curse is Broken? ·	205
Chapter 10	Things Fall Apart ·	227
Chapter 11	Life's a Fitch ·	241
Chapter 12	The Kandi Man Kan't ·	271
Chapter 13	Re-Branding Efforts ·	302
Chapter 14	The Kobe Circus ·	324
Chapter 15	Unchartered Waters ·	339
Chapter 16	One Step Forward, Two Steps Back · · · · · · · · · · · · · ·	369
Chapter 17	Betrayal ·	382

Chapter 18	A New Hope	400
Chapter 19	Everybody Loves Chris	425
Chapter 20	The Fish Rots from the Head	460
Chapter 21	There Are No Hollywood Endings Here	510
Epilogue	Some Things Change and Some Stay the Same	526
	Acknowledgements	535
	About the Authors	541

Foreword

My first email from Mick Minas informed me of his intention to write an historical narrative of the San Diego/Los Angeles Clippers. He was interested in interviewing me to glean some of my personal insights, based on my brief tenure as head coach of the team[1]. Admittedly, I was somewhat puzzled by the intrigue of this Australian writer who wanted to explore the turbulent history of this star-crossed franchise. At the very least, he seemed to be undertaking a daunting task, embarking on a journey with more twists and turns than a modern day roller coaster.

Mick's intent, or more accurately, his mission, was to dissect the inner workings of the team from countless different perspectives- players, coaches, front office personnel and media, all of whom had first-hand knowledge of the franchise. After tracking down and speaking with the various participants, his real challenge was to somehow weave this mass of information into an interesting story. Suffice to say that he has succeeded in admirable fashion- Mick has produced a great read.

I was actually the first head coach who was hired by Donald T. Sterling. To peg him as eccentric would be like referring to Manute Bol as a player with size[2]. Donald T. was truly one for the ages. Many of his idiosyncrasies were beyond description- carrying two telephones, dining at half-

---

1   143 games across one and half seasons.
2   Bol, one of my all-time favorite players, was 7'6" tall.

court during games, The Move, bounced checks and a never-sell-anything philosophy. If the human race were boarding Noah's Ark two at a time, he might be the only passenger in SINGLE file! Yes, that unique- and I honestly liked the man[3].

Over the past few years, the Clippers have enjoyed a meteoric rise. Unfortunately, this dramatic change in fortunes[4] has had a greater impact on the $$$$ column than the win column.

For many of the people involved, the experience of working for "The Clips" was unique unto itself. In chronicling these journeys, Mick has managed to create a book with mass appeal. One need not be an NBA or even a sports fan to enjoy it. Filled with plots and sub-plots that defy the imagination, a more appropriate subtitle might have been: *"You Can't Make This Stuff Up"*.

Welcome to Clipper-land.

Jim Lynam
September 2016

---

[3] Given the difficulties at the end of his tenure as the Clipper owner, I will state on the record that I never once heard him make a comment or statement that was in any way disparaging to ANY race or minority group.
[4] Pun intended.

Author's Note

THIS IS A BOOK ABOUT the history of the San Diego and Los Angeles Clippers. According to official NBA records, that history also includes the period between 1970 and 1978 when the Clippers were known as the Buffalo Braves. For the purposes of this book, the Braves will be treated as if they were a separate franchise, as I believe this aligns with the views of the majority of NBA fans[5]. Therefore, any mention of events occurring for the "first time in franchise history" or players setting "new franchise records" are referring to the period from the 1978-79 season onwards.

---

[5] I think most people are of the opinion that when you take a team, move it to the opposite side of the country and change its name, colors and logo, then it is no longer the same franchise.

PROLOGUE

The Start of Your Ending

"It bothers me a lot that you want to broadcast that you're associating with black people."

Donald Sterling

Saturday, April 26th 2014

It was around 7am when Blake Griffin woke up at the Four Seasons Hotel located in San Francisco. Like a typical Millennial, the first thing he did was reach for his cell phone. Given how well he had played during Thursday evening's game, he was expecting to be greeted by the usual assortment of congratulatory messages. Griffin had led all scorers with 32 points, as the Clippers defeated the Golden State Warriors 98-96 at Oakland's Oracle Arena. The win gave the Clippers a 2-1 series lead and also restored home court advantage in their first round playoff match-up with Golden State. When Griffin checked his phone, he was surprised to see over 40 text messages waiting to be read. This was far more than he anticipated and he quickly realized that something else was going down. Griffin had a fairly good idea of what that something else might be.

Two days earlier, coach Doc Rivers informed the players that the Clippers were once again about to find themselves in the news for reasons that had nothing to do with basketball. Rivers explained that someone had recorded owner Donald Sterling making a number of objectionable comments and it appeared that a prominent media outlet was about to release the audio file. Rivers was not able to provide many details about exactly what Sterling had said and Griffin did not view this update as particularly important. Game 3 against Golden State was set to tip-off in just a few hours, meaning that whatever trouble Sterling had brought upon himself was far from Griffin's primary concern.

Now, in the privacy of his hotel room, curiosity got the better of Griffin. He reclined on the bed, found his way to the TMZ website and clicked on the play button. What he heard was a scratchy recording of a personal conversation between a man and a woman. He immediately recognized the male voice as Sterling's and once he heard what the Clippers' owner had to say, Griffin knew why his inbox was suddenly overflowing with messages.

"Why are you taking pictures with minorities?"

"It bothers me a lot that you want to broadcast that you're associating with black people."

"You can sleep with them…you can do whatever you want. The little I ask is not to promote it…and not to bring them to my games."

It was confronting.

It was disturbing.

Yet unfortunately, it was not surprising.

Blake Griffin first formed the view that Donald Sterling was a man of questionable character five years earlier. It was the eve of the 2009 draft and Griffin was about to be selected as the first overall pick by the Los Angeles Clippers. He wanted to find out as much as he could about the Clippers, so he did what most people do when they need to get answers- he visited Google. When Griffin typed *"Donald Sterling,"* the search engine tried to preempt what he may be looking for and suggested- *"Donald Sterling racist"* as a topic that he might be interested in. This immediately grabbed Griffin's attention and he followed Google's lead. What he found wasn't pretty.

The articles Griffin stumbled across discussed incidents from Sterling's past. There were allegations from former Clippers' general manager Elgin Baylor that Sterling wanted to field a team of "poor black boys from the South" with a white head coach. There was a deposition where Sterling went into great detail describing his sexual encounters with a prostitute whom he was suing. There were also articles outlining the various housing discrimination lawsuits that had been brought against Sterling for allegedly mistreating black and Hispanic tenants.

So, as Griffin lay in his San Francisco hotel room, listening to the gravelly voice of Sterling lecturing his latest female companion on matters pertaining to race in America, he came to the conclusion that this was nothing out of the ordinary. Sure, the NBA would have to take some sort of action. After all, these were not "alleged" comments that could be made to disappear with a posse of high priced lawyers. These were clearly Sterling's own words, recorded as evidence for the entire world to hear.

When Griffin began moving about his room to prepare for the day ahead, he was fairly confident that he knew what was going to happen to Donald Sterling. This latest scandal was going to play out in a way that would be remarkably similar to all the other Sterling-related scandals he had first read about back in 2009. There would be some embarrassing headlines, Sterling would fork over a large sum of money and, eventually, the problem would simply fade away.

Sterling was certainly not going anywhere.

Nor was this most recent incident going to have any significant impact on the Clippers' 2014 playoff campaign.

As Blake Griffin closed the door of his room in order to make his way to a team meeting, he felt secure in his belief that this would all blow over within a matter of days. In reality, he was like a man with an umbrella who was about to head into a hurricane.

CHAPTER 1

An Unconventional Birth

"I traded the Celtics...but that's the price you have to pay to have the pleasure of enjoying a team back home. Besides, I think we're better than the Celtics."

IRV LEVIN

JOHN HAVLICEK WAS ABOUT TO play his final NBA game and the Celtic faithful were determined to give him the send-off that he deserved. It was the last days of winter and Boston Garden was packed to the rafters, though the result of the game between the Celtics and Braves was only a secondary consideration for most of the 15,276 people that were in attendance. The fans had come to say goodbye and pay their respects to a man who had given them so many happy memories over the previous 16 years.

It was Havlicek who stole the ball in 1965, Havlicek who was the leading scorer for the Celtics in the 1968 and 1969 Finals, Havlicek who led Boston to their first post-Bill Russell championship in 1974 and Havlicek's off-balance bank shot that saved the Celtics from defeat in Game 5 of the 1976 Finals[6].

---

[6] This basket helped propel the Celtics to the 1976 championship and also became one of the most iconic moments in a game that is still regarded as one of greatest of all-time.

16 seasons.

13 All-Star selections.

Eight championships.

Boston had a lot to be grateful for.

On this Sunday afternoon, the Celtic fans were prepared to put aside the fact that their beloved team had won a mere 31 games during the 1977-78 season. For a couple of hours, it didn't matter that they were about to miss the playoffs for just the third time in 28 years. This day was about saying thank you to one of the greatest players ever to wear Celtic green.

The crowd's admiration for the man known as "Hondo" was clear for all to see, with an eight minute standing ovation preceding the opening tip. As the thunderous applause washed over a tearful Havlicek, he displayed his respect for the Boston fans by walking to center court and humbly bowing in all four directions. Love was definitely in the air and it seemed unlikely that anything could bring down the mood. All of which made the events that unfolded at half-time even more stark.

The Celtics decided to use the half-time break to give Havlicek a lavish parting gift- a state of the art camper van that would be perfect for his frequent fishing trips. The man who made the presentation was team owner Irv Levin. Boston fans had little time for Levin, with many believing that the Celtics' current declining fortunes were solely attributable to their tight-fisted owner. So no-one was expecting another eight minute round of applause when Levin walked out onto the parquet floor to hand over the keys.

As soon as the owner was introduced, it became painfully obvious that the same fans who adored Havlicek despised Levin and what followed was one of the most awkward scenes in NBA history. With a forced smile plastered across his face, Levin presented Havlicek with his gift while a loud chorus of boos filled the stadium. The jeering only subsided when Levin retreated into the background, in order to give Havlicek the chance to thank the many people associated with his career. When the presentation was finally over, a shocked and humiliated Levin turned to his son and declared, "I've had it. I'm never coming back here again."

And so begins the story of the birth of the least successful organization in American sporting history.

Long before Irv Levin became the first owner of the Clippers, he was a pilot who flew fighter planes in World War II. During this time, Levin was stationed in Southern California and he grew to love the area so much that he decided to move there after completing his active service. When the war ended, there was a dramatic drop in the demand for fighter pilots, which meant that Levin had to find a new way to earn a living. This led to a long and successful career as a movie producer. Levin's physical appearance was exactly what you would imagine of a Hollywood mover and shaker from the 1970s. He wore stylish corduroy suits with partially buttoned shirts that exposed the gold chains that hung from his neck and his perpetual tan. His time in the movie business brought him into contact with the industry's biggest names, including Henry Fonda, Jimmy Stewart and Paul Newman.

Many of Levin's Hollywood colleagues also had ownership interests in the world of professional basketball and he soon became keen on the idea of purchasing a team of his own. He first tried to buy the Celtics in the early 1970s, only to have the agreement voided by the NBA due to conflict of interest concerns[7]. However, after some legal wrangling, Levin was allowed

---

[7] Levin and Sam Schulman, who was the owner of the Seattle Supersonics, were both on the board of directors at the same film production company and the league initially ruled that Levin could not purchase an NBA franchise due to this existing business relationship.

to purchase the Celtics and his first full season as the franchise's owner was like a fairy tale, with Boston winning their 13th NBA title after defeating Phoenix in the 1976 Finals.

Over the next few years, Levin's relationship with the Boston fans soured significantly. When the Celtics' fortunes began to decline after the 1976 championship, many people assumed that Levin was the man who was responsible. And in some respects, they were correct. It was Levin's unwillingness to meet Paul Silas' contract demands that resulted in the All-Star forward being traded to Denver at the end of the 1975-76 season. Silas' presence on the court was a crucial component in the Celtics' success. His dominant inside presence allowed Boston center Dave Cowens to play further from the basket, where he could use his deadly jump shot to draw opposing big men out of the key. Silas' departure for the Nuggets ultimately put an end to the short-lived Celtics' championship era of the mid-1970s[8]. By the end of the 1977-78 season, Levin wanted out of Boston and it was not just because of the frosty reception that he received at Havlicek's retirement ceremony.

Levin's work in the movie business meant that he spent much of the year in Los Angeles, making it extremely difficult for him to attend Celtic games. To Levin, this meant that he was not getting a good return on his investment. After all, what is the point of owning a professional basketball team if you can't sit in the courtside seats and act like a mogul? And while Levin would have loved to move the Celtics to California, the NBA was never going to allow their most successful franchise to re-locate in order to make the owner's game day commute more convenient. This left Levin with two choices- continue to own a team that he hardly ever got to see play

---

[8] The trade took place despite Cowens and coach Tommy Heinsohn imploring Levin to pay Silas the $330,000 he was asking for, with both men letting the owner know that they viewed Silas as an irreplaceable piece to their championship puzzle. Many people in the organization felt that it was team president Red Auerbach, not Levin, who was responsible for the decision to reject Silas' contract demands, as he feared that paying Silas more than Cowens or Havlicek would disrupt the team's natural pecking order. However, regardless of who actually made the final call, in the eyes of many Celtics fans, Levin was viewed as the culprit behind the Silas trade.

and whose fans hated him, or sell the franchise. Or at least, that was the case until an intriguing third option emerged.

Two months after Levin was booed off the court in Boston, he was at the Hotel del Coronado in San Diego. Levin was a regular visitor to the hotel, spending many family vacations there with his wife and three children. However, on this occasion he was not in California to catch-up on some rest and relaxation, he was there for the annual meeting of NBA owners. And it turned out that Levin was not the only person in attendance who was looking for a new home for his team.

John Y. Brown was an entrepreneur who had made a fortune in the chicken business- the Kentucky Fried Chicken business. Brown purchased KFC from Colonel Harland Sanders in 1964 for $2 million and proceeded to build it into one of the world's most popular fast-food chains. Seven years later, he sold his share of the company for $285 million. Brown's first foray into the world of professional basketball came in the ABA, where he owned the Kentucky Colonels for a number of years. When the ABA merged with the NBA in 1976, Brown received a seven figure payout in return for agreeing to fold the Colonels and he subsequently used some of this money to purchase the Buffalo Braves. Brown's stewardship in Buffalo was considerably less successful than his time at the helm of KFC.

In fact, the brief period that Brown spent as the Braves' owner closely mirrored the plotline of "Major League," the 1989 comedy film that starred a young Charlie Sheen. In the movie, the Cleveland Indians are taken over by a new owner named Rachel Phelps, who is desperate to move the franchise to a more desirable location. Phelps discovers that the only way to break the stadium lease is for attendance to fall to record lows. So, in order to ensure that the fans will lose interest and stop attending games, the Indians purposely assemble a roster with as little talent as possible.

At the time that Brown purchased the Braves, the franchise had just signed a new lease that locked the team into playing home games at the Buffalo Memorial Auditorium for the next 15 years. However, the contract did contain one crucial out-clause. The Braves were free to break the lease if they failed to sell at least 4,500 season tickets in any one year. And from the moment Brown took the reins in Buffalo, it was clear that he was committed to ensuring that the number of season ticket holders dipped below this threshold.

Prior to Brown's involvement, Braves' fans had every reason to be optimistic about the 1976-77 campaign. Buffalo had a strong nucleus of young players that included league MVP winner Bob McAdoo, All-Star guard Randy Smith and Jim McMillian, a 27 year old forward with a knack for scoring. The Braves had just come off a season where they had accumulated the league's fifth best record and had subsequently managed to strengthen their roster during the 1976 off-season. Firstly, they used the sixth pick in the draft to secure the services of Adrian Dantley, a talented small forward who had just won a gold medal at the Montreal Olympics, leading the USA team in scoring with an average of 19.3 points per game. The Braves also managed to pick up a promising young center by the name of Moses Malone on the eve of the new season, courtesy of a trade with Portland. On paper, Buffalo had a team that looked capable of contending for an NBA championship.

The shedding of players began almost as soon as Brown walked in the door.

First the Braves traded McMillian to New York for $500,000 in cash. This meant that Buffalo lost one of their best players and received no compensation in terms of players or draft picks[9]. And McMillian was no scrub either. Before arriving in Buffalo, he was a key contributor on the Los Angeles Lakers team that won the 1972 championship, averaging 18.8 points per game. During his three seasons with the Braves, McMillian

---

9 In 1976, NBA rules allowed a player to be traded solely for money.

averaged 16.4 points per game and the team made three consecutive trips to the playoffs.

Next to go was Malone, who was traded away for a couple of draft picks and $100,000. Malone, who would go on to win three of the next seven MVP awards, only got to play two games for Buffalo before he was shipped off to Houston.

A month and a half later, McAdoo was traded to the New York Knicks. As was the case with the McMillian and Malone deals, the Braves gave up an extremely talented player and, with the exception of money, collected very little else in return. In exchange for McAdoo, Buffalo received $3 million and a modestly talented center named John Gianelli, who had career averages of just 8.2 points and 6.3 rebounds per game. Meanwhile, McAdoo had just finished a three year run where he led the league in scoring every season, was named league MVP once and finished second in the award voting on the other two occasions. During this stretch, McAdoo averaged 32.1 points and 13.8 rebounds. The McAdoo-for-Gianelli trade capped off a wild three months, where the Braves were transformed from one of the NBA's up and coming teams to a kind of travelling fire sale.

It's at this point that the narratives of John Y. Brown's Braves and the "Major League" script head in vastly different directions. In the Hollywood version, the decimated playing roster discovers Phelps' plans to relocate the franchise. The remaining players are so annoyed that they somehow summon the power to win a whole bunch of games and eventually defeat the Yankees in the season finale to claim the division title. As a direct result of this on-field resurgence, the fans fall in love with this ragtag collection of underdogs and attendances rise so high that there is no way that Cleveland is going to lose their Indians.

In the real life John Y. Brown/Buffalo version, the Braves never recovered from the gutting of their roster. Over the course of the 1976-77 season,

19 different players suited up for the Braves and three different coaches took turns calling the shots from the sidelines. By the end of the season, Buffalo had compiled the second worst record in the entire league. The only highlight to emerge was in the form of Adrian Dantley, who was named Rookie of the Year after averaging 20.3 points per game. However, even this achievement would be rendered somewhat meaningless, as Dantley was traded to Indiana at the end of the season[10].

The following year proved to be Buffalo's final as the host city for an NBA franchise. For the second consecutive season, there was very little about the on-court product to entice people to come along and support the team. The Braves lost twice as many games as they won and were effectively eliminated from the playoff race by December. As the defeats mounted, fans lost interest and attendances began to plummet. Season ticket sales fell below the 2,500 mark, well short of the 4,500 minimum set out in the recently signed lease.

The decline in attendances meant that Brown was now free to move the Braves to pretty much any city he wanted. The question was no longer whether the Braves were being relocated, it was simply a matter of where they were being re-located to. In the months leading up to the owner's meeting in San Diego, Brown travelled the country fielding offers from consortiums that were interested in bringing an NBA team to their town. At one stage, it seemed like Dallas was going to be the new home of the Braves but this proposed deal quickly fell apart, leaving Minneapolis and San Diego as the new frontrunners.

All of which brings us back to Irv Levin and his desire to get out of Boston. The decision makers at NBA head office were obviously not keen on the idea of seeing the Celtics being moved away from the only city that

---

10 Dantley became the first player in NBA history to win the Rookie of the Year award and start the following season playing for a different team. The only other time this has occurred was in 1994 when Chris Webber was traded to Washington after being named Rookie of the Year while playing for Golden State.

they had ever called home. So a bold plan was hatched. Levin and Brown would swap their respective franchises. Once Levin became the owner of the Braves, he would move the team to San Diego, while the Celtics would remain in Boston. Everyone was a winner[11]. Levin got to have his Southern Californian franchise, the NBA got to keep the Celtics in Boston and Brown was able to own a successful team that played in a market which was much larger than Buffalo.

While Levin was extremely happy with the prospect of owning a team that played closer to his Beverly Hills home, it was pretty clear he was getting the short end of the stick. In order to get his hands on a franchise that he could easily move across the country, Levin had to sever his ties with one of the most successful sporting organizations in the world. In the 20 year period between 1957 and 1976, Boston won an astounding 13 NBA championships. Levin was voluntarily stepping away from this remarkable history, in order to launch a new team in a city with a poor track record of hosting professional basketball.

The newly re-located Braves would not be the first basketball team to call San Diego home. Two other franchises, the NBA's Rockets and the ABA's Conquistadors, had previously tried to make a go of operating out of San Diego and both had failed, primarily due to a lack of public support. The Houston Rockets played their first four seasons as the *San Diego Rockets* and during this time they struggled to generate much interest from the local community. In their first season, the average attendance for home games barely got above the 4,000 mark. And while things improved slightly over the next three years, they were never able to attract the support necessary to sustain an NBA franchise. After four bleak seasons, the owners of the Rockets decided that the NBA in San Diego was not going to work and they moved the team to Houston.

---

11 Well, everyone except for the basketball fans of Buffalo.

One year later, professional basketball was back, in the form of an ABA team called the San Diego Conquistadors. However, the Conquistadors also failed to capture the hearts and minds of the locals and they folded just 11 games into their fourth season. During this time, their average home attendance was just 2,227 spectators, a pitifully low number.

So as Irv Levin and John Y. Brown negotiated the finer details of the franchise swap, it was clear that establishing a viable team in San Diego was going to pose a challenge. If Levin was going to have any chance of succeeding where the owners of the Rockets and Conquistadors had failed, he needed to field a team that was going to capture the imagination of the city of San Diego. And, as history has shown time and time again, the best way to win over a fickle fan base in the world of professional basketball was by finding a star player who could inspire the masses. A player whose feats and deeds transcended those of his peers. A player like Larry Joe Bird.

In an alternate universe, Larry Bird would have been the first great player in the history of the San Diego Clippers, rather than the next in a long line of legends to play for the Boston Celtics. When Bird claimed his first Larry O'Brien Trophy, he would have been wearing a powder blue Clipper uniform instead of Celtic green. And when he won three consecutive MVP awards in the mid-1980s, he would have been representing the city of San Diego rather than Boston. All of the above could have been a reality had Irv Levin decided that Bird was the player whom he wanted to build his new team around.

On top of their agreement to swap franchises, Brown and Levin also decided to include a rather substantial trade of players and draft picks as part of the deal. Marvin "Bad News" Barnes, Billy Knight, Nate "Tiny" Archibald and two second round draft picks were sent from Buffalo to Boston. In return, Levin's new team received Kevin Kunnert, Kermit

Washington, Sidney Wicks and one of the two players whom the Celtics had selected in the first round of the 1978 draft, which was held just a few weeks earlier. The two Celtic draftees were Freeman Williams and Larry Bird and since Brown didn't have a strong preference, he left it up to Levin to make the call on which player would be the final piece in one of the most complex deals in NBA history.

In retrospect, this decision might seem like a no-brainer, but back in 1978 it would have been a much tougher choice. Williams, a 6'4" shooting guard, was considered to be a very strong pro prospect. He had just come off consecutive college seasons where he led the nation in scoring, averaging 38.8 points per game as a junior and 35.9 points as a senior[12]. Just a few months prior to being taken by the Celtics with the eighth overall selection of the 1978 draft, Williams scored 81 points in a game, the third highest individual tally in the history of college basketball[13]. Williams was selected as a second team All-American at the end of his senior season and to this day, he trails only "Pistol" Pete Maravich in terms of total points scored over his college career[14]. Williams was also born and raised in California, which only made him more attractive to Levin, who was keenly aware of the need to generate interest from the San Diego public.

Larry Bird, on the other hand, played at Indiana State, where he posted the impressive averages of 30 points and 11.5 rebounds per game. Like Williams, he was also selected as an All-American, only Bird was given first team honors. However, despite these noteworthy achievements, there were still plenty of people who questioned whether Bird would be able to dominate the professional game as he was doing in college. The doubters

---

12 In the 20 years preceding Williams' feat, the only other college players who were able to lead the nation in scoring for consecutive seasons were "Pistol" Pete Maravich and Oscar Robertson.
13 And this was back when there was no shot clock or three point line in the college game.
14 Williams would also later make a brief appearance in the 1992 movie "White Men Can't Jump." He played the role of playground legend Duck Johnson, who is one of the guys who gets torn to shreds in the movie's final basketball scene, courtesy of Billy Hoyle and Sidney Deane's streetball version of the Princeton offense.

highlighted the fact that Bird was playing in the Missouri Valley conference against largely inferior opposition. The thinking was that his game might not translate to the world of the NBA, which was filled with players who were both bigger and more athletically gifted than those who Bird faced while at college.

Bird also presented a unique set of circumstances for any NBA team that was thinking about acquiring his rights. He had only just completed his junior year and had already declared his intention to head back to Indiana State to play his senior season. In today's NBA, this decision would have made Bird ineligible for the 1978 draft but due to a loophole in the rules at the time, he was available to be picked, provided someone was willing to select him[15].

Bird was considered to be such an attractive prospect that NBA teams were willing to use a draft pick on him, despite the fact that he would be spending the next year playing in Terre Haute. His home state team, the Indiana Pacers, held the rights to the first pick and they made a run at trying to convince Bird to abandon the Sycamores to turn pro. When he turned them down, Indiana decided they no longer wanted the first pick and traded it to Portland. The Blazers then tried their luck by dangling a pot of gold in front of Bird, but they received the same answer that the Pacers had.

Eventually Bird fell to the sixth pick, where the Celtics courageously selected him. Boston was employing an extremely risky strategy because the rules at the time stated that the team which drafted Bird had just 12 months to secure his signature. If no agreement was reached during this time, Bird

---

15 This unique situation was due to the fact that Bird sat out a season after transferring from Indiana to Indiana State. This meant that while Bird still had one season of eligibility left, his college class was set to graduate, which made him available for selection in the draft. The only other way to draft an underclassman at that time was if the player provided sufficient evidence to the NBA showing that they needed to begin their professional career early, due to extreme financial hardship.

could simply put his name back into the pool of players for the 1979 draft, thus leaving the Celtics empty-handed. If Levin opted to take Bird instead of Williams, he would also be inheriting the risk that went with this.

When the time came to make the decision about which player to include as the final piece in the franchise swap, Levin went to see his lawyer, Frank Rothman, for advice. Rothman had worked closely with Levin over the years, including helping win the legal battle that allowed Levin to become the owner of the Celtics. Now he was being asked to evaluate basketball talent, despite having no discernable expertise in this area. Rothman told Levin that Bird was "supposed to be slow and can't jump that well" before recommending that he go with Williams.

In the end, the fact that Bird was not going to be available to play immediately was a large factor in Levin's ultimate decision to opt for Williams. Levin knew that it was crucial that his new team made a good first impression and Williams was a player who could help achieve this. Bird could not. In fact, if Bird wanted to, he could simply refuse to sign with the new San Diegan franchise, which was a risk that Levin was not prepared to take. And so, Freeman Williams became the final piece in the most peculiar trade in NBA history.

Now that which players were being shipped to what team had been sorted out, the final step to making the franchise swap official was getting approval from the other NBA owners. This would prove to be a mere formality. The final vote was 21-1, with the only dissenting voice belonging to the Lakers[16].

After Levin assumed control of the Buffalo Braves, he immediately announced his plans to move the franchise to southern California. The team would henceforth be known as the San Diego Clippers, a selection that

---

16 Three years after the swap took place, the Boston Celtics were again back at the top of the NBA mountain and the trade of players agreed to by Levin and Brown clearly played a large role in the Celtics claiming their 14th Larry O'Brien Trophy. In fact, the two stars on the 1981 championship team were none other than Bird and Archibald.

was inspired by the speedy 19th century sailing ships[17]. When Levin was asked why he wanted to move his new team to a city with such a poor track record of supporting professional basketball, he nominated the reduction in his game day travel time as a key influence. "One of my personal problems with the Celts was commuting 3,000 miles," Levin said. Levin also spoke about his belief that the growing population of San Diego would get behind his new enterprise, while dismissing the failures of the Rockets and Conquistadors, saying that they occurred in "another era."

Levin knew that the best way to generate interest from the basketball fans of San Diego was to ensure that the Clippers were as competitive as possible and he promised that he would "put a winning team on the court from day one". The first step in achieving on-court success was employing a head coach and Levin elected to go with Gene Shue, a former NBA player and five time All-Star, who had become one of the league's most respected tacticians. In his 11 year coaching career, Shue had taken two different teams to the Finals and was named the NBA's Coach of the Year in 1969.

Shue's preferred style of play was fast, with his teams looking to push the ball up the court in search of early scoring opportunities. His other big belief was that you couldn't be successful in coaching without having talented players. When he arrived in San Diego, the Clippers' inaugural roster was filled with serviceable players like Swen Nater, Kermit Washington and Sidney Wicks. Shue thought that the Clippers needed something more if they were serious about fielding a winning team. They needed someone who could compete with the NBA's brightest stars on a consistent basis. Someone with a big personality who would connect with the fans and make the Clippers a team worth watching. Someone who was capable of being the face of the franchise. Fortunately, Gene Shue knew the perfect candidate for the job.

---

17 This new name came courtesy of a competition where fans were asked to send in their suggestions.

World B. Free grew up in Brooklyn, where he developed a love for the game of basketball and learned his distinctive, high-arcing shooting technique by imitating his older brother[18]. By the time Free was 16, he was already well known throughout the playgrounds of New York City for his rainbow jump shot and his ability to throw down spectacular dunks. Free attended Canarsie High School and during his senior season he led the school to a perfect 24-0 record that cumulated in a City Championship. Free's next stop was North Carolina, where he played for Guilford College. His freshman year at Guilford brought another championship, with the Quakers winning the 1973 NAIA title and Free claiming the tournament MVP award. Over the next two years, Free continued to improve and by his junior season he was named the NAIA's Player of the Year.

After three years at Guilford, Free decided to declare for the 1975 NBA draft, where he was eventually selected in the middle of the second round by Philadelphia. Free quickly worked his way into the Sixers' rotation, averaging 8.3 points in a little over 15 minutes per game during his rookie season. The following year, Philadelphia became the center of the basketball universe when the Sixers bought the rights to a 6'6" small forward named Julius "Dr. J" Erving. With the addition of Erving, Philadelphia had assembled one of the most talented rosters in NBA history[19]. They finished the 1976-77 regular season with the Eastern Conference's best record and one of the key contributing factors to the Sixers' impressive results was the form of Free, whose scoring average of 16.3 points per game was almost double that of his rookie season.

Once the playoffs began, the Sixers found themselves in danger of succumbing to a quick elimination when Boston forced a Game 7 in the Eastern Conference semi-finals. The decisive game was a closely contested,

---

18 World B. Free was born Lloyd Free. He legally changed his first name to "World" in the middle of his professional career, as this was the nickname that was bestowed upon him as a youth. With a middle name of Bernard, he now had the catchy moniker of World B. Free.
19 Erving joined a team that featured a host of big names, including George McGinnis, Doug Collins, Caldwell Jones and Steve Mix.

low scoring affair and it was Free who ultimately saved the day, scoring 27 points in an 83-77 victory. The Sixers moved onto the Conference finals where they faced the Houston Rockets. This series did not feature any heroics from Free, who was forced to sit out for three of the six games due to a collapsed lung. Even with Free's absence, the Sixers still had enough talent to prevail, defeating the Rockets 4-2 and booking a spot in the NBA Finals, where Portland awaited.

Free was able to resume playing during the Finals but it was clear that he was not operating at full strength. The Sixers took an early lead in the series before losing four consecutive games, handing the Blazers their first championship in just their seventh year of existence. Afterwards, Erving lamented the fact that Free was not his usual self, saying, "I think we would have won the championship if Free and Steve Mix would have been healthy[20]." Erving went on to add that "a healthy Free just can't be stopped."

When it became apparent during the 1978 off-season that the Clippers needed another scoring threat, Shue immediately thought of Free. Shue had firsthand knowledge of Free from his time coaching in Philadelphia. He believed that Free would be a good fit for the roster and so he asked Levin to explore trading options with the Sixers' front office. On the eve of the Clippers' season opener, Levin pulled the trigger on a trade that brought Free to San Diego in exchange for a future first round draft pick. Shue was hoping Free had learned from his time playing as Erving's understudy and that he was now ready to be the star of his own show.

Season I: 1978-79

While Shue was undoubtedly happy to get his hands on Free, this latest addition only added to the eclectic mix of players that he had to work with. Normally, a coach of an NBA franchise that has been relocated will retain

---

20 Mix was also dealing with an ankle injury at the time.

the majority of the previous year's team, thus providing an established foundation to build upon. However, in this case, only three former Braves suited up for the Clippers during their debut season- Randy Smith, Swen Nater and Scott Lloyd. Besides this trio of ex-Braves, the make-up of the inaugural Clippers squad included four rookies, three former-Celtics and one player each from the 76ers, Rockets, Bulls and Nuggets, along with a guard named Connie Norman, who had not played professional basketball for two full seasons.

Considering the motley crew of players that Shue was asked to coach, it should come as no great shock that the Clippers' first season did not get off to a flying start. Their first win didn't arrive until the fourth game of the season, when they were able to hold off a fast finishing Bulls team to secure a 99-94 victory. Leading the way for the Clippers was Free, who led all scorers with 29 points. This became something of a pattern, with Free's name regularly appearing at the top of the box score as the team's leading scorer. When the Clippers beat the Lakers to record their second win of the season, Free had 35 points. The next night, he put up 38 against Milwaukee. A week later, he had 42 in a loss to the Knicks.

It only took a few weeks for Free to establish himself as the face of the Clippers, and it was not just his scoring exploits that were winning over the fans. Free was the poster boy for 1970s chic. Take, for example, the fact that Free was losing his hair at the time of his trade to the Clippers. For many players, this would be something that they tried to cover-up, either by shaving their head or wearing a strategically placed head band. Not Free. He instead chose to let the back part of his hair grow into a kind of semi-afro, while the area just above his forehead was decidedly bare due to his receding hairline. This is a look that not many people could pull off and yet Free found a way to make it work in his favor.

While Free had no trouble settling in, the team as a whole struggled to find its feet, losing 12 of their first 18 contests and dropping to the bottom of the Pacific Division. Center Kevin Kunnert diagnosed the team's primary problem as an inability to maintain leads, saying that the Clippers had the "killer instinct of a field mouse." And while they did lose some close games over the first month of the season, there were also a number of blowout defeats, including an embarrassing 38 point loss to the Spurs in which they allowed San Antonio to score 163 points. This was clearly not the ideal way to win over fans in a new town.

The on-court results from the first month of the season may have painted a pretty glum picture but behind the scenes, the Clippers were in the process of developing into a cohesive, close-knit unit. One of the key figures in this improving team chemistry was Shue, who worked tirelessly to create an atmosphere that was reminiscent of a large family rather than a collection of well-paid athletes from a variety of different backgrounds. Shue made sure that each player had a good understanding of his individual role and his fast-paced game plan meant that there were plenty of scoring opportunities to go round and keep everyone happy. Away from the hardwood, Shue went beyond the regular duties of an NBA head coach by inviting the team into his home and organizing social gatherings that helped forge bonds between the players.

Shue may have been the architect of the vision to create a harmonious team but his plan needed to have the support of the players in order to be successfully implemented. And there was nobody who played a larger role in turning Shue's vision into a reality than Randy Smith.

The 1978 All-Star game featured 12 future Hall of Fame inductees, including Bill Walton, Julius Erving and Moses Malone[21]. In short, it was a

---

21 The full list of Hall of Famers to play in the 1978 All-Star game is: Rick Barry, Dave Cowens, Julius Erving, George Gervin, Artis Gilmore, John Havlicek, Elvin Hayes, Bob Lanier, Moses Malone, Bob McAdoo, David Thompson and Bill Walton.

contest that was not lacking in star power. The game itself was won by the East and when the time came to hand out the MVP award, the nod went to Randy Smith, who finished with 27 points, 7 rebounds and 6 assists. The fact that Smith was even playing in the NBA defied the odds, being selected as the Most Valuable Player in the league's showcase event was almost too far-fetched to believe. However, for those people close to Smith who had firsthand knowledge of his work ethic and character, it was nothing more than the latest chapter in an amazing life story.

Randy Smith graduated from Buffalo State at a time when the Buffalo Braves were in desperate need of some good publicity. If it wasn't for this geographic coincidence, it is highly likely that Smith would never have played a single game in the NBA, much less win the All-Star MVP award. The Braves' interest in drafting Smith can be traced back to another local college player named Calvin Murphy. Back in 1970, when Smith was about to begin his senior year at Buffalo State, the Braves passed up the opportunity to draft Murphy out of Niagara University, which upset many of their local fans. These emotions were only amplified when Murphy went on to have an exceptional rookie season, averaging 15.8 points and 4 assists per game.

Twelve months down the track, the Braves were presented with an opportunity to make amends when Smith became available for selection. Smith had enjoyed a productive college career, averaging 23.1 points and 13.3 rebounds across the three seasons he spent with the varsity team. But while these raw numbers might seem impressive, it is important to note that they were achieved at a Division Two school, against a standard of competition which was worlds away from that of the NBA. Smith spent most of his time at Buffalo State playing in the frontcourt and the majority of his success had come from exploiting the athletic advantage he held over most of his gravity-bound rivals.

In 1971, the NBA draft did not have a designated finishing point. Instead, teams could continue making selections until they decided that they wanted to stop[22]. When the seventh round of the draft arrived, the Braves decided to take a flyer, using the 104th pick to select Smith. The assessment from the few scouts who had bothered to watch Smith play was that he was an under-sized forward with a shaky jump shot, not exactly the recipe for a long-lasting NBA career. The Braves' selection of Smith was clearly directed at appeasing local fans, rather than any realistic expectation that he would develop into a useful NBA player.

Smith was invited to participate in the Braves' 1971 training camp but the overwhelming feeling was that he was a long shot to make the team. The general perception was that his game would not translate to the NBA level, where he would be required to spend the majority of his time on the perimeter, thus needing to handle the ball more and take plenty of outside shots. When Smith arrived at Darien Lake for the pre-season workouts, he began to turn heads before he even picked up a basketball. Braves play-by-play announcer Van Miller labeled Smith as "the perfect physical specimen," observing that there "wasn't an ounce of fat" to be seen on his body. And Smith continued to impress once the action on the hardwood got underway. He was often asked to match-up against Fred Hilton, another 6'3" rookie who was selected 85 picks ahead of him and he did more than just hold his own against his highly-regarded opponent, he often out-played him.

The first indication that Smith was on his way to earning himself a spot on the Braves' roster came in an exhibition game at nearby Fredonia State University against the Boston Celtics. When Smith checked into the game, he was asked to defend John Havlicek, one of the league's most accomplished players. By the end of the evening, Smith had played so well against Havlicek that he had earned a standing ovation. The idea that Smith was someone who could make a meaningful contribution was quickly gaining

---

[22] Hypothetically, the 1971 NBA draft could have gone on forever. It didn't. Instead it finished after 19 agonizing rounds and 237 picks.

traction. The Braves were originally planning on selecting a roster of just ten or 11 players, but they decided to go with a full complement of 12 to enable them to include Randy Smith.

However, Smith was far from satisfied with just making the team and over the course of his rookie year, he continued to work on his deficiencies. By the end of his first season, he had climbed his way from the end of the bench and into Buffalo's starting line-up. In fact, Smith's improvement was so rapid that he was the Braves' second leading scorer over the final month of the season. Smith's overall rookie numbers were 13.4 points, 4.8 rebounds and 2.5 assists, not a bad return from a guy who was only supposed to generate a few feel-good newspaper stories. Over the next few years, Smith became one of the Braves' most important players. In the 1975-76 season, he received a double dose of recognition when he was picked to play in his first All-Star game and was also selected on the All-NBA second team[23].

By the time the 1978-79 season tipped-off, Smith had come a long way from his days as a unheralded draft pick struggling just to make the team. He was now viewed as one of the NBA's most dominant and well-rounded perimeter players. The varied and demanding on-court assignments that were given to Smith when he arrived in San Diego were a testament to his wide range of abilities. Not only was Smith asked to be one of the Clippers' primary scoring options, he was also expected to shoulder the majority of the ball-handling/playmaking duties and was frequently given the toughest defensive assignment.

On top of all this, Shue wanted his veteran point guard to shoulder a leadership role within the playing group and Smith tackled this responsibility in two distinctly different ways. On the court, his work ethic and professionalism provided a daily example that his teammates could aspire

---

23 To this day, Smith remains the lowest draft pick ever named on an All-NBA team.

to emulate. Away from the hardwood floor, Smith used his humor and easy-going personality to help develop a sense of team camaraderie that is rarely seen in the NBA. It would be Smith's work in this second area that ultimately set the tone for the second half of the Clippers' debut season.

By the middle of November, the playing group that was essentially a collection of strangers at the start of training camp was bonding into a tight unit and this was starting to pay dividends on the court. The improvement was nothing dramatic at first, with the Clippers chalking up slightly more victories than losses and slowly climbing up the NBA standings. They continued to play better throughout December and January and by the time the league paused for its annual All-Star break, the Clippers had won exactly half of their 54 games. This was good enough for sixth spot in the Western Conference standings. However, despite this improvement, not a single Clipper was invited to participate in the league's showcase event[24].

Once play resumed after the All-Star game, the Clippers continued to push for one of the Western Conference's six playoff spots and by the middle of March, they were the hottest team in the entire league. First, they reeled off an eight game winning streak that was eventually broken when they let a late game lead slip at Madison Square Garden. This was followed by a run of five victories that included a crucial win over Portland, who were also chasing one of the last few playoff berths. A 110-98 victory over the Nets gave the Clippers 13 wins from their past 14 encounters. They were now sitting in the Western Conference's fifth position with only ten games remaining and the playoff dreams that seemed like a distant fantasy earlier in the season were close to becoming a reality.

---

[24] The player most deserving of an All-Star spot was clearly World B. Free, who was the league's second leading scorer at the time.

And then the wheels fell off.

Two nights after defeating the Nets at home, the Clippers lost a closely contested game to Portland, reducing their lead over the Blazers in the standings to just a solitary game. The following evening, the Clippers defeated the Warriors to give themselves some much needed breathing room.

The Clippers next stop was Los Angeles, where they were set to face the Lakers. As they prepared for the game, the Clippers had good reason to be optimistic, given that they had beaten the Lakers twice in their three previous encounters. Once the game started, the contest ended. At the end of the first quarter, the Clippers were down by 17 and by half-time the margin had grown to 27. In the second half, the Lakers racked up 88 points ensuring that there would be no miraculous comeback. When the final buzzer sounded, the Clippers had conceded a total of 156 points, as the Lakers cruised to a 37 point victory.

This shocking result turned out to be the beginning of the end for the Clippers' playoff hopes. Over the next two weeks, the Clippers lost five of their six games, while the Blazers were in the midst of a five game winning streak. By the time the Clippers returned to San Diego to play their final game of the season, Portland had locked up the Western Conference's sixth and final playoff spot.

While the Clippers' late season plunge was a huge disappointment for everyone who was connected with the team, Irv Levin had to be happy with the overall results from his maiden season in San Diego. His new franchise had exceeded all expectations by winning 43 games and in the end, they fell just two victories short of an unlikely playoff appearance. Gene Shue's efforts in molding a cohesive team were recognized when he finished second in the voting for the Coach of the Year award. World B. Free, who averaged

28.8 points per game, was the league's second leading scorer and was also named on the All-NBA second team[25].

The Clippers' improved play also led to a rise in the level of community support, with home games over the second half of the season regularly selling-out. There was a growing belief from the locals that they finally had a *real* professional basketball team which they could get behind. The Clippers were not just there to make up the numbers, they were capable of competing against the biggest and best that the NBA had to offer.

As the team prepared for their sophomore season, the overwhelming feeling that surrounded the organization was one of optimism. The fans looked towards the upcoming campaign with a sense of anticipation about what Free, Smith and company might be able to accomplish now that they had a year of playing together under their belts. Levin and Shue were also enthusiastic about the 1979-80 season but for a very different reason. Behind the scenes, they were busy working on a bold and daring plan. A plan to lure arguably the greatest player in the world to come and play for the San Diego Clippers.

---

25 Free more than doubled his career scoring average and finished just 0.8 points behind San Antonio's George Gervin, who averaged 29.6 points per game.

CHAPTER 2

The Homecoming

"I not only visualize a championship here, I expect it. And not just one either."

BILL WALTON

IF THE BASKETBALL GAME PLAYED at the Anaheim Convention Centre on September 27th 1979 was a boxing match, it would have been a heavyweight title fight. After not facing each other for almost two years, Kareem Abdul-Jabbar and Bill Walton were set to do battle in one of the most anticipated exhibition games in NBA history. At the time of the clash, the two big men were widely regarded as the best players in the NBA. Kareem was a five time league MVP and NBA champion, while Walton had a championship and MVP award of his own. The rivalry between these two titans was further fueled by their shared experience of playing under legendary coach John Wooden at UCLA. During Walton's three years as a Bruin, his teams won 86 of their 90 games on their way to two national championships. Unbelievably, Kareem had an even better record, winning 88 of 90 games and all three national titles in his time at Westwood.

On this evening, the Orange County fans were treated to a full repertoire of the Bill Walton show. He went to work on the low block, used his extraordinary court vision to set teammates up for easy scores and even managed to swat away two of Kareem's supposedly unblockable skyhooks.

With just a few minutes remaining in the game, the Clippers clung to a three point lead that looked set to be trimmed to one. Lakers' rookie Magic Johnson caught the ball at the halfway line and saw that the only thing standing between him and an easy two points was a back-pedaling Walton. Johnson was sure that he would be able to speed past the Clippers' newest recruit and so he drove hard towards the basket, before lofting a running, right-handed lay-up. The ball never made it out of his hand. Somehow Walton managed to scramble back and keep himself between Magic and the basket. So when Magic attempted to lay the ball in, Walton was right there to block the shot. Even more impressive was the fact that Walton managed to retain possession of the ball as he landed. Walton quickly fired an outlet pass to Freeman Williams and he threw the ball ahead to World B. Free, who finished the play with a thunderous two-handed dunk. The margin was now five points and this was a lead that the Clippers never relinquished, as the upstarts from San Diego pulled away for a 104-95 victory.

When the final buzzer sounded, there was no doubt about which player took the points in the individual match-up between Walton and Kareem. Despite the fact that it was only Walton's second competitive game in 19 months, he convincingly out-played his long-time rival. Walton finished with a well-rounded stat line of 17 points, 13 rebounds, 5 assists and 3 blocks, while holding Kareem to 13 points on 27% shooting and just 8 rebounds.

The end of the game gave Walton a moment to reflect on his decision to return to San Diego to play for the Clippers and he found it hard to suppress the feeling of rising optimism. The previous 18 months had been the most miserable and frustrating time of his life, as injuries prevented him from doing the one thing that he truly loved- playing basketball. But Walton was ready to put that behind him and move on. As he walked from the court, surrounded by loud cheers from his adoring fans, he glanced at the scoreboard and dared to dream of greatness. It was now just a few weeks until the 1979-80 season tipped off and Bill Walton could hardly wait for it to get underway.

William Theodore Walton seemed destined to succeed at basketball. In his very first game, playing as a fourth grader for Blessed Sacrament Elementary School, Walton scored his first basket when an attempted pass from midcourt inadvertently sailed through the hoop. Even at a young age, Walton towered above his peers and yet he chose to model his game after "Pistol" Pete Maravich, a flashy point guard who handled the ball like a Harlem Globetrotter. In fact, Walton's dribbling and passing skills were so good that his youth coach would often ask him to be the team's primary ballhandler.

Walton spent his formative years in the San Diego suburb of La Mesa, where he was taught by his parents to always think for himself rather than follow the crowd. When the time came for high school, Walton, guided by the allure of female classmates, elected to leave the all-boy Catholic system and enroll at Helix High. Walton's love for basketball was so strong that he signed up to play in five different leagues in the summer between his freshman and sophomore years of high school. This created a situation where he would often have to race out of one gym at the end of a game, in order to get across town in time for the tip-off of his next clash[26]. All of this hard work paid off, as Walton's final two years at Helix resulted in consecutive state championships and a winning streak that stretched out to 49 games.

---

26 At the time, Walton made a promise to his father, who was giving up much of his weekends in order to chauffeur his son around the city of San Diego. Walton said that if he ever won the NBA's MVP award, he would give his dad the car that was awarded as a prize. Years later, when Walton was named NBA Finals MVP, he kept his word, handing over the keys to a brand new Ford pick-up truck that his father proudly drove for the rest of his life.

By the time Walton graduated from high school, he was a hot property, with every college coach in America eager to sign him up. However, despite all of this attention, he only ever gave one school serious consideration. Walton first met John Wooden at a basketball camp when he was in sixth grade and he had dreamed of playing at UCLA ever since. As far as Walton was concerned, UCLA had everything he needed- a proud history of success, an exceptional coach whom he could learn from and the added advantage of being based in Southern California.

Walton's first two years on the UCLA varsity team brought more of the success that he was becoming accustomed to. In fact, the Bruins won all 60 games that they played during the 1971-72 and 1972-73 seasons, claiming two NCAA championships along the way. Walton's performance in the 1973 final is still widely regarded as the best individual game in the history of college basketball. He scored a staggering 44 points while missing only one of his 22 field goal attempts, a feat that no-one has come close to matching since.

It was on this historic evening that Walton met with a delegation from the Philadelphia 76ers, who tried to convince Walton to forgo his senior season at UCLA and turn pro. The Sixers had the rights to the first pick in the upcoming draft and there was no player whom they would rather use it on than Walton. On the same weekend, Walton received another intriguing pitch, this time from representatives of the ABA, who offered to give him his own Los Angeles-based franchise. Walton was told that he would be able to stock the roster with his choice of teammates from other ABA squads, with only Julius Erving being declared off limits. Walton politely knocked back both the Philadelphia and ABA offers and returned to school for what would prove to be his most difficult season yet.

For three years, Walton had been a loyal disciple of John Wooden but by 1973 the star center started to push back against his coach's rigid ways. Walton had always been a free-thinker in areas of campus life that did not relate to basketball, participating in protests and demonstrations connected with a variety of social issues. Now, Walton's rebellious ways began to creep into the UCLA basketball program.

The troubles began on the first day of Walton's senior season when he turned up for the annual team picture with a long hair style that Wooden believed violated team rules. Walton was immediately kicked out of Pauley Pavilion and told he would not be allowed back unless he got a haircut, which he reluctantly did. Throughout the season, there were a range of other incidents that highlighted Walton's new-found willingness to challenge his coach's authority. On one occasion, Wooden confronted Walton about smoking marijuana. Another time, Walton was caught naked in a hotel Jacuzzi by his coach, after a game.

Whether or not these off-court matters had an impact on the Bruins' results can never truly be known but it was clear to all observers that UCLA was not playing as well as it had in the previous two years. In fact, they lost three games during the regular season and then needed three overtime periods to dispatch Dayton in the early rounds of the 1974 NCAA tournament. Still, Walton and the Bruins prevailed and made it through to the Final Four, where they faced a David Thompson-led NC State team in the semi-finals. Midway through the second half, UCLA held an 11 point lead and seemed to be on their way to another NCAA final. Or at least that was the case- until State came storming back and scored a stunning upset victory in overtime. It was a disappointing end to one of the greatest college careers of all-time.

Two months later, Walton was taken with the number one pick of the 1974 NBA draft by Portland, a team that had only been in the league for four years. During this time the Blazers averaged less than 24 wins per season. The arrival of Walton was met with much fanfare in Oregon, with locals believing that their newest addition would lead to a rapid turnaround in the team's fortunes. Unfortunately, this was not the case. Walton missed a total of 78 games across his first two seasons, due to a variety of injuries and while the team improved, they were still unable to qualify for the playoffs.

All of which only served to make what happened in the 1976-77 season even more remarkable.

Walton was healthy enough to appear in 65 of the Blazers' 82 regular season games[27] and he led the league in both rebounds (14.4) and blocks (3.2), while also contributing 18.6 points and 3.8 assists per game. The increase in production from Walton resulted in an improvement in the Blazers' fortunes. They finished the regular season with the Western Conference's third best record and then defeated the Bulls and Nuggets in the first two rounds of the playoffs.

The Western Conference finals saw Portland matched up with the Los Angeles Lakers, which meant that Walton would be going head-to-head with Kareem Abdul-Jabbar. At the time, Kareem was the reigning league MVP and widely considered to be the best player in the league. However, in the space of just eight days, opinion over who was the NBA's most dominant player changed as Walton and the Blazers dispatched Kareem's Lakers in a humiliating 4-0 sweep.

This set up a Finals face-off with the Philadelphia 76ers, a team that featured Julius "Dr. J" Erving, another of the league's truly elite players. When the Sixers won the first two games at home, it appeared that Portland's memorable run was finally coming to an end. At least that was the case until the series shifted to Portland for Games 3 and 4. Led by a near triple-double from Walton (20 points, 18 rebounds and 9 assists), the Blazers convincingly won Game 3 and then followed up with a 32 point blowout that evened the series at two games apiece. Game 5 was back in Philadelphia

---

27 This would remain Walton's personal best in terms of games played in a single season until the eleventh year of his professional career.

and Walton once again led the way, pulling down 24 rebounds as Portland stole home court advantage with a 110-104 victory.

This set the stage for one of the most remarkable individual performances in NBA Finals history. Game 6 was played back at Portland's Memorial Coliseum and Walton produced a dominant display for the home fans, finishing with 20 points, 23 rebounds, 8 assists and 7 blocked shots. The Sixers fought valiantly but they ultimately fell two points short, handing the Blazers their first NBA championship. Walton's contribution to Portland's victory was recognized when he was named as the Finals MVP.

After leading the Blazers to the 1977 championship, Walton became an immediate cult hero in Portland. Whereas previously his long red hair and scruffy beard were a lightning rod for criticism, they were now viewed as the endearing features of a basketball icon. Most people were predicting that the Blazers would remain a league powerhouse for years to come and the team started off the 1977-78 season as strongly as they had finished the last. There was even talk that they might be the first team in NBA history to crack the 70 win barrier.

And then, it all unraveled.

The first sign of a problem came in late February when Walton had to remove himself from a game early in the second quarter due to a pain in his foot. Despite the limited contribution from Walton, the Blazers still won, pushing their overall record to an imposing 50-10. After the game, it was revealed that Walton had a neuroma in his right foot and the decision was made to operate and remove it. While this procedure was a success, Walton began to notice pain in his *left* foot during the recovery period and this kept him sidelined for the remainder of the regular season. Without their leader, the Blazers stumbled, winning just 8 of their final 22 games. Still, Walton had played so well during the early stages of the 1977-78 season that he was named the league's MVP, despite missing almost a third of the Blazers' schedule due to injury[28].

As the regular season wound down and the playoffs approached, the pressure on Walton to resume playing intensified. People around Portland knew that any chance the Blazers had of repeating their championship run hinged on Walton's health. He suited up and played in Portland's first playoff game against Seattle, managing to log 34 painful minutes. And although he was able to pull down 16 rebounds, he was otherwise largely ineffective, struggling with limited mobility due to his aching left foot. The local newspaper reported that Walton was "hobbled like a trotting horse who could break down at any time." Not surprisingly, the Blazers lost and the focus on Walton's injury status only intensified.

Prior to Game 2, Walton consented to having painkilling shots, hoping to increase both his output and the Blazers' chances for success. In hindsight, this was not a good decision. Despite the injections, Walton was in intense pain and eventually had to call it a night midway through the second quarter. The next day, x-rays revealed the cause of the pain- Walton had a stress fracture just below his left ankle. With their star player stuck on the sidelines, Portland was eliminated by Seattle, bringing a swift end to any dreams of back-to-back titles.

In the aftermath of Portland's early playoff exit, questions were raised as to whether the painkilling injections contributed to Walton's stress fracture. Walton blamed the Blazers' medical team for his predicament, believing that they applied subtle pressure in order to influence him to have the painkilling injections. He felt that the interests of the team had been given priority over his long-term health.

---

28 No other player in NBA history has ever been named MVP after missing so many games, a testament to just how good Walton was at the time. In fact, no MVP winner has even come close to Walton's tally of 24 games on the sidelines. Allen Iverson is a distant second on the list for most games missed during an MVP season, sitting out 11 games during the 2000-01 campaign.

Walton was so incensed that he filed a malpractice suit against Robert Cook, the Blazers' team doctor, seeking over $5.5 million in damages. What made the case even more explosive was the fact that Cook and Walton had been close personal friends prior to Walton's latest injury[29]. Walton spent the next seven months in a cast and was ultimately forced to sit out the entire 1978-79 season. He eventually announced his desire to leave Portland and it came as no great surprise when the Blazers said that they would "attempt to abide by his request." The only question now was which team was willing to take a chance on Bill Walton and his seemingly cursed body.

Gene Shue was sitting in his office in San Diego on a Wednesday afternoon when the phone rang. It was Walton's agent, calling to ask a simple question- Would the Clippers be interested in acquiring the services of his client. Shue almost fell out of his chair. If ever there was a player who was born to play in Shue's up-tempo system, it was Walton, who was regarded as the game's premier defensive center and arguably the greatest outlet passer to ever to play in the NBA.

Shue was so excited about the prospect of coaching Walton that he quickly arranged to fly out and met up with him so they could talk face-to-face. The two men met a few days later and they spoke about a range of issues, including Walton's health and what type of role Shue wanted him to play if he was to join the Clippers. By the time Shue returned home, he had formed the opinion that Walton was a perfect fit for the Clippers and that he would be worth the gamble.

Shue went to see Irv Levin to find out if the Clippers' owner would be willing to spend the money necessary to secure Walton's services. Even though Walton had spent much of his professional career sidelined with injuries, his signature would not come at a bargain basement price. He was

---

29 The case was eventually settled in 1982 for an undisclosed sum of money.

still regarded as one of the game's premier players and thus was expecting to be paid accordingly. Levin knew from his time working in Hollywood just how important it was to have a prominent leading man and he agreed to sit down with Walton's representatives to see if they could work out a deal. The contract that the two sides eventually agreed on was the most lucrative in the history of professional basketball- a seven year deal that allowed Walton to earn up to one million dollars per season if certain performance-based clauses were met.

Walton's decision to sign with the Clippers was greeted with considerable hype and fanfare. The team hired a plane that scribed the words "Walton is a Clipper" across the San Diego skyline, while Walton appeared on the cover of Sports Illustrated for the magazine's 1979-80 NBA preview issue. And Walton was not exactly hosing down the city's expectations, making the LeBron-esque proclamation that he expected the Clippers to win multiple championships, now that he was part of the team.

While some of Walton's new teammates shared his optimistic outlook, many others were less than thrilled when they heard the news about the Clippers' latest recruit. The reason for this was that the NBA did not have unrestricted free agency back in 1979. If a team signed a free agent from another team, then some combination of players, money and/or draft picks had to be provided as compensation to the franchise that was losing their player. There were two different ways of determining what an appropriate level of compensation was. Either the two teams involved came to an agreement on what was fair or, in cases where a consensus could not be reached, the NBA commissioner made the final determination. So when the Clippers secured Walton's signature, many of his new teammates began to fret that this was going to mean the end of their days playing in San Diego. And there was no Clipper who was more concerned about being shipped off to Portland than Kermit Washington.

If Moses Malone had been able to stay out of foul trouble on December 9th, 1977, then it is highly likely that one of the most horrific events to ever to take place on a basketball court would not have occurred. Instead, when the second half of the Rockets-Lakers clash got underway, Malone did not take his usual place on the floor with the rest of the starters, due to the four fouls he had accumulated in the first half. With Malone seated on the bench, Kevin Kunnert, the Rockets back-up center, removed his warm-ups and entered the game.

In the opening minute of the third quarter, a Lakers' shot ricocheted off the backboard and Kunnert grabbed the defensive rebound. After throwing an outlet pass to start the Rockets' fast-break, Kunnert and Kareem Abdul-Jabbar got tangled up in the backcourt. While this was going on, the other person trailing the play was Lakers' power forward, Kermit Washington. One of Washington's roles on the team was to act as a quasi-protector for Kareem.

Earlier in the season, Kareem was involved in an altercation with Milwaukee's rookie center Kent Benson that resulted in one broken jaw- Benson's, and one broken hand- Kareem's. The injury kept Kareem out of the Lakers' line-up for the next seven weeks and the team struggled badly during this stretch, winning just eight of their 20 games. The Benson incident made it crystal clear to Washington that one of his primary responsibilities was to put himself between Kareem and any potential conflict.

In an attempt to slow Kunnert's progress up the court, Washington grabbed hold of his shorts, a regulation physical play in the rough and tumble world of 1970s NBA basketball. This in turn led to a scuffle in which Washington landed a punch below Kunnert's eye. When Kunnert's teammate Rudy Tomjanovich saw the commotion at mid-court, he ran over to try and break up the fight. Washington saw somebody approaching out of the corner of his eye, spun around and punched Tomjanovich so hard that it almost killed him. Literally.

Tomjanovich was taken straight to the intensive care unit at Centinela Hospital, where it was discovered that the top and bottom parts of his skull were almost an inch out of alignment and spinal fluid was leaking from his brain. And while Tomjanovich eventually survived, Washington's blow had far-reaching consequences. Tomjanovich was unable to play for the rest of the 1977-78 season and continued to suffer medical problems for years after the event. Meanwhile, Washington went from being a little known role player to one of the most despised athletes in America. He was suspended for 60 days and began receiving hate mail and death threats.

In the weeks that followed the incident, the Lakers moved to distance themselves from Washington by trading him to the Celtics. It was in Boston where Washington took the first steps to resurrect his flailing public image. He played the final 32 games of the 1977-78 NBA season as a Celtic and won over many of the initially skeptical Boston fans with his relentless work ethic. Washington's play was a lone bright spot in an otherwise dismal season for the Celtics and he posted the best numbers of his career during his brief stay in Boston[30].

At the conclusion of the season, Washington was facing an uncertain future as a free agent with a significant black spot on his resume. But, he had played so well over the closing weeks of the season that Boston was keen to have him back. The Celtics offered him a four year deal at $250,000 a season. However, his impressive play had also attracted attention from other teams and Denver presented Washington's agent with an even more lucrative offer of four years at $300,000 per season. Washington's decision would seem to be pretty straightforward. After all, an extra $200,000 in salary was nothing to turn your nose up at, especially back in 1978. However, Washington felt a great deal of loyalty towards the Celtics for taking a chance when many other teams were avoiding him like the plague. He was also not keen on moving to another city and having to win over an entirely new collection of fans. So he took less money and signed with

---

30 11.8 points, 10.5 rebounds and 1.3 blocked shots per game.

the Celtics. And how was Washington's loyalty to the Celtics repaid? He was almost immediately shipped off to the San Diego Clippers as part of John Y. Brown's and Irv Levin's franchise swap[31].

Washington was initially not too keen on the idea of moving cities again. However, the trade from the Celtics to the Clippers worked out pretty well for him. In fact, after one season with Levin's new franchise, Washington was delighted to be playing and living in San Diego. Washington was a big reason behind the Clippers' impressive debut season, averaging 11.3 points and 9.8 rebounds while playing in all 82 games. He had even been voted as the team's most popular player at the end of the season by the Clippers' fans, a feat that would have been unimaginable just 18 months earlier. Washington felt settled and was now looking forward to spending the rest of his career playing in San Diego. Then he heard the news about the signing of Bill Walton and he immediately became concerned about the implications for him personally.

Washington didn't want to go to Portland. The last thing that he wanted to do was move to a new city and start the process of winning over a skeptical fan base all over again. In fact, Washington was so desperate to not be included in the compensation package that he wrote a letter to NBA Commissioner Larry O'Brien. In the letter, he asked O'Brien to consider the upheaval that had taken place in his life in recent years and pleaded not to be one of the Clippers shipped off to Oregon[32]. The Clippers shared Washington's desire that he not be one of the players included in

---

31 Coincidentally, one of the other players who was traded from the Celtics to the Clippers as part of the franchise swap was Kevin Kunnert, who had signed with Boston as a free-agent just a few weeks earlier.

32 To be clear, Kermit Washington was not the only Clipper who didn't want to be sent to Portland as part of the compensation package. In fact, there was almost a consensus view amongst the playing group that whoever was sent to the Blazers would be drawing the short straw. However, there was one Clipper who didn't seem to be too fazed about the prospect of becoming a Blazer. World B. Free was asked about how he would feel if he ended up being sent up to Portland and he responded by saying, "I'll go anyplace they got a disco."

any compensation package, as they viewed him as an essential piece to their championship plans.

The only problem was that the Blazers' desire to extract Washington was equal to that of the Clippers' to keep him. And Washington was not the only player whom the Blazers were after. Portland wanted the Clippers to hand over 1) Washington, 2) Kevin Kunnert or Swen Nater *and* 3) Randy Smith or Freeman Williams. That is potentially three members of the Clippers' starting five from the previous season. The Blazers also wanted the Clippers' next *four* first round draft picks. At this stage, you might be thinking that this seems like a pretty high price to pay for a player who had appeared in just 209 of the 410 regular season games which Portland had played since drafting him. Well, hold that thought because the Blazers were not finished. They asked for money as well, and not just a little bonus cash. They wanted $1 million. Every year. For the next five seasons.

Even if you are looking at Walton's career through the rosiest of lenses, one would have to call the Blazers' compensation request a fairly ridiculous claim. While Walton had demonstrated that he could be the most dominant player in the league when he was healthy, his injury history was so extensive that it simply could not be ignored. With 'good-faith' negotiating like this, it came as no surprise when the discussions between the Clippers and Blazers eventually broke down. In the end, Larry O'Brien had to step in and make the final decision on what was going to be a fair package.

When O'Brien announced his ruling, it was not one that anyone who supported the Clippers felt was fair or reasonable. The Clippers were told to hand over Washington, Kunnert and a first round draft pick (1980) to the Blazers. They were then given the choice of either sending Randy Smith to Portland or hanging onto him. However, if they wanted to keep Smith, they had to give the Blazers $350,000 and another first round draft selection (1982). The Clippers chose to give the Blazers the money and draft pick and then quickly traded Smith to Cleveland for a first round pick in the 1980 draft. In the final analysis, the Clippers lost their starting point guard (Smith), starting power forward (Washington), back-up center (Kunnert), $350,000 in cash and a future first round draft pick.

The compensation package wasn't announced until a couple of days into training camp and the news that Smith, Washington and Kunnert were leaving was a huge blow to team morale. The departures of Smith and Washington represented more than just two fifths of the team's starting five, it was also the loss of the two men who had served as the leaders of the Clippers' playing group. No-one felt more uncomfortable about this news than Bill Walton. As Washington, Smith and Kunnert were summoned off the practice floor and into Gene Shue's office to hear the news that they were no longer members of the San Diego Clippers, Walton could barely bring himself to make eye contact with the rest of his teammates. The Clippers close-knit playing group was being broken-up and Walton placed the blame for this squarely on his own shoulders.

And while Kunnert and Smith were not exactly ecstatic to discover that they were leaving San Diego, Kermit Washington was absolutely devastated. The move to Portland would be his second forced relocation in the space of twelve months. Washington was so upset that he spent the next two weeks holed up in his apartment, contemplating retirement. Washington was eventually talked out of walking away from the game by his agent and he reluctantly reported to Portland. The loss of Washington, Smith and Kunnert made one thing crystal clear; if the Clippers were going to take the next step and qualify for the 1980 playoffs, they needed their million dollar recruit to be in career best form.

Season II: 1979-80

Bill Walton arrived in San Diego looking fit and strong and by the time the exhibition schedule got under way, it appeared that he had finally put his injury issues behind him. Any lingering anger over the players lost via compensation quickly gave way to the realization that the Clippers now had one of the league's strongest rosters on paper. Walton was clearly going to be an upgrade over Kunnert at the center position and the team already had a ready-made replacement at point guard, in former ABA All-Star Brian Taylor[33].

Washington, on the other hand, would not prove as easy to replace. Two weeks after the compensation package was announced, the Clippers pulled the trigger on another deal that they hoped would off-set the loss of their starting power forward. As they had done a year earlier, when acquiring World B. Free, the Clippers sent a future first round draft pick to Philadelphia in exchange for a Sixers bench player. This time around, the Clippers traded their 1986 first round selection for Joe "Jellybean" Bryant, a talented, 6'9" forward whose NBA career had thus far been fairly underwhelming[34]. Bryant was drafted with the 14th overall selection in the 1975 draft but in his four seasons with the Sixers, he had failed to demonstrate that he could be a productive player on a consistent basis[35].

After defeating the Lakers in the exhibition game played in Anaheim, many Clipper fans started to believe that their new-look team was capable of contending for an NBA championship. Season ticket sales were up and for a brief moment, it appeared that the Clippers were heading somewhere desirable.

---

33 Taylor had joined the Clippers at the end of the previous season, however he played a limited role, due to the glut of backcourt talent already on the roster. Randy Smith's trade to Cleveland meant that Taylor was once again set to play major minutes.

34 The Clippers had now traded away four first round draft picks (1980, 1982, 1984 and 1986) in the space of just 12 months in order to acquire Free, Walton and Bryant.

35 One can only conclude that Shue had seen something he liked during the two seasons that he coached Bryant in Philadelphia. Otherwise, it seemed like a completely bizarre move to trade a first round draft pick in exchange for a 25 year old player with career averages of 6.4 points and 3.3 rebounds. Bryant arrived in San Diego with his wife and one year old son Kobe. This was the same Kobe Bryant who would dominate the NBA two decades later.

The following day, the Clippers were scheduled to play another exhibition game against the Lakers, only this clash was not quite as positive as the win in Orange County, with Walton unable to complete the game due to a foot injury. A week later, he was only able to walk with the aid of crutches. Any hope of the Clippers lifting the Walter A. Brown trophy[36] quickly gave way to the realization that life with Walton might not be all cigars and champagne. The pain in Walton's foot turned out to be another stress fracture and it kept him on the sidelines for the remainder of the exhibition schedule.

Opening night of the regular season brought yet another clash with the Lakers, this one broadcast on national television. The game was the first official outing of Magic Johnson's NBA career and was played at the San Diego Sports Arena in front of 8,500 enthusiastic fans. Unfortunately for the Clipper faithful, Walton was still unable to play due to his injured foot. This left Kareem free to impose his will against the undermanned Clippers' frontline and he finished with a team-high 29 points. However, despite Kareem's dominance, the Clippers led for much of the evening and looked set to record an unlikely victory. With just a few seconds remaining, the home team had both possession of the ball and a one point buffer. All they needed to do was hold onto the ball and they could hit the showers with a 1-0 record. Instead, Freeman Williams carelessly dribbled the ball off his foot and out of bounds, providing the visitors with one final chance to steal the win.

The Lakers called a timeout to draw up a play that called for a lob pass to go to Magic, who was cutting off a back-screen. However, when the screen was set, the Clippers opted to switch, making the pass too risky to throw. Instead, the ball went to the second option on the play, Kareem, who was stationed at the edge of the free throw line. What happened next has become part of Laker folklore. Kareem caught the inbound pass, turned

---

36 The original name of the Larry O'Brien Trophy.

and hit a 15 foot skyhook over the out-stretched arms of Swen Nater, giving the Lakers a 103-102 victory.

Magic was so overjoyed at achieving his first NBA win that he raced over to Kareem and began gripping him in a passionate bear hug. Kareem, who was famous for his subdued attitude, was unsure of what to make of his over-exuberant new teammate. When they finally reached the locker room, he warned Magic to take it easy in the victory celebration department as they had another 81 games to go.

This is a story that has been told many times over when reflecting on the career of Magic but a lesser known fact is that it was the undermanned Clippers who played the role of the Lakers' foil on that famous evening. In the space of just 15 days, the Clippers had gone from being the Lakers' feared Southern Californian rivals, to a mere footnote in the first chapter of the Showtime story. This opening night defeat would set the tone for what would be a disappointing second season in San Diego.

Unfortunately, Bill Walton watching games in street clothes would become an all too familiar sight for basketball fans in San Diego. Walton was unable to play a single minute in the first three and a half months of the 1979-80 season. During this time, the Clippers somehow managed to keep in touch with the Western Conference playoff picture despite playing without the services of their star recruit. After getting off to a slow start, the team hit a hot streak in which they won 16 of 22 games over a six week period, bringing their overall record to 27-23.

Perhaps the most bizarre victory during this run of good form came five days before Christmas in a home game against New York. With Walton's absence continuing to have a negative impact on the team's gate receipts, the Clippers' PR team had begun trialing a number of promotional ideas in an attempt to lift attendance figures. When the Knicks came to town, they decided to hold a half-time pie-throwing competition.

It turned out that pies, polished wood floors and professional basketball players are not a good mix.

As the two teams headed off to their respective locker rooms, a tarp was brought out to cover the floor and a local broadcaster named Ted Leitner took his place as the human target underneath one of the baskets. Theoretically, everything could have gone smoothly if the fans selected from the crowd were able to throw the cream pies in such a way that all the debris stayed contained in the area covered by the tarp. Unfortunately, they couldn't and cream ended up everywhere.

The mess was so bad that when the two teams emerged for the second half, the court was deemed unsafe and the game was postponed. While the bemused players stood around and watched, a team of ball boys frantically tried to clean the court. However, the ball boys used damp towels to mop up the mess, which only served to smear the cream across an even larger area, making the court as slippery as an ice-skating rink.

As the delay stretched past the 30 minute mark, New York coach Red Holzman became increasingly frustrated. The Knicks had a game the following night in Seattle and were scheduled to fly out straight after their clash with the Clippers. However, the San Diego airport had a strict 11:30pm curfew, after which no flights were allowed to take off. Holzman knew that his team would be stranded in San Diego if the game didn't get back underway soon. This would force the Knicks to fly to Seattle on the morning of the game, hardly the ideal preparation for a match-up with the reigning NBA champions. As the big clean-up continued, an irate Holzman informed anybody within earshot of exactly how he felt about the Clippers organization, with some of the most colorful language being saved for their promotional department.

Play was finally able to resume after a 53 minute delay which, on top of the 12 minute half-time break, meant the game had been on pause for over an hour. The score remained close until the fourth quarter, when the Clippers came from behind and defeated the Knicks, 128-118. Holzman used his post-game comments as an opportunity to blame his side's defeat on the extended half-time break, while Clippers' coach Gene Shue summed up the evening by declaring, "It was a long game."

On January 29th, with less than two minutes remaining in the first quarter of the Clippers-Suns clash, a spontaneous standing ovation broke out at the San Diego Sports Arena. The reason for this burst of enthusiasm had nothing to do with the action taking place on the floor. Instead, it was in response to Bill Walton rising from his seat on the sidelines, ripping off his warm-up jacket and making his way to the scorer's table. He was about to check-in to an NBA regular season game for the first time in 700 days. After months of rehabilitation, Walton was finally ready to resume his career. The crowd of 11,428 stood and roared, both in appreciation for the hard road Walton had endured in order to return, as well as in anticipation of what his comeback meant for the Clippers' playoff hopes.

Walton was restricted to playing very limited minutes in his comeback game but was still able to make a valuable contribution. He finished with 8 points, on 4-5 shooting, 4 rebounds and 1 blocked shot in just 13 minutes of action. Inspired by the return of their star recruit, the Clippers scored a 133-121 victory, giving them some much needed breathing room in the playoff race with Portland, who were just a game and half behind in the standings. And while everyone was happy to finally see Walton out on court, even better news arrived the next day when he was able to walk without limping. With no games scheduled over the next seven days, due to the All-Star game, Walton had plenty of time to recover from his Clipper debut.

One Clipper who didn't get the chance to have a rest was World B. Free, who was heading off to Washington for his first All-Star appearance.

Free was not only invited to play in the league's showcase event, he was selected as a member of the Western Conference's starting five. Free scored 14 points and played a pivotal role as the West erased a 17 point deficit in the fourth quarter to force the game into overtime. However, the East pulled away in the extra period and secured a 144-136 victory.

The Clipper front office was also busy over the All-Star break, signing up Marvin "Bad News" Barnes for the remainder of the season, a decision that raised more than a few eyebrows around the league. While nobody doubted Barnes' talent, he was also a well-known drug user with a history of erratic behavior. At the time that the Clippers signed him, Barnes had been out of the NBA for over 12 months. This extended period on the sidelines should have set alarm bells ringing in the minds of the Clippers' brains trust. Here was an extremely talented player who was just 27 years of age and yet no one was interested in having him on their roster.

The reason for every other NBA team electing to steer clear of Barnes was because he continued to cause chaos wherever he went. During his time at Providence, it was alleged that Barnes hit a teammate, Larry Ketvirtis, with a tire iron. This resulted in him pleading guilty to assault with a deadly weapon and receiving a suspended one year jail sentence[37]. In his first professional season, playing for the Spirits of St. Louis, he got into a dispute with management over the terms of his contract and walked out on the team. For two weeks, no one knew where he was or if he would ever play for the Spirits again[38]. After the NBA-ABA merger, Barnes' rights were picked up by the Detroit Pistons in the dispersal draft that was held to redistribute the ABA players whose teams were not joining the NBA. During his brief stay in Detroit he was arrested for carrying a handgun through a metal detector at an airport, which earned him a five month stint in prison.

---

37 Barnes later claimed that he actually punched Ketvirtis and that the tire iron was only brandished to prevent the fight from escalating further.
38 Barnes was eventually located in a pool hall in Dayton, Ohio and he re-joined the Spirits after receiving an assurance from the front office that his contract would be re-written.

His final stop before arriving in San Diego was with the Celtics. By this time, his drug use had become so brazen that he even snorted cocaine on the bench during a game, with nothing but a towel draped over his head for the purposes of concealment. It came as no surprise when Barnes was cut by the Celtics in the middle of the 1978-79 season.

Barnes arrived in San Diego having not played a meaningful basketball game in over a year and he was a long way from peak physical condition. He made his debut on February 8th in a crucial home game against Portland. Led by a 29 point performance off the bench from Freeman Williams, the Clippers won, giving them a one game lead over the Blazers in the standings. Barnes did not play a significant role in the victory, scoring just 4 points in limited court time.

For the second consecutive season, the Clippers were clinging to a playoff berth with Portland hot on their heels. And for the second year in a row, they saved their worst form for the closing weeks of the season. Following the win over the Blazers, the Clippers lost 13 of their next 19 games, which allowed Portland to leap-frog them in the standings. And then, just when things looked like they couldn't get any worse, they did, as the Clippers lost the services of their best two players.

The first to go down was Bill Walton. In his final game of the season, a 17 point defeat at the hands of the Lakers, Walton struggled around the court for 31 minutes and was absolutely dominated by Kareem, who had 28 points and 12 rebounds. The following day he could hardly walk and scans would later reveal that he had once again broken a bone in his foot. Walton played a total of 14 games and finished with averages of 13.9 points, 9 rebounds, 2.4 assists and 2.7 blocks.

A week after Walton hung up his sneakers for the season, Free sustained an injury of his own and ruled himself out of the Clippers' last five games. A severely undermanned Clippers team travelled to Seattle, where they almost caused a huge upset, losing a tightly fought contest by just three points. The Clippers were now half a game behind the Blazers in the race for the Western Conference's final playoff berth. However, with four games to play, including two against Portland, the Clippers' fate was still very much in their own hands.

The Clippers' next game was played in Portland and the Blazers held on for a 98-91 victory. This result meant that, in order to keep their playoff hopes alive, the Clippers had to defeat the Blazers when the two teams clashed in San Diego and in the lead-up to the game, the home team's chances were given an unexpected boost when Free declared himself fit to play. This encounter would be a lot closer than the clash in Portland, with the result remaining in the balance until the game's final possession. With nine seconds remaining, World B. Free had the ball, with the Clippers trailing by a single point. Free was not only the team's leading scorer for the season, he was also the man with the hot hand, having already connected on two three-pointers in a 10-0 fourth quarter run that brought the Clippers back into the game.

Kermit Washington, now the starting power forward for the Blazers, had firsthand knowledge of Free's uncanny ability to put the ball in the hole. He decided that it was better to force someone else to take the final shot, rather than give his former teammate a clean look at the basket. Even with Washington rushing out to double team him, Free still considered launching the game's final shot, before deciding to swing the ball to the open man. The player whom Washington had left alone just happened to be Marvin Barnes, who was unguarded on the left baseline, just ten feet from the basket. If Barnes was able to convert he would not only save the season, he would justify Gene Shue's show of faith in him.

Barnes caught the pass, fixed his eyes on the basket and launched the shot.

It was an airball.

And just like that, the Clippers second season was finished.

Season III: 1980-81

The most immediate effect of the Clippers missing out on the playoffs was that it brought an end to Gene Shue's time as the franchise's first head coach. Twelve months after finishing runner-up for the Coach of the Year award, the Clippers and Shue decided to part company by mutual agreement. Shue had done a remarkable job of keeping the Clippers in playoff contention all the way until the last week of the regular season, considering how little time Walton spent on the court. However, his chances of returning to San Diego to coach for a third year were undoubtedly hurt by the team's late season slump. The Clippers ended up losing 17 of their final 23 games, including a run of 7 straight losses to close out the regular season, giving them an overall record of 35-47.

When the time came to appoint a new coach the Clippers would, somewhat ironically, select Paul Silas. This was the same Paul Silas that Irv Levin refused to give a pay raise to all those years ago in Boston. This led to Silas' departure, which brought a premature end to another Celtic championship era and ultimately played a big role in Levin's eventual decision to flee Boston. Now, five years later, Levin was turning to Silas, a man with no coaching experience, in the hope that he could steer the Clippers towards an NBA championship.

Originally, Silas was hired as a player-coach, making him the only person in the league who was attempting to simultaneously perform both of these roles. It didn't take long for Silas to figure out that this arrangement was not going to work. He quickly realized that the demands of coaching the Clippers were more than enough for him to contend with and informed Levin that he was officially retiring as a player, to allow him to concentrate on coaching.

With Silas hanging up his sneakers, the Clippers' front office launched another unorthodox plan to bring in a power forward to play alongside Walton. And the player whom they had their eyes on was no stranger. The Clippers asked the league to send Kermit Washington back to San Diego, by filing an official appeal against the compensation ruling from 12 months earlier. The Clippers' appeal was based on the fact that they believed that the original award of compensation to the Blazers was far too generous. It was easy to see why the Clippers were keen to get Washington back. In his first year with Blazers, he was named as a reserve on the Western Conference All-Star team and finished the season with career highs in points (13.4), blocks (1.6) and assists (2.1), while pulling down 10.5 rebounds per game.

The case was reviewed by Telford Taylor, a lawyer who worked as prosecutor during the Nuremberg Trials and he ruled in favor of the Clippers. However, despite winning the case, the Clippers did not get the prize that they hoped for. Portland was allowed to hang onto Washington and was instead told to return one of the Clippers' first round draft picks (1982) and the $350,000 in cash they had received as part of the initial transaction. The Clippers complained publically that this ruling was also unfair, but privately they had to be happy to have received something back, as they were getting very little out of Walton.

One of Silas' first acts as a head coach was to sit down for a meal with World B. Free, to discuss his vision for the upcoming season and the role that he wanted Free to play. Unfortunately, the dinner did not go well and Silas left the restaurant feeling convinced that it was going to be difficult to have a productive relationship with his star player. Silas told the Clippers' front office to start looking into trading options and in late August, Free was dealt to Golden State in exchange for two-time All-Star Phil Smith and a first round draft pick.

After missing out on Washington and trading away Free, the Clippers were hopeful that Bill Walton would be able to make a greater contribution than the 14 games that he had played in his first season in San Diego. And things started off positively enough at the team's training camp, which was held on the campus of Arizona Western, a small junior college in Yuma, Arizona. For the first couple of days, Walton was able to join in the practice sessions and the mood around the team was fairly positive. However, this optimism was soon replaced with a harsh dose of reality as Walton's feet began to give him problems once again. His foot troubles were so bad that they eventually forced him to miss the entire 1980-81 season. This left the Clippers to once again try and find a way to sneak into the playoffs with a seriously undermanned roster.

The Clippers' third campaign was a case of different coach, same results. Once again, the team hovered around the .500 mark for much of the season and by the end of February they were just two and a half games out of the West's final playoff spot. There are no prizes for predicting what happened next. The Clippers faded badly down the stretch, winning just six of their final 16 games, which was enough to cause them to drop out of the playoff race. They finished the year with a humiliating home loss at the hands of Portland, in which they allowed the Blazers to score 144 points. It was a fitting end to a disappointing season.

For the third consecutive year, the Clippers showed early signs of promise before ultimately failing to secure a playoff berth. However, if the basketball fans of San Diego were concerned that this was going to develop into some sort of long term trend, they needn't have worried. There were about to be some big changes in Clipper-land. Changes that would usher in a new era of Clipper basketball and make the days of narrowly missing out on qualifying for the playoffs seem like a distant memory.

CHAPTER 3

The Don

"Yeah, there is a curse. His name is Donald Sterling."

BILL PLASCHKE

WHEN MICHAEL SPILGER FIRST HEARD the news that the Clippers were holding a free-throw competition, he figured he had a pretty reasonable chance of winning the $1,000 first prize. After all, Spilger had played Division One college ball at San Diego State, while the remaining competitors were a random assortment of real estate agents and lawyers. The contest was part of a function hosted by Donald Sterling, a wealthy 47 year old who had recently purchased the Clippers. The event, held at the San Diego Sports Arena, was designed to build goodwill between the local business community and the franchise's new owner.

Spilger, who had long since hung up his sneakers for a career as an attorney, spent the first part of the afternoon taking advantage of the free sandwiches and hors d'oeuvres on offer. When the time finally came for the shooting competition, he calmly strode to the line and iced nine out of ten attempts, which was good enough to claim the $1,000. Or at least that's what Spilger thought, until later in the day, when he had a conversation with Sterling. The Clippers new owner informed Spilger that the reward for winning the shoot-out was no longer a cash prize, it was now a four night vacation in Puerto Rico. The only problem was airfares were not included, meaning Spilger had to pay for flights if he wanted to collect his new reward. An unimpressed Spilger informed Sterling that he had no interest in forking out for an airfare to Puerto Rico and asked for the money that he was owed.

Sterling, who at the time had a net worth that was estimated to be somewhere between $300 million and $700 million, asked Spilger if he wanted to go double or nothing for the $1,000 prize. Spilger declined. Sterling then offered a couple of season tickets as a new alternative. Spilger was already a season ticket holder so he said no, before again asking for the money that he had won. Sterling said that the Clippers promotional department would be in touch within the next few weeks to sort everything out. Spilger left the Sports Arena feeling like a tourist who had just gone head-to-head with a three card monte hustler, rather than a winner of a promotional event put on by an NBA team.

Two weeks later, Spilger received a chirpy letter from the Clippers congratulating him on winning two nights in Las Vegas. As far as Spilger could see, his prize was shrinking by the minute. He started with a $1,000, was then offered four nights in Puerto Rico and was now down to just two nights in Vegas. Over the next few months, Spilger tried to bring the situation to an amicable resolution by writing letters and calling the Clippers to try and ascertain when he would be able to collect his prize money.

After a year of failed attempts, a fed up Spilger decided that his only alternative was to file a lawsuit. At this point, a Clippers team official offered him a $1,000 payment to his favorite charity, to which Spilger replied, "I'll see you in court." Two days later, Spilger finally received a check for $1,000, over a year after hitting the nine free throws.

The final chapter in this drawn out saga took place a couple of years later, when Spilger ran into Sterling at a party. Sterling instantly recognized the sharp shooting lawyer who was so brazen as to expect the Clippers would hand over the actual prize that they had advertised. He approached Spilger and, instead of offering an apology, told him that his actions were reprehensible.

And so begins Donald Sterling's 33 year reign as owner of the Clippers.

By the spring of 1981, it seemed that Irv Levin had simply run out of patience with his new basketball enterprise. The Clippers were losing games, losing fans and losing money, which was difficult for a man like Levin to process. Up until this point, Levin had been successful in almost every endeavour in his life but it appeared that basketball was destined to be his Achilles heel. First Levin suffered the ignominy of being booed off the court in Boston, which led to his decision to trade away the Celtics and start afresh in San Diego. Now he was facing constant criticism over his decision to sign Bill Walton, who had only appeared in 14 games across his first two seasons with the Clippers. At the time, Levin was also dealing with a personal tragedy, after the death of his second wife. Levin decided that he wanted to devote more of his time to the movie business and so he began to explore ways to off-load the Clippers.

Levin's first attempt at selling the franchise did not go well. The prospective buyer was a man by the name of Phil Knight, owner of a little shoe company up in Oregon called Nike. Levin and Knight reached an agreement on how much the team would be sold for ($13.5 million) and had even gone so far as to draw up a schedule of when the various payments would be made. All of this was done in the presence of a pair of lawyers and the general manager of the Phoenix Suns, Jerry Colangelo, which left Levin feeling pretty confident that his time as an NBA owner was about to come to an end. Then Knight had a change of heart, causing the deal to collapse[39].

The next potential buyer was Donald Sterling, a Los Angeles-based lawyer with a growing real estate portfolio and a desire to move into the world of professional sports. In the weeks leading up to the sale, Levin spent a considerable amount of time courting Sterling, selling him on the joys of owning an NBA team and the positives of the city of San Diego. Sterling was already well aware of the many benefits that came with being an NBA owner through his association with Jerry Buss, a chemist turned investor who had bought the Los Angeles Lakers two years earlier. In fact, Sterling had played an important role in Buss' entry into the world of NBA basketball.

When Buss purchased the Lakers from Jack Kent Cooke, he also bought Cooke's ice hockey team (the Los Angeles Kings), the arena that hosted the Lakers' and Kings' games (the Forum) and a 13,000 acre ranch located in Nevada. The cost of this extravagant package of assets was $67.5 million and the deal was labeled as "the largest single financial transaction in the history of professional sports" by the New York Times. Not surprisingly, Buss did not have the necessary cash to close the deal and so he needed to quickly liquidate some of his assets. Which is where Sterling entered the story. Buss sold Sterling 11 of his Santa Monica apartment complexes and then used the money from this sale to make up part of the $67.5 million that he paid to Cooke.

Buss became the Lakers owner at the start of the 1979-80 season and Sterling watched on as Buss' new team experienced immediate success. During that first season, the Lakers won the NBA championship and Buss

---

39 While Knight's exact reason for backing out of the deal was unknown, it is clear that Levin was not impressed. Levin filed a lawsuit, claiming that he suffered financial hardship as a result of Knight breaking a legally binding contract. The courts eventually found in favor of Knight, saying that there was no actual contract, just a memo that was nothing more than "an agreement to agree."

was so pleased with his decision to buy the team that he encouraged Sterling to join him by purchasing a franchise of his own.

When word began to spread amongst the Southern Californian business community that Levin was looking to sell the Clippers, Sterling was interested. After weeks of discussions, Sterling and Levin met at an upscale San Diego restaurant called Lubach's to nut out the details of the sale. The final deal called for Sterling to make a relatively small cash payment of around $2 million and assume approximately $10 million in existing team debts and deferred compensation. The announcement that the Clippers had a new owner initially created a burst of optimism amongst the basketball fans of San Diego. These positive feelings would prove to be extremely short-lived.

Donald Sterling was once labeled "the Howard Hughes of the NBA" by one of his employees, although it is unclear whether this was meant as a compliment or an insult. Over the years, Sterling has developed a number of unusual habits that probably wouldn't be tolerated by those around him if he were not so insanely wealthy. But money can buy you many things, including the ability to conduct yourself in a manner that most regular folk would not be able to get away with. Sterling is a renowned close talker and a serial toucher, someone who either doesn't respect other people's personal space or is simply unaware that he is encroaching on it. Go for a meal with Sterling and you don't have to bother looking at the menu, as he is likely to order for you and everyone else at the table. Once the food arrives, Sterling is known for helping himself to whatever catches his fancy, regardless of whose plate it is on. Sterling is also a brilliant real estate investor who has made a fortune following a simple buy and hold strategy. But while this real estate empire has brought him some fame and notoriety over the years, there is no doubt that the Sterling brand is built on the fact that, for 33 years, he was the owner of the Clippers.

Sterling was born Donald Tokowitz in Chicago in 1934. When he was two, he moved to Boyle Heights, Los Angeles, where his father supported his family by selling fresh produce to local restaurants. Sterling's mother always dreamed that her son would have a more charmed life and pushed him to go to college so he could become a lawyer. After graduating from Roosevelt High School, Sterling attended Southwestern University School of Law while also moonlighting as a salesman at Harry Stein's Coliseum Furniture. It was during this period of selling couches and coffee tables that Donald Tokowitz decided to change his name to Donald T. Sterling[40], telling a colleague that "you had to name yourself after something…that people have confidence in." Not only did Sterling pick up a new name while working for Harry Stein, he also met his future wife, Shelly, who just happened to be the boss' daughter.

By the early 1960s, Sterling was working as a personal injury lawyer and was busy filing lawsuits against some of the biggest names in Hollywood. He sued singing cowboy Gene Autry for $5.1 million on behalf of a family who was injured in a car accident[41]. He also took on actress Carol Lynley in divorce proceedings, where he won $25,000 on behalf of her ex-husband. Sterling took the money that he was earning via his legal fees and began investing it, purchasing apartment buildings in the area between Beverly Hills and Santa Monica. At the time, the real estate market was slumping and few people thought that buying property in Los Angeles was a good idea. However Sterling was a visionary who anticipated that a lot of Americans would soon be moving west to California. As the population of Los Angeles continued to grow throughout the 1960s and 1970s, the value of Sterling's real estate portfolio appreciated, which allowed him to refinance and purchase even more. His motto was to buy only what he intended to keep. It was a simple plan and, by the spring of 1981, it made Sterling rich enough to become the owner of his very own NBA franchise.

---

40 The "T" standing for his discarded surname.
41 The case was settled before making it to trial.

Season IV: 1981-82

If you lived in San Diego in 1981, it was hard to miss the fact that the Clippers had a new owner, due to a unique advertising campaign that was launched during that off-season. A series of peculiar billboards were erected around the San Diego area with the aim of promoting the Clippers, although they did not feature any of the team's players. Instead, potential fans were greeted with a giant shot of Donald Sterling's smiling face and some accompanying text that read: *"My Promise: I will make you proud of the Clippers."* Sterling also wrote an open letter to the people of San Diego in which he pledged to spend whatever it took to turn the Clippers into a winner. "We are going to go after box office names. Whatever a winning team costs, we are prepared to pay," Sterling said. "If an average player costs $300,000 and an above average player costs $600,000, we'll pay it. We think that we owe that much to the fans

It didn't take long for Sterling to switch his focus from public relations to the basketball-related affairs of his new team. Clippers general manager, Ted Podleski, had shrewdly negotiated a favorable trade with the Denver Nuggets on the eve of the 1981-82 season: a straight swap of Freeman Williams for Alex English. English was a 6'7" scoring machine who had just come off a season where he averaged 23.8 points and 8 rebounds per game. He was just 27 years old and looked to be an ideal fit for the Clippers. The deal was as good as done when Sterling got cold feet and used his position as owner to veto the trade[42].

Having missed out on the services of English, the Clippers were dealt another blow when it was revealed that Bill Walton would not be taking any part in the 1981-82 season. In fact, it was beginning to look increasingly likely that Walton may have played his last NBA game. Doctors had recently discovered that Walton had an unusually shaped left foot with a heel

---

[42] English went on to average over 20 points per game for nine consecutive seasons, play in the next eight All-Star games, lead the NBA in scoring in the 1982-83 season and be inducted into the Hall of Fame. He also missed a total of just nine games in the ten years between his almost trade to the Clippers and the end of the 1990-91 season, when he eventually retired.

that did not flex properly. This meant that every time he ran or jumped, the impact was absorbed by the bones in his foot rather than being dispersed across the various muscles, tendons and ligaments. The effect of this repetitive force over time was to cause these bones to weaken, making them highly susceptible to stress fractures. Around the same time that the doctors began discussing the prospect of amputation, the Clippers declared that Walton was permanently disabled and cashed in a $1.25 million insurance policy[43].

With his playing days seemingly behind him, Walton decided to head back to college, at the urging of David Halberstam, a renowned writer who had formed a friendship with Walton. Halberstam arranged for Walton to enroll at Stanford Law School, leaving the Clippers to once again kick-off a new season without the services of their star center and causing the hopes of the local fans to sink dramatically. Without Walton, it seemed unlikely that the Clippers would be able to mount any sort of serious challenge for a play-off berth. It would soon become apparent that, as far as Donald Sterling was concerned, this was no problem whatsoever.

If Clippers' fans were getting sick of *just* missing out on the playoffs, the first year under Sterling's ownership would drastically change that script. The 1981-82 Clippers managed to eliminate themselves from playoff contention before the month of December had ended. Four days after Christmas, the Clippers were sitting in last place in the Western Conference, with just six wins from their first 27 games.

---

43 Although collecting on this policy was far from straight forward. The insurance company, Lloyd's of London, initially refused to pay the $1.25 million because of an exemption in the policy relating to ankle injuries. Lloyd's claimed that Walton's troubles with his feet were ankle-related and thus denied the Clippers' claim. The Clippers took legal action, asking for the money they were owed as per policy and an additional $11.25 million in damages. This led to an out of court settlement where Lloyd's agreed to pay the initial $1.25 million but nothing further.

In the middle of all of this losing, Sterling decided to publically announce his plans to tank the rest of the season. Sterling's rationale was that the Clippers needed to do whatever they could to give themselves the best chance at landing the first pick in the 1982 draft, where it was expected that Ralph Sampson would be available for selection. Sampson stood at an imposing 7'4" tall and was universally regarded as the best NBA prospect since Kareem Abdul-Jabbar left UCLA. At the time of Sterling's comments, Sampson was in the middle of his junior season at Virginia. "We must end up last in order to draw first and get a franchise maker like Ralph Sampson," Sterling told his assembled audience, before adding, "I don't think we'll have to work very hard to have the worst record."

Bad teams deliberately losing games to try and land a high draft pick has long been a part of NBA history. However, the unwritten rule is that you never publically declare that you are no longer interested in winning. For an owner who had only bought his team a few months ago, to come out and emphatically state that he was trying to finish with the league's worst record was the last thing that the NBA needed. Sterling was immediately fined $10,000 for "conduct prejudicial and detrimental to the NBA" which, at the time, was the largest fine ever levied against an NBA owner. And it was not just the league's head office that was annoyed by Sterling's comments. Tom Chambers, a 6'10" forward whom the Clippers had selected with the eighth overall pick in the 1981 draft, said that Sterling's remarks "left scars that will take a long time to heal." Chambers, the rookie player, also had some words of advice for Sterling, the rookie owner, saying, "Maybe it's better for him not to talk anymore. Maybe it's best to be quiet."

From the moment Sterling made his controversial remarks, it seems that the Clippers did everything in their power to avoid winning games. With both the team's centers already out for the rest of the season with injuries[44], the Clippers shifted their focus to weakening their backcourt. In

---

[44] Swen Nater joined Walton on the sidelines when he injured his knee in the middle of December. He was unable to resume playing until the following season.

late January, Freeman Williams was traded to Atlanta. During the previous season, Williams led the Clippers in scoring with an average of 19.3 points per game, despite only ranking *sixth* on the team in terms of minutes played[45]. Williams was also the first Clipper to win the NBA's Player of the Month award[46]. Over the first half of the 1981-82 season, Williams was again providing the Clippers with an explosive scoring spark off the bench, averaging 16.5 points in just over 21 minutes per game. Meanwhile, it was hard to put a positive spin on the two players the Clippers received in return for Williams. Charlie Criss was a 5'8" guard who was averaging less than 9 points per game, while shooting just 40% from the floor and 25% from three-point range. The second player the Clippers acquired was Al Wood, who was a 6'6" rookie who was shooting 34% from the field and averaging just 4.8 points per game.

The Clippers next big move was to trade away Phil Smith to Seattle for Armond Hill and a second round draft pick. At the time of the trade, Smith, a former NBA champion and two-time All-Star, was starting for the Clippers and playing over 30 minutes a night while averaging 13.2 points and 4.9 assists per game. Meanwhile Hill, who was a only a year younger than Smith, was averaging 2.6 points per game in a little over 11 minutes a night for the Sonics. Once again, this did not look like a trade made by a front office who was interested in putting a winning team on the court.

At the same time that the Clippers were weakening their current team to improve their draft prospects, they were also instructing Pete Babcock, the team's only scout, to cease all travel until further notice. In an era before the internet and prior to the proliferation of college basketball on cable television, this was the equivalent of shutting down the scouting department. If the Clippers were looking at the 1982 draft as the source of a potential savior,

---

45 During the 1980-81 season, Williams was the league leader in points per minute, tied with George Gervin. Both players averaged 28.9 points per 36 minutes played, placing them above such notable opponents as Kareem Abdul-Jabbar, Julius Erving and Moses Malone.
46 Williams won the award in December 1980. It would be 299 months before another Clipper would claim this honor.

it seemed that they were putting all their eggs in the Ralph Sampson basket and giving little thought to what would happen if they were unable to secure his rights. Babcock was told that the Clippers were not spending money on anything related to basketball beyond what was required by the league.

The scouting department wasn't the only area where Sterling attempted to trim the budget to the bare bones. At one stage in the season, Paul Silas was asked if he would be able to tape the players' ankles before games, thus eliminating the need for a trainer. Silas said no.

Then there was the time when the Clippers almost didn't turn up to play a road game in Seattle because the team's management was trying to save money by having the players fly coach. The team turned up at the airport thinking they were about to board a flight from San Diego to Seattle, only to discover that their tickets were not first class. This was a direct violation of a recent agreement between the players' association and the league owners, which stated that players had to be provided with first class tickets for any flight that was two hours or longer. The players, led by Joe Bryant, the team's union representative, refused to board the plane, leaving Silas to fret that he might be the first coach in NBA history to lose a game via forfeit.

This crisis was only averted by some swift talking from Silas, who offered his personal assurance that this would never happen again if Bryant was able to convince his teammates to fly economy just one more time, so that the Clippers-Sonics game could go ahead. Bryant calmed the rest of the team down and the players eventually boarded the flight and squeezed their over-sized bodies into the cramped economy seats. The Clippers flew to Seattle, where they were predictably defeated by the Sonics. When they returned to San Diego, Silas spoke with the team's management and informed them, in no uncertain terms, that trying to save a few bucks by booking coach airfares for the players was no longer an option.

In the midst of all these cost-cutting measures, the Clippers welcomed a new employee, a former model by the name of Patricia Simmons whom Sterling was rumored to have met at the Playboy Club. Simmons started off working in the marketing department, was promoted to the role of business manager and eventually became the team's assistant general manager, despite having no known background in the world of professional basketball.

Some members of the local media thought it would be a bit of a laugh to interview Simmons to put her knowledge of the sport to the test. She refused this request and instead told the reporters to submit their questions in writing. So Bud Poliquin and Nick Canepa, the two San Diego Union-Tribune writers who wanted to speak with Simmons, put together a list of the most basic questions possible, including such mind-benders as "Who was Wilt Chamberlin?" Poliquin and Canepa sent the questions off to the Clipper headquarters and a few hours later, they received a call from Simmons, who informed them that she would not be providing any response.

The act that Simmons was most well-known for was evicting Paul Silas from his office. For months, Simmons had been trying to get Silas to swap offices with her. And for months, Silas had been holding his ground, figuring that as the franchise's head coach he was entitled to what he referred to as "the good office." Simmons decided that since the negotiating tact wasn't working for her, it was time to try a different approach. So, she waited until Silas was out of town and simply took over his office space, moving in all of her stuff and dumping Silas' possessions out in the corridor. Silas returned to San Diego to find his furniture and files stacked haphazardly out in front of what was now Patricia Simmons' new office.

Given this surrounding chaos, it should come as no great surprise to learn that the Clippers did not perform well in the second half of the season. In fact, they managed to lose 36 of their final 40 games to finish with 17 wins and 65 losses.

One of the few bright spots in an otherwise dismal year was the development of Tom Chambers, who seemed to get better as the season progressed. When Chambers was first drafted by the Clippers, he was so unsure about his future as an NBA player that he asked his agent if he was going to be good enough to earn a spot on the team's opening day roster. Chambers did more than just make the team, he quickly became the Clippers' best player, finishing the season as the team's leading scorer with an average of 17.2 points per game. The good form of Chambers was largely responsible for the Clippers falling short of Sterling's stated aim of ending the season with the worst record in the league. That "honor" went to Cleveland, who won just 15 games.

Sterling needn't have worried as the Cavs greater ineptitude was not going to have any effect on the likelihood of the Clippers claiming the first overall selection in the upcoming draft. Back in 1982, there was no such thing as the NBA draft lottery. Instead, the allocation of the first pick was decided by a simple coin toss between the teams with the worst record in each of the NBA's two conferences. While the Clippers had been unsuccessful in their mission to finish last in the league, they did have the worst record in the Western Conference, putting themselves in the best possible position to draft Sampson. The franchise that they would be facing off against in the all-important coin toss was the Lakers, who had acquired the rights to the Cavaliers' first round selection in an earlier trade.

In the lead-up to the coin toss, the question on everybody's lips was whether Sampson would declare for the draft or return to play his senior season at Virginia. Sampson was intrigued by the prospect of playing for the Lakers but he wanted nothing to do with the Clippers. "There was no way I was coming out early to be a Clipper," he said. "I didn't want to spend my life losing game after game." The problem for Sampson was that the deadline on when he had to declare his intentions was five days before the coin toss was scheduled to take place.

The Lakers were keen to get their hands on Sampson and so on May 12th, three days before Sampson had to let the world know whether he was returning to college or not, Jerry Buss invited Donald Sterling to his mansion for dinner. Here, Buss made numerous pitches to Sterling to try and get him to guarantee that the Lakers would end up with the first pick regardless of the coin toss result. $6 million. $6 million plus the number two pick in the upcoming draft. $6 million plus the number two pick in the upcoming draft and the Lakers first round selection in 1984. Sterling said no to each and every offer. With the possibility of ending up on the Clippers' roster still very much in play, Sampson released a statement declaring his intention to return to Virginia for his senior season.

Six days later, the Lakers won the coin toss.

San Diego basketball fans were justifiably disappointed at what had been served up to them by Donald Sterling and his Clippers during the 1981-82 season. They had endured months and months of almost constant losing and still did not wind up with their supposed savior, Ralph Sampson. However, this farce of a season was merely the entrée and when people realized what Sterling had planned for the main course, it was not only the folks of San Diego who would be outraged. It had only been 12 months since Sterling purchased the Clippers and yet he was already looking to put a radical plan in motion. A plan that would not just infuriate the Clippers' fan base but also put Sterling at odds with nearly every other owner in the league. A plan that would ultimately lead to the NBA filing a $25 million dollar lawsuit against the Clippers and their new owner. A plan that, if successfully implemented, would result in the Los Angeles Lakers ending up with some new neighbors.

CHAPTER 4

To Live and Die in LA

"I'm in San Diego to stay and committed to making the city proud of the Clippers."

Donald Sterling

AT FIRST GLANCE, IT SEEMED that the Clippers efforts at tanking during the second half of the 1981-82 season were a wasted effort. The fans in San Diego were led to believe that they would be rewarded with Ralph Sampson if they were able to endure the pain of a season that ended with 65 losses. But with Sampson still very much a student-athlete at Virginia, it appeared that the previous season's losing epidemic was a pointless exercise.

However, not long after the conclusion of the 1981-82 season, the *other* driving force behind the Clippers' sudden drop in form became evident when Donald Sterling announced his latest plan- he was moving the franchise from San Diego to Los Angeles. The Clippers were leaving town and Sterling was hoping that the relocation would take place with as little resistance as possible from the people of San Diego.

When Donald Sterling first purchased the Clippers, he proudly told the media that he had no plans to move the team. "The franchise will stay here in San Diego and we will do everything in our power to bring a winning club to the city," Sterling said. Then, when the Clippers struggled throughout the 1981-82 season, Sterling assured fans that this sudden spike in defeats was necessary to give the franchise the best chance of drafting Sampson.

However, not only did the odds of securing Sampson shorten with each mounting loss, the number of people passing through the San Diego Sports Arena turnstiles also decreased. During the 1981-82 season, the average home crowd plummeted by over 40%, leaving the Clippers with the worst attendance figures in the entire league. With local interest in the team at an all-time low, it seemed like the perfect time for Sterling put his relocation plan in motion.

Sterling broadcasted his intention to move the Clippers at a bizarre press conference, where he attended but did not speak to the media. Instead, his attorney Maxwell Blecher handled all queries[47]. Blecher said that the Clippers would now play their home games at the Los Angeles Memorial Sports Arena. It had taken a mere 13 months for Sterling to go from pledging to keep the Clippers in San Diego, to announcing that the team was relocating to Los Angeles.

It is not hard to see why Sterling was interested in moving the franchise. At the time, he lived in Malibu, thus the shift north would make his regular game day commute significantly shorter. Another reason was the size of the Los Angeles market, which was over six times that of San Diego[48]. On top of these pull factors in favor of the relocation, there was one considerable

---

47 When asked why Sterling was not speaking about the potential shift, Blecher said his client wanted to wait until the move was given the green light by the league's other owners. Which begs the question: if Sterling wanted to get the all clear from his fellow owners before discussing the move, why did he hold the press conference in the first place?
48 San Diego County's population was 1.9 million people, while the population of the Greater Los Angeles area was 11.5 million.

push factor- the condition of the San Diego Sports Arena. The Clippers had a long list of grievances with the facility, including a leaky roof, inadequate locker rooms, broken seats and a poor quality sound system. The Clippers contended that their inability to draw decent crowds was largely due to the arena, which they believed was well below NBA standards. However, this argument seems to be flimsy at best.

Rather than the rundown state of the venue, Clipper crowds seem to be more closely correlated with the team's on-court performance. Across the franchise's first three seasons, the team won 43, 35 and 36 games respectively and during this time, average home attendance was 7,272[49]. However in season four, when the Clippers were victorious on just 17 occasions, their average home crowd dropped to just 4,344. This indicates that the ability to attract customers had more to do with the success of the team than the condition of the arena.

There was one major roadblock that stood in the way of Sterling's vision of a shorter commute to a nicer arena filled with adoring fans. Los Angeles already had an NBA team and the league's constitution stated that you could not relocate a franchise within a 75 mile radius of an existing team, without getting consent from the established franchise.

In the days following the Clippers' relocation announcement, Lakers' owner Jerry Buss failed to make any definitive public statements on the matter. This led to speculation that Buss was planning on using his veto power to keep the Clippers out of Los Angeles, which in turn left the owners of the L.A. Sports Arena feeling very concerned. If Buss blocked the move, the L.A. Sports Arena would once again be left without a regular tenant, so the arena's management took the extraordinary step of filing a $50 million anti-trust lawsuit against Buss and the Lakers. This was done despite

---

[49] While this was below the league average, which hovered around the 10,000 mark, it was comparable to what other infant franchises were achieving, e.g. Cleveland (7,097), New Orleans/Utah (8,071) and New Jersey (6,166).

the fact that Buss had not taken any official steps to try and disrupt the Clippers' plans. The lawsuit barely lasted two days. Buss' attorney wrote to the L.A. Sports Arena and signaled his client's intention to waive his right to veto the Clippers' move, which resulted in the arena's lawyers immediately dropping their complaint against the Lakers. However, this resolution was far from the final act of legal maneuverings related to the proposed move.

The next organization to file a lawsuit was the NBA. They were not happy that the L.A. Sports Arena had lured the Clippers to Los Angeles without their knowledge, so they asked a federal court to award them $10 million in damages. The management of the L.A. Sports Arena retaliated by filing a $120 million counter claim against the NBA for damages relating to the league's attempts to prevent the move from taking place. The San Diego Sports Arena also got in on the action, filing a $17 million lawsuit against the L.A. Sports Arena for inducing the Clippers to relocate.

The final legal battle was a $6 million class action against Sterling on behalf of the team's season ticket holders. The suit was initiated by Sheldon Sherman and Michael Pancer, two attorneys who were also Clipper season ticket holders. They alleged that Sterling had engaged in fraud, misrepresentation and breach of contract by selling season tickets for a team that was based in San Diego and subsequently trying to move that same team to Los Angeles. Sherman and Pancer were able to get a judge to issue a temporary restraining order that blocked any relocation from taking place until the case was heard in court on July 2nd.

On the day the trial was due to begin, the Clippers called a press conference to announce that their planned shift to Los Angeles was no longer going ahead. Whereas Sterling did not speak at the media gathering when the move was initially announced, this time he did not even show up. And given what was to be said, it was not surprising that he decided to stay home. The Clippers general manger, Ted Podleski, informed the assembled media that the team would now be playing the 1982-83 NBA season in San Diego but he gave no further assurances in terms of a longer term commitment. When Podleski was asked about the future of the franchise in San Diego beyond the upcoming season, the best he could offer was, "We're going to be here and I think we are going to be here for a long time. I really believe that, or I wouldn't say it[50]." Regardless of what Podleski believed at the time, this announcement did not exactly fill the basketball fans of San Diego with much confidence.

One possible reason for the Clippers' sudden U-turn was the launching of an investigation by the league's head office into whether Sterling was financially fit to continue as an NBA owner. A panel of six owners was formed and they were given the task of investigating the manner in which Sterling was running his franchise. What they discovered was not pretty. The Clippers owed money to the league, former players, current players, the league's pension plan and a number of third parties, including at least one hotel with a long history of hosting NBA teams[51].

When the time came for the panel to decide whether Sterling should be allowed to continue to own the Clippers, they unanimously voted "no." This meant that the matter would now be forwarded to the annual meeting of NBA owners, which was due to take place in the middle of October. At this get-together, a binding vote would be held which would determine Sterling's fate.

In the lead-up to the owners meeting, it became crystal clear that the vast majority of Sterling's peers were in favor of banishing him from the

---

50 Incidentally, Podleski was fired by Sterling less than four months after fronting this charade of a press conference. So much for being around for a long time. Podleski later filed a lawsuit against the franchise in which he alleged that he was asked to participate in "wrongful and illegal activities" as part of his employment. Podleski claimed he was asked to sign checks even though he knew there was not enough money in the bank to cover them and that he was instructed to stall creditors by deliberately sending them unsigned checks. This case was eventually settled before the trial began, which meant no evidence was ever given in court in support of Podleski's claims.
51 This led to the hotel, the Hyatt House in Oakland, refusing to allow the Clippers to stay there, in the later stages of the 1981-82 season.

league. "The fact that Sterling wants to move the club is a separate issue," said one unnamed owner. "We've been concerned about him and what he's done to the franchise for months. And I'm not just speaking for a handful of owners, I'm talking about 20 of us[52]. There is overwhelming sentiment against Donald Sterling." Another NBA executive offered a more succinct opinion, saying, "He's as good as gone." And then, just when it appeared that Sterling's days as an NBA owner were numbered, he pulled off a strategic retreat that Napoleon would have been proud of.

On the eve of the owners' meeting, Sterling announced that he was now planning on selling the Clippers, saying he would off-load the team as soon as someone made a reasonable offer. "I'm not sure I was ready to own a pro team," he said. "Maybe I can make up for it by selling to someone who can accomplish what I couldn't." If Sterling was aiming to buy himself some time before his franchise was forcibly taken away, he would have been very pleased with the outcome of his latest public declaration.

The NBA decided that there was little point in proceeding with their plans to dump Sterling if he was on the verge of selling the team, so they postponed the vote. Instead, David Stern, the league's vice president at the time, encouraged Sterling to hire Alan Rothenberg, hoping that this would help to steady the ship before the franchise was put on the market. Rothenberg was an attorney with a long association of working in the world of professional basketball, having previously been employed by the Lakers, Blazers and Sonics[53]. Sterling did as he was told and appointed Rothenberg as the Clippers' new president.

---

52 Given that there were only 22 teams in the NBA at the time that were not owned by Donald Sterling, this represents a very large majority.
53 Rothenberg played a key role in bringing Kareem Abdul-Jabbar to the Lakers in 1975 and at one point, he was in the running to succeed Walter Kennedy as the NBA's new commissioner. The Clippers had firsthand knowledge of how effective Rothenberg could be, as he was the person hired by Portland to negotiate the monstrous compensation package that the Blazers received in exchange for Bill Walton.

However, rather than put the Clippers on the market, Sterling sat back and waited for the dust to settle. After stalling for a few months, Sterling attended a meeting with representatives from the league's head office where he gave numerous assurances about the changes that were taking place at the Clippers. Amazingly, it seemed that this presentation was enough to convince the league that Sterling was a changed man. The NBA decided not to proceed with their plans to oust Sterling and the proposed vote of the remaining owners was permanently shelved.

Having narrowly dodged a bullet, one might have expected Sterling to spend the next few years repairing his franchise's damaged reputation, both in the city of San Diego and with players, coaches and executives from around the league. He didn't. Instead, Sterling continued to make decisions which made it clear that moving the team to Los Angeles was still very much a part of his future plans.

Season V: 1982-83

There were a number of ways that Donald Sterling sent the message to the Clipper players that they were still part of a small-time operation. Training camp was moved from Yuma, Arizona to the North Island Naval Station, which was located in San Diego. This change of venues had two noteworthy effects. Firstly, it saved Sterling a bundle of cash, as the Clippers were allowed to use the navy facility free of charge. However, the more subtle impact of the shift was the decline that it caused in the morale of the team. While other NBA players were building team camaraderie by spending time away from their regular home base, the Clippers were stuck in San Diego, practicing in an ancient gym with a grand total of two baskets to shoot on.

At the start of training camp, each player was issued two practice jerseys, two pairs of shorts, two jock straps and four pairs of socks and told there would be no replacements if any of the gear was lost. This meant that the team's trainer had to collect all of the sweaty gear from the morning's practice session and race home, where it would be washed and hung out to dry. The same process was followed at the end of each afternoon session, in order to ensure that the players had clean clothing to practice in for the following day.

The issues occurring at training camp were symbolic of a widespread movement to cut costs across the entire organization. The Clippers' exhibition schedule was shortened from the NBA standard of eight games down to a solitary match. Sterling also reduced the Clippers scouting budget by an astonishing 95%. This act of fiscal frugality was exposed by the San Diego Tribune, who obtained a copy of the Clippers' proposed budget for the 1982-83 season[54]. Some of the other notable penny pinching efforts that came to light were in the areas of advertising (where expenditures were set to drop from $205,000 to $5,000), administrative travel (cut from $33,000 to $100) and medical expenses (from $10,454 to $100).

While all of these cost-cutting measures undoubtedly impacted the franchise's ability to thrive in San Diego, perhaps nothing had as large an effect on the team's on-court performance as the Clippers' inability to sign incoming rookie Terry Cummings to a contract in time for the tip off of the 1982-83 season.

Lost amongst all of the disappointment over missing out on being able to select Ralph Sampson in the 1982 draft was the fact that the Clippers managed to pick up a very talented player with the second overall pick. Terry Cummings was a 6'9" forward who looked like he was born to play in the NBA. Cummings grew up on the South Side of Chicago as one of 13 siblings. As a child, he lived by a simple code- if something was not working for you, stop doing it. It was this philosophy that allowed him to navigate his way through a local community that was plagued with drugs and

---

54 During the 1981-82 season, the Clippers allocated $23,402 for scouting related expenses and for the 1982-83 season this figure was reduced to just $1,100.

violence. He tried smoking marijuana at a young age but quickly gave it up when he realized the negative impact it was having on his life.

This ability to change course when the need arose also played a crucial role in Cummings' selection of which sport he should devote his time to. His early love was ice hockey and he initially dreamed of becoming one of the first African-Americans to play in the NHL. However, any hope of Cummings starring for the Blackhawks took a back seat when, at 14 years of age, he had a growth spurt of almost 6 inches. Seeing that hockey was no longer working for him, Cummings made the wise decision to focus on basketball.

When Cummings graduated from Carver High School, he chose to attend DePaul, allowing him to pursue his basketball goals while staying close to his friends and family in Chicago. During his junior season, he averaged 22.3 points and 11.9 rebounds and it became clear that Cummings' next stop would be the NBA. He also led the Blue Demons to a 26-1 regular season record, which was good enough to be awarded the number one seed for the Midwest region of the 1982 NCAA tournament. However, Cummings' dreams of bringing an NCAA title back to his hometown came to an abrupt end when DePaul was upset in their first game of the tournament, losing to a talented Boston College team.

DePaul fans held out hope that their star player would return for his senior season but Cummings decided to forgo his final year of college eligibility to declare for the 1982 draft. When he was selected with the second overall pick by the Clippers, it was expected that he would immediately play a large role for the struggling franchise. Then the process of negotiating his rookie contract got underway and any hope of Cummings being able to jump start the new season quickly faded.

The inability of Cummings and the Clippers to reach a deal stemmed from not one, not two, but three separate issues. Firstly, there was money.

Tom Collins, Cummings' agent, was seeking a salary that was somewhere between $500,000 and $600,000, while the Clippers were offering a deal with a salary of just a little over $100,000[55]. The second point of contention was the length of the deal. Cummings only wanted to commit for one or two seasons, while the Clippers were trying to lock him into a five year deal. Cummings' reluctance to sign a lengthier deal related to the third sticking point between the two parties- the wording of the contract. Collins had done his homework on the Clippers and was well aware of the franchise's bad reputation when it came to financial matters. Thus, he wanted a clause inserted that stated that the contract was automatically null and void the moment that Cummings did not receive a pay check on time. He was also seeking to have Cummings' salary guaranteed for the full length of the deal.

Collins was trying to do everything possible to protect his client from the behind the scenes shenanigans that many other Clipper players had to contend with. He gave the franchise a September 1st deadline to have the contract situation sorted, which quickly came and went without any resolution being reached. On the day that the deadline expired, Cummings announced his intention to start playing for Athletes in Action, a Christian organization that uses sport as a means of spreading the word of the gospel. The two sides still hadn't reached an agreement when training camp began six weeks later[56].

So while the Clippers went to work in the luxury confines of the North Island Naval base, Cummings continued to travel the country with Athletes in Action. By the end of October, Cummings remained unsigned, meaning

---

[55] Sterling did all he could to convince Cummings that he would have to accept a salary that was well below market rate, explaining that high inflation and a flailing economy had forced the franchise to tighten its budget. Collins explained Sterling's pitch by saying, "Mr. Sterling spent 2½ hours trying to convince Terry that it was Doomsday."

[56] This was the second year in a row that the Clippers had difficulty signing their first round draft pick. A year earlier, it was Tom Chambers who spent the entire training camp on the sidelines while his agent and the team's management went back and forth on terms for his rookie deal.

the Clippers were forced to open their new campaign without the services of their first round draft pick for the first time in franchise history[57].

Cummings' opening night absence was partially off-set by the return of Bill Walton, who had decided to attempt a comeback, of sorts. It had been two and a half years since Walton's last NBA appearance and during this time he had had a number of surgeries performed on his troublesome left foot. By the summer of 1982, Walton's foot was feeling good enough for him to start making the trek to the Loyola Marymount campus, where he participated in full-court games with a variety of other Californian-based NBA players. Once he was able to prove to himself that he could get through these contests unscathed, the idea of a return to the NBA was once again placed on the agenda.

While Walton was keen to resume playing, he was also aware that his foot might not be able to stand up to the rigors of a full 82 game season. So, he pitched a plan to the Clippers' front office that allowed him to resume playing on a part-time basis, while continuing to study. Under Walton's proposal, he would spend his weekdays living in Northern California, studying law at Stanford. On weekends, he would fly out to meet the team and play one game, before returning to Silicon Valley.

The Clippers were initially reluctant to agree to this highly unconventional arrangement, fearing that having Walton constantly moving in and out of the line-up would be too disruptive for their young team. But they eventually conceded, figuring that a part-time Bill Walton was better than no Bill Walton at all. "Some teams might not accept the situation or would find it disruptive," said Paul Silas, "but remember- we won 17 games last year. I don't think we can afford to be choosy."

There were no signs of any cobwebs when Walton finally played his first NBA game in over 31 months. He scored 20 points and pulled down

---

[57] It would not be the last.

8 rebounds in 28 minutes of action and while Walton's left foot managed to make it through the game intact, his face was not as fortunate. In the middle of the third quarter, Walton fractured his cheekbone when he was inadvertently elbowed by a teammate while pursuing a loose ball. The Clippers played the next three games without Walton, who returned to Stanford to rest his sore cheek. Not surprisingly, they lost all three, by a combined margin of 47 points.

The eve of the team's fifth game brought some good news, when it was announced that Cummings and the Clippers had finally agreed on a deal[58]. Cummings made an impressive NBA debut, leading his team in scoring with 19 points in a blowout loss to Milwaukee. This was followed by two more defeats, bringing the Clippers' overall record to 0-7, hardly the ideal way to kick off a new season. This dismal start was followed by another lean stretch in November and December where the team lost 13 of 14 games, giving the Clippers just four wins from their first 27 contests.

One of the factors behind the Clippers' horrendous start was the Bill Walton experiment, which was not going as planned. Walton had only been able to take the court in eight of the Clippers first 27 games and the team was yet to post a victory with their star center in the line-up. While nobody doubted that Walton still possessed plenty of talent, his teammates and the coaching staff were finding it difficult to adjust to him playing on a part-time basis, with some players becoming resentful of their well-paid teammate. "It was very difficult," said Cummings. "We had guys mumbling and criticizing. 'This guy gets to come when he wants, play when he wants, practice when he wants and practice how he wants.'"

In the middle of December, the Clippers front office decided that enough was enough and told Walton that he needed to make a stronger commitment to the team. Paul Phipps, the franchise's new general manager, made this very clear, saying, "He has two choices: either commit himself

---

58 Cummings signed a four year, $1.7 million contract.

fully to his basketball career or...he can retire. And if he retires, of course, he willingly forfeits his salary." Walton was left with little choice and, after getting the all-clear from his doctor, he put his studies on hold so he could resume his career as a full-time NBA player[59].

Given the Clippers' miserable record, it was highly unlikely that the team was going to make a run at a playoff berth. But with Walton back as a permanent fixture, they did manage to show glimpses of the team's potential. Led by a starting frontcourt of Cummings, Chambers and Walton, they reeled off an impressive streak where they won 10 out of 16 games, including a rousing 122-107 home rout of Boston, in front of over 18,000 fans. However, if San Diego's basketball community was beginning to think that there might be a light at the end of the tunnel, they were sorely mistaken. This run of good form ultimately proved to be nothing more than a tease.

Immediately following the win over the Celtics, the Clippers plunged into perhaps the worst sequence of games in the franchise's short history. This slide was preceded by two events that landed damaging blows to the team's morale. In early March, Walton announced that he was going to sit out the rest of the season due to recurring pain in his ankle. Walton finished the season with a final tally of 33 games and averages of 14.1 points, 9.8 rebounds, 3.6 assists and 3.6 blocks per game.

The second problem arose the day after Walton played his last game for the season. Paul Silas called a team meeting where he told the players that the current season would be his last as the Clippers head coach. Silas was informed of the franchise's desire to bring in a new coach when he met with team management earlier that week. The playing group was shocked to discover that their coach was taking the fall for the miserable season that they were enduring.

---

59 Walton never returned to Stanford to finish his degree.

The effect of this latest series of bad news became immediately evident the day after Silas' shocking announcement. The Clippers travelled to Kansas City and suffered a humiliating 39 point defeat at the hands of a fairly mediocre Kings team. This demoralizing result was part of a ten game stretch in which they won just once. Then, just when it looked like things couldn't get any worse, they did. In the closing weeks of the season, Terry Cummings was forced to join Bill Walton on the sidelines with a mystery medical ailment that was so severe, it almost ended his career.

As the 1982-83 season was winding down, the play of Terry Cummings was perhaps the only bright spot in an otherwise wretched year for the Clippers. Cummings led the team in scoring (23.7) and rebounding (10.6), while also averaging 2.5 assists, 1.8 steals and almost a block per game. By the end of the regular season, Cummings' excellent form was recognized when he was named Rookie of the Year, ahead of future Hall of Famers James Worthy and Dominique Wilkins. But, as is usually the case with the Clippers, this silver lining came with an accompanying cloud.

Being given the nod as the league's best first year player might have created the impression that Cummings' debut NBA season was all plain sailing. In fact, nothing could have been further from the truth. While Cummings was starring out on the court, he spent much of the year feeling exhausted. At first, he put this down to the accumulated stress from getting married, moving halfway across the country and dealing with the grind that comes from playing an 82 game schedule. However, after Cummings fainted in the middle of a game in December, the Clippers medical team began to suspect that his problems were more than just the typical rookie fatigue. Cummings was diagnosed with an iron deficiency and he was instructed to take iron supplements as well as make some changes to his diet. He missed just one game and was back playing three nights after his initial collapse.

Over the next few months, Cummings started to feel a little better. But, while his health was improving, he sensed that there was something not quite right, as he continued to experience dizzy spells and feelings of breathlessness. While no one was sure of exactly what was going on, it was becoming apparent that the problem was more serious than just a simple iron deficiency.

With just a few weeks remaining in the regular season, the decision was made to pull Cummings from the line-up. He flew home to Chicago, where he underwent a series of tests at Northwestern Memorial Hospital. When the results came back, they revealed that Cummings was suffering from a condition called cardiac arrhythmia. Essentially this is when there is abnormal electric activity in the heart, which causes an irregular heartbeat. It can lead to cardiac arrest and in some cases can even be fatal.

The diagnosis was shocking for Cummings and it was also a cruel blow for the Clippers organization. After enduring five seasons of relative mediocrity in San Diego, it looked like Cummings might finally give the franchise a player whom they could build around for years to come. Instead, it appeared that the problem with his heart was so serious that it might force him to retire, after playing just one season of professional basketball.

Cummings was initially informed that he would be able to continue his basketball career provided he started taking an extremely strong drug called Amiodarone. However, things quickly became a lot more complicated when Lloyds of London, the same insurance company that refused to pay out on Walton's policy, informed the Clippers that they would not be renewing Cummings' disability policy in light of his heart problems. This posed a huge problem for the Clippers. They asked Cummings to sign an agreement which stated that he would forgo any future compensation owed to him by the franchise if he was forced to retire due to his heart condition. Cummings was obviously not happy with this idea and threatened to walk away from the game if the Clippers could not come up with a better solution.

This dispute dragged on for many months before the Clippers were able to get the appropriate level of insurance coverage for Cummings and thus, any thoughts of a premature retirement were soon forgotten. Cummings continued to take the prescribed heart medication and it proved to be very successful in managing his condition[60].

Season VI: 1983-84

On the eve of the 1983-84 season, it was clear that some combination of factors was conspiring to prevent the Clippers from achieving any meaningful success. In the two years since Donald Sterling purchased the team, they had managed to win just 42 games. If you were looking for possible reasons for these on-court struggles, there were plenty that immediately sprang to mind: Sterling's unwillingness to spend money, Bill Walton's injury plight, a string of seemingly illogical trades and the lack of any real home court advantage due to poor crowd numbers. However, when the time came for the Clippers to make a move to try and reverse their fortunes, they elected to go with the oldest sports cliché of all- they fired their coach. Paul Silas proved to be better at clairvoyance than he was at coaching by successfully predicting his termination six weeks before it was formally announced.

Paul Phipps then embarked on a search to fill what was fast becoming the least desirable coaching position in the NBA. One of the first people he interviewed was Rollie Massimino, who was coaching at Villanova at the time. Massimino flew to San Diego to meet up with Phipps and the interview went quite well. Phipps was impressed with Massimino's coaching philosophy and their discussion certainly didn't do his chances of getting the job any harm.

Sterling was also keen to speak with the potential coaching candidates, so he organized to meet up with Massimino before he flew back to

---

[60] Cummings ultimately went on to appear in 1,183 regular season games across a decorated career that spanned 17 years.

Philadelphia. Phipps had firsthand knowledge of Sterling's personality and he was a little worried about how this meeting would go. In fact he was so concerned that he warned Massimino prior to dropping him off at the airport, telling him that Sterling was "a bit eccentric".

The next contact that Phipps had with Massimino came somewhere between three and four o'clock the following morning. Phipps was woken from his sleep by an unexpected phone call from an irate Massimino. He was calling to officially withdraw his name from the pool of candidates for the Clippers' head coaching job. A groggy and half-asleep Phipps sat up in his bed to try and figure out what could possibly have gone wrong in the brief period since he last spoke with Massimino.

The answer was Donald Sterling.

According to journalist Jeff Pearlman, Phipps claims that Massimino related that a clearly drunk Sterling turned up at the airport with a bottle of champagne in one arm and a "blonde bimbo" hanging off the other. If this was a bad start to the meeting, Massimino recalls things only got worse from here. Massimino says Sterling then said to him, "I wanna know why you think you can coach these niggers." An outraged Massimino states that he informed Sterling in no uncertain terms that he would never work for a man who was capable of uttering such racist remarks and promptly left to catch his plane.

The Clippers eventually decided to appoint Jim Lynam as their new head coach. Like Massimino, Lynam had been working in Philadelphia's college basketball scene, coaching at St. Joe's. Lynam also had experience in the professional ranks, after spending a season as an assistant coach with the Portland Trailblazers. When it was first announced that Lynam would be taking over from Paul Silas, it appeared that he would have a talented, young roster to work with. This did not remain the case for very long.

If there was one area where the Clippers had been experiencing success in recent times, it was the NBA draft. Over the previous two years, they had acquired the rights to Tom Chambers and Terry Cummings, giving them perhaps the strongest forward pairing in the entire league. This trend of making the most of their draft picks continued in 1983, when they shrewdly used their first two selections to pick up two players who would go on to appear in a combined total of 1,909 NBA games. Unfortunately, not a single one of these contests involved either player wearing a Clippers uniform.

The first player taken by the Clippers in the 1983 draft was Byron Scott, a 6'3" guard who was selected with the fourth overall pick. Scott looked to be a perfect fit for the Clippers, with his excellent outside shooting providing the perfect complement for their imposing frontline of Walton, Cummings and Chambers. However, as was the case with Chambers and Cummings before him, drafting Scott and signing Scott proved to be two very different things. Scott was asking for a four year deal that paid a total of around $1.75 million. Sterling, who was far from enamored with the selection of Scott in the first place, thought that this was too steep a price tag. When training camp began, Scott remained unsigned and thus was nowhere to be seen.

Meanwhile, 120 miles up the road, the Los Angeles Lakers were having troubles of their own with one of their backcourt stars. Norm Nixon had played six seasons in the NBA and during this time, he assembled quite an impressive resume. An All-Star selection, two championship rings and six consecutive years of finishing in the league's top ten for assists was definitely not a bad return for a player taken with the 22nd pick of the 1977 draft.

Despite this impressive list of achievements, by the summer of 1983, Nixon had worn out his welcome in Los Angeles. He had always been viewed as somewhat of a prickly personality by Laker management, a player who was tolerated because of his contributions to the team's success rather than embraced. He spent his first two seasons clashing with Jerry West, who was coaching the Lakers at the time and the last four bickering with Magic Johnson. The problems between Nixon and Johnson mostly stemmed from the fact that they both played the same position. For the majority of their time together, the Lakers were winning and the two point guards found a way to peacefully co-exist in the same backcourt. However, every once in a while, Nixon grew unhappy with the fact that he spent most of his time playing off the ball and controversy would flare up[61].

However, the event that preceded Nixon's departure from the Lakers had nothing to do with his relationship with Johnson and everything to do with management's suspicions that he was using cocaine. Nixon first found out about these concerns when he was driving home one night and someone pulled up alongside him, rolled down their window and said that they needed to talk. Nixon instructed this mystery man to follow him back to his house and once there, he proceeded to explain that he had been hired by the Lakers to follow Nixon's every move. At first Nixon wouldn't allow himself to believe what he was hearing. He had poured his heart and soul into his professional career and this was how the Lakers chose to repay him? But when Nixon heard an intricate rundown of his movements from the previous fortnight, he was forced to confront the truth that his employer no longer trusted him.

The next morning, Nixon peered out of his window and immediately noticed a suspicious person sitting in a parked car at the end of his street. He marched outside to speak with this apparent spy, but the car quickly sped away. A few hours later, Nixon confronted West in his office and the

---

[61] Away from the court, the two men also moved in the same social circles, which led to occasions where they were romantically involved with the same woman at the same time. Or as Michael Cooper put it so eloquently, "They were fucking the same girls." Cooper believed that while Nixon and Johnson were good friends, the competition between them also led to friction which put a strain on their relationship.

Lakers' general manager didn't deny that he was in fact using private investigators. Instead, he accused Nixon of hanging out with drug dealers and using cocaine. Nixon continued to protest his innocence but it seemed as if West's mind was made up[62].

Once the decision was made to get rid of Nixon, the next step was to find a team to which he could be traded. Luckily, Lakers' owner Jerry Buss had someone in mind. Ever since Donald Sterling first bought the Clippers, he had kept an eye on Norm Nixon. The two men knew each other through mutual acquaintances and Sterling had often told Nixon that if he ever got the opportunity to trade for him, he would grab it. The Clippers had come close to acquiring Nixon 12 months earlier when Sterling and Buss met to discuss the coin flip to decide the first pick in the 1982 draft. A year later, the two owners negotiated directly on the terms of a trade that had huge implications for both franchises. Nixon was sent to San Diego, in exchange for Byron Scott and Swen Nater.

This was a trade that the Clippers front office was not especially pleased with. If they ever hoped to build a championship contending team, then the age of their roster should have been a crucial consideration. The Clippers best two players at the time were Cummings and Chambers, who were both in their early 20s. Adding Scott to this duo would give them a solid nucleus that they could build around. "I remember saying repeatedly to Paul Phipps that this was a mistake," said Pete Babcock, the Clippers director of player personnel. "Not that Norm Nixon wasn't a great player, but Norm's at the end of the road. Byron's going to play for 10 or 12 years and be a really good player. He said, 'It doesn't matter, it's being done.' We weren't asked for our opinion, it was just done."

---

[62] To this day, Nixon maintains that there was no substance to the Lakers' suspicions, saying, "They were all rumors and it was not true."

The second player taken by the Clippers in the 1983 draft was selected 93 picks after Byron Scott and yet still went on to appear in 653 NBA games. He twice led the league in blocked shots, won a place on the NBA's All-Defensive team and was so unique that his mere presence was enough to completely alter the tactical approach of the opposition. However, in true Clipper fashion, this draft selection was ruled invalid, meaning that the player in question never played a single game for the Clippers.

Manute Bol first came to the attention of Jim Lynam when one of his old coaching buddies, Don Feeley, called to tell him that he had a prospect who was worth considering. Bol was from Sudan, couldn't speak a word of English and had very little experience playing organized basketball. Lynam was polite, but also not interested. He needed good players, not some long-shot who appeared promising but ultimately lacked the talent to make it in the NBA. Then Feeley slipped the player's height into the conversation. Seven feet and seven inches. All of a sudden, Lynam was interested. Very interested.

Feeley explained to Lynam that Bol was not only very tall, he was also very raw. His basketball skills and understanding of the game were both severely lacking. The one thing that he could do exceptionally well was block shots, which was not surprising, given his extraordinary height. But Feeley attributed Bol's shot blocking ability to more than just his stature, telling Lynam that Bol possessed an innate sense for defending, displaying instincts that belied his lack of experience. Lynam asked Feeley who else he had discussed Bol with. The only other person Feeley had spoken to was Utah's general manager, Frank Layden and he was not interested. Lynam asked Feeley not to call anybody else.

Having been persuaded that Bol was worth taking a flyer on, Lynam now had to convince the Clippers front office of the same. This would not be an easy task. Lynam had never actually seen Bol play and he didn't have any video footage that he could show to Phipps or Babcock. In fact, Lynam did not have so much as a photo to share. He would have to win his colleagues over with words alone.

The Clippers had the fourth overall selection in the 1983 draft and then they didn't have another pick until the fifth round. Lynam was eventually able to convince Phipps that Bol was worthy of their fifth round pick selection. On the night of the draft, Lynam was a nervous wreck. He spent much of the evening pacing around the team's office, convinced that someone else was going to snatch Bol's rights away before they had the chance. Babcock tried to calm him down by reassuring Lynam that no one else knew about Bol.

It turned out that Babcock was right and Lynam had no reason to be nervous. Nobody knew who Bol was and when the Clippers announced that they were using the 97th pick to select him, it caused quite a stir. Even the NBA's director of scouting Marty Blake, who had a reputation for knowing every obscure potential NBA player, had never heard of Bol. When Blake was asked to share his thoughts on the Clippers' puzzling selection during the television broadcast of the draft, he was forced to admit that he had no idea who Bol was.

Once it was established that Manute Bol actually existed, his passport also surfaced and this document was not good news for the Clippers. It said that Bol was 19 years of age, which meant that he was ineligible to be drafted. Under NBA rules at the time, anyone who was under the age of 21 had to formally declare for the draft at least 45 days prior to the event. Bol had not lodged the necessary paperwork and therefore his selection by the Clippers was ruled invalid.

Instead of heading to San Diego to make his NBA debut, Bol began playing for the University of Bridgeport, where he stayed for two seasons. The Clippers were obviously unhappy with the NBA's ruling, believing that there were questions to be raised about the legitimacy of Bol's passport.

"That was a legal pick," Lynam said. "The NBA was looking at his passport. Well, his passport also said that he was five foot two."

Two years later Bol was drafted in the second round by Washington. This time, there was no problem with the pick and he was finally free to start his NBA career. In Bol's rookie season, he averaged 5 blocks per game despite playing only 26 minutes a night[63]. Bol developed into a unique weapon, somebody whose defensive play could completely change a game. He went on to play for ten years in the NBA, becoming a much loved fan favorite and something of a cult figure in the process. In 2010, Bol died as a result of a kidney failure. To the NBA community, Manute Bol was a true diamond in the rough. To the Clippers, Manute Bol represented yet another lost opportunity.

The final young star to slip through the Clippers fingers during the 1983 off-season was Tom Chambers, who was shipped to Seattle in exchange for a couple of bench players and a first round draft pick. If this seems like a crazy move, that's because it was. At the time of the deal, Chambers had played two seasons in the NBA and it was clear that he was emerging as one of the league's best young forwards, as indicated by his averages of 17.4 points, 6.8 rebounds and 2.1 assists[64]. The most prominent player the Clippers received in return was James Donaldson, a 7'2" center with career averages of 7.5 points and 5.6 rebounds.

The cumulative effect of the Clippers' off-season maneuvers was that they managed to make their roster both less talented and older, a most undesirable outcome for any sporting team. And yet, they opened the 1983-84 season with three wins from their first four games, including a home victory

---

63 When Bol finally made his debut appearance at the Los Angeles Sports Arena in February of 1986, he fell a lay-up short of producing his first NBA triple double, finishing with 8 points, 13 rebounds and 10 blocked shots.
64 Chambers went on to play in four All-Star games and make two All-NBA second teams.

over the Lakers, in which Norm Nixon scored 25 points and dished off 12 assists, outplaying both Magic Johnson and Byron Scott in the process. Unfortunately, this win proved to be the high point of an otherwise disappointing season.

In early December, the Clippers suffered a major setback when Walton broke his hand after hitting it against the backboard while trying to secure a rebound. This latest injury caused him to spend seven weeks on the sidelines. By the time Walton was ready to resume playing, the season was effectively over, with the team's 13-28 record making the chances of securing a playoff berth nothing more than a mathematical possibility.

Xs, Os and Subpoenas

If there was one thing that Clippers' employees had learned over the years of working for the franchise, it was to always expect the unexpected. There was perhaps no better example of this than the evening of January 11th, 1984. The team was in Phoenix and Jim Lynam was in the middle of giving his pre-game address in the visitors' locker room. While he was outlining the tactical approach for that evening's clash with the Suns, he noticed that there was a stranger standing in the corner.

Lynam needn't have feared that his brilliant game plan had just been laid out in front of a member of the opposition's coaching staff because the mystery man had nothing to do with basketball. He was a process server employed by a Phoenix t-shirt manufacturer, who had grown weary of chasing the Clippers for money they owed for promotional t-shirts. And while Lynam had nothing to do with this unpaid debt, he was the highest ranking Clipper official in Arizona at the time, thus he was person who was served with the subpoena.

Having his pre-game speech interrupted in this manner was too much for even Lynam to put up with. The bewildered players looked on as Lynam was forced to stop giving his instructions so he could accept the legal paperwork. Not surprisingly, the Clippers promptly went out and conceded 39 first quarter points, on their way to another blowout defeat.

The Clippers eventually finished the season with 30 wins and 52 losses, which represented a five game improvement on their tally from the previous campaign. However, they still fell eight games short of qualifying for the playoffs[65]. If one was to write a list of the positives to emerge from the season, they would need a very small piece of paper. Terry Cummings backed up his impressive rookie season with an equally commanding sophomore campaign, averaging 22.9 points and 9.6 rebounds and narrowly missing out on selection for the 1984 All-Star game. Norm Nixon's first season as a Clipper was also a success, with the veteran point guard averaging 11.1 assists per game, second best in the entire league behind only Magic Johnson. And, with the exception of sitting out 21 games with his broken hand, Bill Walton was able to remain fairly healthy, playing in 55 regular season contests, which was the most since his final season with Portland. In terms of good news, that was about it. The Clippers had just completed their fifth consecutive losing season and it appeared that this was a franchise which was going nowhere fast.

In fact, nothing was further from the truth.

---

65 The Clippers missed out on the post-season action, despite the NBA increasing the number of teams that qualified from 12 to 16. With a total of just 23 teams in the league at the time, this meant that only 7 teams missed out, which kind of makes the whole 82 game regular season seem like a big waste of time.

CHAPTER 5

If at First You Don't Succeed

"We are delighted to bring our team of the future to the greatest community in the world, our home- Los Angeles."

Donald Sterling

At the conclusion of the 1983-84 season, Jim Lynam headed back to Philadelphia to stay at his mother's place. It was a chance to reconnect with his family and unwind after what had been a stressful first season as an NBA head coach. However, rather than completely switch off from basketball, he was already thinking of ways to make his second season in San Diego more successful.

Lynam came from a large family and each of his ten siblings loved sports, with the exception of his younger sister Margo. So, when Margo passed on a phone message in early May stating that the Clippers had just moved to Los Angeles, his first thought was that his kid sister had made some sort of mistake. "I just kind of sniggered and said, 'Margo, they don't move teams.'" An unperturbed Margo shot a blank look back at her older brother and handed him a slip of paper with a message to call Pete Babcock, who had recently taken over as the Clippers general manager.

Lynam was still laughing about Margo's misunderstanding as he dialed Babcock's number. "Pete, it's Jim," Lynam hollered in his thick

Philadelphian accent. Babcock paused for a few seconds on the other end of the line before saying, "You won't believe this...but they just moved the team." A shocked Lynam covered the receiver and yelled down the corridor to his younger sister, "Margo, you're right. They moved the team."

While the Los Angeles Lakers and Phoenix Suns were battling it out in the 1984 Western Conference finals, Donald Sterling had already shifted his thoughts to the following season. A few months earlier, the United States Circuit Court of Appeals handed down its ruling in a case between the NFL and its Raiders franchise. And although this finding was related to a completely different sport, it gave new life to Sterling's plans for relocating the Clippers. Al Davis, the owner of the Oakland Raiders, first tried to move his team to Los Angeles in 1980, however, this attempt failed spectacularly. The remaining NFL owners voted 22-0 against the proposed move, thus preventing the shift from occurring[66]. Davis chose to view this result as a solid punch rather than a knockout blow and he continued to investigate alternative methods to make the relocation happen.

Davis' next move was to file an antitrust lawsuit against the NFL. He claimed that the league's attempt to block the Raiders' initial move infringed on his right to run a profitable business. In response, the NFL tried to claim that antitrust laws were not applicable, as the league was actually a single entity rather than a collection of separate franchises. The jury ruled in favor of Davis, clearing the way for him to move the Raiders to Los Angeles, two years after his failed first attempt. Not only was the team free to move, but the NFL was also instructed to pay Davis $49 million in damages.

The NFL's inability to prevent Davis from moving the Raiders rekindled Sterling's dream of having the Clippers play in his backyard. It also gave him a powerful legal precedent that he could use if anyone tried to

---

66 Five owners abstained from voting.

challenge him. Sterling decided that the best way to approach a second attempt at relocation was to move swiftly.

On May 14th, the Clippers informed the NBA that they were moving to Los Angeles, on *the very next day*. The league responded by saying that they wanted to appoint a committee to investigate the logistics of the move. Buoyed by the finding in the Raiders vs. NFL case, the Clippers' asserted that any such investigation would be a violation of antitrust law. The NBA was fearful of any potential liability that might result from trying to stand in the Clippers way, so they made no immediate attempt to block the move. The following day, Sterling signed a ten year lease with the Los Angeles Sports Arena and the San Diego Clippers were no more. Henceforth they would be known as the Los Angeles Clippers.

These changes were announced at a press conference and this time, Sterling decided he would both attend and speak. He told the assembled media that he was "delighted" to be able to bring the Clippers to Los Angeles, which he gushingly labeled as "the greatest community in the world." It seemed Sterling's strategy was to reveal his brash plan and then sit back and see if anyone was willing to challenge him.

He did not have to wait very long.

While the NBA was unhappy that Sterling was once again attempting to move without permission, they also knew that they were operating in a very different legal climate from what they had experienced two years earlier. Consequently, they would have to employ a different set of tactics than those that had been successful in blocking Sterling's first attempt to pull the Clippers out of San Diego.

For the first few weeks, it appeared as if the league had no objections to the move. No public statement was issued by the NBA to suggest that they were going to challenge the Clippers' plans and the league even printed up schedules for the 1984-85 season with the words "Los Angeles" replacing the "San Diego" that went next to the Clippers name. But anyone who thought that the NBA was going to take Sterling's provocative actions lying down was sorely mistaken.

A month after Sterling announced that he was now the owner of the *Los Angeles* Clippers, the NBA fired back in the form of a multi-million dollar lawsuit. The league claimed that moving a second franchise to Los Angeles was a violation of its by-laws and sought $25 million in damages from both the Clippers and the management of the Los Angeles Sports Arena. The NBA also asked the courts to make a determination on whether they had the power to terminate the Clipper franchise. Essentially the lawsuit centered around one question: did the Clippers have to seek approval from the NBA's Board of Governors before relocating to Los Angeles? One thing was clear- if the league was successful in court, Sterling's days as an NBA owner appeared to be numbered.

It took nearly three years for this legal battle to be settled, but there is no doubt about who landed the first blow. Just a few weeks after the Clippers' move to Los Angeles was announced, a San Diego jury awarded the fleeing basketball organization almost $500,000 in damages. This payout was the result of a lawsuit between the Clippers and the San Diego Sports Arena and it proved to be a substantial asset in the team's ongoing battles with the NBA. The Clippers now had a legal ruling to back their long-standing assertion that the condition of the San Diego Sports Arena was well below accepted NBA standards, thus giving their recently announced relocation some sense of legitimacy.

In amongst all this legal wrangling, the NBA held its annual draft and the Clippers had two first round selections, courtesy of the trade with Seattle during the previous summer. They used their first pick on Lancaster Gordon, a 6'3" shooting guard who went on to start a total of just six games across his entire NBA career. Gordon would have been considered a bust as the eighth overall selection in any draft, let alone in 1984, which is still regarded as the best draft class of all-time[67]. Thankfully the Clippers fared better with their second pick (14th overall), which they used to snare Michael Cage, a bruising 6'9" power forward with a knack for rebounding.

With the draft out of the way, the Clippers had one more move to make before launching themselves into the Los Angeles market. They were about to trade away their best player.

The realization that it was time to leave the Clippers came to Terry Cummings in his sleep. Cummings was a deeply religious man who believed that Jesus communicated with him via his dreams, using them as a way of showing him the future. So, when Cummings dreamt he was playing basketball wearing the distinctive green and red uniforms of the Milwaukee Bucks, he took it as a sign. He woke up convinced that Milwaukee was going to be his next NBA destination and promptly went about implementing a plan designed to get him to Wisconsin.

At the time of the dream, Cummings had played two seasons for the Clippers and his individual form was nothing short of exceptional. There was just one small problem- he no longer enjoyed playing basketball. A big reason for the decline in Cummings' passion for the game was his relationship with head coach Jim Lynam. "He was the first coach that I played for that I felt didn't like me as a player," Cummings said. Add in the fact that the Clippers had a 55-109 record in the two years since Cummings' arrival and it was easy to see why he wanted out.

In contrast, the appeal of playing in Milwaukee was obvious. The Bucks had one of the league's most respected young coaches in Don Nelson, who had been named as the NBA's Coach of the Year 12 months earlier. Behind

---

67 This was the same draft that produced seven All-Stars and four eventual Hall-of-Famers (Hakeem Olajuwon, Michael Jordan, Charles Barkley and John Stockton).

the astute coaching of Nelson, the Bucks were coming off consecutive trips to the Eastern Conference finals, losing to Philadelphia in 1983 and Boston in 1984. Finally, playing in Milwaukee meant that Cummings would be just 100 miles away from his family and friends in Chicago.

Having come to the conclusion that it was his destiny to play for the Bucks, Cummings decided to pay a visit to Donald Sterling to see if he could turn it into a reality. He shared his recent dream with Sterling and said, "I need you to trade me because I can't do this anymore. I can't play under these conditions." Sterling dismissed the idea, saying that he viewed Cummings as a franchise player and thus he couldn't entertain the idea of trading him away. "You can trade me," Cummings replied. "And when you do, trade me to Milwaukee." Sterling repeated that they would not be making any moves that involved getting rid of the team's best player and a disappointed Terry Cummings left the owner's office.

While it was true that Sterling wanted to hang onto Cummings, he was also conscious of the fact that they were about to start playing in Los Angeles. This meant that they needed to field a team that would be able to compete with the Lakers, both on the court and at the box office. And when it came to putting asses in the seats, there was no bigger name in the world of professional basketball than Julius "Dr. J" Erving. While Erving may have been at the tail end of his career, he was still someone whom basketball fans would pay to watch on a nightly basis. So the Clippers offered the 76ers Cummings in a straight swap for Erving. Philadelphia's owner Harold Katz loved the idea of Cummings playing for the Sixers, so he agreed to the deal, with one important proviso. Katz said he would have to speak with Erving to see if he was prepared to end his career playing for the Clippers. If Erving gave his consent, the trade would go ahead. If not, the deal was dead.

Some members of the Clippers' inner sanctum spent that evening visualizing Erving's high wire act thrilling a packed Los Angeles Sports Arena but Pete Babcock was not one of them. "I remember telling everybody,

'We're not going to make this deal tomorrow morning,'" said Babcock. "It's just not going to happen because Erving is not going to agree to be traded to the Clippers." Babcock's assessment of the situation proved to be spot on. Erving declined the opportunity to ride off into the NBA sunset with a Clippers jersey on his back and the dream of having Dr. J as the face of the franchise ended before it had the chance to begin.

With Erving no longer an option, the Clippers began to look for other players who would generate interest from the fans of Los Angeles, which brought them all the way back to Cummings' initial request to be traded to Milwaukee. It just so happened that the Bucks roster featured a former UCLA star who was one of the most popular athletes in Los Angeles area. If the Clippers couldn't have Erving as their starting small forward, then Marques Johnson was probably the best consolation prize imaginable.

Marques Johnson was born to play basketball. Named after Marques Haynes, the former-Harlem Globetrotters star, Johnson was raised in a modest home that was located just a few miles from the Los Angeles Sports Arena. The Johnson family were Lakers season ticket holders, which meant Marques was able to regularly attend games. He would marvel at Elgin Baylor's ability to seemingly score at will and then try to replicate these moves on the family's backyard court. Johnson and his dad spent hours together, working on the game's fundamentals and driving their neighbors crazy, as the noise of a rubber ball pounding against cement echoed throughout their street.

Marques initially attended Dorsey High but transferred to Crenshaw for his final two years, where his father oversaw his development as an unofficial assistant coach. In the final game of his senior season, Johnson scored 36 points despite playing with a painful back injury, as Crenshaw

High capped off an undefeated season by winning the prestigious City Championship. Next stop for Marques was UCLA, where he won every major player of the year award at the end of his senior season. Johnson was a sports star who was both talented and personable, an increasingly rare combination, and by the time he was ready to graduate, he had built a considerable fan base in the city of Los Angeles.

Had it been up to Johnson, his next stop would have been a professional career with the Los Angeles Lakers. However, the Lakers had the sixth pick in the 1977 draft and Johnson's rights were snatched up by Milwaukee with the third overall selection. Johnson was an immediate star in Milwaukee. In his rookie season, he averaged 19.5 points and 10.6 rebounds and finished in the top ten in MVP voting. The following year, Johnson played in his first All-Star game, finished third in the league in scoring and was named to the All-NBA first team. He went on to make four All-Star appearances in his seven years with the Bucks, while the team improved from winning just 30 games in the year before his arrival to posting four consecutive seasons of 50 wins or better. However, despite this on-court success, Johnson still yearned to return to Los Angeles.

As the years went by, Johnson knew that it was less and less likely that he would ever be able to play for the Lakers. Then, in the summer of 1984, the Clippers moved north and the odds of Johnson playing for an NBA franchise based in his hometown immediately doubled. When Johnson heard that the Bucks and Clippers were discussing a potential deal, he "literally prayed it would happen."

However, whereas the Sixers were willing to part with Erving in a straight swap for Cummings, dealing with the Bucks proved to be a little more complicated. Milwaukee's front office was not interested in a Cummings for Johnson trade and instead requested that extra players be brought into the deal. The two franchises eventually agreed on a six player swap, with Cummings, Ricky Pierce and Craig Hodges going to the

Bucks and Johnson, Junior Bridgeman and Harvey Catchings heading to the Clippers[68].

By swapping Cummings for Johnson, the Clippers were losing a 23 year old forward who was averaging 22.9 points and 9.6 rebounds per game and picking up a 28 year old forward with averages of 20.7 points and 6.5 rebounds. The trade did not get any better once the focus shifted to the other players involved. Pierce and Hodges were excellent outside shooters who had shown great promise in the early stages of their careers, while Bridgeman and Catchings were both on the wrong side of 30[69]. With the Clippers likely to be years away from participating in any meaningful playoff action, it was hard to see what they hoped to achieve by giving up three emerging stars in exchange for a collection of players who were clearly approaching the tail end of their careers. This latest transaction meant that the Clippers had now traded away Tom Chambers, Byron Scott, Terry Cummings, Craig Hodges and Ricky Pierce in the space of just 14 months, transforming their roster from one of the youngest in the entire league to the sixth oldest.

At first glance, it appeared that the Clippers were pinning their hopes for a successful first season in Los Angeles on a bunch of aging veterans. However, the player who turned out to be the Clippers' star performer during the 1984-85 season was not Bill Walton, Marques Johnson or Norm Nixon. Instead, it was a little known 23 year old who was about to complete one of the most remarkable ascents from fringe to franchise player in NBA history.

---

68 This trade doubled the number of Clippers who featured in "White Men Can't Jump," with Johnson joining Freeman Williams as former players from the franchise who had small roles in the movie.
69 Pierce and Hodges went on to play a combined total of 26 NBA seasons in which they claimed two NBA titles, an All-Star selection and two Sixth Man of the Year awards between them. On the other hand, Catchings retired after one year with the Clippers while Bridgeman played for just three more seasons before hanging up his sneakers.

Season VII: 1984-85

Derek Smith had already committed to dunking the ball when he spied Michael Jordan making ground on him out of the corner of his eye. Suddenly, what appeared to be an easy breakaway score turned into an aerial duel between two of the league's most promising young players. With a little over three minutes remaining in the fourth quarter and the Clippers clinging to a one point lead, the Smith vs. Jordan contest was likely to be crucial in determining the outcome of the game.

It appeared that Jordan had made up enough ground to put himself in a position to either block Smith's shot or send him to the free throw line. However, as Smith elevated on the left side of the basket, he protected the ball by keeping it down by his waist while hanging in the air long enough to allow Jordan to soar past. With Jordan now out of the picture, Smith sailed underneath the hoop before emerging on the right hand side and emphatically slamming the ball home. This play was more than just a jaw dropping highlight, it was the exclamation mark at the end of an impressive individual performance that made it clear Smith was ready to join the ranks of the NBA's elite.

On this one night in late November, the Sports Arena was the center of the NBA universe. Michael Jordan was playing his first professional game in the City of Angels and a crowd of 14,366 had shown up to see the rookie sensation for themselves[70]. Jordan's evening was filled with a number of spectacular plays that thrilled the fans and yet, he was on the verge of suffering a defeat. Smith's dunk gave the Clippers a three point lead with less than three minutes to play and it also pushed Smith's individual scoring tally to 33 points, more than double Jordan's total of 14.

But as would be the case throughout his career, it was Jordan who had the last laugh. He scored six of the Bulls' final seven points, including an

---

[70] The Clippers actually drew a larger crowd than the Lakers, who were playing at the Forum on the same night in front of just 12,766 people. Even the Lakers biggest fan, Jack Nicolson, chose to head to the Sports Arena so he could witness the Michael Jordan show.

amazing three point play with just over a minute left in the game[71]. Jordan's late game heroics were enough to secure a four point Chicago win but much of the postgame discussion focused on the performance from the previously unheralded Smith.

Smith went toe to toe with a player who was rapidly emerging as the league's biggest star and more than held his own. While not many players would have had the self-confidence to believe that they could take on Jordan, for Smith it was just another chance to show the world that you underestimated him at your own peril.

Derek Smith was born in Hogansville, Georgia, a small town near Atlanta. He and his six siblings were raised by their single mother, who worked at a local sewing factory. Money was always tight and when Smith was just four years old, he was sent off to school, allowing the family to save on the cost of childcare. Smith started playing basketball when he was in the seventh grade and by the time he graduated from Hogansville High, he had led the school to two state championships. Despite this on-court success, there was little recruiting interest shown for Smith. He spent most of his time at high school playing center and at just 6'4", there was considerable skepticism about whether his game would translate to the next level.

For a while it looked like Smith was going to attend Gardner-Webb, a small college in North Carolina with very little basketball history, before fate intervened. One of Smith's local friends had just received a football scholarship to play at Louisville and he approached the school's basketball coach, Denny Crum, to tell him about a prospect from his hometown.

---

71 Jordan appeared to be streaking in for an easy fast break score before Smith chased him down and applied what can best be described as a tackle. Rather than take the foul and head to the free-throw line, Jordan somehow managed to keep his arms free from Smith's bear hug and converted an improbable scoop shot that had the entire Sports Arena gasping in amazement. It was the perfect answer to Smith's spectacular dunk from just a few minutes earlier.

Crum sent an assistant coach out to Hogansville to investigate and not long after, Smith signed a letter of intent to become a Cardinal.

Smith arrived on campus as a 16 year old freshman, courtesy of his early start at school all those years ago and Crum planned to redshirt him. Or at least that *was* the idea until Crum watched Smith's first intra-squad scrimmage. After seeing Smith convert his first 12 shots, Crum realized that he was ready to contribute right away. It didn't take long for Smith to snatch a starting spot from one of his senior teammates and he was soon playing almost 20 minutes a game.

Despite this early success, Smith remained driven. He kept a copy of a team photo and whenever he passed a teammate, in terms of court time, he would mark the occasion by crossing out his colleagues' face. By the end of his sophomore season, there were many more red crosses than smiling faces looking back at Smith. That year, Louisville won the national championship and Smith, still only 18 years of age, led the team in rebounding (8.3 boards per game) and was second in scoring (14.8 points a night).

Smith's final two years at Louisville resulted in similar levels of on court production and heading into the 1982 NBA draft, Smith was optimistic that he was going to be a first round selection. However, most NBA experts viewed Smith, who was now 6'6", as a classic 'tweener', someone who was stuck *between* being a guard and a forward. They feared that Smith lacked the skills to play guard and was not tall enough to play in the front court. The first round came and went without Smith's name being called and he was eventually picked by Golden State with the 35th overall selection.

Smith earned himself a spot on the Warriors' roster but once the season got underway, he received very few chances to show what he could do. For Smith's entire rookie year, he clocked a grand total of just 154 minutes, playing mostly as an under-sized power forward. At the end of the 1982-83 campaign, the Warriors had given up on Smith and he was released.

Most people in the NBA expected that this would be the last they heard of Derek Smith but he remained optimistic of receiving a second chance. Enlisting the help of former Chicago Bulls coach Ed Badger, Smith went to work on improving his ball handling and outside shooting. Throughout the summer, in a gym that reached scorching hot temperatures, Badger ran Smith through a series of tortuous drills that slowly transformed his game. As the 1983-84 season approached, Smith felt like he was playing the best basketball of his life and yet no one was willing to take a chance of him. He couldn't find a single coach who was prepared to give him a spot on their summer league team, much less get an NBA general manager to offer him a contract.

Smith's big break came when Jim Lynam reluctantly agreed to allow him to join the Clippers' summer league entry midway through the competition. Lynam didn't think Smith had any chance of making the Clippers' regular season roster and only agreed to take a look at him as a favor to an old colleague named Stu Inman. In fact, Lynam initially told Inman that Smith would only be able to participate in practice sessions, stressing that he would not get to play in any of their actual summer league games.

When Smith heard that he was able to start practicing with the Clippers summer league team, he was relieved that he finally had a foot in the door. Smith saw Lynam at the Loyola Marymount gym, the site of the summer league, and went over to introduce himself and thank the Clippers coach for giving him the opportunity. Lynam began passing on the details about the time and venue for the next day's session when he was struck by the intense look in Smith's eyes. Lynam's intuition was telling him that Smith may have more to offer than just an extra body for practice and so made a split second decision that changed the trajectory of Smith's life. He decided to hold an informal tryout on the spot.

Lynam took Smith to a deserted practice court and put him through his paces for around half an hour. As Smith put on a dunking exhibition that would have made Dominique Wilkins blush, a shocked Lynam could barely comprehend what he was witnessing. "He displayed incredible strength and athleticism," Lynam said. "You didn't have to be a basketball expert to see that, a lawyer watching him would get that." It wasn't just Smith's explosiveness that captivated Lynam, it was also his ability to consistently knock down mid-range jump shots. Once the session was over, Lynam knew that a special player had just fallen into his lap. He said goodbye to Smith and then made his way outside to a payphone, where he placed a call to his wife. "Kay, I'll tell you the story when I get home," Lynam said as he looked up to the clear blue sky above him, "but I may have just been hit by lightning."

Having been convinced that Smith was a bona fide NBA player, Lynam now needed to persuade the front office to take a chance and sign him up. The crux of Lynam's big sell was Golden State had used Smith incorrectly and that this was the reason for his underwhelming rookie season. Lynam wanted to convert Smith from a back-up power forward into a starting shooting guard. The Clippers' front office had heavily scouted Smith in the lead-up to the 1982 draft and, while they liked what they had seen when it came to Smith's character, they were doubtful that he could be converted into an effective perimeter player. "I had no reservations about signing him as a person, because the research on him was terrific," said Babcock. "I just didn't know many players who made the transition from being a power player to a guard." Smith's outstanding form during the remaining portion of the Clippers' summer league schedule eventually clinched the deal and the Clippers signed him for the 1983-84 season.

However, when the regular season started, Smith's impact was barely noticeable. While Lynam knew how good Smith was, he was also trying to establish himself in a league that is notoriously unforgiving of rookie coaches who don't perform. So instead of starting the season with an ex-power forward alongside Norm Nixon in the backcourt, Lynam went with safer, more conventional options like Ricky Pierce and Craig Hodges. Still,

Smith was far from discontent. Instead, he was happy to be in the league and glad for any opportunities that he did receive to play. "I never looked at myself as an NBA starter, much less a star," Smith said. "I always compared myself to Michael Cooper, a guy who's willing to stick around and do the hard things, like taking charges and playing good defense."

Smith continued to impress the coaching staff with his astounding work ethic and by the latter stages of the 1983-84 season, Lynam decided to throw caution to the wind. He inserted Smith into the starting line-up for the final 19 games and during this time, he averaged 17.4 points, giving the rest of the league a glimpse of his true potential.

Smith's impressive form over the final weeks of the season caught the attention of coaches and general managers from around the league. The Nuggets tried to lure Smith away by signing him to an offer sheet worth $800,000 over two years, which was a substantial salary upgrade. Given Sterling's hesitancy to spend large sums of money on players, many people speculated that Smith was about to head to Denver. However, it took the Clippers just two days to match the Nuggets' offer and retain him.

Which brings us back to the 1984-85 NBA season. If the game played at the Sports Arena against Jordan and the Bulls was Smith's coming out party, then the entire season was a six month festival to announce his arrival to the rest of the NBA. In the space of just three years, Smith went from scoring a total of 59 points across an entire NBA season, to averaging 22.1 points per game[72]. Smith's rise to prominence was so sudden and dramatic that it is worthy of being given the Vince Papale treatment from the folks at Disney. But while Derek Smith's emergence was the feel-good story of the Clippers' first season in Los Angeles, the player at the opposite end of the spectrum was undoubtedly Marques Johnson.

---

72 Along with 5.3 rebounds, 2.7 assists and 1 steal.

When Marques Johnson first heard that he was being traded to the Clippers, he was ecstatic. He had long dreamed of being able to play in his hometown in front of his family and now it had become a reality. However, once Johnson arrived in Los Angeles, things began to sour. Quickly.

The problems started at the beginning of Johnson's very first day of training camp. "We had a two-on-one kind of drill where I had to reach in and slap the ball away," Johnson said. "I remember telling the assistant coach, 'This is dangerous.'" Johnson was assured that this was a great way to improve players' reaction times and the drill continued. A few minutes later, Johnson broke the pinkie finger in his shooting hand. This injury did not cause Johnson to miss any games but it had a lasting impact, disrupting his ball handling and shooting for his entire first season with the Clippers[73].

Johnson's broken finger was followed by a hamstring injury that caused him to spend six games on the sidelines in the middle of December. Then, after only a month back in the line-up, Johnson sprained his ankle, forcing him to sit out another four games. At the halfway point of the season, a bruised and battered Johnson was on pace to finish with career lows in almost every major statistical category.

Meanwhile, halfway across the country, the Bucks couldn't have been happier with the play of Terry Cummings. Milwaukee was sitting atop of the Central Division and Cummings, who was averaging over 24 points per game, was the star of the show. In fact, Cummings' form was so impressive that he was now being mentioned as arguably the best power forward in the NBA[74]. The stark contrast in the fortunes of Cummings and Johnson was making the Clippers' front office look like bumbling fools. Then, the

---

73 The effect of this injury on Johnson's shooting was dramatic. In his first seven years in the league he converted 53% of his field goal attempts but, after breaking his finger, this figure plummeted to just 45% during the 1984-85 season.
74 Cummings' was eventually named on the All-NBA second team at the end of the 1984-85 season, alongside icons such as Kareem Abdul-Jabbar and Michael Jordan.

Clippers were presented with a novel way of dealing with this case of buyer's remorse.

In early February, Alan Rothenberg was contacted by a journalist from the Los Angeles Times, who asked if he was aware that Johnson had spent some time at a drug rehabilitation center while playing for the Bucks. Apparently, the Clippers had no knowledge of this but, armed with this new information, the team's management set about announcing their moral indignation to the rest of the league. "I think for sure the Bucks were obliged to tell us," proclaimed Rothenberg, before adding, "If that's true, we would have looked at the trade very carefully before completing it." General manager Carl Scheer said, "There is an ethical factor involved, if not a legal one."

The Clippers were initially undecided on what to do but Rothenberg clearly stated that if they opted to pursue the matter, they would not be requesting that the initial six player trade be reversed. "You can't unscramble an egg," said Rothenberg. "If we decide to take some action, it won't be that."

A few months later, the Clippers filed a lawsuit against the Bucks that sought to have the original trade overturned.

The Clippers asked the courts to force the Bucks to send Cummings, Pierce and Hodges back to California. If this was deemed to be too impractical, they wanted to be compensated for Milwaukee's deceit in the form of draft picks or money. The Clippers' latest courtroom drama may have been good for generating newspaper headlines but it appeared that their case was lacking in legal merit. Information about Johnson attending a drug rehabilitation facility while he was playing for Milwaukee was contained in his file, which was kept at NBA head office. Standard procedure called for the Clippers to look in this file before completing the trade but, for some inexplicable reason, they choose not to. Therefore it was hard to see how they were going to make the case that the Bucks were responsible for withholding or concealing information from them.

The decision to try and get the courts to rescind the trade certainly did no favors for the public perception of the Clippers. Johnson was an immensely popular player, as well as the face of the franchise's marketing campaign. And while Johnson was understandably upset by this turn of events, he handled himself with dignity throughout the entire affair. He chose to say very little about the matter but did tell the media he felt unwanted, while also saying that he believed his "name had been dragged through the mud." Johnson also provided an explanation as to why he spent time at a drug rehabilitation facility, saying that he voluntarily attended a program after the Bucks had raised some concerns about rumors that he was experimenting with drugs. Those close to him could see that the intrusion into his personal life and the Clippers' choice to try and have him sent back to Milwaukee were deeply hurtful to Johnson.

Ultimately, the Clippers case against the Bucks was decided in arbitration by the league's new commissioner, David Stern. Stern said he found no proof of any misrepresentation on behalf of the Bucks and ruled that the original trade would stand. Milwaukee did not have to compensate the Clippers in any way, shape or form.

This whole embarrassing chapter was one that the Clippers would rather have forgotten and was the last thing the organization needed as they tried to find their feet in a new market that was already inhabited by one of the league's powerhouse franchises. While the Lakers were winning the 1985 NBA championship, the Clippers were busy trying to force another team to swap back players from a trade that was made almost a year earlier. In the process, they were fast losing what little credibility they had when they arrived in town just 12 months earlier.

While this latest saga was keeping Clipper management occupied with matters away from the court, out on the hardwood the team continued to struggle. On the day that the Marques Johnson story broke, the Clippers were in the midst of a horror stretch in which they lost nine out of ten games. Preseason hopes of seriously challenging the Lakers for the hearts and minds of Los Angeles had given way to the reality that the Clippers were going to once again fall well short of qualifying for the playoffs.

Given the team's poor results, it came as no surprise to Jim Lynam when he became the first Clipper coach to be sacked in the middle of a season[75]. Lynam first realized that he was on shaky ground back in February, when an article appeared in the Los Angeles Times that stated his days were numbered. In it, Scheer acknowledged that he "would prefer to have (his) own man" coaching the team. Not exactly the sort of comment that would make Jim Lynam want to take out a mortgage on a house in the Hollywood Hills. Luckily for Lynam, fate intervened 48 hours later when the Times published their revelations about Marques Johnson and any thought that the Clippers had of sacking their coach gave way to trying to manage this latest scandal.

Lynam's reprieve would be extremely short-lived. At the start of March, with the team in the middle of another long losing streak, the speculation about Lynam's job began to grow once again. Scheer decided that the best way to deal with the constant chatter about whether Lynam would hold onto his job was to call him and offer a personal reassurance that his position was safe, until at least the end of the current season. Scheer shared the contents of his and Lynam's discussion with the media, saying, "I told Jimmy, once and for all, that he doesn't need to worry. It would take 46 straight blowout losses and a riot in the locker room to replace Jimmy now." With only 23 games remaining on the Clippers' schedule, Scheer's message was clear- Lynam was not going anywhere anytime soon.

---

75 He would not be the last.

A week later, Jim Lynam was canned.

When the termination was announced, Scheer was asked about the assurances that he had given just a few days earlier. He responded by saying, "When I said that, I meant it." Apparently things had changed in the ensuing seven days. After firing Lynam, the Clippers rallied to win nine of their final 21 games under interim coach Don Chaney. Even with this late season flurry of victories, the first year in Los Angeles was a decidedly ordinary one. It was case of different setting, different cast, same plot line. The Clippers won a total of 31 games, a marginal improvement from the previous year but still well short of securing a playoff berth.

As the 1984-85 season drew to a close, Donald Sterling once again turned his attention to the ongoing legal dispute with the NBA over his decision to move the team to Los Angeles. Sterling decided to adopt the "best form of defense is to attack" philosophy, filing a $100 million counter suit against the league in early March. He was seeking $50 million in actual damages and $50 million in punitive damages, claiming that the league had committed "various fraudulent acts" and was conspiring to terminate the Clippers franchise. Having thrown a $100 million legal haymaker, Sterling sat back and waited for the NBA's response.

The conclusion of the 1984-85 season also marked the end of an era, as Bill Walton and the Clippers decided to go their separate ways. While Walton had managed to play 67 games during the 1984-85 season, a personal best at this point in his career, he also came to the realization that he was not the same player he once was. The Clippers had spent most of their short history trying to build a championship roster around their red-headed center, but Walton could see that he was no longer capable of being the franchise player on a contending team.

Walton had a clause in his contract that granted him restricted free agent status at the end of any season in which the Clippers failed to qualify for the playoffs. He was hoping to use this to place himself on the roster of a title contender, where he could play a smaller role but hopefully experience more success. His preferred destination was the Lakers. Walton loved the idea of being able to continue living in Southern California while playing for one of the NBA's elite teams. However, after a physical test raised concerns about his durability, the Lakers quickly lost interest.

Walton then shifted his attention to the second team on his wish list, the Boston Celtics. He decided to opt for the direct approach and so he picked up the phone and placed a call to the offices of Red Auerbach, who was the Celtics' president at the time. It was the day after the Celtics lost the 1985 NBA Finals and Auerbach was meeting with Larry Bird to discuss plans for the following season. When Auerbach heard that Walton was keen to join the Celtics, he was intrigued. However, as is often the case when dealing with the Clippers, the Celtics found that the process of securing the rights to Walton would not be a straight forward process.

In fact, negotiations between the Clippers and Celtics dragged on for three months before both sides were able to finally agree on a deal. The Celtics knew that their best chance of landing Walton was via a trade, as they believed that if they tried to sign him as a free agent, the Clippers would simply match their offer and retain his rights. The Celtics thought they had the perfect player to send to the Clippers- Cedric Maxwell.

Maxwell was not only a former Finals MVP and a key contributor on two Celtic championship teams, he was also an ex-teammate of interim coach Don Chaney, the man who looked to be the most likely candidate to coach the Clippers in the coming season. The Celtics were looking to make a deal for their likable power forward, due to a falling out between Maxwell and Auerbach. The Celtics' president was furious at Maxwell, believing that he had not put his best effort into his rehabilitation after having knee surgery midway through the previous season. Auerbach now viewed Maxwell as somewhat of a malingerer and thus wanted to get rid of him as soon as possible.

The Clippers, on the other hand, thought that Maxwell would be a good addition to their roster, believing that he would be able to slot nicely into their starting line-up. However, despite the Clippers' interest in Maxwell, the trade talks between the two sides seemed to be heading nowhere. "We'd talk regularly, but with quite a bit of frustration on our part because every time we'd make progress, they'd come back with, 'Yes, we'll do that, but need this too,'" said Celtics general manager Jan Volk. "They'd keep adding something to the deal and we didn't think we could get it done unless it was exceptionally lopsided and probably imprudent from our point of view."

By early August, the Celtics' front office had grown tired of the long, drawn out process and they informed their Clipper counterparts that they were pulling out of the trade discussions. Scheer then told a disappointed Walton that he should start preparing for another season of playing for the Clippers.

Meanwhile, Volk got in touch with Maxwell to try and extend an olive branch to bring him back into the fold. Maxwell was invited to attend the Celtics' rookie camp, which was being held at Camp Milbrook, a former lumber mill with very basic facilities, including asphalt courts and metal backboards. The only problem was that Maxwell was not keen on holding hands around the camp fire and singing Kumbaya with Auerbach. In fact, as an eight year veteran, he found the idea of being asked to attend rookie camp to be a little absurd and so he declined the offer. This only served to further infuriate Auerbach, who instructed Volk to re-open trade discussions with the Clippers. Volk called Scheer and they picked up where they left off.

A few weeks later, the two sides reached a general consensus on what the major pieces of the trade were going to be. Boston would get Walton in exchange for Maxwell and the Celtics' 1986 first round pick. However, rather than this bringing an end to the months of haggling, the Clippers now shifted their focus onto fiscal matters. Before they would sign off on the deal, the Clippers were asking Boston to pay some of Maxwell's salary for the upcoming season and also wanted to get Walton to cough up some cash as well. They were eventually successful in both endeavors. The Celtics agreed to pay half of Maxwell's salary, while Walton surrendered a year and half worth of deferred payments that the Clippers owed him in order to get the trade done. Eventually on September 6th, 89 days after Walton first placed a call to the Celtics, the deal was finalized. Bill Walton could breathe a sigh of relief, his days with the Clippers were officially over.

Years later, Walton still looked back on the six years that he spent with the Clippers as the most disappointing stage of his entire career. Here was an athlete who had proven himself as a winner at every level he had competed in, winning championships at Helix High School, UCLA and as a professional in Portland, and yet he could not lead the Clippers into the playoffs. "The biggest failure of my professional life," was how Walton referred to his stint with the Clippers[76].

Thus the 1985-86 season marked the beginning of a new era for the Clippers, one that would be played without the services of Walton. Not only was Walton gone, the franchise was also in the midst of a multi-million dollar conflict with the league's head office and if the Clippers did not prevail in this legal battle, their future as an NBA franchise looked to be

---

76 Walton returned to his winning ways as soon as he hit the ground at Logan Airport, as the Celtics put together a magnificent season that eventually resulted in their reclaiming of the NBA championship. Amazingly, Walton was healthy enough to play in 96 of the Celtics 100 regular season and playoff games and his contribution to the team's success was recognized when he won the Sixth Man of the Year award. To provide some perspective on just how remarkable a turnaround this was, it took Walton 1,536 days to play 96 games as a Clipper.

questionable at best. On the court, they had now been trying to reach the playoffs for seven seasons and success had thus far proven to be elusive. In these types of difficult times, people often console one another by saying things like, "The only way to go from here is up." However, in this case, these words of encouragement were way off the mark. Over the next few seasons, the Clippers were headed in one direction- down. In fact, they were about to crash catastrophically and, in the process, mount a serious challenge for the title of the worst NBA team of all-time.

CHAPTER 6

Thank God for the 1973 Philadelphia 76ers

"It's a constant feeling of impending doom. You know, Murphy's Law. Whatever can go wrong is gonna go wrong. There was this Sword of Damocles kind of hanging over all of us."

MARQUES JOHNSON

NO ONE CAN ACCUSE THE Clippers of being idle during the summer of 1985. On top of their ongoing legal battle with the NBA's head office and the complicated Walton-Maxwell trade, the franchise had to negotiate contracts for a new coach, an All-Star point guard and a promising rookie.

The front runner for the vacant head coaching position was Don Chaney. He had performed well as the interim coach at the end of the previous season, with the Clippers winning nine of their final 16 games and had also proven to be very popular with the players. So when Chaney was presented with a contract for the upcoming season, most people expected that he would be quick to sign. However, nothing is ever that simple when dealing with the Clippers.

Although Chaney desperately wanted to land an NBA head coaching position, he still declined the Clippers' offer of a one year, $75,000 contract, as he considered it to be insulting. "I definitely had a desire to be a head coach," said Chaney, "but at the same time, I wasn't going to take a job and get paid beans for doing it[77]." When Chaney rejected the offer, acting upon the advice of his agent Larry Fleisher, it became a news item in Los Angeles, which only further consolidated the growing public perception that the Clippers were a small-time operation. To most observers, it appeared as if the Clippers were trying to use Chaney's lack of experience to force him to accept a salary that was *well* below the going rate for an NBA head coach.

What ensued from here was a saga that dragged on for weeks. The Clippers went out of their way to show the world that Chaney needed them more than they needed him. They made public comments about looking at other candidates, which created the impression that they were pretty much indifferent as to whether Chaney ended up coaching the team. As the weeks went by, Chaney's alternate employment options began to rapidly disappear, as other vacant coaching jobs started to be filled. Eventually, the Clippers upped their offer to three years at $90,000 a season and this was enough to secure Chaney's signature.

While at first glance it may appear that Chaney had extracted a victory, he was only marginally better off. Just one of the three years was actually guaranteed and the $15,000 improvement in salary simply moved him from being the outright lowest paid head coach in the league, to tied for last[78]. In reality, there were no winners, as these prolonged negotiations only served to further tarnish the franchise's already damaged reputation.

---

[77] Had Chaney accepted this first offer, he would have been the lowest paid head coach in the league. In fact, some assistant coaches were making more than what the Clippers were offering. On top of the relatively poor financial compensation, Chaney was also put off by the length of the deal. It is hard to think of a less secure sports-related job than having a one year contract as the head coach of the Clippers.

[78] Along with Golden State's John Bach.

Securing a contract for Chaney would not be the final chapter of Larry Fleisher's summer of discontent. Almost immediately after Chaney's deal was finalized, Fleisher had to go through the whole frustrating process again, this time on behalf of his newest client, Benoit Benjamin. Benjamin, an imposing 7'0" center from Creighton University, was the third overall pick in the 1985 draft. He was born in Monroe, a small city located in the north-east of Louisiana, and raised by his single mother, Carolyn Benjamin, with considerable help from both his aunt and grandmother who lived nearby. His father passed away in a car accident when Benoit was just 9 years old. Without a father figure in her son's life, Carolyn had to fill both parental roles, a challenge that led to her being somewhat overprotective of her only child.

When Benjamin enrolled at Carroll High School he found the male role model that he had been looking for. During the four years that Jimmy Jones coached Benjamin, he filled various roles that would normally be reserved for a father, from driving Benjamin to school each day to offering him relationship advice. This partnership eventually led the Carroll Bulldogs all the way to the 1982 Louisiana State Championship, with Benjamin the star of the show, averaging 29 points and 19.5 rebounds.

When the time came to choose a college, Benjamin selected Creighton for one reason- the chance to be coached by Willis Reed. Reed was a fellow Louisiana native who had gone on to one of the most successful careers in NBA history, winning two championship rings and an MVP award as a member of the New York Knicks. As Jones had done, Reed assumed a mentoring role in Benjamin's life, starting from the star center's first few days on campus. When Benjamin arrived at school weighing approximately 280 pounds, almost 40 pounds above his optimal playing weight, Reed informed him that he needed to get in shape and change his ways if he was going to ever reach his potential.

Benjamin's first two seasons at Creighton were solid but unspectacular but by his junior year, he was playing so well that he made people sit up and take notice. He put up consecutive 40 point games in early January, scoring 43 against Southern Illinois and 45 two nights later against Indiana State. Then, after a 29 point, 12 rebound, 12 block triple double against Bradley, opposition coach Dick Versace said Benjamin would be his first choice if he was assembling an NBA roster from scratch. Benjamin finished the season with averages of 21.5 points, 14.1 rebounds and 5.1 blocks per game and with a stellar professional career seemingly awaiting, he made the decision to forgo his senior year and enter the NBA draft.

When the Clippers selected Benjamin, they were buoyant about his prospects. "I guess we have to be careful in hyping him up and putting a lot of pressure on him," said Carl Scheer, before adding, "He could turn out to be as good or better than (Patrick) Ewing." Even Benjamin himself joined in, proclaiming, "I want to become one of the greatest players in the NBA. That's my goal." However, these optimistic proclamations ignored the questions about Benjamin's work ethic and attitude, which had hovered around him throughout his time as a college student. Video footage of his playing days at Creighton provided clear evidence of him yelling at teammates, arguing with his coaches, complaining to referees and putting in a sub-standard effort on occasion. Benjamin was about to find out that the world of professional basketball was a lot more complicated than the supportive environment of a college campus.

His first task was to agree on terms for his rookie contract, never a straightforward process for a new Clipper draftee. Different organizations have their own traditions and rituals designed to help welcome a new employee. Some hold social functions so new staff can meet their colleagues in a relaxed setting. Some provide mentors to answer any questions and show the newbie the ropes. When it came to the Clippers, the standard orientation process for newly acquired personnel seemed to be offering them a contract with remuneration terms well below the current market rate and then refusing to budge from this initial low-ball figure. From here, things usually drag out for weeks or months on end until it becomes a battle of wills to see who will blink first. While this approach may have been successful in helping the Clippers to suppress their salary costs, it also gave new employees the impression that they were not valued by the organization. This, in turn, created considerable bad blood or as Michael Cage put it, "After this franchise negotiates with a player, what they end up with is damaged goods."

If the employee in question is an equipment manager who can be easily replaced, perhaps this "take it or leave it" style of negotiation makes some sense. However, if the worker in question is a 20 year old prodigy who possesses a rare combination of physical attributes and basketball skills, it is harder to understand the desire to quibble over money and risk alienating the player in question. However, as the Clippers had previously done with Tom Chambers, Terry Cummings, Byron Scott and Michael Cage, this is the approach they took to signing Benoit Benjamin.

Benjamin was seeking a three year deal at $1 million a season. The Clippers were offering significantly less. While the two sides tried to find some common ground, training camp got under way and Chaney was not impressed that he was forced to start pre-season practices without Benjamin. "To miss even two or three days of practice will set him back half a season," Chaney said. In all, Benjamin missed ten days of training camp before Fleisher and the Clippers finally agreed on four year deal that that paid around $800,000 a season.

Season VIII: 1985-86

An offer of four years at $700,000 a season was what Norm Nixon was hoping to get. While this represented a considerable upgrade on his existing salary of a little over $400,000, Nixon's form since he was traded from the Lakers was clearly deserving of a pay rise. When the Clippers acquired Nixon, they were hoping that he would be able to provide steady, veteran leadership and this was precisely what he had delivered. Nixon played in

163 of the Clippers' 164 games during this two year stretch, while averaging 17.1 points and 10 assists per game[79]. He also became the first Clipper to play in an All-Star game since World B. Free in 1980, when he was selected for the 1985 showcase.

However, despite all of these positives, when the regular season tipped off, Nixon still did not have a new contract. This meant that while the Clippers were up in Sacramento launching their new campaign with a rare road victory, Nixon was sitting on his couch back in Los Angeles. After the win over the Kings, the Nixon-less Clippers returned to the Sports Arena for a four game home stand and won all four games, propelling them to the top of the Western Conference standings.

There was no doubt about which player was the driving force behind this surprisingly good start to the season. Derek Smith began the 1985-86 campaign like a man on a mission. 36 points on opening night against Sacramento. 26 in a one point victory over Houston. 28 points and 6 assists against Clyde Drexler and the Blazers. After Michael Jordan watched Smith put up 21 points in a Clippers' win over the Bulls, he described his opponent as "the most underrated player in the NBA," before predicting that he was just a few months away from being selected as a first time All-Star.

By the time the 1986 All-Star break came around, Derek Smith had already played his last game as a Clipper.

In the middle of November, Seattle visited Los Angeles to play the Clippers and Derek Smith must have felt like the loneliest man in professional basketball. He was the only member of Chaney's preferred starting line-up who was on the court for the game's opening tip. Benjamin had not yet

---

[79] Nixon was one of just three players who averaged at least 15 points and 10 assists during this time. The other two were Isiah Thomas and Magic Johnson.

been able to work himself into a reasonable physical condition, limiting his contribution to a few short stints off the bench. Nixon remained stuck on the sidelines, courtesy of the still unresolved negotiations for a new contract. And the team's forward pair of Marques Johnson and Cedric Maxwell were both unable to play due to injury.

Rather than complain about the lack of support, Smith put his head down and produced another exceptional performance. With a little over three minutes remaining, he had contributed 26 points, 8 rebounds, 4 assists and 3 blocks, almost singlehandedly keeping the undermanned Clippers in the contest. The Sonics were up by four points when Smith aggressively drove into the key, looking for points number 27 and 28. He planted his left foot prior to elevating but instead of exploding towards the basket, Smith heard a loud popping noise and crumpled to the floor.

An eerie silence descended over the 5,240 fans in attendance and as Smith clutched his left knee and screamed in agony, he happened to catch the eye of Donald Sterling, who was sitting in his regular courtside seats. Six days earlier, Sterling had offered Smith a $5 million contract that would have set him up financially for the rest of his life. Smith had not yet signed the contract and he correctly suspected that, with a knee injury hanging over his head, this lucrative offer would no longer be on the table. The diagnosis was a torn cartilage and Smith underwent arthroscopic surgery later that week. If all went well, it was expected that he would be out of action for a little over a month, meaning he was likely to miss around 20 games.

The injury had a devastating effect on the psyche of the Clippers. Smith's teammates knew how good he was, even if the rest of the league was a little slow in catching on. Over the first nine games of the season, Smith was averaging 27.1 points, 4.3 rebounds, 3.1 assists and 1.4 blocks while shooting 56% from the field. One of the immediate effects of Smith's absence was that it placed more pressure on the Clippers' front office to work out a deal with Nixon. However, while the Clippers now desperately needed

Nixon, it was beginning to look increasingly likely that he had played his last game for the franchise.

A few days after Smith hurt his knee, Nixon signed an offer sheet with Seattle worth $2.7 million over five years. This was considerably more lucrative than anything that had been tabled thus far by the Clippers. This left the Clippers with two options: either give Nixon a lot more money than they were intending to or watch him leave to play for one of their Pacific Division rivals. After months of haggling, the Clippers realized that Nixon was too important a player to let go, and so they matched Seattle's offer. Five months after negotiations had first begun and 13 games into the regular season, Nixon was finally able to return to the court.

By the time Nixon re-joined the team, their 5-0 start to the season seemed like ancient history. And while the Clippers managed to break an eight game losing streak in Nixon's comeback appearance, this was followed by a three week period in which they only won twice, bringing their overall record to just eight wins in 25 outings. And the Clippers were not just losing, they were getting humiliated. They lost by 32 points in Seattle, 28 points in San Antonio, 39 points in Denver and a whopping 40 points against Utah at home.

The Clippers front office decided that something had to be done.

And this is what they came up with.

Chaney was told that he had one week to prove himself or he was going to be fired. Exactly what Chaney was being asked to achieve in this week remained unclear. Did the Clippers have to win a single game? Or did they have to win all three in which they were scheduled to play? Could Chaney save his job if the team continued to lose but they were able to lessen the margins of defeat? It seemed no-one was 100% sure and nobody was prepared to elaborate.

Marques Johnson knew all too well what it felt like to be the subject of negative media attention courtesy of Clipper management and he labeled this latest brainwave as "purely a scapegoat move." Any doubts about whether Chaney's job was on the line disappeared when Carl Scheer began publically speculating about whether they would hire an interim coach or seek to make a more permanent appointment if they fired Chaney. Clearly, not many people expected Chaney to have a job come Christmas Day. Somehow, he managed to survive.

In fact, Chaney did not even have to wait the full seven days before getting word from Sterling that his job was now safe[80]. The Clippers won the next game they played after Chaney was given the "win or else" warning, a 103-99 home victory over Golden State, another team stuck in the basement of the Pacific Division standings. Two nights later, they put up a brave fight against San Antonio before eventually going down by 15 points. These two results were apparently enough to convince Sterling that Chaney was still the best man for the job. Sterling called Chaney and told him that there wouldn't be any changes in the immediate future. And just like that, Chaney's job was saved.

The other big news to come out of the win over the Warriors was the short-lived comeback of Derek Smith. Amidst a lot of speculation about whether his knee was fully healed, Smith played 13 minutes against Golden State and he looked like a shadow of his former self. He converted just three field goals and was barely a factor in the Clippers' four point victory. Smith then sat out the next two games before returning to play on Christmas Day against Portland. The clash with the Blazers was even less productive. Smith was limited to 11 minutes of court time and his stat line of 5 points, 2 turnovers, 2 personal fouls and 1 assist clearly indicated that something was not right. This was not the same Derek Smith who had gone head to head with Clyde Drexler and outscored him 28-16 just

---

80 Well, as safe as any job can be when your employer is the Los Angeles Clippers.

a few weeks earlier. This loss to the Blazers turned out to be Smith's last outing in a Clipper uniform.

Smith was initially placed on the injured reserve list to give his knee more time to recover. However, he was soon reporting feelings of unexplained fatigue to the Clippers' medical staff, to go along with the pain in his knee. The reason for this lethargy was unknown, so the Clippers sought outside help in order to get an accurate diagnosis. For two months, the Clippers sent Smith to a variety of doctors and for two months, no one could detect anything that would explain the sudden feelings of exhaustion that Smith was describing. This caused some people within the Clippers organization to start spreading rumors that there was nothing physically amiss with Smith.

When the doctors finally figured out what was wrong, they discovered that Smith had contracted a rare form of mononucleosis. This quickly put an end to the scuttlebutt and gossip that was circulating about Smith. The franchise's focus now shifted onto what was the best course of action to ensure that their star player made a full recovery. Given that the Clippers were once again out of the playoff race, the decision was made to sit Smith for the rest of the season. This would give him some extra time to both get over the virus and build up strength and confidence in his surgically repaired knee.

It might come as a shock to learn that the biggest headache Don Chaney had to deal with during his first full season as an NBA head coach was not Derek Smith's health or Norm Nixon's holdout or his own job security. It was Benoit Benjamin. When Benjamin was selected with the third overall pick in the 1985 draft, the Clippers had high hopes, envisioning that he might one day be the centerpiece of the franchise's first championship team. It did not take long for the reality of working with Benjamin to erase these lofty visions from the collective heads of all associated with the Clippers.

The first half of Benjamin's rookie season was bad. Really bad. After his first 28 games as a professional, he was averaging a little over 5 points and 5 rebounds per game- astoundingly low totals for someone with Benjamin's physical tools. "He was gifted with good talent," said Chaney. "He had good size, could score, good passing skills and could block shots. He just didn't have drive." Chaney tried every trick he could think of to motivate Benjamin but nothing seemed to be working.

On Christmas Day, Chaney stumbled across a potential solution. The Clippers were in Portland, where they were set to take on the Blazers that evening and Chaney was enjoying a casual lunch with one of the greatest players of all-time, Bill Russell[81]. Russell was also in town for that evening's game, where he would be working as a broadcaster. During the meal, Chaney discovered that his old friend was planning on spending a few weeks in Los Angeles over January and so he asked if Russell was prepared to swing by Clipper practice to do some work with Benjamin[82]. Russell agreed and over the next few weeks he conducted some intensive one-on-one sessions with Benjamin.

If Chaney was hoping that spending some time with the greatest winner to ever play in the NBA was going to rub off on his young center, he would have been happy with the short term results. For a two week period in the middle of January, Benjamin showed signs that he might actually be capable of being a productive NBA center and this sudden improvement was instrumental in the Clippers winning five out of seven games[83].

---

81 Russell and Chaney's careers intersected during the 1968-69 season, when they were teammates on a Celtic squad that claimed the franchise's 11th championship banner. Russell was an aging veteran who was also the team's coach, while Chaney was a rookie who played a limited role off the bench. Russell also shared a connection with Benjamin, as both men spent their formative years growing up in Monroe, Louisiana.

82 This was the mid-1980s Clippers, so it would be an unpaid role, of course.

83 Included in these five wins were four consecutive victories against the Jazz, Spurs, Mavericks and Lakers, all teams who eventually qualified for the 1986 playoffs.

However, it didn't take long for Benjamin to revert back to his pre-Russell form. He followed up an 18 point effort in a win over Kareem and the Lakers with a series of insipid performances. This resulted in another run of blowout defeats for the Clippers, leaving Chaney both frustrated and disappointed. He had gone out on a limb to give Benjamin the chance to work with one of the game's all-time greats and yet it seemed to have no lasting impact.

A few days later, Chaney's emotions evolved into outright anger when Benjamin casually sauntered into a practice session 15 minutes late, with his shoes untied. Instead of hustling over to the middle of the court, where Chaney was addressing the team, Benjamin plonked himself on the sidelines and began to leisurely lace-up his high-tops. No explanation as to why he was so late and no apology. Chaney called Benjamin to come and join the rest of the team and then proceeded to deliver the type of tongue lashing that many an exasperated coach has handed out over the years. However, while Chaney was shouting, Benjamin's facial expression barely changed. "He just didn't have any awareness of the effect of not being on time and not caring for the team," said Chaney. "He just didn't care."

Sensing that his verbal tirade was having zero impact only served to make Chaney even more incensed. In the middle of the rant, Chaney snapped and made an attempt to lunge at Benjamin. As Chaney tried to wrap his hands around Benjamin's throat, a stunned collection of players looked on and wondered what was happening. "It was an eye opener, a jaw dropper, whatever you want to say," said Kurt Nimphius, a marginally talented power forward who had been starting at center for the Clippers due to Benjamin's indifferent play. "He turned a really nice coach into a madman."

"I was so angry, I just wanted to put my arm around his throat," Chaney said. "I can still see myself, arms outstretched, trying to reach for Benoit." Luckily for Benjamin, Cedric Maxwell leapt into action, possibly saving the

NBA from its first case of homicide by coach. Maxwell used his 6'8" frame to wrap Chaney up in a bear hug, preventing the incident from escalating any further. And while it is doubtful that Chaney was expecting anything productive to result from his violent outburst, it seemed to be the alarm that finally woke Benjamin from his slumber.

Over the final month of the season, Benjamin's form was nothing short of outstanding. In fact, he played so well that he was selected as the league's Rookie for the Month for March, ahead of future Hall of Famers Patrick Ewing, Chris Mullin and Karl Malone. And looking at his averages over the last quarter of the season (19.9 points, 12 rebounds and 4 blocks) it is easy to see why he received the award. Benjamin's impressive play helped the Clippers win six of their final nine games but this mattered little in the grand scheme of things, as they still finished with one of the worst records in the Western Conference.

The only real positive to emerge from the season was the rejuvenation of Marques Johnson. His first year with the Clippers could best be described as the season from hell. However, Johnson managed to put this behind him and during the 1985-86 season he returned to his high flying best. After Smith went down with his injured knee, Chaney decided to swing Johnson from his regular small forward position to the two guard spot. This meant that on most nights Johnson was matched up on a smaller opponent, allowing him to use his size and strength to bully his way to easy points in the paint. Johnson's scoring average increased to over 20 points per game and his field goal percentage also returned to above 50%. He was selected as an All-Star for the fifth time in his career and won the last ever NBA Comeback Player of the Year award[84].

The Clippers finished with a 32-50 record, a slight improvement on the 31 wins that they posted 12 months earlier and the 30 wins from the season

---

84 The very next season, the Comeback Player of the Year award was replaced by the Most Improved Player award.

before that. It appeared that the Clippers were travelling in the right direction, even if they were moving at a Zydrunas Ilgauskas-like pace. However, this impression did not last for very long.

There is an old saying that bad luck travels in threes and in this case, it turned out to be true. Derek Smith's injury was merely the first in a trio of mishaps that led to one of the worst single season performances by a team in the history of the NBA.

Season IX: 1986-87

The biggest move made by the Clippers during the 1986 off-season was hiring Elgin Baylor as the franchise's new general manager. Baylor was considered to be sporting royalty, especially in Los Angeles, where he had mesmerized fans across the 14 years that he played with the Lakers. The impact of Baylor's career was wide reaching, covering everything from playing style to race relations.

Baylor is widely credited as the first player to successfully transfer the one-on-one style from the playgrounds to the professional game. His combination of height, speed, athleticism and strength made him a match-up nightmare and from the moment Baylor was selected with the first overall pick of the 1958 draft, he was a force to be reckoned with. In his debut season, Baylor finished in the NBA's top ten for points (4th), rebounds (4th) and assists (7th), won the Rookie of the Year award and placed third in MVP voting. He also led a Lakers team that had won just 19 games during the previous season all the way to the NBA Finals, where they were defeated by the Celtics.

This was the first of eight trips to the NBA Finals for Baylor between 1959 and 1970. Unfortunately, on each and every occasion, the Lakers failed to capture the league's ultimate prize. In Baylor's first seven Finals appearances, he ran up against Bill Russell and the Celtics. And despite giving Boston all that they could handle, including extending the series to seven games on three different occasions, the Lakers always came up short[85]. By 1970, Russell had retired, giving Baylor and his Laker teammates hope that this might finally be their year. They made it back to the Finals, where they faced off against New York. For the Lakers, it was a case of different opposition, same result, as they lost to the Knicks in another tight seven game series.

Baylor's playing career came to an end in the early stages of the 1971-72 season. After averaging just 11.8 points across the first nine games, Baylor could see that he was no longer the dominant player that he once was. When coach Bill Sharman informed Baylor that he was being moved out of the starting line-up, he chose to retire. Baylor explained his decision by saying that he was not interested in prolonging his career if he couldn't play up to his usual high standards. In a cruel twist of fate, the Lakers went on to win the 1972 championship, leaving Baylor to ponder what might have been if he had hung around for a few more months and agreed to play a lesser role.

Baylor's influence on basketball extends far beyond his hardwood exploits. Halfway through his rookie season, he became the first player to refuse to suit up for an NBA game on the grounds of racial discrimination. Baylor's decision to sit out came after he was forced to confront two separate incidents of bigotry in the lead-up to a neutral-court game played in Charleston, West Virginia. The first occurred when the Lakers tried to check into their hotel and were informed by a clerk that "colored fellas" were not welcome. This conversation took place just a few feet from where Baylor was standing, prompting the star forward to approach the desk for clarification. However, when Baylor attempted to speak with the clerk, he was insulted further, this time by being completely ignored. The team

---

85 The closest Baylor came to winning a championship was in 1962, when Boston defeated the Lakers in overtime of Game 7. During that series, Baylor scored over 30 points in all seven games and finished with averages of 40.6 points and 17.9 rebounds per game.

left the hotel, found another place to stay and at this point in time, Baylor was still intending to play. However, any remaining goodwill soon drained away when Baylor went out for a meal and found the only place that would serve him was a concession stand at the local Greyhound station.

This was the last straw.

Baylor informed Lakers coach John Kundla that he was not going to play in that evening's game. He explained his stance by saying, "All I want to do is be treated like a human being. I'm not an animal put in a cage and let out for the show. They won't treat me like an animal." That evening, Baylor watched from the bench in street clothes as the Lakers were defeated by Cincinnati, 95-91.

Despite finishing his career without a championship or an MVP trophy, Baylor is widely regarded as one of the greatest players in NBA history. His career scoring average of 27.4 points ranks third on the all-time list, behind only Michael Jordan and Wilt Chamberlin, while his ten All-NBA first team selections trails only Kobe Bryant and Karl Malone, who were both selected on 11 occasions.

After hanging up his sneakers, Baylor was employed as part of the inaugural coaching staff of the NBA's newest expansion team- the New Orleans Jazz. He spent two and half seasons working as an assistant coach before he was elevated to the top job midway through the 1976-77 season[86]. At the time, the star of the Jazz's roster was Pete Maravich, whose flashy approach was clearly influenced by Baylor's playing career. In Baylor's first game in charge, Maravich posted a new career high of 51 points. A few weeks later he scored 68, joining Wilt Chamberlin and Baylor as the only players to score over 65 points in an NBA game. These scoring explosions were a sign of things to come, with Baylor leaning heavily on Maravich throughout his

---

[86] Baylor's opportunity arose when Butch van Breda Kolff was fired amid rumors of player discontent.

time at the helm. Maravich finished the season as the league's leader for both minutes played (over 41 per game) and scoring (31.1 points per game).

The following season was Baylor's first full year as head coach and at the halfway mark, it appeared that the Jazz were on track to qualify for the playoffs. On January 31st, they had the 5th best record in the East and were cruising to an easy victory over Buffalo when Maravich hurt his knee, while attempting to throw a Globetrotter-esque pass. The injury put an end to Maravich's season and any hope the Jazz had of making the playoffs. Maravich returned the following season but continued to be plagued by knee problems. With their star player hobbled, New Orleans slumped to a 26-56 record, the worst in the NBA. At the end of the season, Baylor was fired and in the seven years since leaving New Orleans, he had been working as the vice president of a package delivery firm.

Baylor was the latest in a long string of general managers employed in the five years since Donald Sterling bought the Clippers[87]. He returned to Los Angeles hoping that his new role would finally deliver the championship that had been just out of reach for most of his professional career. Initially, Baylor had little choice but to try and build around the group of players he had inherited, as the Clippers had already traded away their first round pick in the upcoming draft[88]. With no high profile rookies joining the team, Baylor's plans to assemble a playoff caliber roster centered around three players: Norm Nixon, Derek Smith and Marques Johnson.

---

87 The full list of GMs to work for Sterling in this short time period is- Ted Podleski, Paul Phipps, Pete Babcock, Carl Scheer and Baylor.
88 This pick turned out to be the first overall selection of the 1986 draft. The Clippers traded the pick to Philadelphia in exchange for Joe Bryant, back in 1979. When it was revealed that the Sixers would be selecting first, Philadelphia's general manager Pat Williams said, "I guess the Clippers felt that seven years would never come. Joe Bryant, where are you now?" After making these wisecracks, Williams inexplicably traded the first overall selection, handing it to Cleveland in exchange for Roy Hinson, a modestly talented forward who averaged just 13.3 points and 6.3 rebounds during his short stay with the Sixers. Meanwhile, the Cavs used the first pick to draft Brad Daugherty, who went on to be selected as an All-Star on five separate occasions.

Baylor wasted little time in getting started, renewing Chaney's contract for another season on the same day that his own hiring was announced. However, the signing of Baylor and Chaney was overshadowed by comments made at the press conference by a very disgruntled Derek Smith, who was also in the process of negotiating a new contract. "I'm not happy with the way I've been treated," Smith said. "I'm leaving L.A. tomorrow for Louisville and I'm taking all my clothes and everything with me." Smith was hoping that the next time he was in Los Angeles would be for an overnight stay as a member of another NBA franchise.

Smith's displeasure stemmed from the fact that he had recently joined the "I-want-to-leave-the-Clippers-because-of-an-insulting-contract-offer" club, a group whose membership was growing very rapidly. Smith was initially offered a salary of around $700,000, which would have made him just the fifth highest paid Clipper[89]. Smith believed that, based on his performances, he was entitled to a much higher level of compensation.

Over the next few months, the situation between Smith and the Clippers escalated from a dispute over the terms of a new contract to an all-out war. Predictably, this dramatic downturn was due to a disagreement over money. Smith's previous contract was structured so that he received a bonus payment of around $250,000 for any season where he was on the court for more than 2,000 minutes[90]. Smith easily reached the 2,000 minute mark during the 1984-85 season and thus received his bonus.

But during the 1985-86 season, he fell well short of target, playing a total of just 339 minutes due to his knee injury and battle with mononucleosis. This should have meant no bonus payment. However, Smith and his agent claimed that the Clippers agreed to pay him $175,000 of the bonus in exchange for taking out a new insurance policy. Not surprisingly, team

---

89 The four players who would have still been earning more than Smith were Nixon, Johnson, Benjamin and Maxwell.
90 This translates to around 24 minutes a night over 82 games

officials disputed that there was any agreement in place. "We don't owe him one cent," said Clipper attorney Arn Tellem. "His claim has no factual or legal basis." One thing was certain- the disagreement left Smith feeling furious and the chances of him playing for the Clippers again were looking less likely by the day.

Smith's comments at the time illustrate the depth of his anger. Here is a sample of what he had to say:

"I don't want to play for the Clippers."
"They have done everything to destroy the relationship we had."
"They would be stupid to sign me."
"No money they can give will make me happy."
"I can't think of anything positive to say about them."

Former Clippers general manager Carl Scheer inserted himself into the debate and his take on the matter cast the franchise in the familiar role of chief villain. "My position is there is at least a moral obligation to pay (Smith)," Scheer said. "There was a verbal agreement to pay that bonus, but it was never put into writing." It is likely that Scheer would have had first-hand knowledge if any agreement had been reached, considering he was the general manager at the time that the bonus payment discussions were alleged to have taken place.

This dispute and the explosive comments made by Smith further complicated matters for Baylor, who was trying to re-sign the star guard for the coming season. It now appeared that any prospect of Smith returning to play for the Clippers was shot to pieces. With this in mind, Baylor shifted his focus from signing Smith to trying to trade him.

In the midst of all this Derek Smith-related drama, the Clippers were dealt an extremely cruel blow when Norm Nixon suffered a potentially career threatening injury while playing softball. Nixon hurt himself when he stepped in a pot hole and the impact twisted his left knee and ruptured a tendon. He was operated on the next day but the injury would eventually keep him on the sidelines for the entire 1986-87 season.

Meanwhile, Smith continued to tell anyone who was willing to listen that he would rather sit out the season than play for the Clippers. With Nixon lost for the year and Smith basically refusing to play, Baylor's plans of building a team around the trio of Nixon, Smith and Johnson were unravelling before his eyes. And opening night was still three months away. Just a few weeks after Nixon's softball mishap, Baylor granted Smith's wish and traded him. Smith was sent to Sacramento and in return, the Clippers received Larry Drew, Mike Woodson and the Kings' 1988 first round draft pick.

With the Clippers now deprived of the services of both of their backcourt stars, greater responsibility would undoubtedly fall on the shoulders of Benoit Benjamin. The thinking within the organization was that the slow start to Benjamin's rookie campaign was related to missing a large chunk of training camp, due to the prolonged contract negotiation process. But with Benjamin already locked into a deal for the upcoming season, hopes were high that he would have a productive training camp and build on his excellent form from the closing weeks of his rookie campaign.

It was clear that, with Nixon and Smith not playing, the Clippers expected Benjamin to carry a much bigger load for the 1986-87 season. When Benoit Benjamin arrived for the first day of training camp that is exactly what he was doing- carrying a much bigger load. Literally. Benjamin weighed in at 272 pounds, which was 26 pounds above his playing weight from his rookie year. "Evidently, he spent a great deal of time this summer at the dinner table," Chaney said, "rather than the basketball court."

If Clippers' fans were beginning to sense an ominous vibe about the upcoming season, these feelings would only intensify once the exhibition schedule got underway. The Clippers played six games and lost them all by an average margin of 19 points. The lowest point of the exhibition schedule came when the Clippers travelled to Fresno to take on the Warriors. Benjamin gave a pretty clear indication about what fans could expect from him in terms of professionalism when he turned up to the game armed with two left shoes. With not enough time to return to the team's hotel to get the *right* shoe, Benjamin sat on the sidelines and watched another defeat. Clearly, Benjamin was not going to challenge Patrick Ewing or Hakeem Olajuwan for the mantle of the NBA's best young center anytime soon.

Opening night only brought more misery for the Clippers, as Derek Smith's new team, Sacramento, came back from an eight point deficit in the final 90 seconds to secure a one point victory. And even though Smith did not produce the 40 point haul that he was planning on, he still had a nice all-round game, finishing with 18 points, 8 rebounds, 6 assists, 3 steals and 2 blocks. This victory would prove to be one of the few highlights of Smith's post-Clipper playing days.

Smith played another four seasons with the Kings and 76ers before finishing his career with a couple of cameo appearances for the Celtics, but he never came close to scaling the heights that he had while playing for the Clippers. Smith was unable to regain all of his speed and explosiveness after his knee surgery and he spent his final four plus seasons playing primarily as a role player. After retiring in 1991, Smith was once again given a helping hand by Jim Lynam, who was coaching the Washington Bullets at the time. He hired Smith as one of his assistant coaches.

Tragically, Smith's life was cut short when he passed away at the age of just 34. Smith collapsed and never regained consciousness while on a promotional cruise with Bullets players, coaches and season-ticket holders.

Perhaps Charles Barkley said it best when he reflected on the Derek Smith that he knew and played with[91]. "Usually when you go to a funeral, people will say good things about a person who really wasn't a good person. With Derek, it's the opposite. You can't say enough good things about him. The world is a poorer place now."

By late November, the Clippers' depleted line-up had managed to win just three of their first ten games, placing them at the bottom of the Western Conference standings. It was clear that they were headed for another dismal season, unless something dramatic happened to change their fortunes. During their next game something dramatic did happen. But far from saving the Clippers' ailing season, this latest incident only added to their pain.

The first 23 minutes of the Clippers-Mavericks encounter was best described as unremarkable. This Thursday night clash, played in front of a crowd of just 5,000 people, had all the atmosphere of an unpopular library. The Clippers fell behind by ten points early in the game but, with half-time approaching, they rallied to cut Dallas' lead to just a single basket.

With less than 40 seconds remaining in the second quarter, Marques Johnson pulled down a defensive rebound and turned to head up court. As soon as Johnson spun to face the opposite basket, he was immediately aware that Benoit Benjamin was blocking his path. After making a split second judgement that he had enough room to maneuver around his teammate, he proceeded to make his way up court. However, instead of dodging past Benjamin, Johnson collided with his teammate's large stomach. The last thing Johnson remembered seeing was the large double zeroes from Benjamin's jersey in front of him and then he was lying on the floor, his body numb from the waist up.

---

91 Barkley and Smith were teammates when they were both in Philadelphia.

Johnson was obviously hurt, although nobody could have predicted just how damaging this impact would be. The crowd at the Los Angeles Sports Arena could only shake their heads in disbelief as they watched their team's one remaining star being carried on a stretcher, with his neck in a brace. The initial diagnosis was a bruised spinal cord and it was expected that Johnson might miss just two-to-three weeks of action. However, upon performing more tests, the Clippers' medical team discovered that Johnson had actually ruptured a disk in his neck- a much more serious injury. This left Johnson with a decision to make, either have surgery to remove the disk, which would effectively end his season, or retire from the game at just 30 years of age. Either way, Johnson would not be suiting up for the Clippers anytime in the near future.

This latest injury felt like a knockout blow for a team that was already swaying and stumbling like Sylvester Stallone in the final minutes of every Rocky movie. The fact that it occurred just one week after the first anniversary of Derek Smith's knee injury only further highlighted just what a miserable run the Clippers were experiencing. This 372 day period was unprecedented in NBA history. Never before or since has a team had its best three players suffer serious injuries in such a short space of time. Prior to Smith getting hurt, the Clippers had arguably the best trio of perimeter players in the entire league. Now, just 12 months down the track, they would be forced to play out the remainder of the 1986-87 season without the services of Nixon, Smith or Johnson, leaving Clippers fans wondering if they were ever going to catch a break[92].

Once it was confirmed that Johnson was going to be spending an extended period on the sidelines, the decision was made to add someone else

---

92 It is also worth reflecting on just how these three injuries actually occurred. While Smith's was your standard basketball-related injury, Nixon's and Johnson's were the result of two freakish events. Stepping in a pot hole or colliding with a teammate's bulbous stomach are not exactly the usual ways that NBA players hurt themselves.

to the roster. The player who the Clippers elected to sign as Johnson's replacement caused more than a few raised eyebrows around the league.

Quintin "Q" Dailey grew up in Baltimore as the youngest of four brothers. Tragedy struck Dailey at the age of just 16, when both of his parents passed away within a month of each other. This left the young basketball star without a mother or father to provide the guidance that he would so desperately need in the coming years. After graduating from high school, Dailey accepted a scholarship from the University of San Francisco and, once he arrived on campus, he was an immediate star. During Dailey's three years in San Francisco, he averaged over 20 points and the Dons won 71 of the 91 games that they played. At the start of his junior season, Sports Illustrated published an article on Dailey that labeled him as "possibly the finest all-round player to wear the emerald-and-gold[93] since Bill Russell."

However, Dailey's lasting legacy at the school was not related to his basketball achievements but rather to a disturbing incident that took place away from the bright stadium lights. Just a few weeks after the SI article was published, Dailey was accused of sexually assaulting a young woman on campus. The nursing student claimed that a drunken Dailey had entered her room in the middle of the night and tried to initiate unwanted sexual contact. She said that when she went to call the police, he wrapped his fingers around her throat.

Dailey denied this allegation, claiming that it was a case of mistaken identity. He even agreed to take a polygraph in order to prove his innocence. In California, the results of a lie-detector test are not admissible as evidence but any statements made by the suspect while in police custody are. When Dailey was informed that the polygraph showed that it was

---

93 USF's colors.

likely that he was being deceptive, he told police, "All right, I was there. But I didn't mean to harm her, I never did anything like that before." Facing a possible seven year jail sentence, Dailey opted to accept a plea bargain agreement. He pled guilty to the lesser charge of aggravated assault and received three years' probation, but managed to avoid any jail time. The judge responsible for the case signed off on the plea bargain deal, just four days before the 1982 draft.[94]

Dailey was drafted by Chicago with the seventh overall selection and he enjoyed a productive rookie season, averaging 15.1 points and earning a selection on the All-Rookie first team. Away from the court was a very different matter. To put it mildly, Dailey was not the most popular person in the city of Chicago. His legal troubles had been big news and many Chicagoans were not keen on rolling out the welcome mat for someone who had pled guilty to assaulting a female student.

When he first arrived in Chicago, Dailey couldn't find a place to live after numerous apartment complexes rejected his residency applications. After he finally found somewhere willing to take him, he began receiving anonymous death threats over the phone. Dailey was also the subject of protests from groups who picketed outside of Chicago Stadium and was often booed by fans during games. On one particularly humiliating evening, he looked on as a fan dressed in a Bulls jersey bearing his number (44) chased another fan, who was dressed in a nurse's costume, around the

---

[94] Dailey also paid the woman that he assaulted $100,000 and issued an apology as part of a civil suit initiated by the victim. Meanwhile, this incident had huge implications for the University of San Francisco basketball program. While Dailey was being interviewed by a probation officer, he revealed that he had been paid $1,000 a month to work at job where he was not actually required to turn up. It turned out that this "job" was organized by one of the USF boosters and this proved to be the last straw for a basketball program that was already on NCAA probation for a range of other offenses. At the conclusion of the 1981-82 season, the president of the university announced that USF would be suspending the basketball program due to the damage it had caused to the integrity and reputation of the entire institution. This decision meant that USF would not field a basketball team for three full seasons.

arena. This public backlash took an emotional toll on Dailey and one of the ways that he chose to deal with it was by using cocaine.

When the Bulls became aware of Dailey's drug use, they sent him to a rehabilitation center for eight weeks during the summer of 1983. Initially, Dailey seemed to rebound well and during his second season, he boosted his scoring average up to 18.2 points per game. But, in Dailey's third season, a new player joined the Bulls and it seemed that Dailey was not too pleased when he perceived that the new guy was receiving preferential treatment from the coaching staff. The rookie's name was Michael Jeffery Jordan. "Michael didn't ask for it," explained Dailey, "but he was their boy. And I was on the other end, the one who could do nothing right." After a training session where he felt like he had been treated especially poorly by the Bulls coaching staff, Dailey decided it was time to take a stand. His form of protest was to fail to show up to that night's game against the Bucks, a move that did not endear him to the coaches, his teammates or the Bulls' fans.

It goes without saying who won the battle between Q and MJ to be the alpha-male of the Bulls' locker room. By 1985, it seemed that instead of concentrating on cementing his spot on an emerging Bulls team, Dailey was more focused on providing material for a book like this. During a game against San Antonio, Dailey actually sent a ball boy to purchase him a bag of popcorn. As the game headed into the fourth quarter and Dailey sat on the bench munching his popcorn, he looked less like an elite athlete playing in the best basketball competition in the world and more like your average fan.

The following season, things continued to go downhill as Dailey's behavior became more erratic. He failed to turn up for practice sessions, missed team flights and had two separate stays at a drug rehabilitation center, causing him to miss more than half of the season. The Bulls eventually cut him loose and, when no other team was willing to take a risk on him, it appeared that, at just 25 years of age, Dailey's NBA career was over. He was unemployed, broke and unsure of what to do next.

At one stage, Dailey considered enrolling in the army but he ultimately decided that he was not ready to draw the curtain on his basketball career just yet. So he swallowed his pride and signed with the Jacksonville Jets of the Continental Basketball Association. It was while Dailey was playing for the Jets that the Clippers came calling. They decided to recruit the talented but troubled guard, offering Dailey what would most likely be his last chance at NBA redemption.

When the Clippers' added Dailey to their roster to cover for the loss of Johnson, the team's management looked like a bunch of hypocrites. Huge hypocrites. Remember, it was only two years earlier that the Clippers tried to get the Cummings-Johnson trade rescinded, on the grounds that they were not aware that Johnson had *once* stayed at a drug rehabilitation facility. It seemed that a lot had changed in the ensuing twenty four months because now they were apparently okay with acquiring a player who had made *three* visits to rehab. And that's not to mention Dailey's guilty plea for assaulting a female student or his history of missing flights, failing to turn up to games and arriving late to practice sessions. Whatever little credibility the Clippers had left was declining faster than Antoine Walker's bank balance.

When Dailey reported for duty in Los Angeles, he was 30 pounds overweight and the Clippers had lost their past eight games. Dailey's presence did little to improve the situation. In fact, the Clippers lost the first 13 games that Dailey played, part of a stretch where the team went nine weeks with just one solitary victory. During this time, their record went from a respectable 3-3 to a dismal 4-31. Chaney labeled this run "embarrassing" and said, "I don't like to walk out of here and have people laughing at us."

There may have been some people around the league who were snickering at Chaney's plight but clearly these bad results did not give a true indication of his coaching ability. Chaney himself probably gave the best explanation as to why the Clippers were finding it so hard to win when he said, "Sometimes I look out on the floor at all these no-names and I can't believe my eyes. I'm literally working myself to death trying to win with mediocre players."

By the middle of January, it had become obvious that the 1986-87 season was a lost cause and so Baylor shifted his focus towards trying to acquire as many future first round draft picks as possible. Cedric Maxwell and Kurt Nimphius were both traded for future first round selections, leaving the Clippers in the enviable position of having five first round picks in the next two drafts.

Baylor's emphasis on securing and retaining draft picks indicated that the Clippers were now taking a longer term view when it came to building their roster. This represented a dramatic philosophical shift for a franchise that had previously used draft picks as trade bait to secure older, more experienced players. Alan Rothenberg described the new approach by saying, "There was a history of trading away draft picks under the previous ownership and it will be nice to start hoarding them ourselves."

While it was all very well for Rothenberg to criticize the Clippers for trading valuable picks under the stewardship of Irv Levin, this only partially told the story of why the franchise was in its present predicament. In the five and a half years since Sterling bought the team, the Clippers had shown an amazing willingness to trade away talented players who were still in the very early stages of their careers. This "buy now and pay later" attitude was clearly one of the major reasons why their current roster lacked anything in the way of an emerging star.

To illustrate how short-sighted the Clippers had been over the previous eight and a half seasons, consider what their 1986-87 roster might have looked like in an alternate universe. Below is an example of the team the Clippers could have fielded if their front office had simply made a commitment to hang onto all first round draft picks and retain any young players who were showing signs of promise or potential[95].

<u>Starting Five</u>
Center-   Brad Daugherty
Forwards-   Tom Chambers & Charles Barkley
Guards-   Ricky Pierce & Byron Scott

<u>Bench</u>
Center-   Benoit Benjamin
Forwards-   Terry Cummings & Michael Cage
Guards-   Craig Hodges & Derek Smith

This would have been a pretty impressive collection of players back in 1987 but imagine how good it would have looked in the early 1990s if the group had been able to stay together. And while it is true that the Clippers lost the chance to draft Barkley and Daugherty due to trades made while Levin was the owner, six other players listed in the hypothetical team above were dealt away in the time since Sterling bought the team. Making matters even worse was that fact that Scott, Chambers, Cummings, Pierce, Hodges and Smith were all between 22 and 25 years old at the time that they were traded.

To get an idea of the level of talent that the Clippers had voluntarily parted with, consider the following numbers. Scott, Chambers, Cummings,

---

95 It is worth noting that the Clippers' position in each draft was dependant on where they finished at the end of the previous season. Therefore it is highly likely that, had the front office retained more of these good players, they would have won more games and thus had lower selections in subsequent drafts. However, for sake of illustrating just how much talent the franchise let slip through its fingers, let's just assume that the Clippers draft slots remained unchanged.

Pierce, Hodges, Smith, Barkley and Daugherty all enjoyed NBA careers that spanned from good to outstanding. Between them, they appeared in a combined total of 7,056 regular season games, made 16 All-NBA teams, were named as All-Stars on 23 different occasions and won five NBA championships as well as a league MVP award.

The reality that faced Chaney was that neither Charles Barkley, Byron Scott nor Brad Daugherty was around to help as the Clippers tried to avoid becoming only the second team in NBA history to lose 70 games in a single season. At one stage, when they had won just four of their first 35 games, it appeared that they might make a run at the NBA record of 73 losses, set back in 1973 by Philadelphia. However, a mid-season resurgence put to rest any thoughts that the Clippers were going to seriously challenge the 1973 Sixers for the title of the "Worst Team of All-Time".

February was a particularly good month, with the Clippers securing three wins in the ten games that they played[96]. Their win over Sacramento on the last day of the month was their tenth for the season, making Philadelphia's record of futility unattainable with a third of the season still to play. In fact, with the Clippers sitting on a 10-44 record, it seemed unlikely that they would get close to clocking up 70 defeats. But, from this point on, the Clippers only won two of their final 28 games to finish the season with exactly 70 losses.

In the case of the 1986-87 Los Angeles Clippers, the numbers really do tell the story. On top of 14 consecutive losses to close out the season, the team had losing streaks of 12 and 16 games. They also went for almost three months without winning a game on the road, dropping 17 straight. Over a third of the Clippers' losses were by margins of 20 points

---

96 Read that last sentence again.

or more and their longest winning streak was just one game[97]. However, the one number that best sums up the Clippers' season above all others is 70. Three decades later, there are still only six teams in the history of the league who have managed to lose 70 games in a single season[98]. The Clippers had made their way into the NBA record books, but it was not for an accomplishment that would be a source of pride for anybody who was connected to the franchise.

"My off-season is to kick back and relax and do whatever I want."

These were the words that were uttered by Benoit Benjamin on the same day that Don Chaney was fired as head coach of the Los Angeles Clippers. Four days into the 1987 off-season, Clipper management decided that somebody had to be held accountable for the dismal season that had just taken place. If you were looking for someone to blame for the team's 12 win effort, Benjamin appeared to be a fairly reasonable place to start.

The depleted state of the Clippers' roster had provided Benjamin with the chance to fast-track his development. Unfortunately, when opportunity knocked, Benjamin was lying on the couch, eating a hot dog. He turned up to training camp overweight and seemed to be generally disinterested for most of the year. Benjamin posted an almost identical set of statistics as he had produced during his rookie year, despite being given more court time and becoming a greater focal point in the team's offensive structure. "Overall, I'm happy with the way I played," was Benjamin's comical effort at critically reflecting on his sophomore season.

---

97 Which is really just another way of saying that at no stage in the 82 game regular season were the Clippers able to win two games in a row.
98 The other five were Philadelphia in 1972-73 (73 losses), Dallas in 1992-93 (71 losses), Denver in 1997-98 (71 losses), New Jersey in 2009-10 (70 losses) and Philadelphia in 2015-16 (72 losses).

But alas, Benjamin was in the middle of a multi-million dollar four year deal, so he was not going to be the person who wore the blame for the Clippers' struggles. Instead, Chaney was shown the door. Everyone associated with the Clippers said all the right things about how Chaney was not to blame for the disastrous season that had just taken place but it was hard not to read between the lines and assume that he was being made the fall guy[99].

When the time came to replace Chaney, the Clippers decided that they wanted a more experienced coach to lead the rebuilding efforts and so they re-hired Gene Shue. Shue had thus far been the most successful coach in the short history of the franchise, compiling a 79-85 record in the Clippers' first two years of existence.

Luckily for Shue, the Clippers had not only retained their own first round draft pick for the upcoming draft, they had also managed to accumulate two more first round selections via trades. Unluckily for Shue, the Clippers front office already had a pretty good idea about which players they wanted to use these picks on and were not overly interested in receiving input from the new coach. Shue wanted to implement a fast-paced style of game and was hoping that the Clippers would draft a small forward who was capable of pushing the ball and triggering the offense. After watching some tape of the players who were going to be available, he became very interested in one prospect in particular, an athletic 6'7" forward named Scottie Pippen.

Baylor was not keen on gambling with any of the first rounds picks he had worked so hard to acquire. "Elgin was always cautious," said assistant coach Don Casey. "He would draft names who played good in college and appeared to be safe picks…but safe picks are not always good picks."

---

[99] Just four years later, Chaney would prove to the basketball world that he was a more than competent coach, when he received the NBA's Coach of the Year award for leading Houston to a 52-30 season.

Pippen was far from a safe pick. In fact, he didn't even attend a Division One college. Instead, he was attempting to become the first player to make the jump from the University of Central Arkansas, a small Division Two school, to the NBA. When the time came for Baylor to make his maiden first round selection, Pippen was still available. However, the Clippers used the fourth overall pick to select Reggie Williams, a 6'7" swingman whom Donald Sterling labeled "a Michael Jordan-type player."

Williams played for four years at Georgetown and during this time, he had put together a very impressive resume. In his freshman season, he played on an NCAA championship winning team, scoring 19 points and grabbing seven rebounds in the title clinching win over Houston. As a senior, he was named the Big East Player of the Year and also led the conference in scoring. Williams played as a forward for most of his time at Georgetown but the Clippers planned on transforming him into a guard, much like they had done a few years earlier with Derek Smith. Baylor used the other two first round picks to select Joe Wolf, a 6'11" forward/center from North Carolina, and Ken Norman, a 6'8" forward from Illinois[100].

On the day he was drafted, Williams showed scant regard for the Clippers' nine year history of struggles when he declared, "I think the Clippers will be a team to be reckoned with." If Williams was a little naïve about just how difficult it was going to be to transform the Clippers into a winning franchise, his debut professional appearance would make the size of the task abundantly clear.

---

100 No-one was more surprised to hear that the Clippers had selected Joe Wolf than Joe Wolf himself. In the lead-up to the draft, Wolf flew out to Los Angeles with his Tar Heel teammate Kenny Smith, to work out for the Clippers. However, when they landed in L.A., there was nobody at the airport to pick them up. The confused pair went down to baggage claim to see if anyone was waiting with a "Joe Wolf & Kenny Smith" sign and found nothing. In the era before cell phones, the two prospects chose what they thought was the best option- they sat and waited. One hour went past, then two. Finally, they decided to give up. They hopped back on a plane and headed home to the UNC campus, firmly believing that this was going to be their first and last Clipper experience.

Season X: 1987-88

The Clippers opened the 1987-88 season on the road playing against Denver at McNichols Arena. Prior to the game, there was a lot of talk about how important it was to make a statement on opening night, to show the rest of the league that last season's 12 win effort was a thing of the past. This was a new team. A team of youth. A team of promise. A team of the future.

The new, youthful version of the Clippers went out and lost by 46 points, with Benoit Benjamin's four turnovers his greatest statistical contribution to the game. So much for starting the new season off on the right foot. However, considering the problems faced by the Clippers in the lead-up to the season opener, a blow-out defeat was really not all that surprising. In fact, a one-sided result was always going to be in the cards, given that they were starting the season without the services of either of their two marquee players.

Norm Nixon was looking forward to resurrecting his NBA career. After 15 months of strenuous rehabilitation, his surgically repaired knee was back to full strength and he appeared to be ready to once again take his place as one of the Clippers' on-court leaders. His form during the exhibition schedule had been good and he looked set to be a big part of Shue's plans for the coming season. The Clippers' new coach was hoping that Nixon could quarterback his up-tempo offense as well as provide a steadying veteran influence, both on the floor and in the locker room.

With five minutes remaining in the second-to-last practice prior to the Denver game, Nixon was running at full speed, when he planted his foot to change direction. However, when he went to push off with his right foot, he heard a "Bumph!" noise and toppled to the ground. As Nixon was carried from the court, he heard a teammate say, "He popped his Achilles," and a quick inspection from the Clippers' medical team confirmed this. He had ruptured his right Achilles tendon, ruling him out for another season. Instead of playing in the season opener, Nixon was left to face the prospect of another lengthy period on the sidelines, filled with more grueling rehabilitation work.

Making matters worse was the fact that Nixon was not the only former All-Star who was not going to be playing any time soon. In fact, it turned out that Marques Johnson's collision with Benoit Benjamin was the last time that anyone ever saw him in a Clipper uniform.

Marques Johnson had his afternoon all planned out. He was going to sit back on his couch and watch his former teammates from Milwaukee play against Boston in Game 6 of the 1987 Eastern Conference semi-finals. As he walked towards the front door of the family's Bel Air home to help a departing electrician with the front gate, he told his son Kris to keep an eye on his youngest brother. Johnson had three children, Kris was 11, Josiah was 4 and Marques Jr. was 15 months old. When Johnson returned to the house and asked where Marques Jr. was, Kris looked up from the video game that he was playing and said, "In your bedroom." However, when Johnson went to the bedroom, he discovered an empty room with an external door that was open. This door led into the family's backyard, where the swimming pool was located.

Johnson rushed into the backyard.

Marques Jr. was in the pool.

Johnson raced to the pool and scooped his son out of the water. When he got back in the house, Marques Jr. was motionless and Johnson frantically yelled for Kris to call 9-1-1. The paramedics took him to UCLA

Medical Center where the doctors performed cardiopulmonary resuscitation for more than an hour.

Marques Jr. died the next day.

Clearly it would not be an exaggeration to say that the summer of 1987 was the worst time of Johnson's life.

Not long after Marques Jr.'s funeral, Johnson received a request from an intermediary asking him to call Donald Sterling. Johnson and the Clippers were in the midst of a dispute and while basketball was probably the furthest thing from his mind, he called to see what Sterling had to say.

Johnson and Clippers had spent the previous few months beefing about two separate but related matters. The first was a disagreement about the best way to treat Johnson's neck injury. When Johnson first hurt his neck, the Clippers' medical team presented him with two options: either have corrective surgery to fuse two of his vertebrae together or retire from the game. Johnson was keen to continue playing but he also had serious reservations about the fusion surgery, which had a certain degree of risk attached to it. This led Johnson to consider a third option of returning to play without having the surgery. While Johnson sought alternative medical opinions to help him make an informed decision, the Clippers remained adamant that they would only clear him to play if he underwent surgery.

The second element to the dispute between the Clippers and Johnson centered on money. Nearly three million dollars' worth of money. Prior to injuring his neck, Johnson believed that he had reached a verbal agreement to change the terms of his contract. The alterations were as follows: Johnson would defer 30% of his salary in exchange for the Clippers guaranteeing the final two years of his contract, which were only option years at that stage.

With Johnson's injured neck placing his career in limbo, the question of whether or not these last two years were guaranteed suddenly became extremely important. Johnson was scheduled to earn $2.9 million over this two year period and, not surprisingly, the Clippers were claiming that no agreement to guarantee the final two seasons had ever been reached.

While this dispute over the exact terms of the contract was continuing, the Clippers were growing increasingly frustrated with Johnson's indecisiveness in relation to his injured neck. "He has been to three or four specialists and they've all told him to have the surgery," said Rothenberg. "I don't know why he hasn't had it." Initially, Johnson was scheduled to have the fusion surgery in January of 1987, before he cancelled it. By the time March came around, the Clippers had run out of patience.

They sent Johnson a letter stating that they were declaring him to be permanently disabled, thus effectively giving up any hope of him returning to play. This allowed the Clippers to significantly reduce the amount of money that they owed Johnson, as they would now only have to pay one more year of his salary. Johnson responded by once again postponing the neck surgery and filing a grievance with the players' association.

All of this back and forth between Johnson, the Clippers, the doctors and the lawyers preceded the death of Marques Jr. So when Johnson was asked to call Sterling, he was hoping that they were going to discuss how they could settle the financial and medical disputes so Johnson could resume playing. However, Johnson soon discovered that Sterling was not reaching out in the spirit of peace, he was reaching out so he could make a declaration of war. "I called Donald up and he told me he was going to ruin me," recalled Johnson in an interview broadcast of Fox Sports in 2014. "He was going to crush me financially and that I needed to go ahead and settle on his terms if I wanted to have any money left. He talked to me like I was a piece of bat guano."

Given the nature of Sterling's comments coupled with what was going on in Johnson's personal life at the time, it shouldn't come as any great shock to learn that he never played another game for the Clippers. The bitter dispute between the franchise and their one time star player was not resolved until August 1988, 20 months after Johnson collided with Benjamin. The two parties reached an out of court settlement, although the exact amount that the Clippers paid Johnson was never publically revealed. Johnson later reflected on the process of negotiating with the Clippers, saying that it wore him down "psychologically, spiritually and financially[101]."

With Nixon and Johnson playing a combined total of zero games for the 1987-88 season, the Clippers' primary goal was to provide the maximum amount of opportunities for their younger players. However, rather than lead some sort of Clipper revival, their top two draft picks spent most of the year dealing with injury problems of their own. Reggie Williams hurt his left knee in January and his right knee in March and played a total of just 35 games. Even when he was healthy, Williams struggled to make the transition to the backcourt, shooting a miserable 35.6% from the field and just 22.4% from three point range. Things weren't a whole lot better for Joe Wolf either, who sat out a total of 40 games due to knee problems of his own.

Perhaps the only piece of good news to emerge from the season was the resolution of the Clippers' long-running legal dispute with the NBA over their move to Los Angeles. The two parties reached an out of court settlement which allowed the franchise to remain in L.A. on the condition that they forfeited their share of the upcoming expansion fees from the four new NBA franchises based in Charlotte, Miami, Minnesota and Orlando. This equated to a relatively meager penalty of around $6 million. David Stern even attended a party at Donald Sterling's Beverly Hills mansion, where

---

101 The other effect of the settlement was that Johnson was now a free agent, meaning he was able to finish his playing days on his own terms. Johnson chose not to have the neck surgery but he still got the opportunity to make a brief, ten game comeback with Golden State during the 1989-90 season.

he told guests, "I'm here to welcome them to Los Angeles and wish them well." After making a reasonable start to the 1987-88 season, the Clippers fell away badly and they finished with a record of 17-65, meaning they had a grand total of just 29 wins over a two year period.

Then, during the off-season, the unthinkable happened. The Clippers actually won something. The envelope with the Clippers' logo inside was the last one drawn out at the league's draft lottery, which gave them the right to select first in the upcoming NBA draft. Even the potential problem of how to use the pick did not appear to be an issue, as this draft contained one of those consensus number one picks, whom everyone was projecting would have a long and successful career. It seemed that not even the Clippers could screw this up. I mean, what could possibly go wrong?

CHAPTER 7

If I Have to Play for the Clippers, Let's Just Forget the Whole Thing

"I'm dead."

RON HARPER (UPON DISCOVERING THAT HE
HAD BEEN TRADED TO THE CLIPPERS)

THERE WAS NEVER ANY DOUBT about who the Clippers would select with the first overall pick of the 1988 draft. In fact, the decision to take Danny Manning was such a no-brainer that they didn't even wait until the day of the draft to announce it. The Clippers welcomed Manning aboard at a press conference held over a month before the draft took place. At this gathering, Manning spouted all the regular sporting clichés, talking enthusiastically about the bright future that lay ahead for his new team.

Manning also spoke about his desire not to have his upcoming Olympic campaign disrupted by negotiations for his first professional contract, saying that he would like to have it sorted out "as quickly as possible[102]." However, when Manning's agent Ron Grinker told the assembled media that he expected his client to be "the highest paid player of all time," it became immediately apparent that there was trouble on the horizon. Anybody with a passing knowledge of Clipper history could have guessed that Grinker and the franchise's management were not quite on the same page. In fact, their respective views on Manning's likely level of compensation seemed to be so far apart, that they appeared to be reading from two different books.

The world of professional basketball was not new to Danny Manning. He enjoyed a childhood filled with memories of Julius Erving, Wes Unseld and Earl Monroe, courtesy of his father's nine year career in both the NBA and ABA. As a young boy, Danny spent many an afternoon in gymnasiums across America, in the company of some of the greatest players and coaches in the history of the sport.

Ed Manning was far from an All-Star, as indicated by his career average of 5.9 points per game. Instead, he specialized in the intangibles- setting good screens, making the extra pass and boxing out an opposing rebounder. In time, this attention to the details that don't show up in box scores would also come to define Danny's approach to the game.

When Ed finally decided to hang up his sneakers, the Manning family settled in North Carolina. Ed initially pursued a career in coaching but after briefly working as an assistant at North Carolina A&T, he found it difficult to find employment in this highly competitive field. With money getting shorter and a young family to support, he was forced to take a job as

---

102 Manning was the captain of the men's basketball team team, the last collection of amateurs that the US ever sent to an Olympics Games. Manning's Olympic experience did not end with a gold medal around his neck, as the US lost in the semi-finals to the Soviet Union. Manning played one of the worst games of his career in this shocking defeat, finishing with 0 points, 3 rebounds and 0 assists.

a long-haul truck driver. Most people wouldn't think that playing professional basketball and driving an 18 wheeler have very much in common, but for Danny there was one crucial and painful similarity- both jobs required his father to spend extended periods of time away from home.

Ed took the truck driving job at around the same time that Danny started to blossom as a player. This meant that there were many occasions when he was forced to miss his son's games, which was always a sore point for both men. Danny was quickly becoming one of the most sought after prospects in the country. He led Page High School to a 26-0 record and a state championship while he was still a junior. Danny's impressive play led to him being recruited by a number of major colleges, including local powerhouses North Carolina and NC State. Throughout this time, Ed had tried to maintain some type of connection to the world of college basketball. He helped out at friends' camps so he could build up his network of contacts, with the hope of landing another coaching position.

The offer that Ed was waiting for finally arrived between Danny's junior and senior years of high school when Larry Brown, the newly appointed Kansas coach, hired Ed as one of his assistants. Brown was upfront about the fact that his recruiting of Danny was a factor in this decision but he was also quick to dismiss the idea that this was the *only* reason for Ed getting the position. "What really makes me mad is when people say I hired a truck driver," said Brown. "They act like Ed never played or coached. He did both. They act like I never heard of Ed Manning before I came to Kansas. He played for me. He was a friend. I knew that if I hired him, even if we didn't get Danny, that he'd be my friend and work hard for me[103]."

Not long after Ed Manning was hired as a Jayhawk assistant coach, Danny Manning announced that he too would be going to Kansas. He arrived on campus carrying the weight of expectation that went with being

---

[103] Ed played for two years under Brown as a member of the Carolina Cougars of the ABA.

the player projected to be the next big thing. Over the ensuing four years, he found a way to live up to the considerable hype.

By his senior season, Manning was not only viewed as the best player in college basketball but as someone who just might change the way the game was played. He was now 6'10" tall, which meant that he had the size necessary to play as a power forward and yet he also possessed the ball-handling and passing ability of a point guard[104]. During his senior year, he averaged 24.8 points, 9 rebounds, 1.9 blocks and shot over 58% from the field, while also leading Kansas to an NCAA title. Danny's sizable contribution to the team's success was recognized when he was named the Final Four's Most Outstanding Player. He also won both the Naismith and Wooden College Player of the Year awards and was selected as a first team All-American. Manning was the type of prospect that NBA coaches fantasized about and the Clippers were hoping that he would be the person to finally lift the franchise out of the doldrums.

―――――

Before the Clippers could get around to the inevitable business of squabbling over the terms of Manning's contract, they first had to draft him. June 28th was a good day for the franchise and not just because this was when they made their selection of Manning official. The Clippers also landed the 3rd and 15th selections, courtesy of some wheeling and dealing from Baylor, who negotiated a complicated three team trade with Philadelphia and Seattle. In order to acquire these two picks, the Clippers had to send their other first round draft slot (the 6th overall selection) to Philadelphia and ship Michael Cage off to Seattle.

These trades were another huge step in Baylor's plan to stockpile as much young talent as possible, although they were not very popular moves

―――

104 One NBA scout declared that once Manning hit the pros he would be "a whole new concept in basketball."

at the time. Cage had become a fan favorite amongst the Clippers' supporters and he was one of the few players on the roster who could hold his head high after the recent miserable run that the franchise had endured. When the deal was announced, the crowd of 1,000 fans who had gathered at the Sports Arena to watch the draft proceedings loudly made their displeasure known. Cage was also not shy about making his feelings known, saying he was "glad" to have been traded. Later, he compared his time with the Clippers to playing for a minor league baseball team.

Despite losing the services of Cage, the draft was undoubtedly a good day for the franchise. They used the third pick to select Charles Smith, a 6'10" prospect from the University of Pittsburgh who was considered so versatile that he could comfortably play all three front court positions. The Clippers' final first round selection was Gary Grant, a first team All-American point guard from Michigan who averaged 21.1 points and 6.9 assists per game during his senior year. With the selections of Manning, Smith and Grant, the Clippers had secured the rights to three highly respected college players for the second year in a row. The franchise's brain trust was extremely happy with this outcome. Gene Shue called draft day "sensational", while Baylor chose to go for the understated approach, saying it was "probably the best draft any team has ever come up with in history."

Having drafted three potential stars, the Clippers now had to negotiate contracts with each of them. Securing the signatures of Smith and Grant proved to be a relatively pain-free process, with both players agreeing to terms prior to the start of the 1988 exhibition schedule. Danny Manning's contract would be another matter entirely.

If you lived in Los Angeles during the summer of 1988, you may have come to the conclusion that Manning had already signed a contract with the

Clippers and was ready to take to the floor for opening night of the new season. In fact, nothing could have been further from the truth. The reason for the confusion about Manning's status was the Clippers' decision to make him the focal point of an aggressive marketing campaign. Manning's face was featured on billboards, in newspaper advertisements, on the cover of the team's media guide and in television commercials, despite the fact that he was an uncontracted player.

Agent Ron Grinker was initially hoping to secure a ten year, $35 million contract for his client, which would have surpassed the rookie deals given to both Patrick Ewing and David Robinson[105]. The Clippers were not as keen on setting a new NBA record for the most lavish contract ever given to a rookie. As the start of the regular season approached, the negotiations between Manning, Grinker and the Clippers were becoming increasingly tense and bitter.

Years later, it was alleged that at one particular meeting Manning was told by Donald Sterling that the franchise was offering him "a lot of money for a poor black kid." This revelation was made by Elgin Baylor in 2009 during a deposition which was part of legal action that he launched against Sterling and the Clippers. Baylor claimed that, upon hearing this racially charged remark, Manning stormed out of Sterling's mansion and never returned.

Season XI: 1988-89

While the Clippers were forced to begin the new season without the services of Manning, they were able to welcome back Norm Nixon. Perhaps no player epitomized the miserable run of luck that the Clippers had endured for the past few seasons better than Nixon. After working tirelessly

---

[105] Both players signed for ten years, Ewing for a total of $33.5 million and Robinson for $26 million.

to rehabilitate his injured knee throughout the 1986-87 season, it appeared that Nixon was ready to resume his professional career, only to snap his Achilles tendon just days before the start of the 1987-88 season. This additional setback would have spelled the end of many professional athletes' careers, especially when you consider that Nixon was 32 years of age at the time that the second injury occurred. But Nixon was determined to play on. He went through another long winter of rehabilitation and was fully fit and ready to play a valuable role on the eve of the 1988-89 season. Nixon played well in his first game in over two years, finishing with 11 assists and 4 steals, although the Clippers still lost by 19 points.

With the new season under way and Manning, the league's latest star attraction, still not in uniform, David Stern decided that enough was enough. The league's commissioner inserted himself into the negotiations, hoping that his influence would help speed up the process. Stern's intervention proved to be the Midas touch, as just a few days later, the Clippers were proudly announcing that Manning had signed a five year, $10.5 million contract, just in time for the team's first home game. Alan Rothenberg did his best to play down the four months of acrimonious negotiations which had preceded the signing, telling the media that the feeling between Manning and the franchise was "all embracing and joyous." It is doubtful that Manning endorsed these comments or shared these positive feelings.

The Clippers had already played four road games by the time Manning joined the team, losing three of them. When Manning was introduced to a crowd of almost 14,000 at the home opner, his name was greeted with a healthy serving of catcalls and boos, mixed with just a sprinkling of applause. But while Manning was not an immediate fan favorite, his inclusion brought about an immediate change in the fortunes of the team. Manning finished his first NBA game with 12 points in 27 minutes off the bench, as the Clippers pulled out an 11 point victory.

Over the next few weeks, Manning's role gradually expanded. By the end of November, he was elevated into the Clippers' starting line-up and by the middle of December, he was beginning to look like one of the league's top forwards. Manning's play was attracting attention and earning praise from all across the league. After he put up 23 and 8 against the Lakers, Pat Riley said, "Manning's got the potential to be better than great, he can be another Magic (Johnson)." This was lofty praise indeed, especially considering that Magic was in the middle of another MVP season.

However, despite Manning's good form, the Clippers continued to struggle. By early January, their record had slumped to 10-19 and they were in serious danger of losing touch with the playoff race before the season had reached its halfway mark. Their next game was on the road in Milwaukee and when the Clippers fell behind by 12 points in the first quarter, the signs were not good.

They were about to get a whole lot worse.

With just over a minute remaining in first period, Manning drove to the basket and scored his only two points for the evening. As the ball passed through the net, Manning landed awkwardly and jarred his right knee. He hobbled over to the bench and after having his knee checked out, the decision was made to rest him for the remainder of the evening. The initial diagnosis of a hyperextended knee had both the Clippers and Manning breathing a sigh of relief. "I was able to put some pressure on it, so I know it's not that bad," Manning said after the game, before ominously adding, "At least, I hope not."

The next day, Manning began to suspect that the injury was something worse than just a simple hyperextension and further medical examinations revealed his intuition to be correct. He had torn his anterior cruciate ligament, one of the most severe injuries that a basketball player can suffer. With this shocking piece of news, Manning's rookie campaign was over, after just 26 games.

Manning's injury kick-started a losing streak that would eventually stretch to 19 games and ultimately cost Gene Shue his job. Never mind that Shue was coaching the youngest roster in the entire league or the fact that his best player had gone down with a season-ending injury. The Clippers were losing and someone had to be held accountable.

Not only did the Clippers fire Shue in the middle of the season and halfway through his three year contract, they also didn't bother to call and inform him that he had lost his job. Shue only discovered his fate after *he* placed a call to Elgin Baylor to find out what was going on. Shue decided to phone Baylor after seeing media reports saying that he was no longer the Clippers' coach, which was news to him. "I called Elgin and said, 'Am I fired?'" said Shue. "And Elgin sort of hemmed and hawed and said, "Yeah, I think so.'" Shue was replaced with his only assistant, Don Casey, who said that he came close to turning the job down before he realized that the opportunity to land a head coaching position was simply too good to pass up. It wasn't long before Casey started to second guess his decision.

After six weeks in the job, Casey had coached 22 games and won on just one occasion.

Casey's 21st defeat would also mark the last game in Norm Nixon's illustrious NBA career. During his final NBA season, Nixon was forced to accept a much smaller role than he had become accustomed to and as the season dragged on, his frustrations grew. "On our team, young guys would twist their ankles and miss practice," Nixon said. "I didn't come from that type of environment and I didn't want to be around that." With his minutes declining with each new week, Nixon decided to walk away with 18 games remaining on the schedule. It was a sad way to draw the curtain on what had been a very impressive NBA career[106].

The Clippers finished at the bottom of the Pacific Division for the third year in a row, with a final record of 21-61. However, things were not all doom and gloom in Clipperland as Baylor's vision of rebuilding via the draft appeared to be taking shape. The team's greatest strength was undoubtedly their trio of young forwards. In fact, the loss of Manning to a knee injury proved to be a blessing in disguise for Charles Smith and Ken Norman. Smith played so well in the second half of the season that he was selected on the All-Rookie first team, after averaging 16.3 points and 6.5 rebounds per game. Meanwhile, Norman led the team in scoring (18.1 points), was second in rebounding (8.3 rebounds) and was one of the leading candidates for the Most Improved Player award. With Manning set to return early the following season, it looked like the Clippers now had three talented and versatile forwards whom they could build a contending team around.

Season XII: 1989-90

They say a picture is worth a thousand words and that is definitely true in the case of the photograph of the player selected with the second overall pick in the 1989 NBA draft. In the photo, the young man is wearing a red Clippers cap while speaking to someone on a telephone. If you did not know any better, you might think that this person had just been informed of some really bad news, like he was being told that a close relative had been diagnosed with a terminal illness. His expression is one of shock and

---

106 At the time of his retirement, Nixon was second amongst active players for totals assists, behind only Magic Johnson.

looming dread, clearly not the face of a happy man. And so begins the short saga of Danny Ferry and the Los Angeles Clippers.

Danny Ferry did not want to play for the Clippers, which was a problem. It was a problem because Ferry was widely considered to be one of the best prospects in the 1989 draft, a draft in which the Clippers had the second overall selection. Ferry, a skillful 6'10" forward, had just completed his senior season at Duke, where he won the Naismith College Player of the Year award. He had also twice been named the Atlantic Coast Conference's Player of the Year and was the only player in the history of the powerful ACC to finish his college career with totals of 2,000 points, 1,000 rebounds and 500 assists.

Ferry had numerous reasons for not wanting to join the Clippers. He was all too aware of the franchise's well-earned reputation for dysfunction, via his father Bob Ferry, a former NBA player who now worked as the general manager of the Washington Bullets. Danny knew all about the Clippers-the difficulties that rookies faced when negotiating their contracts, the seasons of losing 50 or 60 games and the general feeling of instability and low morale that hung around the franchise like a bad smell.

In the lead-up to the draft, Bob decided to see if he could help his son out. He contacted David Falk, an agent whom he knew from his time working in the Bullets' front office, to ask if Falk could dissuade the Clippers from drafting Danny. Falk placed a call to Donald Sterling and told him, in no uncertain terms, that Ferry did not want to play for the Clippers. An unfazed Sterling told Falk that once Ferry had visited Los Angeles and looked out at the majestic view from the balcony of his office, he would fall in love and want to stay.

As the day of the draft approached, Ferry was like a man at a swingers' party who was unable enjoy the event due to one unattractive female who was eyeing him off from across the room. Ferry made his feelings about his predicament known, saying it was unfair that players were given no say in where they would start their professional careers and labeling the NBA draft system as un-American.

Despite these misgivings, Ferry headed off to Madison Square Garden on the evening of the draft feeling reasonably confident that he was not about to be drafted by the Clippers. On top of Falk's call to Sterling, Ferry also took comfort from the make-up of the Clippers' roster. If there was one position where they were already overloaded with talent, it was at power forward, which just happened to be where Ferry played. It appeared that in Manning and Smith, the Clippers already had two future All-Stars at this position. And with Norman, the team's best player from the previous season, playing at the three, it was unlikely that there would be many additional minutes up for grabs at small forward.

Sacramento started the proceedings by using the first overall selection to take Pervis Ellison. A few minutes later, Ferry heard David Stern utter the following sentence: "With the second pick in the 1989 NBA draft, the Los Angeles Clippers select…Danny Ferry from Duke University."

The Clippers.

Danny Ferry was going to be stuck playing for the Clippers, basketball's equivalent of being sent to death row.

The crowd of around 2,000, who were watching the draft at the Sports Arena, greeted the selection of Ferry with a chorus of boos. Ferry shared the sentiments of the Clipper fans but was careful to keep these thoughts hidden in the immediate aftermath of the draft. The closest Ferry came to revealing his true feelings was when he said he was "a little surprised" to hear his name called out as the Clippers' first round pick. In the days and weeks that followed, it became apparent that Ferry was more than just a little surprised.

He was working on a get-away plan.

A few weeks after the draft, Danny Ferry headed off to Europe in what was initially reported as nothing more than a vacation. However, while Ferry undoubtedly used some of this time to put his feet up, the primary reason for this overseas trip was to explore what playing options were available outside of the NBA. Danny and his father were flown to London in a Concorde by a wealthy Italian businessman named Raul Gardini. Gardini told the Ferrys that he was planning on buying Rome's basketball team and he was prepared to offer Danny a very lucrative deal in order to get him to launch his professional career in Europe. Gardini presented Ferry with a five year deal that paid a total of $10 million in salary. This offer also came with an out-clause that allowed Ferry to sever the contract at the end of any season if he so desired, giving him the flexibility to return to the NBA at some point in the future.

When news of this proposal became public knowledge back in Los Angeles, most people didn't take it very seriously. Agents had been using European teams as bargaining ploys for years, threatening to send their clients to Italy or Spain if they could not get the team that they were negotiating with to agree to their demands. It seemed to most observers that Ferry was simply trying to force the Clippers' hand and get himself traded to another team.

While Ferry was contemplating a move to Italy, Falk, who had by now been hired as his agent, was searching for a way to allow his client to remain in America by trying to convince Sterling to consent to a trade. A number of teams were interested in acquiring Ferry, including San Antonio and

Cleveland, but no one was able to put together a package that Sterling was willing to sign off on.

All the while, Gardini was growing increasingly impatient. After waiting a few weeks to hear whether Ferry was going to accept his offer, Gardini decided to go all out. He sent a business colleague named Enzo DeChiara to Falk's office to try and finalize the deal. Falk knew he needed the Italian offer to remain on the table, in order to keep pressure on the Clippers to make a trade, and so he attempted to stall. When DeChiara arrived at his office, Falk tried to buy some time by going through an outrageous list that contained every perk that he could think of- a luxurious palazzo to live in, two chefs to prepare meals, cars, drivers, tickets on the Concorde for Ferry's family- the list went on and on. Falk figured that DeChiara would have to take these requests back to Gardini, which would give him a few extra days to persuade Sterling that it was in his best interests to make a trade.

Amazingly, DeChiara agreed to each and every one of Falk's demands on the spot. He then told Falk that Ferry had three hours to accept their offer or it would be permanently revoked. With all of these additional perks, the total package was now valued at around $4 million per season, an astoundingly high figure for 1989[107]. Falk tried to call Ferry but was unable to reach him, so DeChiara granted a 24 hour extension to the deadline. When Falk presented the updated offer the next day, Ferry was still not too enthused about the idea of playing in Italy. However, with the likelihood of a trade growing slimmer by the day, Ferry reluctantly signed the papers.

The luring of Ferry was big news in Italy, with one Rome newspaper labeling it the "Coup of the Summer." Ferry publically said all the right things about his impending move being motivated by his desire to travel around Europe, learn a new language and experience different cultures.

---

[107] To put this into perspective, at the time, there wasn't a single NBA player who had cracked the $4 million barrier for salary.

Still, it was hard to escape the feeling that the stench of the Clippers played a large role in driving Ferry across the Atlantic.

From the Clippers' perspective, perhaps the most worrisome aspect of Ferry's decision to choose Italy over the NBA was not that they lost the services of their prized rookie but that the move appeared to start some sort of a trend. A few months after Ferry announced that he was off to Rome, Benoit Benjamin hopped on a plane bound for Italy to play for Philips Milano. It seemed that the Clippers were on the verge of becoming a feeder team for the emerging Italian league. Benjamin's stay in Italy would turn out to be significantly shorter than Ferry's. In fact, he was there for a total of just three days before returning to the United States. Sadly for the Clippers, the dispute over Benjamin's second professional contract would drag on for a much longer period of time.

As the final weeks of the 1988-89 regular season approached, Benoit Benjamin found himself in a difficult spot. The four year contract that he had signed as a rookie was due to expire, which meant that he was about to become a restricted free agent. This was not good news. Over the past four seasons, Benjamin had done little to suggest to the various front offices around the league that he was a player who was deserving of a lucrative, long-term deal. In fact, his reputation for lackluster effort had reached legendary proportions in NBA circles.

Benjamin knew that his current body of work was not going to be enough to secure the type of pay day that he was looking for. So, with about 20 games remaining, he set about proving that he still had the physical tools to be one of the league's most dominant players. When Charlotte visited the Sports Arena in the middle of March, Benjamin played his best game since arriving in the NBA, hitting 15 of his 18 field goal attempts to finish with 34 points, 23 rebounds and 8 blocked shots. Two weeks later, he led the Clippers to victory over the Spurs with his first professional triple double[108]. And while Clipper fans were not so foolhardy as to get *too* excited, Benjamin's form over the latter part of the season did provide some hope that he might finally start living up to his vast potential[109].

When the season ended, it became apparent that the Clippers' front office and Team Benjamin, the self-appointed name given to Benjamin's new management group, were not on the same page in relation to a new contract[110]. Team Benjamin were pushing for a long-term deal, while the Clippers' were only willing to offer one or two years, as they were concerned that Benjamin's motivation might wane if he secured a contract that ran for any longer than this. "I'm scared to death that he'll sign for several million dollars and then we'll get more of the same," said Rothenberg.

When Team Benjamin accepted that the Clippers were not going to commit to anything longer than two years, the two sides began to bicker over what was an appropriate salary. The Clippers were offering around $1.25 million per season, which Benjamin's representatives believed was well below what their client deserved. The Clippers attempted to bridge the gap by suggesting that incentive clauses be added to the contract, allowing more money to be earned if Benjamin was able to meet certain weight-related targets. This idea went down like Benoit Benjamin on a see-saw and his agents began publically campaigning for their client to be traded.

In amongst these contract discussions, Benjamin held a press conference where he announced that he had signed a one year deal with a team

---

108 25 points, 10 rebounds and 10 blocks.
109 His averages over the last quarter of the season of 21 points, 11.8 rebounds, and 3.8 blocks proved that he could be one of the league's premier players, provided he was focused and put in the required amount of effort.
110 Larry Fleisher, Benjamin's agent for his first four years as a professional, had passed away just a few months earlier after suffering a heart attack while playing squash. Benjamin's new representation was an assortment of agents and lawyers and even included Don King, the infamous boxing promoter who worked with both Muhammad Ali and Mike Tyson.

based in Milan and said that he would be flying to Italy immediately[111]. "I don't think the Clippers treated me fair," Benjamin complained. "I got dragged in the mud, talked about in the papers like I was a dog. I went through seasons such as 12-70[112]."

Not surprisingly, the Clippers had a very different take on Benjamin's decision to leave town. "We now have a young, dedicated and well-conditioned team in camp which is hustling, enthusiastic and hard working," Baylor said. "We made it clear to Benoit that we wanted him as part of our team only if he fit the same mold. We made a fair offer and structured a contract to assure that he would be well conditioned, hard-working and motivated. He was not willing to accept those terms and we did not want him on any other terms." On the day that Benjamin announced that he was heading to Italy, Gary Grant and Don Casey spoke with him and both got the feeling that he did not want to leave. Grant said that Benjamin told him, "I'll be back."

And he was, just three days later.

According to Benjamin, when he arrived in Italy, Philips Milano tried to change many of the key stipulations that were contained in his contract. Benjamin did not like this, so he left. When asked what went wrong in Milan, Benjamin said, "I just want to concentrate on the positives with the Clippers." It seemed that a lot had changed in the space of just three days.

When Benjamin returned to America, there were still two weeks remaining before the Clippers' regular season opener. Most people assumed that this was plenty of time for a deal to be worked out. However, two weeks passed and still no contract had been signed. This frustrating delay was due to a disagreement between the two parties about how much of

---

111 Benjamin turned up 45 minutes late for his own press conference, giving reporters a little taste of what the Clippers had been forced to endure for the past four seasons.
112 *Went through* was an interesting choice of words, suggesting that Benjamin had not been able to see the correlation between his own sluggish form and the Clippers' poor results.

Benjamin's salary should be guaranteed and how much should be linked to incentive clauses[113]. The upshot of all this was that the Clippers were forced to begin another regular season without the services of one of their key players due to an ongoing contract dispute.

The Clippers opened the new campaign with a weaker version of the team that had struggled its way to just 21 wins during the previous season. Their starting center was not playing. Their most experienced player from the previous season, Quintin Dailey, had been waived. Their most talented player, Manning, was still injured. And the player they selected with their first round draft pick was riding a Vespa somewhere around Rome.

It was hard to see what the Clippers could say to their fans to get them excited about the new season. So, they offered nothing. Casey did his best to hose down any expectations by saying, "I make no predictions. All we can promise is effort and excitement." Then, just five games into the new season, Baylor closed two separate deals that significantly upgraded the level of talent at Casey's disposal.

Firstly, the franchise and Team Benjamin were finally able to agree on terms and conditions for a new contract. The final deal was for two years and worth a total of $2.5 million in base salary. However, the contract also featured a number of bonus incentives that allowed Benjamin to receive significantly higher pay checks, provided he was able to meet a range of targets, including maintaining a weight below 265 pounds. Importantly, the contract also allowed the Clippers to fine Benjamin if he exceeded this target weight.

The second move engineered by Baylor was a blockbuster trade that saw the Clippers acquire Ron Harper and two first round draft picks from Cleveland, in exchange for Reggie Williams and the rights to Danny Ferry.

---

113 One of the participants in this second phase of negotiations described the process as "like stirring cement with an eyelash."

This trade was a masterstroke, perhaps the finest front office move made by Baylor in his long career as a general manager. Ferry was proving to be nothing more than a headache for the Clippers. He was obviously not providing them with any help on the court and his presence in Italy continued to be a lightning rod for criticism. With this trade, the subject of how to lure Ferry back to the States suddenly became somebody else's problem. Meanwhile, the Clippers were happy to see the back of Williams, who had thus far struggled throughout his time in the NBA.

Conversely Harper seemed to be a great fit for the Clippers. He was an athletically gifted wing player who was still just 25 years of age. This meant that Harper was young enough to offer the promise of many more seasons of productive basketball, while also having accumulated more NBA experience than most of the other players on the Clippers roster. His form over the first few weeks of the 1989-90 season was nothing short of exceptional, with averages of 22 points, 7 assists, 6.9 rebounds, 2 steals and 1.3 blocks. All of which made the Cavs' decision to trade Harper somewhat perplexing.

The primary motive behind Cleveland's decision to make this trade had nothing to do with basketball and everything to do with who Harper was hanging around with in his spare time. Early in the 1989-90 season, Wayne Embry, Cleveland's general manager, received some concerning news from Horace Balmer, the NBA's vice president of security. It seemed that Harper had been spotted socializing with people who were suspected drug traffickers. Balmer told Embry that Harper's associates were being actively surveilled by law enforcement and that the DEA wanted to interview Harper in order to gather information on one of his friends.

When Harper was confronted with this news, he protested his innocence and even volunteered to take a drug test to remove all suspicion. Neither Embry nor head coach Lenny Wilkens believed that Harper was actually using drugs but this situation still posed a significant dilemma. If, at some point in the future, arrests were made and Harper was involved in some shape or form, the Cavs faced a public relations nightmare. Wilkens and Embry both urged Harper to distance himself from the friends in question and hoped that the problem would go away.

It didn't.

A few weeks later, Embry was told that Harper was about to be subpoenaed to appear before a grand jury. Balmer again stressed that this was about the star shooting guard's friends, rather than anything that Harper had personally done, but this latest development was still the final nail in his coffin. Embry and Wilkens attended a meeting with team owner Gordon Gund to discuss Harper's future. Embry recommended that they start exploring trade options immediately while Wilkens tried to convince Gund that they should stick with Harper, as this was a simple case of guilt by association. Wilkens stressed that Harper was showing no signs of any drug usage. Gund's opinion on the matter was made crystal clear to all in the room when he roared, "I WANT THAT S.O.B. OUT OF HERE!" A few days later, Embry pulled the trigger on the trade, sending Harper to professional basketball's version of Siberia.

The trade for Ron Harper paid immediate dividends for the Clippers. They beat New Jersey in Harper's debut, with the new recruit finishing with 21 points, 15 rebounds, 5 assists and 4 steals[114]. That performance was merely an appetizer for what Harper served up four nights later when the Clippers thrashed Chicago by 24 points. On top of the convincing nature of the win, the crowd of over 15,000 at the Sports Arena also got to witness an extremely rare occurrence, as Harper went head-to-head with Michael Jordan and came out on top. Harper finished with 36 points and 7 assists, while Jordan had 26 points, 4 assists and 7 turnovers. The team received another

---

114 Benjamin also chipped in with 1 point, 2 rebounds, 0 assists and 2 blocks in his first game for the new season.

piece of good news towards the end of November, when Manning made his long awaited comeback, 11 months after injuring his knee. Manning did not disappoint, converting his first six shots on the way to a total of 21 points in just 20 minutes of action. The Clippers remained within striking distance of a playoff berth throughout December, finishing the month two and half games outside the West's top eight with a 10-16 record.

The New Year saw the team head east for an extended road trip which had become a tradition over the past four seasons. And, like most Clipper traditions, it was not one with a proud history of success, with the Clippers posting just one win in 26 games over this four year period. However, the new-look Clippers showed scant regard for the franchise's previous struggles on the road, winning five out of eight games. This included the franchise's first win in Atlanta since 1981, their first victory in Milwaukee since 1980 and their first win at Boston Garden since 1979. Most of the credit for the Clippers' impressive form fell at the feet of one man, Ron Harper. "That S.O.B. doesn't let you lose," was how Casey described the experience of coaching Harper after he scored 37 points in a tight win over the Hawks.

The Clippers returned to California with an unusual air of excitement surrounding the team. They were even greeted with a standing ovation when the starting line-ups were announced for their first game back at the Sports Arena, against the lowly Charlotte Hornets. Harper headed into this clash having just been named the NBA's Player of the Week, the first Clipper to claim this award since Derek Smith, who won his third and final POW award way back in November 1985. Unfortunately, just a few days after receiving this honor, Smith suffered a knee injury that derailed his career. If you are beginning to think that this was something of a bad omen for Harper, you are spot on.

Early in the fourth quarter, things were looking good. Harper had already scored 33 points and the Clippers were leading by 5 points. It appeared that Harper might be on his way to scoring 40 for just the second time in his career. However, when he attempted to catch a pass on a fast break, he landed awkwardly, causing his right knee to buckle underneath him. Harper struggled to his feet and headed into the locker room

The injury was initially diagnosed as a sprained knee and Harper even told the medical staff that he felt good enough to return for the final few minutes of the game. Luckily, the Clippers decided to opt for the cautious approach and prevented Harper from checking back in. Within 24 hours, it was clear that the injury was actually a lot more sinister than just a simple sprain. In fact, Harper had torn his ACL, the exact same injury that Manning had suffered the previous season. This meant that Harper would need to have surgery and was unlikely to return to action until midway through the following season.

Each of the Clippers past five seasons had now been negatively impacted due to a series of serious injuries suffered by key players. "I don't believe in curses or jinxes," Casey said, "But this is the closest thing to it." Between November 1985 and January 1990, Derek Smith, Norm Nixon, Marques Johnson, Norm Nixon (again), Danny Manning and Ron Harper all suffered season-ending injuries. And in each case, the player who was hurt was arguably the team's most important player at the time that their injury occurred.

The team admirably refused to throw in the towel and over the next two weeks, the undermanned Clippers managed to squeeze out enough victories to keep themselves in touch with the Western Conference playoff picture, including a stunning 121-104 upset over the Lakers. The star of that win was undoubtedly Grant, who recorded his first triple double with 22 points, 17 assists and 10 rebounds.

Just three days after leading the Clippers to victory over the Lakers, Grant was writhing in agony on the floor of the Miami Arena. He had just suffered a fractured left ankle, the result of an opposition player landing on his leg while Grant was pursuing a loose ball[115]. He had surgery later that week, leaving the Clippers to play out the remainder of the 1989-90 season without the services of either of their starting guards and killing off any slim chance that they had of making a push for a spot in the playoffs.

If the injuries to Harper and Grant didn't extinguish the Clippers' playoff hopes, then the meeting that took place at Donald Sterling's office in the middle of February most certainly did. At this extraordinary meeting, which was moderated by Elgin Baylor and attended by Sterling and the vast majority of the players, the case was made that Don Casey should be fired. The complaints were numerous, as indicated by the two hour length of the meeting, and they included concerns over Casey's substitution patterns and a lack of trust between the players and their coach.

Shortly after the meeting, Casey was called into Sterling's office, handed written notes of the complaints that had been levelled against him and then given a verbal assurance that he would remain the franchise's coach for the rest of the season. And while Sterling said that he thought Casey "really appreciated" being told that his job was safe, the disharmony created by this meeting was evident for all to see. The team fell away badly over the second half of the season, losing 28 of their last 39 games.

When the season finally concluded, it came as no great surprise to learn that Casey's contract was not going to be renewed. Once again, it seemed as if the Clippers were changing coaches without giving proper consideration to the range of factors that impacted on the team's performance. The six week period from early December to mid-January demonstrated that, when everyone was healthy, Casey could achieve success with the roster that Baylor had assembled. However, injuries meant that Casey rarely had anything close to a full strength team at his disposal, with his preferred starting

---

115 At the time of the injury, Grant was averaging 13.1 points, 10 assists and 2.5 steals.

line-up of Grant, Harper, Manning, Smith and Benjamin playing a total of just 23 games together[116].

As the franchise headed into the 1990 off-season, Donald Sterling clearly believed that the Clippers had assembled the right mix of players and were on the verge of joining the NBA's elite. For the past few years, Sterling had hosted an annual draft lottery party, a cringe-inducing tradition where an assortment of B-grade celebrities and hired hostesses gathered to celebrate the latest edition of Clipper failure. Sterling was so confident that that the Clippers were about to start a new era of success that he labeled the 1990 shindig the "Farewell to the Lottery" party. He also told the assembled crowd to enjoy the event as "this (lottery party) is the last one there will ever be!"

Season XIII: 1990-91

The big announcement of the 1990 off-season was the decision to hire Mike Schuler as the team's new coach. Schuler learned his trade working as an assistant under Bobby Knight at Indiana University and like his mentor, he had a reputation of being a hard-task master. Schuler's NBA career got off to a good start when he won the Coach of the Year award in his very first season in charge at Portland. However, just a year and a half later, he was fired in the middle of the season after ongoing conflicts with players threatened to derail an up-and-coming Blazers team. When Schuler was appointed as the Clippers' head coach, he labeled his new position the best job in the NBA. "It's not a situation where you have to come in and rebuild," said Schuler. "It's a team that's ready to take off." Schuler signed a four year deal, which was in stark contrast to the one year contract given to Casey a year earlier.

---

[116] Even Magic Johnson spoke out publically in support of Casey, saying that he believed that the Clippers were on track to do some damage in the playoffs before Harper and Grant went down. Johnson said that no coach "could recover from those injuries."

The next item of business was the 1990 draft and the Clippers had two first round picks. They used the eighth overall selection on Bo Kimble, a 6'4" shooting guard who had built a formidable reputation as an unstoppable scorer, averaging 35.3 points per game as a senior at Loyola Marymount. With the 13th pick that they received from Cleveland as part of the Ferry-Harper trade, the Clippers drafted Loy Vaught, a 6'9"power forward from Michigan. Schuler compared Vaught to Charles Oakley, the ultimate compliment for any blue collar player in the early 1990s.

The Clippers' chances of finally qualifying for the playoffs was made all the more difficult by the fact that they would have to play the first few months of the season without Ron Harper, who was expected to return sometime in January. The Clippers were hoping that they could stay within striking distance of the playoff race and then make a late run once Harper was back on-court.

For the first six weeks, everything seemed to be going to plan. The team took advantage of a favorable early season schedule to accumulate a 10-10 record, which had them sitting eighth position in the West, two games ahead of Dallas. However, two extended road trips in December and January caused the Clippers to come undone and by the time Harper was ready to return, the team was 13 games under .500 and effectively out of the playoff hunt for yet another season[117].

The only piece of noteworthy news to emerge from the second half of the season was the franchise's decision to trade Benoit Benjamin. Ironically, Benjamin was playing some of the best basketball of his career at the time of the trade. In fact, his form was so impressive that he came close to earning an unlikely All-Star selection after Hakeem Olajuwon was ruled out with an eye injury in early January[118]. Baylor was able to find a very favorable

---

117 Harper eventually played a total of 39 games during the 1990-91 season and while it appeared that he had lost some of his speed and explosiveness he was still a very effective player. He finished the season with averages of 19.6 points, 5.4 assists and 4.8 rebounds.
118 Kevin Duckworth eventually got the nod as the West's second center.

deal for Benjamin, securing Olden Polynice from Seattle, as well as another two future first round picks. Polynice did not possess the same level of talent as Benjamin but he was just the type of center that Schuler was looking for, a fierce rebounder who could run the floor and thrive in the open court.

Benjamin used his departure as an opportunity to take a final few swipes at Clipper management. He expressed lingering resentment over the way the front office handled his two sets of contract negotiations and then made what is perhaps the greatest understatement in Clipper history: "I feel like I never reached my potential here[119]."

The Clippers had now been based in Los Angeles for seven years and they had spent this entire time in the formidable shadows of their crosstown rivals. In fact, it hardly seems fair to refer to the relationship between the Lakers and Clippers as a rivalry, given the vast differences between the two franchises. The Clippers finished the 1990-91 season with a total of 51 losses, their tenth consecutive year of accumulating at least 50 defeats. Meanwhile, the Lakers were coming off another NBA Finals appearance, their ninth in 12 years. Only a brave person could have predicted that the Clippers were about to finish the following season with a better record than the mighty Los Angeles Lakers, but this is exactly what happened. However, this was not an indication that the Clippers were about to spend the next twelve months sailing across an ocean of calm waters. There were plenty of choppy seas ahead.

---

[119] The Los Angeles Times' Scott Howard-Cooper provided the best summary of Benjamin's time with the franchise, labelling him "the walking epitome of the Clippers," for his ability to consistently deliver disappointing showings despite his unquestionable talent.

CHAPTER 8

One Riot, Two Playoff Wins and Three Head Coaches

"A good deodorant covers up a lot of stink."

OLDEN POLYNICE

AS THE CLIPPERS PREPARED FOR the start of their 1991 training camp, an air of optimism hovered over the franchise. They were about to head into a new season with the deepest and most talented roster in their fourteen year history, prompting Elgin Baylor to declare, "If we don't win with this team, something is wrong." The Clippers' backcourt featured two promising young players in Ron Harper and Gary Grant. Meanwhile, their frontline was stacked with talent, including Danny Manning, Charles Smith, Ken Norman, Loy Vaught, Olden Polynice and James Edwards, a veteran center acquired from Detroit via trade.

Another trade engineered by Baylor during that off-season made arguably the greatest contribution to the sense of expectation surrounding the team. Doc Rivers, an All-Star point guard, was acquired from Atlanta in exchange for a first round draft pick[120]. Rivers had eight years of NBA

---

120 The Clippers gave the Hawks the ninth overall pick in the 1991 draft and they used it to select Stacey Augmon.

experience, including 44 playoff games, and Baylor was hoping that he would be a steadying influence on what was otherwise a fairly young roster. However, when a disgruntled Rivers departed Los Angeles without playing a single game for the Clippers, it left the rest of his new teammates to wonder if he would ever return.

Glenn "Doc" Rivers was the type of child who found it difficult to sit still for long periods of time[121]. He was always on the move, always up to some sort of mischief. So, the trance-like state that he entered into when he went to watch his first basketball game came as quite a surprise to those who knew him well. Rivers grew up in Chicago and was still in kindergarten when he went to watch his uncle, Jim Brewer, play for Proviso East High School. Rivers stared intently at the game, from the opening tip to the final buzzer, with an expression of deep concentration that belied both his age and personality. He didn't get up to use the bathroom, didn't go to the concession stand to buy sodas or snacks, in fact, he hardly uttered a word throughout the entire evening. It soon became obvious to Rivers' mom that her son was not just watching the game, he was *studying* it.

It didn't take long for Rivers to decide that he wanted to follow in the footsteps of his uncle, who was on his way to a nine year NBA career, with stints with the Cavs, Pistons, Blazers and Lakers. There was just one tiny problem with this plan- unlike his uncle, Rivers wasn't very good.

Despite being one of weakest players on the court, Rivers would play at the local playground for hours on end. He quickly learned to find small

---

121   Rivers was given the nickname "Doc" after wearing a Dr. J shirt to a basketball camp that was run by Hall of Fame coach Al McGuire. When McGuire was looking for an additional player to make up the numbers for a scrimmage, he shouted, "Where's that kid, 'Doc'?" The name has stuck ever since.

successes where others would have only seen defeat. If he drove in the lane and had his shot blocked, he would take solace from the fact that his improved ball handling had allowed him to penetrate, rather than dwell on the small issue of his shot being swatted away.

One day, when Rivers was a fourth grader at Garfield Elementary, his teacher, Mrs. Willis, asked each student to write a sentence on the blackboard about what they wanted their future career to be. For Rivers, this was a no-brainer and when it was his turn, he proudly wrote that he wanted to be a professional basketballer. Mrs. Willis thought this was the perfect moment to explain to the class about the importance of being realistic when setting goals. After explaining why Rivers was misguided, she erased his sentence and asked him to come up and try again.

On the way to the blackboard, Rivers intended to change his statement to something that would make his teacher happy but when he got up the front, he found himself writing the same eight words- *I want to be a pro basketball player.* Now, Mrs. Willis was mad. It was clear to her that Rivers was not taking the task seriously, so she sent him to the principal's office. Rivers was suspended and sent home, where his father was waiting for him. Grady Rivers told his son that he should listen to his teacher, as she knew better than he did about what was a sensible choice of occupation. Rivers agreed to go back to school with his dad, so he could make things right. Grady walked Doc back to the classroom and told Mrs. Willis that his son would like to have another try at writing his goal.

Doc wrote the same sentence, for a third time.

The room fell completely silent as Grady stared at his son for what seemed like an eternity. And then Grady said, "I guess that's what he wants. I guess that's the truth. I guess that's realistic for him." When they got home, Grady sat his boy down and said, "If you're going to stand up for something like that, make sure you stick with it."

As Rivers grew older, his game gradually improved and all of a sudden his dreams of playing in the NBA no longer seemed so far-fetched. His time growing up in Chicago coincided with an amazingly large collection of talented teenagers playing on the local blacktops. Isiah Thomas, Mark Aguirre, Terry Cummings, Craig Hodges, Darrell Walker and Rod Higgins are just a few of the 14 players that Rivers competed against as a youth who would go on to play in the NBA. Fueled by this high standard of competition, Rivers became a star at Proviso East just like his uncle, whom he had watched so intently just a decade earlier.

After graduating from high school, Rivers moved on to Marquette University and his first two seasons with the Golden Eagles were outstanding. In fact, his form was so impressive that he was selected to play on the US national team that competed in the 1982 World Championships in Colombia, where he led the team in scoring with an average of 16.8 points per game[122]. However, away from the court, all was not well in the world of Doc Rivers.

Rivers had begun dating Kris Campi, the woman who would eventually become his wife. However, while this story had a happy ending, its beginning was anything but a fairy tale. Campi was white, Rivers was black. And while this didn't concern either of the two people who were actually in the relationship, it seemed to bother many others. Adding to the controversy was the fact that Campi had previously been in a relationship with one of Rivers' Marquette teammates, who also happened to be white. This caused tension on the team, with some of Rivers' teammates believing that he had acted unethically and "stolen" Campi away. This resulted in a variety of ugly behavior directed towards Campi and Rivers. One day, the tires on Campi's car were slashed and "NIGGERLOVER" was scrawled across the sidewalk. Glares and racial slurs became a regular occurrence as

---

[122] The Americans ultimately fell short of their goal of winning a gold medal, losing in the final to the Soviets by one point. Rivers scored 24 points in the final but missed a shot at the end of the game that would have sealed the win for the Americans.

Campi and Rivers made their way around campus. Rivers began receiving crank calls at his house. In short, it was not a pleasant time.

All of this negativity began to have an impact on Rivers' on-court performance. By his junior year, he found it increasingly hard to concentrate on basketball and for the first time in his life he could see that his play was regressing. After a disappointing third college season, Rivers decided that he had had enough and declared himself eligible for the 1983 NBA draft. Twelve months earlier, Rivers appeared destined to be an early first round selection but his indifferent form during his final season at Marquette had many general managers second guessing whether to pick him or not. Rivers eventually tumbled all the way to the middle of the second round, where Atlanta snatched him up and he quickly set about showing those who had passed him over that they had made a big mistake.

Rivers was a starter midway through his rookie year, became a team captain in just his fourth professional season and was selected as an All-Star in the middle of his fifth campaign. Perhaps the high point of Rivers' career came in the second round of 1988 playoffs when Atlanta took on the Boston Celtics. In Game 4, his 22 assists played a large role in the Hawks' 118-109 victory that levelled the series at two-all. Two nights later, he had 21 points and 7 assists as the Hawks shocked most observers by winning in Boston Garden, thus pushing the Celtics to the brink of elimination. In Game 6, Rivers again played exceptionally, scoring 32 points, but it was not enough. The Celtics managed to hold on and win by 2 points, allowing them to return home, where they won Game 7 by the same margin.

When the Clippers traded for Rivers, they were hoping he would provide the same leadership he had demonstrated while playing for Atlanta. However, while this plan sounded great in theory, there was one fairly major problem- Rivers wanted nothing to do with the Clippers. "I just didn't want to play there," Rivers said.

Hoping to force the Clippers hand into trading him to a more desirable destination, Rivers asked for a contract extension of one season, despite having four years remaining on his current deal. Given that Rivers was about to celebrate his 27th birthday, the Clippers were not too keen on this idea, preferring to avoid locking themselves into a five year deal. However, they were also not willing to trade the player they had just brought in to be their new starting point guard.

By the time training camp got underway, the issue remained unresolved. So Rivers decided to sit out of the first few days of practice and it was initially reported that he had a swollen toe. However it soon became apparent that his presence on the sidelines was connected to an entirely different issue.

Rivers said that he planned to fly back to Atlanta and remain there until a new deal was worked out and he made it abundantly clear this decision had everything to do with the fact that he was negotiating with the infamous Clippers. When asked if he would have continued to participate in training camp if he was dealing with another franchise, Rivers responded, "Some teams, I probably would because they're good businessmen. I would give them the benefit of the doubt." He then added, "I remember when I was traded, everyone said, 'Sorry about going to the Clippers.' I said, 'Well, things do change.' They said, 'No.' I don't know now if they're not right."

Over the next three weeks, Rivers made a number of combative comments that had many observers questioning his ability to be a locker room leader if he ever returned to the team. A few days after leaving training camp, he publically asked to be traded. When it appeared that there was no trade on the horizon, he upped the ante in his war of words, saying, "I want to win. But I don't see it happening with the Clippers. It is not a classy organization."

In the end, this public condemnation of the Clippers accomplished very little. In fact, all Rivers' actions seemed to achieve was to cost him almost

$10,000 in fines and to somewhat alienate him from his new teammates. The stand-off finally came to an end on the eve of the regular season, when Rivers conceded that the Clippers were not going to extend his contract and reluctantly reported for duty.

Season XIV: 1991-92

With Rivers back on deck, the Clippers got off to a great start, winning five of their first seven games. However, it did not take long for the more familiar version of the Clippers to resurface. In the middle of November, they lost a contest they were heavily favored to win, against a dismal Dallas Mavericks team. Afterwards, reporters headed to the locker room expecting to hear the same tired clichés about the need to stay mentally focused when playing lesser opponents. Instead, they were confronted by an explosive verbal tirade from Olden Polynice. Number one on Polynice's list of complaints was Mike Schuler's substitution patterns. "I'm tired of being played like a damn yo-yo," Polynice declared, slamming locker doors as he spoke. "I'll tell you right now, I ain't no Benoit Benjamin. I'm Olden Polynice and I need to be treated like Olden, not like other people are used to be treated on this team." Polynice then added, "I'm not going to have this every night. They can trade my butt back to Seattle."

At first glance, Polynice's outburst seemed to be little more than a frustrated player blowing off steam, an incident that is hardly out of the ordinary in the pressure packed environment of the NBA. However, in reality, Polynice was simply the first player to publically voice what many others were whispering- Schuler was not up the task of being an NBA head coach and had already lost the team. Alas, Polynice's comments did nothing to resolve the issues that have been bubbling beneath the surface, they simply brought them to the public's attention. Following the defeat in Dallas, the Clippers lost six of their next seven games, causing Schuler's level of frustration to increase. But the more Schuler yelled, the more the team tuned him out.

As the Clippers' record slumped, the volume of the rumblings from the players only increased. This led to speculation that Schuler was on the verge of becoming the third Clipper coach to be sacked in the middle of a season in the past eight years. Comments from inside the organization only fueled this gossip, with one anonymous source quoted as saying, "If there is no improvement, we will have to take appropriate action."

The start of December saw Charles Smith return from a knee injury and for a brief moment, it looked like he was the cure for all of the team's problems. His comeback coincided with an eight game winning streak, which set a new franchise record. Their eighth victory came against Orlando and with this win, the team moved back into the Western Conference playoff picture, pushing the talk of Schuler's termination into the background. Unfortunately for Schuler, the win over the Magic turned out to be one of the last times that he ever coached an NBA team to victory.

The Los Angeles Clippers team that arrived in San Antonio on January 20th was not a happy collection of players. They were unhappy with their coach. They were unhappy with the fact that they had lost 10 of their previous 16 games. They were unhappy when they discovered that some of their luggage had failed to arrive in Texas with them. But mostly they were unhappy that the practice that was scheduled for that afternoon had been switched from an optional session to a compulsory one.

It was Martin Luther King Day and the players were looking forward to having some time off. Once they realized that this was no longer the case, an impromptu players-only meeting was called to determine whether the now-mandatory practice should go ahead. Contrasting views were expressed, with some players feeling strongly that the team should not practice due to the significance of the day, while others believed that Dr. King's memory was being disrespected so that a group of professional athletes could have some extra time off. At some stage in the discussion, a vote was held and a large majority of those present decided that the practice should not go ahead. Team captain Danny Manning called Mike Schuler to inform him of the decision.

There was just one tiny problem with this case study of democracy in action- Schuler never asked the players if they wanted to practice or not. The Spurs were most certainly practicing on MLK Day. There were 12 other NBA teams that were playing games on MLK Day. And yet the Clippers had decided to give themselves the day off.

Schuler was furious. The team's decision not to train had many outsiders questioning whether this act of player defiance was more about trying to undermine their coach's authority than paying tribute to the memory of Martin Luther King. Regardless of what the players' true motives were, from the moment the scheduled practice failed to go ahead, it was clear that Schuler's days as the Clippers' head coach were numbered.

While the Clippers' front office had been considering replacing Schuler since way back in November, they had been hesitant to pull the trigger for a few good reasons. The first was related to concerns about the franchise's reputation for instability amongst both the general public and the basketball community. When Baylor employed Schuler, he hoped that this would put an end to the cycle of hiring and firing coaches. Another reason for the front office's hesitancy to fire Schuler was their uncertainty about whom to replace him with. They were worried that if they promoted another assistant, the players would end up challenging that new coach's authority somewhere down the line. If Baylor was going to terminate Schuler, he wanted to be sure that there was a high-profile, experienced coach who was ready to step in and take the job.

On the day of the Clippers' clash with the Spurs, it seemed like all of Baylor's prayers had been answered. That morning, San Antonio announced that their head coach, the highly regarded Larry Brown, would not be seeing out the season and was being replaced immediately by assistant coach Bob Bass. The circumstances that surrounded this coaching change in San Antonio were highly unusual, with Spurs owner Red McCombs initially firing Brown, before changing his mind and re-hiring him. However, Brown quickly came to the conclusion that he no longer wanted to work for an owner who did not have faith in him, so he went to see McCombs and asked to once again be terminated.

The clash that took place between the Spurs and Clippers on January 21st was a match-up between two teams in a state of turmoil. The Spurs had just replaced their coach and the Clippers were on the verge of doing the same. San Antonio was able to produce a 14 point win for Bass, who had been put in charge of the Spurs only a few hours earlier.

Meanwhile, Schuler coached another four games before he was finally put out of his misery. The Clippers were 21-24 on the day that Schuler's termination was announced and he joined Paul Silas, Jim Lynam, Don Chaney, Gene Shue and Don Casey on the growing list of coaches to lose their jobs since Donald Sterling purchased the franchise. On this occasion, Baylor was left with little choice but to let Schuler go, as the mood around the team had become particularly toxic, even by Clipper standards. In the weeks before Schuler was sacked, players were purposely disrespectful towards him, openly mocking him on the team bus and ignoring his instructions during games. When explaining his decision, Baylor said that the tension between Schuler and the players was having a negative impact on the team's results, thus forcing him to make a move.

Schuler's axing meant that assistant coach Mack Calvin would have a chance to slide into the hot seat, even if it was for just a few games. Baylor made it clear that Calvin was only being given the role on an interim basis, in order to give the front office enough time to search for a more suitable candidate. Not surprisingly, Calvin saw it a little differently, saying that he thought he was "the best man for the job."

In reality, the Clippers had their eyes on one person- Larry Brown. The front office contacted Brown just a few hours after he was terminated by San Antonio, to gauge whether he was interested in jumping straight back on the saddle, albeit with a different horse. And from the moment that Brown expressed interest in the Clippers' job, Calvin's time in charge was always going to be short-lived. Calvin coached the team to a 97-80 victory over Dallas in his first game calling the shots. However, the following evening, Baylor appeared on the televised broadcast of the Clippers-Lakers clash and announced that Brown had been hired as the franchise's new coach.

No one seemed more shocked that Larry Brown was being introduced as the Clippers' new head coach than Larry Brown himself. "When you lose your job, you don't expect people to be knocking on your door," Brown said. "I was very surprised." Surprised maybe, but once the job offer was on the table, there was little chance that Brown was going to knock it back. Despite the team's struggles and internal chaos, the Clippers' coaching job was still seen as an attractive proposition due to the impressive ensemble of talented players on their roster. Brown was also set to be handsomely rewarded, as he was given a five year, $5 million contract that made him the second highest paid coach in the entire league, behind only New York's Pat Riley[123].

Brown arrived at the Clippers with two decades of experience coaching in the NBA, ABA and college ranks under his belt. And everywhere he went, his teams won. In college he led two different programs to the national championship game, finishing runners-up with UCLA in 1980 and winning the national championship with Kansas in 1988[124]. His Carolina

---
123 Upon signing with Clippers, Brown also entered the history books as the only person to coach two different NBA franchises in the same season.
124 Although the UCLA result was later scrubbed from the record book when a number of the Bruins' players were declared ineligible.

and Denver teams made the playoffs for the last four ABA seasons. When the ABA and NBA merged in 1976, Brown was still coaching in Denver and the prevailing wisdom was that the four ABA franchises would struggle against the established NBA teams. However, Brown's Nuggets finished on top of the Midwest Division for their first two seasons in the NBA. In the early 1980s, Brown coached the New Jersey Nets into the playoffs. His final stop before landing the Clippers' job was San Antonio, where he led the Spurs to consecutive playoff berths before he was fired.

Accepting the Clippers' offer gave Brown the chance to re-unite with Danny Manning, whom he had coached while they were both at Kansas. And while Manning publically praised the hiring of Brown, saying he was "one of the best teachers in the game," privately his view on the appointment was a lot less straightforward. He knew that his greatest success on a basketball court, capturing the 1988 NCAA championship, was achieved while playing for Brown, but he was also wise enough not to look back on his four years with the Jayhawks through rose-colored glasses. Manning remembered what it was like working in close quarters with Brown on a day-to-day basis- his intense personality, the seemingly constant yelling and the pushing and prodding to assume a greater role as a locker room leader. He knew that he found some aspects of Brown's approach to the game difficult to deal with back when he was still a college student, which left him to wonder whether the two of them could peacefully co-exist now that he was an established NBA star.

Despite Manning's personal reservations, the hiring of Brown brought an immediate change in the team's fortunes. While the rest of the league's attentions were focused on the NBA's annual All-Star game, the Clippers participated in a mini-training camp at UCLA's Pauley Pavilion. And once play resumed after the All-Star break, the transformation in the team's attitude and approach was clear for all to see. The Clippers reeled off five straight wins against quality opponents, including an emotional 124-110 victory of the Spurs and a 125-94 blow-out of the Lakers.

Brown elected to use a more mobile starting line-up, replacing Olden Polynice with Ken Norman and having Charles Smith slide over to play the center position. This gave the Clippers a quick, versatile frontcourt of Norman, Manning and Smith who were big enough to rebound and defend but also fast enough to beat their opponents down the floor, thus generating a lot of easy baskets. All of a sudden, the Clippers were the hottest ticket in town. Crowds were flocking to the Sports Arena to see their up-tempo and aesthetically pleasing brand of basketball. Even Donald Sterling was pleased with what he saw, saying, "I like this coach, I think he'll be with us for a decade."

The Clippers closed out the regular season with 23 wins in the 35 games that they played under Brown, pushing their overall record to 45-37[125]. This was good enough to secure the franchise's first ever playoff berth. They qualified as the Western Conference's seventh seed, earning themselves a first round match-up with Utah. And while most Clipper fans were ecstatic just to have qualified for the playoffs, Brown, Manning and the rest of the team quietly went to work on causing, what they hoped would be one of the biggest upsets in NBA history.

THE PLAYOFFS: ROUND 1 VS. UTAH

The Clippers headed into their first ever playoff series feeling positive about their chances. Their form since the All-Star break had been excellent, they had no major injury concerns and the players knew that they had the necessary weapons to defeat their highly-regarded opponents from Utah. As they prepared for Game 1, the team's biggest concern was the prospect of playing the majority of the series at the Delta Center, which was regarded as one of the NBA's most hostile venues for opposition teams[126]. The Clippers were well aware that they needed to win at least one game

---

125 The Lakers finished one position below the Clippers, with a 43-39 record. This was the first time that the Clippers were able to win more games in a season than their Southern Californian rivals.
126 The Jazz's home record of 37-4 was the best in the entire league.

in Utah in order to advance to the second round. Game 1 would not be that game. The Jazz raced out to an early lead, before cruising to a 115-97 victory. John Stockton was the catalyst for Utah's win, finishing with 10 points, 21 assists and just 1 turnover.

In the lead-up to Game 2, Brown made a change to his starting line-up, replacing Gary Grant with Doc Rivers in an attempt to curtail the influence of Stockton. It mattered little, as Stockton was still able to do whatever he pleased, falling just two rebounds short of a triple double (21 points, 19 assists and 8 rebounds). Meanwhile, Karl Malone dominated in the paint, finishing with 32 points and 13 rebounds. Despite the dominance of Malone and Stockton, Game 2 was a much closer contest. The Clippers led by as many as 8 points in the first half and the score was knotted at 84 with a little over five minutes remaining, before the Jazz pulled away for a 103-92 victory.

As the two teams headed to Los Angeles for Game 3, most pundits were predicting that the Jazz were about to complete a 3-0 sweep. But the confidence level amongst the Clippers remained high. After all, the series was about to shift to the familiar confines of the Sports Arena and the Jazz were not a good road team, as indicated by their 18-23 record when playing away from the Delta Center. In front of a boisterous crowd of over 14,000, the Clippers defeated Utah 98-88 in Game 3. The win was fueled by a balanced Clipper attack, with all five starters scoring in double figures, led by Manning's 17 point haul. Attention now shifted to Game 4.

On the morning of Wednesday April 29th 1992, the Los Angeles Clippers woke up feeling pretty good about themselves. Their victory in the previous evening's game was not only the franchise's first post-season win, it also kept their hopes of qualifying for the second round alive. However, the Clippers would not be able to spend too long basking in the glow of their ground-breaking triumph, as they had just one day to prepare for Game 4. If they were going to successfully avoid elimination and send the series back to Salt Lake City for a decisive Game 5, they needed to find a way to produce another win. The Clippers could not afford to spend that spring day celebrating. Instead, they headed straight back to the practice court.

Just over 40 miles away from where the 12 Clipper players were preparing for their next game, a jury of 12 men and women were meeting for their seventh day of deliberations in a high-profile police brutality case. By the middle of that afternoon, the jury had arrived at a decision that would have far-reaching implications for the city of Los Angeles. The four officers in question were all found not guilty of assault and three of the four were also found not guilty of using excessive force[127]. This verdict set off six days of civil unrest that resulted in 2,383 people sustaining injuries and 60 deaths. It was also estimated that over $1 billion in property was damaged or destroyed as a result of the trail of destruction caused by widespread fires and looting[128].

By April 1992, the video footage of Rodney King being beaten by four Los Angeles police officers had been shown so many times, it would have been difficult to find somebody in America who had not seen it at least once. Over the years, there had been many instances where it was alleged that Los Angeles police officers had been heavy-handed when interacting with African-American or Latino citizens. What made the Rodney King case so different was that it was not just one person's word against another's, this time the incident in question had been captured on tape. Thus Americans were able to view exactly what occurred and draw their own conclusions as to whether the officers had acted appropriately[129]. And while

---

127 The jury was deadlocked on whether the fourth officer, Laurence Powell, had used excessive force, so a mistrial was declared on this final charge.
128 Over 11,000 fires burned in Los Angeles during this six day period.
129 The video footage was shocking. King lay helplessly on his stomach as the four officers stood over him, kicking and striking him over 50 times with their batons.

there were some people who believed that the officers had not used excessive force, this group was clearly in the minority[130].

The jury's verdict was announced at 3:15pm and it did not take long for the public's anger to translate into action. By 3:45pm, a group of over 300 people had formed at the front of the Los Angeles County Courthouse to protest the outcome of the trial. Within hours, crowds were gathering in locations all around the city and as the afternoon turned into evening, non-violent protests began transforming into increasingly more aggressive acts.

At 6:45pm a truck driver named Reginald Denny was dragged from his 18-wheeler and brutally beaten by a group of rioters. A television news helicopter hovered above the scene, broadcasting the horrific images from the street below live into lounge rooms around America. People watched on helplessly as a concrete brick was thrown at Denny from close range, striking him in the temple and almost killing him.

By Thursday it appeared that Los Angeles was on the brink of total anarchy. Fires and looting continued to spread across the city, while gun battles were taking place between store owners and would-be looters. In an attempt to regain some sense of control, Mayor Tom Bradley announced that there would be a dusk to dawn curfew until further notice.

Earlier that day, Bradley also spoke with representatives from the NBA to try and figure out what they should do about Game 4 of the Clippers-Jazz series, which was scheduled to take place that evening. It was becoming increasingly clear that nobody could say for sure when order was going to be restored, so the decision was made to postpone the game until Saturday afternoon.

---

130 A telephone poll, conducted the week after the verdicts were announced, found that 73% of white respondents and 92% of black respondents believed that the jury had made the wrong decision in the Rodney King case.

When it was announced that the game had been pushed back two days, the Jazz briefly considered flying home, before deciding to remain in Los Angeles. With the riots continuing, there was very little for the Utah players to do besides hang around their Marina del Ray hotel and watch footage of the unfolding crisis on television. The Jazz did venture out once for what was meant to be a closed practice session. However, when the bus pulled up at Inglewood High School, the players, coaches and members of the press who were travelling with the team were greeted by a scene straight out of a disaster movie. The streets were deserted and yet they seemed to be surrounded by the sound of sirens and the smell of smoke. It was decided that it was too dangerous to ask anyone to wait outside and so, the frazzled media members were ushered into the safety of the gym, where they tried their best to pay attention as the Jazz went through their paces.

On Friday, Game 4 was re-scheduled once more, this time to Sunday afternoon. The only question now was where it was going to be played. It was clear that the Sports Arena, which was located in one of the worst riot affected areas, was not going to be a safe option. The Lakers, who were in the midst of a playoff battle of their own, had already opted to move Game 4 of their series with Portland to Las Vegas. However, the Clippers were not keen to follow suit. "Our organization was vehemently opposed to moving the game out of state and giving up home court (advantage) in a playoff game," said Carl Lahr, who was the vice president of sales for the Clippers at the time.

The challenge was to find an arena that was close enough to allow the Clipper fans to attend, but far enough away from the riots to ensure their safety. UCLA was contacted about the possible use of Pauley Pavilion, the option of using the Long Beach Arena was explored and the Jazz even kindly offered to help, suggesting that the game could be played at the Delta Center[131]. In the end, the game was moved to the Anaheim Convention

---

131 It seems that no-one took this final option very seriously, not even the Jazz themselves. Utah's General Manager Tim Howells said that if he was in charge of the Clippers he would opt to play the game at a "neutral site with nobody in the arena" rather than hand home court advantage over to the opposition.

Center, which had a seating capacity of a little under 8,000. The Clippers-Jazz match-up was only the second NBA game to ever be played at the venue, with the other being an unforgettable pre-season clash from 13 years earlier. In that game, Bill Walton outplayed Kareem Abdul-Jabbar, as the Clippers toppled the almighty Lakers. Everyone connected with the franchise was hoping for a similar result when Game 4 tipped off on Sunday afternoon.

There may have never been a more emotionally-charged lead-up to a game of basketball than the hours that preceded the opening tip of Game 4 of the Clippers-Jazz series. The Clippers had spent the past four days watching the city that they called home tearing itself to shreds. All the while, they were being prevented from doing the one thing that they knew how to do best- play basketball. They woke on Sunday morning feeling like 12 jack-in-the-boxes with cranks that had been continuously turned but whose lids refused to open.

By this time, the rioting had begun to settle down, allowing both teams to make the trek down to Anaheim in relative safety. However, while the streets of Los Angeles were reasonably calm, the players and coaches came across plenty of reminders of the mayhem that had ensued over the previous four days. Police officers on every corner, burnt out businesses and armed soldiers on the roofs of buildings combined to create the impression that they were travelling through a war zone rather than driving through America's second largest city.

When the Clippers arrived at the Convention Center, they were greeted by the comforting sight of the Sports Arena's polished wooden floor. Amid the surrounding chaos, Carl Lahr had somehow managed to arrange for the floor to be transported to Anaheim without telling any of the players or coaches. The distinctive red, orange and yellow "L.A." logo that occupied the center circle was the equivalent of a "Welcome Home" doormat for the emotionally drained Clippers. As the team dressed in the unfamiliar surroundings of the Convention Center's change rooms, they felt a surge of confidence.

This was a game of basketball that they simply could not lose.

A modest crowd of just over 7,000 crammed into the small arena, but what they lacked in numbers they more than made up for with their enthusiastic support[132]. The warm-ups concluded with the Clippers throwing down a series of powerful dunks as the sounds of "Jump" by Kris Kross blared from the Convention Center's modest speakers. There was no question in anyone's mind, the Clippers were ready to play.

Once the game began, it was like watching an arm wrestling contest between two evenly matched opponents and at half-time the Clippers clung to a three point lead. The start of the third quarter saw the game open up, with the Clippers extending the margin out to 12 points. But the Jazz were not a team that would be easily pushed aside. Led by back-to-back three pointers from Stockton, the Jazz went on a run of their own and by the end of the third quarter, the Clippers' advantage was down to three points.

The final period was close throughout. When Jeff Malone scored and put the Jazz in front by a solitary point with less than two minutes to play, it appeared that the Clippers' season was about to come to an end. They had shown a toughness that had not been previously associated with the franchise and along the way had earned respect from around the league. But it seemed to be a pretty safe bet that the playoff tested veterans from Utah would be better equipped to close out this pressure filled contest.

Ten seconds after Utah took the lead, Manning calmly converted a pair of free throws to put the Clippers back in front. Charles Smith then made

---

[132] Doc Rivers would later describe the crowd as the loudest he had ever played in front of.

a lay-in to push the lead out to three, before Mike Brown scored for the Jazz to again cut the margin to one. Brown's lay-up would be Utah's last basket for the evening. Over the next 30 seconds, Rivers scored five points to seal a 115-107 victory for the Clippers. They had survived a 44 point scoring barrage from Karl Malone, including a 22 of 24 effort from the free throw line, to tie the series up at two-all. In the final 1:44, the Clippers outscored their more seasoned opponents 11-2. Manning led the way with 33 points and 10 rebounds, closely followed by Harper's 26 point contribution.

As the final seconds ticked off the clock, delirious fans chanted "We want Seattle! We want Seattle!" Just a week earlier, the Clippers were trailing 0-2 and a second round date with Sonics appeared to be out of the question. A week later, the Clippers had survived a riot and evened up the series, meaning a match-up with Seattle and their old friend Benoit Benjamin was now just one win away.

The Clippers boarded a chartered flight to Salt Lake City, feeling confident that they were about to become only the fourth team in NBA history to comeback from a two-nil deficit and win a five-game series. The forced re-scheduling of Game 4 left very little time to prepare for the series decider, which was set to take place at the Delta Center the very next evening. In the lead-up to the game, most of the talk coming out of the Clippers' camp was about pressure or more specifically how little pressure they were feeling relative to their opponents. The Clippers knew they had already exceeded everyone's expectations just by extending the series to a fifth game. Now, they looked to etch their names in the NBA's record books for an achievement that the franchise could finally be proud of.

When Game 5 commenced, it looked like the pre-game proclamations from the underdogs were spot-on, as a poised and relaxed-looking Clippers team raced to an early 14-2 lead. Surprisingly, it was the Jazz who appeared to be both tense and unsure of themselves in the game's opening minutes, failing to score on each of their first nine possessions. The margin grew to 15 points at one stage before the Clippers settled for a 30-18 quarter time advantage. At the half-time, the margin remained steady at 12 points. In the first 24 minutes of Game 5, the Clippers managed to contain Karl Malone, something they had been unable to do at any other point in the series. Malone headed to the locker room with just 4 points next to his name on 1 for 9 shooting.

In the third quarter, some cracks started to appear in the Clippers' defense, as they gave up 33 points and allowed the Jazz back into the game. However Utah still found themselves trailing 77-73, as the game headed into its final period.

The Clippers were about to play the most important quarter of basketball in the history of the franchise. They were now just 12 minutes away from eliminating the Jazz and booking a second round match-up with Seattle. One more quarter of good basketball and all the jokes about Clipper ineptitude would become a thing of the past.

During the fourth quarter, the Clippers attempted a total of 21 field goals.

Two of them went in.

That is a conversion rate of 9.5%.

With a little over nine minutes remaining, the Jazz took the lead for the first time in the game. From here, they quickly went about ensuring that they would not relinquish it for the rest of the evening. With 4:29 remaining David Benoit, a scarcely-used bench player, hit a crucial three-pointer to stretch Utah's advantage from four to seven. A little over a minute later, the game was all but over when Manning picked up his sixth foul. He left having out-scored Malone for the first time in the series, yet it mattered little[133]. It would be Malone and the Jazz who were moving onto to the second round, courtesy of the 98-89 victory.

When Larry Brown said that he was "really proud of the team" in his post-game press conference, he could have been speaking on behalf of the city of Los Angeles. The unlikely, albeit short-lived, playoff run of the Clippers had given the city a reason to smile during an otherwise somber time. The Clippers returned from Salt Lake City to find their hometown slowly putting itself back together after a truly horrific week. And while the players were disappointed that they were not able to extend their season any further, they still felt an unmistakable sense of pride in what they had achieved over the second half of the season.

As the Clippers prepared to head into the 1992-93 season, there was plenty for their fans to be excited about. They had one of the most respected tacticians in all of basketball signed up to coach for the next four seasons and a team that was stacked with talented, young players who were about to head into their physical primes. However, the Clippers were about to learn that the jump from cellar dwellers to respectability was nowhere near as difficult as making the leap from respectability to being a genuine championship contender.

---

133 Manning scored 24 points to Malone's 19.

CHAPTER 9

The Curse is Broken?

"You just made the biggest mistake of your life."

DANNY MANNING (WELCOMING STANLEY ROBERTS TO THE CLIPPERS)

THE CLIPPERS WERE GETTING BLOWN out.

Twelve months after losing a closely contested series decider in Utah, the Clippers were once again trying to win a Game 5 on the road and progress to the second round of the playoffs. The venue for this year's decisive clash was The Summit and the opponent was the Houston Rockets, led by Hakeem Olajuwon, arguably the league's best player whose name was not Michael Jordan.

A year earlier, the Clippers had earned the respect of the basketball world by forcing the Jazz to play hard right up until the final minutes of Game 5, before a winner could be decided. This time around, it seemed as if they were going to bow out without putting up much of a fight.

The Clippers entered the fourth quarter trailing by 11 points. Just over a minute into the final period, Houston increased their lead to a seemingly insurmountable 16. Barring some sort of miracle, the Rockets were heading to the second round for the first time in six years, where they would take on Seattle for a spot in the Western Conference finals.

And then, the comeback started.

A jump shot. A driving lay-in. An offensive rebound and stick-back. All of a sudden, the margin was trimmed to just nine points.

With a little over three minutes remaining in the game, Ron Harper nailed a baseline jumper to pull the Clippers within seven.

A step-back jumper from the top of the key- Clippers down by five.

A Harper steal at the halfway line that resulted in a breakaway lay-up- Clippers down three, two and half minutes on the clock.

Another stop led to an isolation play for Danny Manning against Rockets power forward Otis Thorpe. And while the crowd was on its feet, their chants of "De-fense" were beginning to sound less like confident support and more like desperate pleas. *Just hold on for a few more possessions.* Manning took two strong dribbles to his left, rose up and hit a baseline jumper. Clippers down one. One minute and forty seconds to play.

When the Rockets failed to score on their next possession, the Clippers were given the chance to take the lead. Their defense had been outstanding, holding Houston to a total of just seven points over a nine and half minute stretch.

Harper aggressively drove down the middle of the lane and elevated. The ball rolled off the fingertips of his right hand. It hit the front of the rim, the back of the rim and the front of the rim again.

Then it settled softly into the basket.

Clippers up by one.

Seventy-seven seconds away from winning their first playoff series.

As the summer of 1992 approached, it seemed to be a fairly safe bet that the Clippers were not going to make any major changes to their roster. Over the past five years, Elgin Baylor had worked hard to assemble a young team and now a large proportion of this group was about to enter into the prime of their careers. Given that the 1991-92 season had been the most successful in the history of the franchise, conventional wisdom suggested that the Clippers' best move was to make no move at all, allowing their current group of players more time to develop and improve. However, this plan went out the window after Donald Sterling balked at meeting Charles Smith's salary requests when negotiating a new contract.

Smith entered the 1992 off-season as a restricted free agent and he was hoping to stay with the Clippers. Smith was considered to be a crucial component in the team's surge over the second half of the previous season. However, when the time came to negotiate a new deal, Smith was left feeling undervalued by the front office's attempts to low-ball him. So, he made the strategic decision to sign a one year contract extension with the Clippers. This meant that at the end of the 1992-93 season, Smith would be an unrestricted free agent, thus allowing him to sign with whichever team he pleased, which was exactly what he was intending to do. Smith was so displeased with how the contract negotiations had gone that he even sent a letter to the Clippers' front office, outlining his plan to leave at the first available opportunity.

Armed with this information, Baylor was left with little choice but to trade Smith as quickly as possible, to ensure that they were not left empty-handed in twelve months' time. In late September, the Clippers made a trade that brought in two new starters- Mark Jackson and Stanley Roberts. They were hoping that Jackson would be an upgrade over Rivers at the point guard position. Jackson was four years younger than Rivers and had already assembled a fairly impressive resume in his short NBA career- winning the Rookie of the Year award, playing in an All-Star game and leading the Knicks into playoffs in each of his first five seasons in the league.

Whereas the addition of Jackson seemed to make a lot of sense, the second player heading to the Clippers was a slightly more puzzling acquisition. Stanley Roberts was an extremely talented center who often struggled with his weight and conditioning. After enduring five and a half years of Benoit Benjamin, the decision to trade for Roberts was a curious choice to say the least.

Stanley Roberts never went looking for basketball, instead the game found him, the way it always seems to find those who tower above their peers. In fact, Roberts had not shown much interest in playing any sort of sport while growing up in Hopkins, South Carolina. By ninth grade, Roberts was already 6'7" tall and he was soon being pressured into playing for his high school's basketball team. Roberts was not overly keen on the idea, but he did agree to go along to the Alex English basketball camp, which most of the Lower Richland High players were attending. Roberts' performance at the camp was underwhelming and when he returned to school, his grades were so poor that any thoughts of joining the varsity team were put on hold for at least 12 months.

A year later, Roberts was back at the Alex English camp and it was plain for all to see that he had come a long way in a short space of time. In fact, Roberts played so well that his team won the camp championship and he was named camp MVP. This was the start of a three year period where Roberts completely dominated the high school basketball scene in South

Carolina. As a 6'10" junior, Roberts led Lower Richland all the way to the state championship. His play was so impressive that by the end of the season, he was one of the most sought after recruits in the entire country. As Roberts prepared for his senior year, it seemed as if the world was at his feet.

And then, tragedy struck.

On April 21st, 1987, Stanley's older brother, Wayne, was charged with murder after he shot and killed a man. If found guilty, Wayne was facing a life sentence.

While Wayne awaited his day in court, Stanley was trying to continue going about his day-to-day business as best he could. In the summer of 1987, this meant trying to decide which scholarship offer he should accept. Stanley had narrowed his choice to just three schools- LSU, Georgia Tech and the University of South Carolina, which was located less than 15 miles from where the Roberts family lived. And while it might seem that Wayne's legal issues and Stanley's basketball dilemma had little to do with one another, the two matters were about to collide.

Harold Hill, the magistrate who presided over Wayne's preliminary hearing, placed a call to the Roberts' family home to try and persuade Stanley to sign a letter of intent to play for South Carolina. Hill later claimed that he was only calling Stanley as a South Carolina fan. However, Stanley interpreted this phone conversation very differently, believing that Hill was using his position as someone with legal authority in his brother's case to influence his decision.

Not long after this highly unusual phone call was made, Isabella Davis, Stanley and Wayne's mother, claimed that somebody paid a visit to their home and told her that it would be in Wayne's best interests if Stanley attended South Carolina. Davis, who worked at USC as a custodial supervisor, thought that the mystery man was somebody she had previously seen around the South Carolina campus. Authorities investigated these claims but no action was taken, due to the lack of solid evidence.

All of this put the Roberts family under considerable stress. Davis was fearful that Wayne's upcoming court proceedings might be adversely affected if Stanley signed with any other school besides South Carolina and so she tried to convince her youngest son to hold off on announcing his decision until the trial was completed. Ultimately, it was Wayne who convinced Stanley to stand strong. The two boys were sitting at home one night, talking about the uncertain future that lay ahead for both of them when Wayne said, "Look, I made a mistake and it shouldn't affect your life. Go to school where you want. If I go to jail, I go." That night, Stanley called LSU coach Dale Brown and said that he was coming to play for him.

Wayne's murder trial cast a dark cloud that lingered over Stanley's final year at Lower Richland. His mother believed that Stanley had jeopardized his older brother's case by announcing his decision to attend LSU and she didn't speak to him for close to three months. Wayne was ultimately found not guilty by a Richland County jury and Stanley led Lower Richland to another state championship but it was still a year that both brothers would prefer to forget. Stanley spent his final few weeks as a high school student in the company of two FBI agents, who were assigned to keep watch over him amidst fears that there might be some form of retaliation from the friends or family of the man who was shot by Wayne. After receiving his high school diploma, Stanley was whisked away to the airport, where he immediately flew to Baton Rouge to start the next phase of his life.

However, when Roberts arrived in Louisiana, he was unable to play during his freshman year because his grades were below the NCAA-mandated level. The upshot to this was that he would have a full year to adapt to demands of college life without having to worry about his performance on the basketball court. Roberts regained eligibility at the start of his sophomore season and he was joined on LSU's roster by a freshman named Shaquille O'Neal. Together, these two giants formed one of the most imposing frontcourts ever seen in the college game. Not only did LSU have Roberts and O'Neal patrolling the paint, they also featured Mahmoud Abdul-Rauf, a sharp shooting guard who went on to average 14.6 points across an NBA career that spanned over 500 games[134]. However, despite fielding a team with three future NBA stars, LSU struggled throughout the 1989-90 season and were eventually eliminated in second round of the NCAA tournament.

This defeat turned out to be Roberts' final game at LSU. Facing academic problems that could potentially force him to sit out another season, Roberts decided to end his college career and turn professional[135]. There was just one problem- by the time Roberts reached his decision to turn pro, it was too late to declare for the NBA draft. So instead, he headed off to Europe to play for Real Madrid in the Spanish league. Roberts was now away from the supportive environment of college, in a foreign country where he couldn't speak the language and he found this to be a difficult transition. When scouts from the NBA came over to watch him play, they were shocked at his poor conditioning and apparent lack of effort during games. After just one season with Real Madrid, Roberts returned to America in time for the 1991 draft.

Roberts arrived home carrying both the weight of the excess pounds he had put on while in Europe, as well as a growing reputation of someone with a questionable work ethic. In fact, NBA front offices were so put off by what they had seen from Roberts that he eventually slid all the way to the 23rd overall selection, where he was taken by Orlando.

His rookie campaign featured a number of dominant displays that left people wondering just how good a player Roberts could be. Arguably his most impressive performance came in late March when the Magic travelled

---

134 Adbul-Rauf was known at the time as Chris Jackson. He would later change his name after converting to Islam.
135 Roberts finished his brief stay as a Fighting Tiger with averages of 14.1 points on 57.6% shooting, 9.8 rebounds and 1.9 blocks per game.

to Chicago Stadium to take on the defending champion Bulls. This was a game that most people expected Orlando to lose, and early in the fourth quarter, they fell behind by 20 points. And then, just when it looked like the game was over, the Magic stormed back and stole the victory. It was one of the most remarkable comebacks of the season and no player was more instrumental in this unlikely win than Roberts, who scored 10 of his 18 points in the fourth quarter, to go with 9 rebounds and 2 blocks. After the game, both Michael Jordan and Scottie Pippen sought him out to tell him that if he brought his A-game every night, he could be one of the league's truly great players.

The problem for the Magic was that more often than not, Roberts seemed to turn up without his A-game in hand. Magic coach Matt Guokas was shocked when he saw the poor physical condition that Roberts was in when he turned up to training camp. Guokas said, "I've seen a lot of guys come to camp in my 26 years in the NBA, but none have been this bad out of shape." His weight and conditioning remained constant areas of concern throughout the season and Guokas often had to play Roberts fewer minutes than he would have liked, due to his lack of fitness.

If Orlando was sick and tired of searching for ways to motivate Roberts, then the 1992 draft lottery was a godsend. When the Magic won the right to select first, they won the right to draft Shaquille O'Neal. And as soon as Orlando selected O'Neal, Roberts became expendable. When the Magic began shopping Roberts around the league, one of the first teams that expressed interest was the Clippers.

The Clippers believed that in order to take the next step and join the NBA's elite, they needed to have a legitimate center who could match-up against the Olajuwons, Robinsons and Ewings of the league and they were hopeful that Roberts could be that player. In order to get their hands on Roberts, and Mark Jackson, the Clippers traded Charles Smith, Doc Rivers and Bo Kimble to New York and gave a future first round draft pick to

Orlando. At first glance, it seemed like a good trade that would benefit all three teams. The Knicks picked up three promising, young players, the Clippers acquired two new starters and the Magic had managed to turn Stanley Roberts into two first round draft picks[136]

It seemed like a done deal.

And then, it wasn't.

A few months earlier, Stanley Roberts signed an offer sheet with Dallas, only to have Orlando match it and retain his rights. Roberts took this as a sign that he was considered to be an important part of the Magic's plans for the future and so he began house hunting in the Orlando area. When Roberts found a place that he liked, he spoke with Magic general manager Pat Williams, asking if there were any plans to trade him in the near future. Roberts told Williams that if a trade was even a slight possibility, he would not buy the house and instead purchase a smaller apartment. Roberts claimed that Williams offered an assurance that they had no intention of trading him and so he went ahead and bought the house.

Two weeks later, Roberts was shopping with his mother when he got a phone call informing him that he was about to be traded to the Clippers. Roberts felt betrayed. But unlike most NBA players, who have no say in where or when they are traded, Roberts had control over his destiny, courtesy of a clause in his contract that allowed him to block any trade involving him. A disgruntled Roberts notified the Magic of his plans to veto the trade. "I'm staying (in Orlando) this year," a defiant Roberts told the media. "Whether they play me or hold this against me, that's fine."

---

[136] The Clippers gave Orlando their 1994 pick, while the Knicks threw in their 1993 first round selection.

Initially it looked as if Roberts had effectively killed off the trade but, over the next few weeks, his stance softened. Roberts flew out to Los Angeles and met with Larry Brown, who told him that he was a big part of the Clippers' plans for the upcoming season. At the same time that the Clippers were trying to woo Roberts, the Magic were doing everything in their power to try and shove him out the door. "Orlando told me straight out that they were going to sit me on the bench and let my career die," Roberts said. Faced with the prospect of staying where he was with a team that clearly didn't want him or going to Los Angeles, where he looked set to be a crucial player on an emerging team, Roberts acquiesced and allowed the trade to go ahead.

The acquisition of Roberts was seen as a huge gamble by most pundits around the league. He arrived in Los Angeles with a five year, $17.2 million contract that did not contain *any* weight-related incentive clauses. Baylor chose to address comparisons being made between the Clippers new center and Benoit Benjamin, telling the press that Roberts deserved to be judged by his own performances.

After this blockbuster trade was finally completed, the Clippers headed into the new season with a roster that looked very different from the team that played Game 5 in Salt Lake City just six months earlier. In all, there were seven new faces, including Jackson and Roberts who were both set to become part of Larry Brown's starting line-up. Given the team's excellent form at the end of the previous season, this roster shake-up was clearly a risky move. The Clippers front office was hoping that their two new starters would prove to be the missing pieces required for the franchise to become a legitimate championship contender.

Season XV: 1992-93

The new-look Clippers got off to a great start, winning 12 of their first 19 games, including victories over both Phoenix and New York- the only two teams who went on to win 60 games that season. No player was more crucial to this early success than Mark Jackson, who was averaging 15.5 points, 9.5 assists, 5.3 rebounds and 2.2 steals per game. But while Jackson was playing just as the Clippers had envisioned he would when they traded for him, Stanley Roberts was proving to be less of a success story.

Roberts turned up to training camp weighing somewhere around 310 pounds, which was approximately 17 pounds heavier than his playing weight in Orlando. It was clear that this extra weight was affecting his ability to contribute to the team's on-court efforts. In fact, Larry Brown was often forced to restrict Roberts' minutes, in order to ensure that he could keep up with the play when he was on the floor. "He would make three trips down court and look over at me to get him out," said Brown. Despite the fact that Roberts was the team's starting center, he averaged less than 16 minutes per game across the first month of the season, while also contributing just 6.7 points and 3.1 rebounds[137].

Unfortunately for the Clippers, the first five weeks of the season turned out to be their best stretch of basketball for the entire 1992-93 campaign. From the outside, their early good form may have created the impression that the team was starting to gel, but just beneath the surface, problems were brewing. And nothing brings the internal issues of a basketball team into the light faster than a string of defeats.

---

137 Years later, it was discovered that Stanley Roberts suffered from exercise induced asthma, a condition that had gone undiagnosed for the majority of his career. "This weight thing had followed me from LSU," Roberts said. "My weight was pretty much on target but the problem was when I got in the game, my asthma kicked in within the first ten minutes. My lungs locked up and I couldn't breathe. So in their eyes, I wasn't in shape. Once they labelled me, it just followed me." And while it is true that Roberts spent most of his time in the NBA battling to keep his weight from ballooning, it is also clear that trying to play with undiagnosed asthma would have greatly affected his ability to make it up and down the floor and thus is likely to have impacted on people's perception of his general fitness.

On December 15th, the Clippers lost to the Warriors in Oakland. The following night, they played the Warriors back in Los Angeles. Again they lost. Then they lost in Seattle. And in Boston. And Indiana. The Clippers were losing games all across America. Between the middle of December and the first week of January the Clippers lost seven out of the eleven games that they played. And as the defeats began to mount, the tensions that had previously been hidden from the public eye quickly started to come out into the open. At the center of this disharmony were the two people whom the Clippers could least afford to have a public falling out-Larry Brown and Danny Manning.

The Clippers might have been playing some of their worst basketball for the season but on an individual level, Manning was in the best form of his career. So it came as quite a shock in early January when Manning was informed by Brown that he was being moved out of the starting line-up for their game against the Pistons. Manning had just scored 30 points in two consecutive games for the first time in his career, making his demotion even more puzzling. The Clippers eventually lost to the Pistons, with Manning playing 24 minutes, 11 below his season average. This defeat brought the Clippers' record to just a single win above .500 and it was followed by one of those players-only meetings that teams tend to hold when their season is collapsing around them. When Ron Harper was asked to describe the tone of the discussion amongst the players, he replied, "Blunt, nasty, rude, disgusting, frustrating."

The Clippers were dealing with a number of issues, the most concerning of which was the strained relationship between Brown and Manning. Despite the shared history between the two men, it was becoming increasingly clear that neither one was particularly enjoying working with the other. Manning had long believed that Brown's coaching style was both relentless and excessively negative. He had been prepared to put up with it while he was a college student but did not want to spend his professional career being shouted at. During the 1992-93 season, Brown publically questioned both Manning's defensive play and his leadership qualities.

The volatile relationship between the two men reached a boiling point in a Milwaukee hotel lobby during an east coast road trip. Passers-by looked on in shock as Brown and Manning stood nose to nose, loudly arguing with one another. Brown told Manning he was sick of his poor on-court effort, while Manning said he had put up with enough of Brown's pessimistic approach.

Any doubts about just how bad this relationship had become were quickly erased when Manning asked to be traded. Manning's agent, Ron Grinker, said the main reason his client wanted to play for another team was due to the lack of rapport between the star forward and his coach. Grinker called the relationship "irreconcilable", before adding that Manning felt "he has no future with the team." Manning said he was not trying to make Brown lose his job, he just felt that they had been together for "too long." Manning was so keen to get out of L.A. that he even offered to restructure his contract in order to help facilitate a trade. Brown denied there was a communication problem with Manning and said that the trade request would have no impact on how he approached his job.

Then, two days after Manning announced that he wanted out of Los Angeles, he changed his mind and told the media that he no longer wanted to be traded. Manning said his trade request was nothing more than a frustrated player speaking out after a loss.

This sudden change of heart far from resolved the issue from the perspective of the Clippers' front office. Manning's rookie contract was due to expire at the end of the season and thus far, he had shown no interest in signing a long-term extension. In fact, Grinker had been pretty clear about his client's intentions to do exactly what Charles Smith had done prior to being traded; sign a one year extension with the Clippers, which would allow him to walk out the door as an unrestricted free agent 12 months later. So, when Manning said that he did not want to be traded, he was actually only committing to the franchise for another season and a half.

Larry Brown expressed the exasperation that was felt by many members in the Clippers' front office when he said, "I don't know what that means, he doesn't want to be traded. Does that mean he wants to be here forever?" The Clippers soon found out that it did not. When Elgin Baylor met with both Manning and Grinker the day after the trade demand was retracted, Manning told the Clippers' general manager that he was sticking with his original plan of only signing a one year extension.

Unfortunately for Brown, Manning was just one of many players whose future with the Clippers was very much up in the air. In total there were five members of the regular rotation, four of whom were starters, who could potentially leave at the end of the current season[138]. Brown believed that having so many players heading into free agency was having a detrimental impact on the team. When negotiating new contracts, both agents and team management will often use a player's statistics as a starting point for determining salary. Therefore, players who are about to become free agents can sometimes develop a selfish mentality, where their primary focus becomes accumulating individual statistics rather than playing the role that their team needs them to play.

Brown's preference was for management to either make a commitment and re-sign the players in question or trade them. With neither of these two options occurring, and the trade deadline fast approaching, the Clippers continued to play an increasingly mediocre brand of basketball.

Behind the scenes, the front office was desperately trying to move Manning before the trading deadline passed. But in spite of his obvious

---

138 The five Clippers on the verge of free agency were Ken Norman, Danny Manning, Ron Harper, Mark Jackson and Gary Grant.

talents, it was proving difficult to find a suitable deal. The major sticking point was the fact that Manning's contract was due to expire at the end of the current season. So while the Clippers were asking for major assets in exchange for Manning, other general managers were understandably cautious. They did not want to trade away their own franchise players for someone who might only stick around for a few months. The Clippers spoke to Charlotte, Phoenix, Minnesota and Dallas but in each case, the other team did not want to go through with a trade unless Manning was willing to commit to a new contract- something that he was reluctant to do.

In early February, Manning was selected as an All-Star for the first time in his career. He was also the first Clipper to play in the league's showcase event since Marques Johnson's appearance back in 1986. Manning performed well in his All-Star debut, scoring 10 points on perfect 5 for 5 shooting from the field. Just a couple of days after the All-Star break, the trading deadline passed and despite months of speculation about a variety of possible transactions, the Clippers were unable to swing a deal.

This left Larry Brown fuming.

Brown knew that the Clippers' inability to move any of their soon-to-be-free-agents meant that the feelings of uncertainty amongst the players would linger for the remainder of the season. Brown made his displeasure about the situation known by lashing out in the media. He accused the franchise of having no long-term plan, saying that nobody knew which players they were aiming to retain and which ones they were happy to let leave. He also claimed that no one was sure who was responsible for making these types of decisions. Brown believed that there was a perception around the league that the Clippers "don't take care of their own," which made it highly likely that the five free agents in question would walk as soon as they got the chance.

When play resumed after the All-Star break, the Clippers' players came up with a plan that was designed to help the team to break out of their funk. In an attempt to change their luck, they decided that they were going to switch from wearing their regulation black sneakers to white ones. In the short term, this wardrobe change produced results, with the team winning their first two games in white sneakers. However, this was followed by another horrid stretch in which the Clippers lost seven of eight, leaving them just three and a half games ahead of the ninth-placed Nuggets and in danger of missing the playoffs altogether. This prompted more discussion from the players about the merits of switching back to black shoes. Lester Conner, a ten year NBA veteran who had recently signed with the Clippers as a free agent, overheard this debate about shoe colors and offered the team some timely advice, "Why don't we just start playing harder?"

The Clippers eventually finished the season with a 41-41 record, a four game drop on their win total from the previous season but still good enough for them to squeeze into the playoffs for the second year in a row. However, while the Clippers were undoubtedly happy to qualify for the post-season, their lower-than-expected seeding meant that they once again faced a match-up with one of the Western Conference's elite teams. This time around, it was the up-and-coming Houston Rockets who were waiting for them in the first round.

The Clippers had played the Rockets four times during the regular season and lost on each occasion. No single player had more influence in these four games than Hakeem Olajuwon, who was widely regarded as the best center in the entire league. If the Clippers were going to have any chance of causing an upset, they would have to find a way of curtailing Olajuwon's impact.

THE PLAYOFFS: ROUND 1 VS. HOUSTON

The series began ominously for the Clippers, with Houston cruising to a 117-94 victory in Game 1. The ease of the win was largely attributable to the Clippers' poor defense, which allowed the Rockets to convert 62.7% of their field goal attempts. In fact, Houston forward Carl Herrera even commented on the lack of intensity from the Clippers during a post-game interview. The Rockets were led by Olajuwon, who completely dominated the Clippers' frontline to finish with 28 points, 11 rebounds, 6 assists, 4 steals and 9 blocked shots.

Compounding the bad news for the Clippers was a knee injury suffered by Ron Harper which limited him to just 16 minutes of action. After the game, the team doctor speculated that it was unlikely that Harper would be able to take part in Game 2. With news that Harper was likely to be sidelined, not many experts were predicting that the Clippers would secure the franchise's first road playoff victory in Game 2, yet this is exactly what they did. And it was not hard to pinpoint the two reasons for the dramatic turnaround in form.

One was defense.

The other was Ron Harper.

Through aggressive trapping and double-teaming of Olajuwon in the post, the Clippers held the Rockets to just 31.5% shooting from the field, approximately half what they had shot in Game 1. Houston finished the game having connected on just 23 field goals, an astoundingly low number[139]. At one stage, the Rockets went almost seven minutes without scoring from the field, a stretch that Brown called the "best minutes of defense this team has ever played." On offense, the Clippers were led by a player who most fans expected to see sitting at the end of the bench wearing street clothes. Harper spent a large proportion of the 48 hours between Game 1 and Game 2 getting treatment on his injured knee and it responded well enough to allow him to play. He finished with 29 points, 6 rebounds, 4 blocks and 3 steals.

---

139 At the time, this was tied for the fewest field goals made by an NBA team in a playoff game, since the 1963-64 season, when this statistic was first collected.

It was a confident Clippers' team that flew back to Los Angeles to play Games 3 and 4. They had won nine of their past 10 games at the Sports Arena and they knew that if they could hold serve and win the next two games at home, they would be heading to the second round. Brown decided against holding a practice session on Sunday, the off-day between Games 2 and 3, due to the fact that the team had arrived from Houston late on Saturday evening. However, the players talked amongst themselves and decided that they wanted to practice, so a light 45 minute shoot-around was scheduled. In 16 months, the team had gone from holding a players-only meeting in order to cancel a scheduled practice against their coach's wishes, to asking for an extra practice session to be organized when they had been given the day off.

Unfortunately the extra work on the practice floor did not pay off. The Clippers were soundly defeated in Game 3, handing home-court advantage back to the Rockets. The Clippers' main problem was the limited contribution from Stanley Roberts. He played just seven minutes in the first half, due to foul trouble and the Clippers headed into the break trailing by 15 points. Brown started Roberts at the beginning of the third period and it took him just 16 seconds to pick up his fourth foul. A little over two minutes later, he had his fifth. Roberts eventually fouled out after playing less than 18 minutes. He finished the game with 0 points, 5 rebounds and 0 blocks, while Olajuwon had 32 points, 12 boards and 4 blocked shots, as the Rockets cruised to a 111-99 victory.

Game 4 marked the resurrection of Stanley Roberts. The same player who had been so ineffective in Game 3, finished Game 4 with 20 points, 13 rebounds and 2 blocks. The primary reason for this rapid increase in production was a defensive switch made by the Clippers' coaching staff that allowed Roberts to stay out of foul trouble. Instead of trying to guard Olajuwon, Roberts spent most of the game covering Rockets power forward Otis Thorpe. This left Manning with the monster task of trying to contain

Olajuwon. Manning managed to somewhat restrict Olajuwon to 25 points, his lowest scoring output for the series.

The game was close throughout and was ultimately decided at the free throw line. Mark Jackson broke a 90-all deadlock with 33 seconds remaining when he sank one out of two from the charity stripe. On the next possession, the Rockets had three separate opportunities to score the winning basket but all three attempts missed. With six seconds remaining, Jackson snared the elusive defensive rebound and was fouled again. This time he calmly converted both free throws and, when a desperate three point attempt from Scott Brooks missed the hoop altogether, the Clippers walked away with a 93-90 win, sending the series back to Houston for Game 5.

Across the first four games of the Clippers-Rockets series, Vernon Maxwell had played a total of six minutes, due to a broken wrist sustained at the end of the regular season. Maxwell, Houston's second leading scorer and the team's best perimeter shooter, was forced to spend the first three games of the playoffs watching from the bench. In Game 4, he wrapped up his wrist and valiantly tried to return but was largely ineffective, converting just one of his three field goal attempts during the six minutes that he spent on the floor. However, this minimal contribution over the first four games of the series was not enough to silence Maxwell. In the lead-up to Game 5, he proclaimed that the Rockets were going to "kick the Clippers' butts" in the series decider.

With a little over a minute remaining in Game 5, Maxwell's brash comments were beginning to look increasingly foolish. He had thus far missed 11 of his 14 field goal attempts, including a woeful 1 for 7 from three-point range. After Ron Harper's running scoop shot went in, the Rockets found themselves trailing by a point and in desperate need of a score. However on the next Houston possession, the Clippers once again played excellent defense and it looked like the Rockets were going to struggle to get a reasonable look at the basket. With just six seconds remaining on the shot clock, Kenny Smith drove down the right hand side of the lane and kicked the ball out to Maxwell, who was stationed behind the three-point arc, directly in front of the Clippers' bench.

A less confident player might have looked to swing the ball to the teammate who was having a better game. After all, Maxwell was shooting just 14% from three point range. But of all the issues that Vernon Maxwell had to deal with throughout his career, a lack of belief in his own abilities was not one of them. Smith's pass was a little low, forcing Maxwell to reach below his waist to catch it. Once the ball was in his hands, he shot it without hesitating.

It hit nothing but the bottom of the net.

Rockets up two. Fifty-six seconds remaining.

The onus was now on the Clippers to find a way to answer Maxwell's dagger or face the prospect of an immediate end to their season. The ball went down low to Roberts, who drew a crowd of players and passed to Jackson, who was wide open for a straight on three. However, rather than take the open shot, Jackson drove into the lane and threw up a contested floater that missed.

Throwing caution to the wind, all five Clippers players charged into the paint, desperately trying to secure the offensive rebound. But as the ball came off the glass, it was controlled by Otis Thorpe, who quickly threw an outlet pass. With no Clipper in a position to rotate back and play transition defense, Kenny Smith sailed in for the easiest two points you will ever see in the final minute of a close playoff game.

Rockets up four.

The Clippers attempted five three-pointers in the final 34 seconds of the game, none of which went in, and the Rockets held on for a nail-biting 84-80 victory. For the second consecutive year, the Clippers had narrowly been defeated in a series-deciding game against a Western Conference powerhouse. And no Clipper had performed better in the hostile surroundings of The Summit than Danny Manning, who finished with 24 points and 12 rebounds.

As he had done 12 months earlier in Salt Lake City, Larry Brown spoke of how proud he was of his team's efforts. "We've been through a lot this year," said Brown. "A lot of it hasn't been really nice or fun, but the effort (over) the last part of the season and what happened in the playoffs meant a lot to a lot of people. I just wish we could have gotten it done. This franchise needs something good to happen." If something good was to happen to the Clippers organization, Brown was not going to be around to be a part of it. The final chapter of the 1992-93 season centered on Brown's swift and controversial departure from the City of Angels.

Speculation that Larry Brown would not be coaching the Clippers for the 1993-94 season began almost as soon as the buzzer sounded at the end of Game 5 in Houston. These rumors were initially dismissed by Brown as having no merit. What happened next depends on whether you believe Brown's version of events or the account provided by Clipper management.

The Clippers' story went something like this- a week after the team was eliminated from the playoffs, Brown met with the front office to discuss trade prospects, free agents and potential draft picks for the upcoming season. Nothing Brown said or did at this meeting gave anyone from the Clippers the slightest inkling that this would be his last official act as the franchise's head coach. Brown then headed to Hawaii for his end-of-season vacation. While Brown was holidaying, he had his agent call the Clippers to inform them that he was resigning, despite the fact that he still had two years remaining on his contract.

According to Brown, the Clippers should not have been surprised by his resignation, as he told Donald Sterling and Elgin Baylor three months earlier that he was going to step down once the season was over. Brown said that this conversation took place shortly after the passing of the trading deadline, when he was feeling frustrated by the front office's inability to either sign or trade any of the Clippers' impending free agents. Brown claimed that Sterling responded by offering him a lifetime contract, which was enough to smooth things over at the time. However, when this lifetime deal never materialized at the conclusion of the season, Brown simply followed through on his original plan to resign[140].

Despite the continued presence of a variety of off-court dramas, including yet another search for a new head coach, the Clippers remained hopeful that their time as professional sport's longest running joke might be over. However, any thoughts that the Clippers were on the verge of becoming a legitimate NBA contender did not last very long. The 1993-94 edition was a return to more familiar territory. The Clippers, as fans across America had come to know them, were well and truly back.

---

140 Less than three weeks after turning his back on the Clippers, Brown was unveiled as the Pacers' new head coach.

CHAPTER 10

Things Fall Apart

"I don't want my career to end like this."

MARK JACKSON

As THE REST OF HIS teammates were being put through their paces at the Clippers 1993 training camp, Danny Manning sat on the sidelines with his left knee heavily wrapped in ice. At first glance, this appeared to be a worrisome scene. Manning had already missed almost 12 months of action just a few seasons back due to an injured right knee. The last thing the Clippers needed was for him to start having troubles with his left. But, as the saying goes, looks can sometimes be deceiving.

It turns out there was absolutely nothing wrong with Manning. In fact, he was feeling fantastic. The ice was nothing more than a prop, part of a ruse to throw the media off the scent of the real reason why the star forward was being held out of practice on that Friday morning. Manning was not out on court because he was about to be traded to Miami and all parties involved didn't want a last minute injury to jeopardize the deal. After five long years, he was finally getting what he wanted. Danny Manning was leaving the Los Angeles Clippers.

A few months earlier, it looked like the Clippers may have been able to hang on to Manning. At the conclusion of the Houston playoff series, and after five years of consistently saying that he was planning on leaving the franchise as soon as he could, Manning appeared to have a sudden change of heart. When asked if he would consider signing a new deal with the Clippers, Manning said it was a possibility. "I've been here five years," Manning said. "It's gotten better. I'd like to be part of something good with this organization."

In June, the Clippers offered Manning a five year contract worth around $26 million, which would have made him the fourth highest paid player in the NBA, behind only David Robinson, Patrick Ewing and Shaquille O'Neal. Even Ron Grinker called the Clippers' offer "very, very generous." However, if Manning was to re-sign with the Clippers, he was not only concerned with his financial position, he also wanted to be sure that the franchise was committed to fielding a winning team. Manning spoke to Clipper management about a number of issues that he wanted them to address, including securing a regular practice facility, re-signing Ken Norman and Ron Harper to long-term deals and seriously exploring the option of moving to Anaheim and making the recently constructed Honda Center the team's new home court[141]. "There were a couple of things that I wanted them to do," Manning said. "Sterling came back with, 'You sign first and then we'll take care of all those things.' So that was that."

Manning rejected the five year offer, saying it was not about money but that he wanted to play "in a place where I feel we're all moving in the right direction." Grinker took the opportunity to re-state that his client was planning on sticking to his initial plan of signing a one year qualifying offer, which would allow him to become an unrestricted free agent at the end of the 1993-94 season. True to their word, Manning and Grinker flew to Los Angeles and signed a one year extension on July 1st. The good news was that Manning was going to be suiting up for the Clippers for another year. The

---

141 See Chapter Eleven for the full story of the Clippers' flirtation with the City of Anaheim.

bad news was that Manning had clearly indicated that he was deadly serious about walking out at the end of the upcoming season. And when Grinker began making public comments about teaching the Clippers a lesson, the chances of Manning remaining in Los Angeles seemed to be slimmer than Manute Bol's forearms.

Faced with the prospect of losing Manning to free agency without any compensation, the Clippers began looking at trade options. They spoke with a number of teams before settling on a deal with Miami, who agreed to send Glen Rice and Willie Burton to the Clippers in exchange for Manning. Given that everyone in the league knew that the Clippers were desperately trying to trade Manning, this was a very good deal. Rice was one of the league's best outside shooters and he looked to be a perfect fit for a Clippers team that was badly in need of help in this area[142].

As Manning sat on the side of the court at UC Irvine, the venue for the Clippers' 1993 training camp, he was excited about becoming the newest member of the Heat. His bags were packed and he had said his goodbyes to his teammates. After leaving the campus, Manning planned on taking the short drive to John Wayne Airport, where he had a first class seat booked on the 11:05am flight to Miami. The Heat were scheduled to play an exhibition match that evening and they were hoping to introduce Manning to their fans during this game.

And then they changed their minds.

Exactly who "they" refers to depends on whose version of events you to choose to believe. Grinker claimed that "they" was actually just Donald Sterling, who pulled the plug on the trade because he was convinced that Manning would eventually come to his senses and sign a long-term deal with

---

[142] Over the previous two seasons, the Clippers converted a grand total of just 287 three-pointers. Meanwhile, Glen Rice knocked in 303 all by himself, making him the only NBA player to crack the 300 barrier during this time.

the Clippers. "I was in the training room and Sterling came in," Manning recalled. "He looked at me and said, 'I'm not trading you.'"

According to the Clippers, the last minute decision to back out of the trade was made by an "executive committee" consisting of Sterling, Elgin Baylor and new Clipper coach, Bob Weiss. They claim that Manning spoke with this trio just prior to the deal being finalized and offered them a glimmer of hope that he might consider remaining with the franchise. "Danny said, 'Well, I don't know if I really want to go,'" recalled Weiss. "I don't know if his mind was made up, he was in a state of flux." Apparently, this was enough for the Clippers to cancel the trade.

Regardless of who decided to kill it, the trade was officially dead, meaning that Manning was still a Clipper. Grinker described his client as "comatose" upon hearing this news. Grinker went on to say that the Clippers had butchered their "last opportunity to get something in return for Danny," promising that his client would no longer co-operate with any potential trades that the franchise was pursuing. This stance effectively made it impossible for the Clippers to get a reasonable return for Manning, as any team that was considering trading for him would want some assurance that he would commit to them for longer than the one year that was remaining on his current contract.

Unfortunately for the Clippers, Manning was not the only star player who was heading into the new campaign less than thrilled to still be playing for the team. Ron Harper was also back for another season, after the Clippers agreed to pick up his option year at a cost of $4 million, thus making him the NBA's equal highest paid guard, along with Michael Jordan. One might expect that receiving such a generous salary would have made Harper a happy man.

It did not.

Harper publically complained about not receiving a long-term deal and issued the front office an ultimatum- sign me to a contract extension before training camp is over or watch me walk out the door at the end of the season. When Baylor was asked about Harper's demand, he said he believed that it would be sorted out before the end of training camp.

It was not.

With no new contract forthcoming, Harper entered the new campaign feeling disgruntled. And as the season progressed, he would make sure that the world knew just how much he hated playing for the Los Angeles Clippers.

One Clipper who did receive a long-term contract offer during the 1993 off-season was Ken Norman. Norman was presented with a $13 million, five year contract, a good deal for a player of his stature and one that he was tempted to accept. But, having waited six years to become an unrestricted free agent, Norman wanted to see what type of salary he could attract on the open market.

The highest bidder for Norman's services turned out to be Milwaukee, who offered a six year deal valued at just under $16 million. For Norman, this was simply too good an offer to refuse. Unlike many other departing Clippers, Norman had nothing but nice things to say about the organization. Upon announcing his decision to join the Bucks, Norman said that the Clippers had been great to him and that he loved the franchise "like a father."

Baylor did manage to have some success in retaining free agents, signing both of the team's point guards to multi-year deals prior to the start of the 1993-94 season. Mark Jackson was rewarded for an excellent first season with the Clippers with a five year, $13 million contract extension. Across the 1992-93 season, Jackson played in all 82 games and surpassed his career averages for points, assists, rebounds, steals, blocks and both field goal and free throw percentage. The Clippers also gave Gary Grant a two year deal that paid him a little over $1 million per season.

When all was said and done, four of the Clippers' five potential free agents were returning to play for the franchise which, at first glance, seems like a fairly positive result. However, with their best two players, Manning and Harper, clearly displeased and most likely playing out their final 82 games in Clipper uniforms, it did not bode well for a happy and harmonious season ahead.

Season XVI: 1993-94

Larry Brown's departure meant that the Clippers were heading into the 1993-94 season with yet another new coach. And the man who eventually got the position was clearly not the franchise's first choice. In fact, it appeared that Bob Weiss was not even their second or third preference. But ultimately, Weiss was willing to take the job and thus he would be the one calling the shots from the sidelines. There was a period of approximately six weeks between when Weiss was first interviewed for the position and when he was actually appointed. During this time, the Clippers pursued a number of the big names in the coaching world, including Hubie Brown, Lenny Wilkens and Rick Pitino, before finally settling for Weiss.

At the press conference to announce his appointment, Weiss was asked about how it felt to know that he was not the team's first choice. He responded by saying that his wife had been on a couple of dates before she asked him to marry her. "That marriage has worked out well," said Weiss, "and I don't see why the same thing won't happen here[143]."

---

143 Elgin Baylor was slightly less tactful when dealing with the curly question of why it had taken so long to appoint Weiss, simply refusing to answer it.

Weiss had a long history of working in the NBA, dating all the way back to the 1960s. As a player, he carved out a 12 year career as a journeyman point guard. His greatest success came in the 1966-67 season, when he won an NBA championship as a bench player with the Philadelphia 76ers. After he retired from playing, Weiss had stints as an assistant coach in Buffalo, Dallas and San Diego, where he was part of Gene Shue's staff in the Clippers' inaugural season. In 1986, Weiss was given his first opportunity as a head coach, taking over for Cotton Fitzsimmons in San Antonio and coaching the Spurs for two years. Next, he moved on to Atlanta, where he was in charge of the Hawks for another three seasons. Stylistically, Weiss had a very different approach to Larry Brown. He was renowned for his sharp sense of humor, an ability to build good relationships with players and adopting a fairly laid back approach.

Weiss' first few weeks in charge went reasonably well, with the Clippers finishing November with a 6-6 record that could have been even better had it not been for a number of narrow defeats. However, any sense of optimism that may have been lingering around the team did not last very long. On December 4th, the Lakers travelled to the Sports Arena and early in the first half, disaster struck the home team. Stanley Roberts had just pulled down his fourth offensive rebound of the game and was about to elevate for a dunk when he heard a loud pop and collapsed to the floor. The diagnosis was not good. Roberts had completely ruptured his right Achilles tendon, ruling him out for the remainder of the season. Without the services of their starting center, it didn't take long for the Clippers to lose touch with the playoff race. By the end of December, it seemed like Weiss was only a few steps away from having a full-scale mutiny on his hands.

After suffering a 13 point defeat against Milwaukee at home, Ron Harper was no longer able to contain his feelings about playing for the embattled franchise. "Smell it," he said. "We stink, point blank. We stink. Ain't no way to hide it." Harper then offered his novel suggestion that the franchise should cease hosting home games. When prompted on why this would be a good idea, he responded, "Do *you* like driving down here every day?" Harper was asked if he was referring to the Sports Arena. He replied, "It's everything. We got a lot of bullshit we just don't like as players. I don't care how many nice planes you fly on or nice hotels you stay at, there's still something that stinks." Even by Clipper standards, Harper's remarks were unprecedented. During his post-game comments, he made at least six references to the Clippers stinking. This was the same organization that was paying him $4 million a year to play basketball[144].

The problem for Weiss was that Harper was not alone in sharing his exasperation with the current state of affairs. After the Bucks loss, Mark Jackson said, "We have a bunch of problems and if it's going to stay this way then get me out of here." Weiss received the award for understatement of the evening when he added, "Right now, we're very fragile."

Three nights later, the Clippers travelled to Oakland and were completely embarrassed by the Warriors, falling behind by 50 points before finally losing by 46. Harper once again provided some choice quotes for the media, saying that the game was like a "YMCA team (playing) against a very good team." However, rather than using their time in the locker room to quietly reflect on this horrendous result, the players loudly laughed and joked like old friends at a high school reunion. All of this took place within earshot of a frustrated and disappointed coaching staff.

Clearly somebody needed to take action if the Clippers had any chance of salvaging something from what was fast becoming one of the more farcical seasons in franchise history. After another embarrassing defeat, this time in Portland, Weiss decided that he had seen enough and announced that the Clippers would be taking advantage of a small break in the schedule to convene a mid-season training camp. And while the

---

[144] At the time, Harper was averaging 18 points and 3.5 assists per game while being paid at the same rate as Michael Jordan. One could easily have formed the opinion that a player in such a position would have been wiser to keep his opinions to himself and concentrate his energies on justifying his substantial salary.

three-day camp was well-intentioned, it had little tangible impact on the team's play. The Clippers opened the New Year by losing their first five games by an average margin of 14 points, dropping their overall record to 11-21.

In February, the franchise finally got some good news when Manning became the first Clipper selected to play in consecutive All-Star games. And for the second year in a row, Manning performed well against the best of the best, contributing 8 points in 17 minutes. This All-Star recognition should have been a ray of sunshine in an otherwise grey and gloomy season but when Manning arrived back in Los Angeles, it too morphed into another controversy.

The All-Star game was played on a Sunday evening in Minneapolis and the Clippers had booked Manning on a flight back to California early Monday morning, to ensure that he would be able to practice with the team that same afternoon. But after arriving home, Manning decided that he was feeling tired and did not want to fight the notorious Los Angeles traffic, so he skipped practice. To make matters worse, he failed to inform anyone from the coaching staff that he was giving himself the day off. When Harper, who had spent the past few days visiting family in Ohio, also failed to attend, Weiss realized that he had to take some sort of a stand.

The next night, the two Clippers stars dressed and prepared to play against the Lakers, but despite being in uniform, Manning and Harper did not take to the court for a single minute of action. Weiss decided to hold both players out of the game as a penalty for skipping the previous day's practice session. The rest of the team responded with a stirring 100-89 victory and after the game, Manning and Harper left quickly without making any comments about their unofficial suspension.

If there were any doubts about how the pair was feeling about Weiss' disciplinary action, they were cleared up the very next day.

Both players returned to the starting line-up for the team's clash with Utah and while Manning played reasonably well, Harper turned in a clunker, finishing with just 4 points on 1 for 7 shooting. After the game, Harper unleashed one of the more bizarre analogies ever heard in the history of professional sports, comparing playing for the Clippers to serving time in jail. "In about 65 or 70 more days," Harper said, "I'll be out on… good behavior[145]." When Harper was asked how someone could compare earning a salary of $4 million for playing basketball to being incarcerated, he responded, "Jail time is jail time, no matter how much you're getting, right?"

The subject of getting benched for the Lakers game was brought up and Harper said that he enjoyed his day off, adding that the fans were the ones who had been cheated, as they had missed out on seeing him play. He then accused the Clippers of changing the team rule relating to whether you had to attend practice if you were sick. However, when quizzed on whether a medical condition had prevented him from turning up to Monday's session he replied, "No, I was healthy. I just missed my flight and I don't feel sorry I missed it." The Clippers were furious that their highest paid player was comparing his employment with the franchise to a prison sentence. They promptly suspended him for one game without pay, costing him almost $50,000 in lost salary.

Harper sat out the Clippers' loss at home to the Hawks and then returned to play against Utah the following evening. In his first game back from suspension, he produced his best individual performance for the season, finishing with 30 points and 10 rebounds. However, it was still not enough to secure a victory, with the Clippers eventually losing by 7. After the game, Harper began implementing his latest public relations strategy, the "if-you-haven't-got-anything-nice-to-say-about-somebody-don't-say-anything-at-all" policy. He was asked a range of questions relating to the team's decision

---

145 At the time, there was exactly 67 days remaining in the regular season, demonstrating just how keen Harper was to escape Clipper-land.

to suspend him and he offered the single word reply of "whatever" to each and every one.

When the conversation moved to other topics, Harper did open up and provide some more expansive answers. One reporter inquired about what he did while he was suspended and Harper replied, "None of your business." Someone else asked whether he had tuned in to watch his teammates play against the Hawks. Harper said, "No, I watched Shaquille (O'Neal). He was awesome." For the rest of the season, Harper answered any questions from the media with the same single word response: "Whatever[146]." And while he may have been acting like a petulant child, at least he was no longer publically criticizing the franchise.

In the final week of February, the long-running soap opera of Danny Manning and the Los Angeles Clippers finally came to an end, when he was traded to Atlanta in exchange for Dominique Wilkins. At first glance, this move seemed to be a puzzling one from the Hawks' perspective. At the time, Atlanta had the best record in the Eastern Conference and Wilkins was arguably the most beloved figure in the franchise's history. However, like Manning, Wilkins was in the final year of his current contract and was also about to become an unrestricted free agent, where he was hoping to receive one final big pay day. But, while Hawks' management was keen for Wilkins to finish his career with the franchise, they were not prepared to offer him the kind of long-term, lucrative deal that he was after. So, they began shopping him around the league. However, they quickly discovered that there was not too much interest in a 34 year old former high-flyer who was in the twilight of his career. In fact, the only team that presented any sort of serious offer was the Clippers. When Manning's name was mentioned as a possible piece in exchange for Wilkins, the Hawks were immediately excited. They

---

[146] Harper was so impressed with this innovative way of dealing with the press that he distributed custom-made t-shirts to the rest of his teammates with the word "Whatever" printed across the front.

loved Manning's unselfishness and believed that he would be a nice fit for their emerging roster.

Manning probably offered the best summary of his time with Clippers, labeling it "bittersweet". Sweet because no one had achieved more in a Clipper uniform than Danny Manning had. He was selected for two All-Star games, led the team to consecutive playoff appearances and along the way, became the franchise's all-time leading scorer. The bitterness was due to a variety of factors: a serious knee injury, an overall losing record, the team never being able to win a playoff series and the constant tension between Manning and the Clippers' front office. As Manning was leaving Los Angeles, he said he felt relieved that his time as a Clipper had finally come to an end.

With no real chance to make the playoffs, the final two months of the 1993-94 season became little more than an opportunity for Clipper fans to watch Dominique Wilkins do what he did best- score lots of points. And Wilkins did not disappoint, finishing the Clippers' phase of his season with an average of over 29 points per game. Wilkins' good individual form mattered little though, as the Clippers' overall winning percentage remained virtually unchanged.

The final game of the season was an embarrassing kick in the guts for a team that was already sprawled on the canvas. San Antonio arrived at the Sports Arena for a clash that had no impact on the playoff picture, with the Spurs having already secured fourth spot in the Western Conference and the Clippers out of the playoff race months ago. The only story of any interest was the race between David Robinson and Shaquille O'Neal for the league's scoring title. Heading into the final day of the regular season, O'Neal had a 0.06 edge on Robinson. But Robinson held a valuable ace up his sleeve- the Spurs' final game of the season was a clash with the Clippers.

This proved to be the decisive factor in determining the winner of the scoring crown.

The Spurs-Clippers match-up was so lacking in intensity that, at times, it barely resembled a professional sporting contest. From the opening tip, it was clear that San Antonio's sole focus was trying to help Robinson secure the scoring title. It was also evident that the Clippers were not going to offer very much in way of resistance. Robinson shot the ball early and often, scoring his team's first 18 points. He added just 6 more in the second period, before picking up the pace in the third, scoring another 19 to bring his game total up to 43 points. Robinson spent much of the final period chasing down George Gervin's franchise record of 63 points, which he surpassed when he converted a pair of free throws with a 1:33 remaining. It was at this point that things became a little absurd.

The Spurs held a comfortable lead and the game, for all intents and purposes, was over. Robinson's tally of 64 points was not only a new Spurs' record, it also seemed to be more than enough to ensure the center's first scoring title. However, San Antonio coach John Lucas was keen for Robinson to keep piling on the points. Not only did Lucas leave Robinson in the game, his players also began intentionally fouling the Clippers in order to stop the clock and regain possession. The Spurs were treating the Clippers with contempt and it seemed as if no one in a white jersey was capable of doing anything to stop the embarrassment. Over the next 56 seconds, Robinson added another 7 points to bring his final tally up to 71, becoming only the fourth player in league history to crack the 70 point barrier[147]. This left O'Neal needing to score 68 in the Magic's final game in order to win the scoring crown. He ended up falling well short, finishing with just 32[148].

---

147 He joined David Thompson, who had 73 points on the final day of the 1977-78 season, Elgin Baylor, who scored 71 back in 1960 and Wilt Chamberlin, who achieved the feat on six separate occasions.
148 Afterwards, a disappointed O'Neal labeled the Clippers' effort a "farce" and it is hard to argue with this sentiment.

This loss to San Antonio gave the Clippers a final record of 27-55 and the comments from the locker room offered a glimpse of just how demoralized the players were. "There's no pride here," observed Wilkins. "I've never seen anything like this in my career." Mark Jackson said, "If you're not committed to winning, I don't want to be here. And I think tonight shows no commitment to winning."

However, the final words for the 1993-94 season were best left to the man who had made a point of saying so little over the previous two months. The humiliation of watching David Robinson score 71 points prompted Ron Harper to finally offer the press something more expansive than his standard response of "whatever." When asked to share his thoughts, Harper uttered five simple words that not only described how he felt about the game he had just played in, they were also equally applicable to the season as whole.

"I'm just glad it's over."

CHAPTER 11

Life's a Fitch

*"People always ask me, 'Why did you to go to the Clippers?',
like they're asking, 'Why did you jump off that building?'"*

BILL FITCH

SEASON XVII: 1994-95

TWO THINGS IMMEDIATELY STOOD OUT about the players who were gathered in the home team's locker room at the Sports Arena on December 5th, 1994. The first was that none of them were smiling. Not a single person. Some were visibly frustrated, others looked despondent and some simply stared off into the distance. A variety of different facial expressions, none of which could be classified as happy. This was not surprising when you consider that the locker room belonged to the Los Angeles Clippers, who had just suffered their 16th defeat in a season that was 16 games old. This was the second worst start to a season in NBA history, only one loss behind Miami's 0-17 effort during their inaugural campaign back in 1988.

The other attention grabbing feature of the faces inside the Clippers' locker room was their lack of familiarity. In the two seasons since the Clippers' playoff series against Utah, there had been a huge turnover of players. Charles Smith, Doc Rivers, James Edwards, Olden Polynice, Ken

Norman and Danny Manning had already departed prior to the conclusion of the 1993-94 season. And while this may seem like a large number of players for a team to lose in such a short space of time, the exodus was only just getting started. During the summer of 1994, Clipper players fled from the troubled franchise like it was a burning building.

First to go was Mark Jackson, who was re-united with Larry Brown courtesy of a trade with Indiana. In exchange for Jackson, the Clippers received point guard Pooh Richardson, swingman Malik Sealy and Eric Piatkowski, a sharp shooting rookie from the University of Nebraska[149]. When Jackson returned to the Sports Arena a few months later as a member of the Pacers, his post-game comments left no doubt as to how he felt about his time playing for the Clippers. "I'm very blessed to be out of here," he said after the Pacers inflicted the Clippers 14th straight loss. Next to depart was Dominique Wilkins, who signed with Boston after he was unable to agree on terms for a new contract with the Clippers.

The final star to walk out the door was Ron Harper, which given his "jail time" comments, came as no great shock to anyone. Before leaving, Harper went through the motions of attempting to negotiate a new deal, asking for $20 million over five seasons. For the Clippers, this was too much to pay for a player with a history of disruptive behavior. But while Harper's present team may not have thought that he was worth $20 million, at least one other NBA front office did, with Chicago offering him a deal that was almost identical to what he was seeking from the Clippers. The Clippers countered with an offer of $16 million over five years, and then

---

149 One person who was unlikely to have been in favor of making this trade was Donald Sterling, who voiced his opposition to selecting Piatkowski on the day of the 1994 draft. The Clippers' coaches and front office staff were discussing the prospect of using the 7th overall pick on Piatkowski when Sterling interjected and asked, "Is this guy white?" Barry Hecker, who was an assistant coach at the time, responded by asking Sterling if he knew any Polish guys who were black. Having had Piatkowski's race confirmed, Sterling then proclaimed, "Why would we draft him? Let's pick the black guy."

tried to convince Harper that this contract was actually better than the Bulls', to which Harper replied, "It sounds $4 million worse." Not surprisingly, Harper opted to sign with Chicago.

The changes in Clipper-land were not just limited to the playing group. When Bob Weiss was first introduced as the franchise's new coach back in July of 1993, it was announced that he had signed a three year deal. Ten months later, Weiss was fired, proving once again that Clipper contracts were hardly worth the paper they are printed on. Weiss labeled his brief time with the Clippers the "most frustrating" experience in his coaching career, saying that the team's me-first attitude destroyed any chance of achieving success[150].

The firing of Weiss meant that the Clippers were once again forced to search for a new head coach and no one could accuse the front office of excess haste in this pursuit. In fact, two and a half months passed between Weiss being handed his walking papers and the day when his replacement was finally revealed. Bill Fitch was the most accomplished coach to take the reins in the 27 year history of the Clippers, having already won two Coach of the Year awards and one NBA championship. He had a reputation of being a hard taskmaster and something of an innovator[151]. Prior to being employed by the Clippers, Fitch had served as a head coach for four other NBA franchises and on each and every occasion, he had presided over a period of

---
150 After firing Weiss, the Clippers also stopped paying him, despite the fact that he still had two years remaining on his contract. This resulted in Weiss employing a lawyer in order to get the Clippers to pay the approximately $1.2 million that he was owed. This matter was eventually resolved when the two sides reached a confidential settlement.
151 Fitch was one of the first coaches to make extensive use of video footage, which earned him the nickname of Captain Video.

significant improvement[152]. It didn't take Fitch very long to realize that his latest assignment was going to be the most challenging of his entire career.

The summer of 1994 should have been a happy time for Stanley Roberts. His right Achilles was now fully healed and he was on the verge of making his NBA comeback. However, as the start of the new season approached, Roberts was anything but happy. After rupturing his Achilles, Roberts was fearful that his career might be over, causing him to enter into a state of deep depression. He spent the majority of his time holed up in his home and on some days, he barely made it out of bed. Not only did Roberts isolate himself from his friends and family, he also stopped attending practices and cut off all contact with his teammates.

This meant that by the time the medical staff gave Roberts the all clear to resume training, he was once again overweight and out of shape. The Clippers would not reveal exactly how many excess pounds Roberts was carrying and Baylor responded to questions about this issue by saying, "He weighs too much, that's what he weighs." It was estimated that Roberts was tipping the scales at around the 345 pound mark, hardly the sort of physical condition one would expect to see from a professional athlete.

The Clippers sent Roberts to a weight loss clinic where he was placed on a low calorie, fat-free diet and put through daily training sessions designed to help him shed the excess weight. At first, this seemed to work

---

152 In Cleveland, he was the first coach ever hired by the expansion Cavs and by the franchise's sixth season, Fitch had led them into the Eastern Conference finals. His next stop was Boston, where he took over a Celtic team that had only won 29 games during the previous season. With the help of a rookie named Larry Bird, Fitch coached a four year stretch in which the Celtics averaged over 60 wins per season and also won an NBA championship. In Houston, the Rockets had won only 14 games the season before Fitch's arrival. Within three years he had them playing in the NBA Finals. His most recent assignment was with New Jersey. During Fitch's first year with the Nets, they won just 17 games. However, by the end of his third season, New Jersey was back in the post-season.

wonders, with Roberts losing approximately 20 pounds. However, after a few weeks, Roberts began to complain about feeling pain in his right heel. When doctors examined him, they couldn't find anything that would explain this discomfort, so he was instructed to continue with his assigned program. Roberts felt like he was not being taken seriously, so he packed up his belongings and left the weight loss clinic. He flew back to his home in Florida, where he stopped taking calls from anyone connected with the team.

Therefore, it came as no great surprise when Roberts turned up for the first day of training camp in poor condition, which meant that he was unable to participate in many of the physically grueling sessions that Fitch had planned. While the rest of his teammates sweated it out on the courts at UC Irvine, Roberts spent much of his time doing low-impact exercises in the pool. At the same time as he was being kept out of parts of training camp, Roberts was telling the world that he planned to be "the next Magic or Kareem." He went on to add, "When everybody thinks L.A., I want them to think Stanley Roberts."

However, despite these confident public proclamations, Roberts was still a very unhappy man. In the lead-up to the 1994-95 season, long-time Clipper broadcaster Ralph Lawler ran into Roberts in the lobby of the team hotel and jokingly asked him if was going to be stuck on the sidelines for another season. Roberts answered with two simple words that revealed much about his state of mind at the time: "I wish."

Stanley Roberts' comeback lasted all of 13 minutes of playing time, all of it before the regular season even began.

Roberts was attempting a free throw early in the fourth quarter of an exhibition game against Atlanta. The moment the ball left his hand, he knew that his shot was going to fall short, so Roberts instinctively charged towards the backboard in order to pursue the offensive rebound. But when he went to push off with his left foot, it immediately buckled underneath him, sending Roberts crashing to the floor.

The diagnosis was almost too cruel for anyone to comprehend. Eleven months after snapping his right Achilles tendon, Roberts managed to achieve some sort of perverse symmetry, with his left Achilles tendon now also ruptured. The injury meant that Roberts was ruled out for the entire season, forcing Fitch to start his rebuilding project with a roster that was beginning to look more like a CBA squad.

In fact, the Clippers' starting five for their opening night clash with Portland may have been the least talented collection of players to start a season-opening game in the history of the NBA. At point guard there was Pooh Richardson, a former first round draft pick who had enjoyed a few good years while playing for Minnesota, before being traded to Indiana. Richardson's form had dropped off so significantly since joining the Pacers that he was left off the team's playoff roster at the conclusion of the previous season. Terry Dehere, the Clippers' new starting two-guard, was entering his second professional season and there was very little about his rookie campaign that suggested he was ready to assume a larger role. Dehere averaged just 5.3 points per game while converting less than 38% of his field goal attempts.

Things did not get much better once the focus switched to the frontcourt. At center, the Clippers went with Elmore Spencer, a player with a 6.5 point per game scoring average and a reputation for engaging in bizarre behavior. Forward Tony Massenburg had not played in the NBA for two full seasons and during his last year in the league he had been cut or released on four separate occasions. His career averages at the start of the 1994-95 season were a measly 2.1 points and 1.6 rebounds per game.

Power forward was the only position where the Clippers were fielding a player who appeared to be up to the task of starting in the NBA. Loy

Vaught was the son of a construction worker and his father's influence was clear for anyone to see. Vaught's blue-collar approach to the game made him popular with fans, coaches and teammates. After spending much of his first four NBA seasons playing in the shadows of Charles Smith and Danny Manning, Vaught looked set to make the most of the increased opportunities that were about to come his way.

The Clippers' line-up was considered to be so weak that many experts were predicting they would make a run at the league record for fewest wins in a season. One Las Vegas bookmaker was so convinced that the Clippers were on track for one of the worst seasons of all-time, that he offered odds of a million-to-one for them to claim the 1995 NBA championship[153].

The Clippers were not afforded the opportunity to quietly ease their way into the new campaign. Instead, they opened the season with two showcase games against Portland in Yokohama, Japan[154]. In front of nearly 15,000 fans, the Clippers surrendered meekly in the first encounter, falling behind by 35 points in the fourth quarter before eventually losing by 21. The result from the following evening was only marginally better, with the Blazers winning by 17.

The Clippers departed Japan with an 0-2 record and when they arrived back on American soil, the losses kept on coming. Most of their early season defeats were not even close, with an average losing margin of over 14 points across the season's first 16 games. They were playing truly horrendous basketball and, despite the fact that there were still 66 games remaining on the schedule, it was hard to see where the season's first victory

---

153 Forward Harold Ellis adamantly stated that the Clippers were not going to break Philadelphia's record of winning just nine games in a season and he justified this claim by saying, "I've never been part of a losing team." Just to clarify, Ellis spent his rookie season as a member of the 1993-94 Clippers, who compiled a 27-55 record.
154 This was only the third time in NBA history that the league had scheduled regular season contests outside of North America.

was going to come from. But if there is one thing that long-time Clipper observers have learnt, it is always to expect the unexpected.

If you walked into the Sports Arena as the final buzzer was sounding on December 9th, 1994, you could have been excused for thinking that the Clippers had just claimed their first NBA championship. Fans flooded the court as "I Love L.A." blared from the P.A. system. Teammates embraced Pooh Richardson, who just nailed the jump shot that secured the 96-94 overtime victory. Coach Bill Fitch was presented with the game ball. There was even talk of popping open some champagne, as Loy Vaught promised to buy the team bottles of Dom Perignon to celebrate this historic win.

But this was not the NBA Finals. It was not even a playoff victory. These wild celebratory scenes took place after a regular season game played in early December against Milwaukee, who arrived in Los Angeles on an eight game losing streak of their own. The game was knotted at 88 at the end of regulation and again at 94-all with just a few seconds remaining in overtime. Fitch called a time-out to set up a play but the Clippers were unable to execute and instead almost turned the ball over. Luckily, Lamond Murray was able to recover the loose ball in the ensuing wild scramble and he quickly passed it to Richardson, who nailed a 20-footer from the top of the key as time expired. The Clippers had finally secured their first win of the season, thus improving their overall record to 1-16.

Two nights later, the Clippers won again, this time against the Lakers at the Forum. The game was not even close, with the visitors dominating from opening tip to the final horn. The Clippers' 25 point victory moved their record to 2-16, prompting Vaught to proclaim that they were "capable of beating any other team in the league." It turned out that Vaught's confidence was horribly misplaced. This two game winning streak proved to be the high point for an otherwise disappointing season.

Fitch described his first season in charge of the Clippers as "not a fun year." However, most observers believed that he had done an impressive job, squeezing 17 victories out of a roster that many people expected would struggle to reach double digits in the wins column. The good news was that the team was still relatively young and, in Loy Vaught, they appeared to have found a player whom they could build around. For the first time in his five year career, Vaught was a regular member of the starting line-up and he grabbed this opportunity with both hands. He finished the season as the team's leading scorer (17.5 points per game) and rebounder (9.7) and was perhaps the only player who was able to provide Clipper fans with at least *some* hope that a brighter future might be on the not too distant horizon.

SEASON XVIII: 1995-96

If Tom Daly had his way, the 1995-96 season would be the last time that the NBA featured a team named the Los Angeles Clippers. Daly, the Mayor of Anaheim, was hoping that he could convince Donald Sterling to move his franchise 30 miles south and play their home games at Orange County's brand new arena, the Honda Center[155]. Under this bold plan, the league's most troubled franchise would be reincarnated as the Anaheim Clippers.

The Clippers first visited the Honda Center back in October 1993, when they played an exhibition game against Golden State. The stadium was managed by the Ogden Corporation, which was keen for the Clippers to make a one-off appearance at their brand new venue. The hope was that Sterling would enjoy the experience of watching his team play in the state of the art facility and this would assist Ogden in achieving their long-term goal of convincing him to permanently move the Clippers to Anaheim. This

---
155 Née the Pond.

first exhibition game went well, with a larger than expected crowd of close to 17,000 people flocking to the venue to watch the game.

The Clippers next foray into Orange County occurred due to an unexpected intervention from Mother Nature. When the Northridge earthquake struck Los Angeles in January of 1994, it caused over 50 people to lose their lives as well as up to $20 billion worth of property damage. One of the buildings damaged was the Sports Arena, which meant that the facility was temporarily unavailable while it underwent repairs. This left the Clippers with a home game against the Knicks and no venue to play in. Not surprisingly, the proprietors of the Honda Center rolled out the red carpet for the Clippers and, once again, the game was a huge success. A franchise record 17,507 fans packed into the arena to see New York win a nail-biter, 103-101.

It was around this time that Sterling began to take the overtures from Ogden and the City of Anaheim more seriously. During the 1994 off-season, the Clippers announced a three year deal to play a selection of home games in Orange County. The contract called for one exhibition and six regular season games to be played at the Honda Center each season. At the time of the announcement, the Clippers were careful to reassure their Los Angeles supporters that they were not looking to permanently relocate to Anaheim, with Andy Roeser, their executive vice president, saying, "We're more interested in expanding our fan base rather than substituting it for another."

The first year of the Clippers' dual home court experiment went very well from the perspective of the people who were trying to lure the franchise to Anaheim. The average crowd for the seven games played at the Honda Center (17,821) was almost double what the Clippers were drawing at the Sports Arena (9,333).

On the eve of the 1995-96 season, the option of a permanent move to Anaheim was beginning to appear progressively more attractive. The Clippers sought permission from the league to shift two additional regular season games to the Honda Center, giving them a total of nine games in Anaheim for the upcoming season. During the second year of the Anaheim trial, there was a drop in the number of fans who passed through the turnstiles at both the Honda Center and the Sports Arena. However, despite this decline, the average crowd figures for Orange County (14,389) were still considerably better than those for games played in Los Angeles (9,074).

The City of Anaheim and Ogden sensed that their moment had arrived and as the 1995-96 season drew to a close, they made their pitch to Sterling. They were no longer content to be a part-time NBA host, they wanted Sterling to move the Clippers to Anaheim and play all 41 home games at the Honda Center. Mayor Daly attempted to sell the plan to his constituents, saying that "having the NBA in Anaheim on a full-time basis and having Anaheim included in the team name will be good for the local economy."

The Anaheim group was willing to offer considerable financial incentives in order to make the relocation happen. Sterling was presented with a proposal that was rumored to be in the vicinity of $95 million, in order to make a 12 year commitment to play in Anaheim. This worked out to be a little under $8 million per season in guaranteed revenue across the life of the deal.

If the Clippers did make the move to Anaheim, they would go from having the league's oldest home venue to playing in a brand new, state of the art arena. The Honda Center was filled with a variety of amenities that were noticeably absent from the Sports Arena: luxury suites, club seating, video scoreboards and a restaurant/bar where patrons were able to wine and dine while watching the game. Not only was the Honda Center a newer venue, it also had a better track record when it came to attracting fans. Over the previous three seasons, the Clippers drew an average crowd of 15,954 spectators to the 15 regular season games played in Anaheim. Meanwhile, the average crowd at the Sports Arena during this time was just 10,009.

Perhaps the most persuasive reason in favor of shifting to Orange County was that it provided the franchise with a chance to re-invent itself. After 18 years of playing in Southern California, the Clippers' brand had about as much credibility as Latrell Sprewell's feigned concern about his ability to feed his family. However, if Sterling moved his team to Anaheim, the organization had an opportunity to make a fresh start. It was clear that the fans of Orange County were prepared to embrace the Clippers. With a new name, new arena and perhaps even some new uniforms, there seemed to be a reasonable chance that the franchise's long history of failure might be able to be pushed to back of everyone's memory, even if the changes were mostly cosmetic.

As the Bulls and Sonics were battling it out in the 1996 Finals, most experts were predicting that the announcement of a deal between the Clippers and the management of the Honda Center was imminent. Lou Lopez, a member of the Anaheim City Council, said that his "gut instinct" told him that the Clippers were going to make the move. Meanwhile, officials from both the Clippers and the Honda Center had become noticeably quiet about the potential relocation, further fueling the rumors that a deal was about to be revealed.

When the announcement was finally made, it was not what most people had expected. The Clippers decided to remain in Los Angeles. They were still happy to play a small proportion of their home games in Anaheim, but that was it. Ogden and the City of Anaheim officials were understandably devastated at being rejected by the Clippers, although they kept their public comments to a minimum.

It seemed that one of the main reasons for the collapse of the deal was Sterling's reluctance to drive the extra miles to Orange County in order to watch the Clippers play. During the negotiation process, an official from the Honda Center commented on Sterling's apprehensions over the longer drive, saying "He still has some reservations about the commute for him and some of his friends. Unfortunately, those concerns are hard for us to alleviate." With the Clippers staying put in Los Angeles, Sterling did not have to worry about battling the notoriously bad traffic to travel to Anaheim. It was a case of same short drive, same second-rate product.

When Brent Barry took flight from the free throw line and sailed towards the basket with the ball held high above his head, it evoked memories of a young Julius Erving or Michael Jordan. Barry was awarded a score of 49 out of a possible 50 for his free throw line dunk, which was good enough to win the NBA's Slam Dunk competition in 1996. Unfortunately, Barry's victory in this novelty event was the lone significant piece of good news in what was an otherwise wretched season for the Los Angeles Clippers.

Barry was only wearing a Clippers' uniform due to a huge draft day gamble made by Elgin Baylor. The Clippers entered the 1995 draft with the rights to the second overall pick. Initially Baylor said that he planned to keep the pick, before ominously adding, "If something comes up we feel we just can't refuse, you have to do it for the good of the club."

Golden State drafted first, opting for Joe Smith, a 6'10" forward out of Maryland. Baylor then selected Antonio McDyess, a 6'9" forward out of Alabama who possessed an imposing level of athleticism. Bill Fitch immediately praised the selection, comparing McDyess to All-Stars Karl Malone and Otis Thorpe. After a number of years of serving up nothing but bad news, the Clippers finally had something they could hang their hats on.

Antonio McDyess would be the new face of the franchise.

For a few hours at least.

McDyess barely had time to place the Clippers cap on his head before a trade was announced. Considering that Baylor had previously said that they would only part with their prized lottery pick if they were presented with an offer that was too good to refuse, the deal he eventually made was shocking, to say the least. Denver received McDyess, seldom used bench guard Randy Woods and center Elmore Spencer and in return, the Clippers welcomed aboard Rodney Rogers, Brent Barry and Bison Dele[156].

Rogers was an improving young player who would provide the Clippers with some additional versatility, due to his ability to play at either forward position. However, considering that he had posted averages of just 10.2 points and 3.8 rebounds across his first three professional seasons, it was unlikely that he was going to suddenly morph into a franchise player. Dele had played four years in the NBA at the time of the trade and had proven himself as a serviceable back-up at either the four or five spot. The final piece of the package was Barry who, as a rookie, was somewhat of an unknown commodity. What *was* clear about Barry was that he was not in the same class as McDyess. This was reflected in the fact that Barry was drafted with the 15th overall selection, exactly 13 spots lower than McDyess[157].

The Clippers' rationale for this seemingly ridiculous trade went something like this: they parted company with one projected starter, McDyess, and received two starters back, in Barry and Rodgers. Apparently, both Baylor and Fitch believed that Barry was a potential star in the making. During his four years at Oregon State, Barry played primarily at either shooting guard or small forward. However, the Clippers believed that he had the court vision and ball handling to become the team's starting point guard.

The trade was universally regarded as mind-blowingly bad. If one thing has been proven over the course of NBA history, it's that you never trade

---

156 At the time of the trade, Dele was known as Brian Williams. He changed his name to Bison Dele a few years later, in recognition of his African and Native American ancestry.
157 When McDyess found out that he had been traded, he immediately removed the Clippers cap from his head, threw it to nearest person in room and said, "Yuck, you can have this."

away one great player for a collection of average-to-good players. And while it was unclear whether McDyess would turn out to be a franchise player, the consensus around the league was that he had the potential to become one.

After the trade was announced, Baylor did not even confront the media to explain his reasoning[158]. Instead, Fitch was left to justify this perplexing deal. "I know it's tough for you guys to understand," Fitch said, although it was unclear who he was referring to, as the majority of the basketball world was having trouble wrapping its head around the Clippers' latest transaction. Fitch went on to label the trade a "shortcut that will stand the test of time."

History shows that this draft day deal was indeed a poor move, with none of the three players acquired by the Clippers ever approaching the form displayed by McDyess at the peak of his career[159]. In fact, in an outcome that surprised almost everyone, including the Clippers' front office, the most productive member of the trio acquired in this trade turned out to Dele, who finished the 1995-96 season with averages of 15.8 points and 7.6 rebounds.

The decision to trade away McDyess proved to be the perfect prologue to another season that ended with over 50 defeats. The team's final record of 29-53 gave them a grand total of just 46 wins over a two year period. If you looked at the Clippers' recent results and the state of their roster, there was very little evidence to suggest that one of the franchise's most successful seasons was just around the corner.

---

158 Apparently Baylor lost his voice due to the extended period of time he spent on the phone discussing the deal with Denver.
159 McDyess went on to have a 16 year NBA career. During his first six seasons, he was selected as an All-Star once, had two separate seasons where he averaged 20 and 10, was named on an All-NBA team and won an Olympic gold medal. At the start of his seventh season he suffered a serious knee injury which caused him to spend considerable time on the sidelines. When he was able to resume playing, he had lost much of his athleticism but was able to make a successful comeback by re-inventing himself as a role player.

Yet, amazingly it was.

Not many people would have predicted it, but the Clippers were about to make their third trip to the NBA playoffs.

Season XIX: 1996-97

Across Bill Fitch's 25 years working in the NBA, he has done it all. From calling the shots for a newly formed expansion team to winning a title with the league's most storied franchise, Fitch has enjoyed many seasons where he could look back and be proud of his coaching efforts. But perhaps the most remarkable achievement of Fitch's long and successful career was piloting the 1996-97 Clippers into the playoffs.

In the months leading up to the season, it appeared unlikely that Fitch would be able to coach at all. In early August, he was rushed to hospital after complaining of chest pains. Doctors discovered that three of the vessels leading to his heart were completely blocked and he underwent emergency triple bypass surgery. The surgery was successful and in order to avoid more heart troubles, Fitch was told to watch his diet, exercise more often and take steps to reduce his blood pressure. "I would say he should try and relieve all stress," said Dr. Connie Hutton, "but being an NBA coach, it would be hard to do." Fitch's heart problems lead to rumors that he might be forced to retire but when training camp opened in early October, he was back on the sidelines, ready to take up the challenge of trying to get the Clippers back into the playoffs.

One of the only good news stories to emerge from the previous season was the emergence of Bison Dele. After coming across from Denver in the McDyess trade, Dele had performed so well that he not only won a spot in the Clippers' starting line-up, he also frequently looked like one of the best players in the entire league. There was the night in the middle of December when he went head-to-head with Juwan Howard and finished with 33 points, 14 rebounds and 4 steals. Or the game at the start of January, when he had 24 points, 14 rebounds, 4 assists and 4 steals against Rik Smits. Or the clash against Boston in early February, when Dele's 35 points single-handedly outscored the entire starting frontcourt of the Celtics.

As Dele headed into the 1996 off-season, he seemed to have the world at his feet. He was about to become an unrestricted free agent and he could rest assured in the knowledge that his recent impressive form would have many teams clambering for his services. All of which meant one thing from the Clippers' perspective- if they wanted to hold onto Bison Dele, they were going to have to cough up a considerable amount of cash.

Dele initially asked for a seven year, $101 million contract. The Clippers said no thanks. Instead, they countered with an offer of $12 million over 3 years. Not surprisingly, Dele declined. With the two parties going back and forth, it seemed like your normal Clipper free agent dance, which usually ends somewhere in the middle of November with the player in question signing a new deal after missing all of training camp and the first few weeks of the season. Only this time, it was different.

While Dele was negotiating with the Clippers, he was also in the process of trying to land a deal with Los Angeles' other professional basketball team. The Lakers were interested in Dele but they were also in the middle of discussions with another center by the name of Shaquille O'Neal, who was a free agent at the time. O'Neal was the Lakers' homerun swing and if they didn't connect, Dele was a nice double that they knew they could land on a subsequent pitch.

In the meantime, Seattle decided to add another variable into the mix by offering Dele a seven year deal worth around $35 million. However, Dele was still feeling relatively optimistic about his chances of becoming a Laker and so he turned the Sonics down. This prompted Seattle to use the money they had put aside for Dele to sign Jim McIlvaine, a modestly talented center with career averages of just 2.1 points and 2.5 rebounds per game. Around the same time that McIlvaine was putting pen to paper in Seattle, the Lakers announced that they had lured O'Neal from Orlando, meaning that they too no longer had any interest in signing Dele.

All of a sudden, Dele was like a child who is too slow to react when it goes silent during a game of musical chairs. With both the Lakers and Sonics no longer interested in his services, Dele shifted his attentions back to the Clippers. In early November, with the regular season already under way, he dropped his asking price down to $36.8 million over seven years. The Clippers responded by raising their offer to $16.8 million over four years. This left the two sides twenty million dollars away from seeing eye-to-eye on what constituted fair compensation for Dele's services. Ultimately, this proved to be too great a chasm to cross. By the middle of November, the Clippers publically stated that they were giving up any hope of signing Dele, leaving Fitch without the services of his starting center.

Walking Away

Dele ended up sitting out nearly the entire 1996-97 campaign before signing with the defending champion Chicago Bulls and playing the final nine games of the regular season. Once the playoffs started, he emerged as a key contributor in a run that ultimately resulted in a fifth championship ring for Michael Jordan and the Bulls. Dele's post-season form caught the attention of many front offices around the league and he eventually secured a seven year, $50 million deal with Detroit.

A few years later, Dele decided that the life of a professional basketballer was not for him and he announced his immediate *retirement from the NBA, despite having five years still remaining on his contract. Ironically, after sitting out nearly an entire season due a dispute over money, Dele proved that he did not place too much value on dollars and cents by walking away from over $35 million in salary that he was due to receive[160].*

Dele then embarked on a three year adventure, travelling across the globe and sampling all that the world had to offer. Tragically, Dele died under mysterious circumstances a few years later while sailing the Pacific Ocean. It is widely suspected that Dele's brother, Miles Dabord, was responsible for murdering Dele and the two other passengers on board. However, the criminal investigation into Dabord's culpability was prematurely halted when Dabord passed away a few months later in a suspected suicide. Bison Dele will be remembered as a generous individual who marched to the beat of his own drum.

The Clippers failure to re-sign Dele saw Stanley Roberts once again thrust into a prominent role. During the 1995-96 season, Roberts had made a somewhat successful comeback from his two Achilles injuries, playing around 15 minutes a night as Dele's back-up. Now, with Dele gone, Roberts looked to have the inside track to resume his role as the team's starting center. Roberts celebrated his re-emergence as a player of relevance by continuing his annual tradition of turning up to training camp out of shape. This time he tipped the scales at over 300 pounds, leaving Fitch feeling understandably frustrated. From here, things only deteriorated.

Roberts was given permission to skip the first day of training camp so that he could return to South Carolina to attend a funeral. The service was on Thursday and Fitch was expecting Roberts to be back in time for Friday's

---

160 Such was the Pistons' regard for Dele that they never filed his retirement papers, hoping that he might one day change his mind and return to play for Detroit.

morning session. Not only did Roberts not turn up Friday morning, he also failed to make an appearance at the Friday evening and Saturday morning sessions. When Roberts finally reappeared on Saturday evening, Fitch was not impressed. Compounding matters was the fact that Roberts was also hobbled by a back injury which the team didn't know about.

As Roberts' injury had not been diagnosed by the team's medical staff, Fitch was operating under the assumption that his late-arriving center was fully fit. So when Roberts was struggling to run during a scrimmage, an irate Fitch called the team into the middle of the court to make his displeasure known. "Some of you guys came to training camp late and out of shape," Fitch said. Roberts knew that this was not a message that was being directed to the wider group, this was a personal message for him. So he told Fitch that if he had something to say about his late arrival or his conditioning, he should do it directly, rather than addressing the entire team. This quickly turned into a heated verbal disagreement. At one point, Roberts yelled, "Fuck you, you bad-heart-having son of a bitch." It turned out that these ten words almost put an end to Roberts' NBA career.

Fitch's immediate reaction was to forcefully tell Roberts to leave the gym and hand in his uniform on his way out. Fitch did not have the power to fire players but he was signaling to everyone else in attendance that, as far as he was concerned, Roberts was no longer part of the team. Roberts tore off his practice jersey, threw it on the floor and was about to make his way to the exit, when he thought he heard Fitch say something else. At this point, Roberts snapped. "I just remember turning around and heading directly for him," Roberts said. "I was pulling back my fist and getting ready to punch him."

The other players watched on in horror, shocked at the sight of a 300 pound teammate charging at their 62 year old coach. Luckily, Lorenzen Wright, the Clippers' latest lottery pick, had enough presence of mind to prevent the incident from escalating any further. "Lorenzen came and hit me from the side," Roberts recalled. "He said, 'No, Stan. No.' and then took me to the sidelines." From here, Roberts stormed out and headed back to the team hotel.

In the days that followed, Roberts was suspended and told that he would not be allowed to re-join the team until he apologized to Fitch. Meanwhile, Fitch didn't seem to be overly concerned about whether things could be patched up, saying that he was no longer able to "coach a guy who doesn't want to be coached[161]."

A few weeks later, Roberts was allowed to resume playing after sitting down with Fitch and saying he was sorry. And while Fitch accepted the apology, he also noted that Roberts' physical condition had worsened during the time he had spent away from the team. Given that there was now just two weeks until the Clippers' first regular season game, the chances of Roberts sliding into the vacant starting center position appeared to be close to zero.

Roberts was relegated to the bench for the first month of the season but towards the end of November, Fitch inserted him back into the starting five. This lasted all of two games. With his back still giving him problems, Roberts missed 8 of his 11 field goal attempts and finished with just 8 points in his first game back as a starter. The following evening, the pain in his back was so intense that he was limited to just 16 minutes of action. After this second game in the starting line-up, Roberts was placed on the injured list and was eventually sent to have surgery, bringing a premature end to both his season and his time as a member of the Los Angeles Clippers.

---

161 "He'll be gone until he makes a total commitment to basketball," Fitch said. "That doesn't mean he's all of a sudden become a bad guy. He's a good guy to have a chocolate sundae or banana split with. But when he's out here and he's frustrated, he's a bad guy."

It was not just the frontcourt that was proving to be a problem for Bill Fitch and the Clippers. The other area of major concern was the point guard position, with Brent Barry struggling badly. Barry's troubles began when he sprained his thumb so severely that his left hand had to be placed in a cast, causing him to miss the first month of the season. When Barry resumed playing, he discovered that his shooting touch had completely deserted him[162].

After 21 games, the Clippers were sitting on a 7-14 record and Fitch decided that it was time to make a change. With Barry unable to find consistent form, Fitch opted to start a virtually unknown player. Someone whose journey from an undrafted college senior to starting point guard on an NBA playoff team is as improbable as it is inspirational.

At first glance, Darrick Martin looked like he would be more at home competing in a rec league than walking out on court for the opening tip of an NBA game. For one thing, he was short. In fact, Martin was so diminutive that midway through his first season with the Clippers he had to be issued a new, smaller jersey because the numbers on his original one would disappear into his shorts whenever he tucked himself in. But it was not just his 5'11" stature that made professional basketballer an unlikely career choice for Martin.

As a college senior, Martin was demoted from UCLA's starting line-up and he finished his final year as a student-athlete with the averages of just 5.6 points and 3.9 assists per game. Thus when the 1992 draft was held, it came as no great surprise that the name "Darrick Martin" was not called in either the first or second rounds. With the direct route to the NBA no longer an option, Martin was forced to head to the CBA to continue pursuing

---

[162] Barry went from hitting 47.4% of his shots from the field as a rookie to 40.9% in his sophomore year, while his three-point percentage plummeted from 41.6% to 32.4%.

his dream. Only there was one fairly significant problem: it appeared that the CBA did not want him either. First he was cut by the Rapid City Thrillers. His next stop was a try-out with the Oklahoma City Cavalry, where he was also told, "Thanks, but no thanks."

At this point, Martin moved out of the world of competitive basketball and joined Magic Johnson's team of travelling NBA veterans. He spent the next 18 months playing a series of exhibition matches across the globe and learning the game from the player who is widely regarded as the best point guard to ever lace up a pair of high-tops. In 1994, Martin finally got his chance to play in the CBA, signing on with the Sioux Falls Skyforce and he grabbed the opportunity with both hands. Martin averaged 21 points and 7.8 assists and this impressive form led to a ten-day contract with the Minnesota Timberwolves.

On February 14th, 1995, 1,053 days after playing his last game of college basketball, Martin finally made his NBA debut. He played well enough to turn this first ten-day contract into a spot on the Timberwolves' roster for the remainder of the season. The following year, he briefly played for the Vancouver Grizzlies, before once again returning to Minnesota.

At the start of the 1996-97 season, the Clippers signed Martin, although with both Barry and Pooh Richardson already on the roster, he was not expected to play very many minutes. In early December, Richardson was forced to sit out for a few games with an ankle injury and Martin was given the opportunity to start. Martin had been here before and he knew how this worked. He was being given a small chance to show the coaching staff what he could do. If he made the most it, he could cement a spot in the team's rotation for the rest of the season. If not, he would most likely find himself buried at the end of the bench.

In late December, Martin matched up against future Hall of Famer John Stockton and finished with 38 points and 8 assists, leading the Clippers to an unlikely 14 point victory over the Utah Jazz. A few weeks later, he produced a 31 point, 9 assist effort as the undermanned Clippers caused another huge upset by defeating Gary Payton and the Sonics. In between these headline performances were plenty of solid outings and by the time that Richardson was ready to return, the starting point guard position belonged to Martin.

With Martin leading the way, the Clippers continued to gradually improve and by the middle of February, a late season run at a playoff berth switched from being a fanciful idea to an achievable goal. Fitch was finding a way to win against the NBA's best with a roster of over-achieving role players. The starting line-up featured Martin, Malik Sealy, Rodney Rogers, Loy Vaught and Lorenzen Wright, a collection of names that would be familiar to only the most ardent basketball fans. Not a single Clipper averaged over 15 points per game and yet by the end of the season, this rag-tag collection of NBA-nobodies had somehow scrambled their way to 36 wins. Even more remarkable was the fact that this was enough to earn the franchise a playoff appearance- just their third in 19 years[163].

Waiting for the Clippers in the first round was Utah, who had steamrolled through the season to finish with a 64-18 record. As the Clippers prepared for Game 1, they could at least look back on Martin's 38 point explosion against the Jazz and draw some confidence that beating Utah was within the realms of possibilities. Now they just had to find a way to do it three times in the next 11 days.

THE PLAYOFFS: ROUND 1 VS. UTAH

The Clippers' 1997 playoff battle against Utah offered none of the drama or tension that was a feature of the franchise's previous two playoff appearances. Prior to the start of the series, a Las Vegas bookmaker was offering 50-1 on

---

[163] The 1996-97 Clippers narrowly missed the record for lowest win total by a playoff team over a full 82 game season. That distinction went to the 1994-95 Boston Celtics, who managed to sneak into the post-season with just 35 victories.

the Clippers advancing to the second round and when Rodney Rogers was told of these odds, he replied, "I'm surprised it's not more than that." Game 1 did little to change the perception that the Clippers were nothing more than a rung on the ladder that the Jazz had to climb in order to reach the NBA Finals. The Clippers fell behind by 14 points early in the second quarter, before eventually losing 106-86. Karl Malone was the star of the game with 27 points and 10 rebounds, while Loy Vaught, the only remaining Clipper from the 1992 playoff campaign, led the road team with 20 points and 11 rebounds.

Game 2 started out in much the same manner as Game 1. At halftime the Clippers were trailing by 16 and things were beginning to look a little hopeless. However, the visitors quickly showed their opponents that they were not going to concede defeat without putting up some sort of a fight. They outscored the Jazz 30-12 in the first seven and half minutes of the third quarter to briefly take a two point lead. From here, the Clippers managed to keep it close before a late Utah surge put them away for good. Malone was once again exceptional. In fact, he was such an imposing force that he caused Vaught to foul out in the third quarter. Vaught played just 22 minutes and exited the game with more personal fouls (6) than points (5). Meanwhile, Malone finished with 39 points and 11 rebounds.

Game 3 was preceded by a string of bravado-laced predictions that athletes who are facing impossible odds sometimes like to make. Martin said, "We're down two games, but we've got two games at home, then it'll be 2-2." Fitch reminisced about the time when he was coaching back in 1981 and Boston came back from a 1-3 deficit to defeat Philadelphia, thus booking a spot in the NBA Finals. According to Fitch, all the Clippers had to do was "win three games to get to the next round." Whether anyone on the team actually believed these public declarations was another matter entirely.

As it turned out, Game 3 was never really a contest. The Jazz were up by 8 at quarter time, 16 at half-time and midway through the third quarter, they had built a 23 point lead. A late rally cut the margin to 10 but by that stage, the game was over. The final score was 104-92, which meant Utah was moving on and the Clippers season was finished.

The post-game comments reflected the level of respect that the overachieving Clippers had managed to command in a short space of time. Malone spoke about the Clippers "playing their butts off," while Fitch said that he wouldn't trade his job for Utah's head coaching position because of the way he felt about the players in his locker room. Commissioner David Stern even got in on the act, labeling the Clippers "a very good, young team." While it may have seemed that there were sunny days ahead, students of Clipper history knew that any predictions of a positive future should be ingested with a grain of salt.

Season XX: 1997-98

The reputation of an NBA head coach is often as much a reflection of that coach's sense of timing as it is their understanding of X's and O's. When it comes to coaching jobs, the immortal words of Kenny Rogers ring true- one needs to know when to hold 'em and when to fold 'em. If ever there was a case of a coach holding on for one season too long, Bill Fitch's final year with the Clippers seems to be it.

By the end of the 1996-97 season, Fitch was considered Clipper coaching royalty. In the space of just three years, he had transformed a 17 win team into a playoff squad, joining Larry Brown as one of only two coaches to lead the Clippers into the post-season. At 63 years of age, Fitch could have easily chosen to end his career on a high note. However, instead of walking off into the sunset, Fitch became the first Clipper coach to have his contract extended, signing on for an additional two years and thus tying himself to the franchise until the end of the 1999-2000 season.

The team that Fitch took into the 1997-98 season was significantly different from the group that qualified for the playoffs a year earlier. The first move made by the front office was getting rid of Stanley Roberts. As they had done six years earlier with the Benoit Benjamin-Olden Polynice trade, the Clippers decided to go with a less talented player whom they could rely upon, rather than persist with someone who spent more time battling dietary demons than opposition centers. Roberts was traded to Minnesota in exchange for Stojko Vrankovic, a 33 year old center with career averages of 2.7 points and 2.4 rebounds per game [164]. Bo Outlaw, an athletic forward who had emerged as a key contributor for the Clippers during the previous season, also departed after accepting a two year offer to play for Orlando. Finally, the Clippers elected not to retain starting shooting guard Malik Sealy, who eventually signed with the Pistons. Sealy had averaged 12.7 points per game across his three seasons with the Clippers and was also widely regarded as the team's best perimeter defender[165].

The Clippers were hoping that the loss of Roberts, Outlaw and Sealy would be off-set by their two big acquisitions of the summer- Maurice Taylor and Keith Closs. Taylor, a 6'9" power forward, was selected by the Clippers with the 14th pick of the 1997 draft. He had shown considerable promise during his three years at Michigan and the Clippers planned to use him as an understudy to fellow Wolverine Loy Vaught. Meanwhile, the Clippers signed Keith Closs, an undrafted 7'3" center, to a five year, $8.5 million contract. This was quite an upgrade in terms of salary, as

---

164 Vrankovic arrived in Los Angeles armed with a ridiculously generous contract that was set to pay him $7.5 million over the next two seasons, making him the highest paid player on the Clippers' roster.
165 Sealy tragically died just three years later, after his car was struck by an SUV that was driven by a man who was heavily intoxicated. Shockingly, Sealy was one of four players from the Clippers' 1996-97 team who passed away before seeing their 45th birthdays. Eight years after Sealy's death, Kevin Duckworth died from heart failure when he was just 44 years of age. Meanwhile, Lorenzen Wright was only 34 years old when he was murdered in 2010 and Dwayne Schintzius was 43 when he died in 2012 due to a rare form of leukemia

Closs spent the previous season making $80 a game while playing for a semi-professional team called the Norwich Neptunes[166].

The remodeled Clippers headed into the season full of optimism, believing that a second consecutive trip to the playoffs was within their reach. These high hopes did not make it to the end of November. The new campaign got off to a bad start, with 12 losses from the first 13 games. And if that was not enough to kill off the team's playoff dreams, the premature end to Loy Vaught's season was.

Vaught had been battling back problems for years, surviving on a steady diet of pain killers and anti-inflammatories. However, after appearing in just ten games at the start of the 1997-98 season, the pain finally became unbearable. Vaught was sent off for surgery to fuse two of his vertebrae together, meaning that the Clippers would be forced to play the remainder of the season without their leading scorer and rebounder from each of the past three years.

By early February, with the team sitting on an abysmal 11-41 record, Baylor traded Brent Barry to Miami in exchange for Ike Austin. As they had done with Danny Manning four years earlier, the Clippers decided to move Barry, who was about to become a free agent, amidst fears that he was likely to sign somewhere else at the end of the season. Barry's two and a half seasons with the Clippers could best be described as disappointing. Any plans to convert Barry into a point guard had been abandoned long ago and by his third professional season, he was utilized almost exclusively in the two spot. Barry departed the Clippers with averages of 10.1 points and 2.9 assists across 179 games.

---

166 Closs' lavish contract meant he was set to earn more in the upcoming season than the combined salaries of Brent Barry and Darrick Martin, the two players who comprised the Clippers' starting backcourt. Even Closs himself was surprised at the money that the Clippers were willing to pay him. "I thought I was going to be a multi-thousandaire," Closs said. "I didn't expect anything more than $450,000 at the most."

The Clippers now had two months to show Ike Austin, who was also about to become a free agent, that theirs was the best organization for him to sign his next contract with. Austin had spent most of his NBA career coming off the bench. However, when Alonzo Mourning was injured at the start of the 1997-98 season, Austin moved into the Heat's starting line-up, where he performed extremely well[167]. The Clippers were hoping that Austin would thrive once he was given a starter's role on a full-time basis and that this would lead to him signing a long-term deal to remain with the franchise. Austin played well over the final 26 games of the season, averaging 15.2 points, 8.7 rebounds and 3.4 assists, but it did little to improve the Clippers' overall win-loss record.

The Clippers finished with 17 wins and 65 defeats, an identical record to Fitch's first Clipper campaign, four years earlier. Fitch described the season as "terrible," saying the loss of Vaught hurt the team and that they simply did not have the required depth to overcome this type of injury. Baylor had a very different interpretation, saying, "Injuries are part of it, but even without Loy Vaught, we believe the team should have done better."

At the conclusion of the regular season, Fitch was informed that his coaching services were no longer required, just 11 months after the front office gave him to a two year contract extension. Having fired Fitch, the small problem still remained about what to do in relation to the $4 million that was owed to the outgoing coach. When Fitch was initially asked about this matter, he didn't seem overly concerned, naively answering, "They told me the contract just takes care of itself." Fitch would find out the hard way that nothing ever takes care of itself when it comes to the Los Angeles Clippers.

When Fitch was terminated, a financial settlement was reached whereby the Clippers would continue to pay his salary for the final two years of the contract. The agreement also stated that any money earned by Fitch from other basketball-related work would off-set the amount that the franchise

---

167 During the 22 games that Austin started, he averaged 18.9 points and 9.3 rebounds.

was liable for. A few years later, the Clippers filed a lawsuit alleging that Fitch had failed to act in good faith because he had not been actively seeking other coaching work. At the time, Fitch was just a few weeks away from celebrating his 67th birthday. Fitch responded by launching his own legal action against the franchise to recover the remaining portion of money that he was owed.

As part of this legal battle, Donald Sterling was asked during a deposition whether he knew if the contract extension given to Fitch back in 1997 was guaranteed or not. He replied, "No." He was then asked if he had any idea what a guaranteed contract was. He again responded with a simple, "No." When prompted to elaborate on his answer, Sterling said, "I really don't understand what 'guaranteed contracts' means. I'm really not sure exactly what that means with relation to players[168]." Sterling also claimed not to have known whether coaches who are fired while still under contract continue to get paid or not. The dispute was eventually settled on the eve of the trial via a confidential, out of court settlement.

There was one piece of good news to emerge from the 1997-98 season, with the Clippers once again winning the NBA's draft lottery. Ten years earlier, they used the number one selection on Danny Manning, launching the most successful era in the franchise's 20 year history. This time around there was no consensus pick, no gleaming All-American whom the scouts were drooling over. If the Clippers were going to draft someone whom they could build a successful team around, they were going to have to figure out who this should be all by themselves.

---

168 It seems a little far-fetched that Sterling truly had no idea what the term "guaranteed contract" meant, given his experience as a lawyer, property developer and NBA owner.

CHAPTER 12

The Kandi Man Kan't

"Look at the big men out there...Alonzo Mourning, Shaquille and Tim Duncan. I think Olowokandi will be in that elite group in three years."

Elgin Baylor

MICHAEL OLOWOKANDI HAD DEVISED A unique way to celebrate his 20th birthday. He was going to land himself a spot at a Division One college program, the first step in achieving his ultimate goal of playing in the NBA. However, given that Olowokandi was living in London at the time, the logistics of this operation were not going to be easy. He went to a nearby library and borrowed "Peterson's Guide to American Colleges and Universities", which he used to find the contact details that he needed. Olowokandi then began placing calls to a number of prominent schools, hopeful that he would find someone who was willing to take a chance on him. He contacted Georgetown and Duke but couldn't get a coach at either school to take his call, much less entertain the idea of having him play on their teams. It is not difficult to figure out the reason for this lack of interest.

Olowokandi had never played a single game of basketball in his life.

Sure, he had fooled around with some of his buddies at a local court a few times, but that was it. To most 20 year olds who dreamed of playing in the world's best basketball competition, this fact would be viewed as an insurmountable hurdle. However, Olowokandi possessed an unwavering self-belief and so he saw it as nothing more than an inconvenient roadblock.

Frustrated at his inability to get John Thompson or Mike Krzyzewski on the phone, Olowokandi decided that it was time to try a different approach. For his next phone call, he would leave it up to fate. He closed his eyes, opened the guide book to a random page and plonked his finger down. When Olowokandi opened his eyes, he was pointing at the University of the Pacific.

On the other side of the globe, Tony Marcopulos was sitting at his desk, eating a cheese and salami sandwich. Marcopulos could think of a hundred other places where he would rather be spending his lunch break. However, his boss, Pacific head coach Bob Thomason, had a policy that an assistant coach needed to cover the phones whenever their secretary was out of the office. Thomason was fond of saying, *"You never know when a seven-footer might call,"* a comment that was usually met with a combination of laughter and eye rolls from the rest of the coaching staff. After all, what were the chances of a seven foot student calling Pacific out of the blue and offering his services? One in a million? One in a billion?

At around 12:30pm, Marcopulos' lunch was suddenly interrupted by the sound of a ringing phone.

When Marcopulos picked up the receiver, he was greeted by a male voice with a thick British accent. "I know this sounds peculiar, but I'm seven feet tall and I want to play basketball." As an assistant coach at a struggling Division One school, Marcopulos was used to receiving unsolicited offers from people who thought they could play for Pacific. Many times, these delusional youngsters had watched the Tigers play on television and formed the view that *they* were the missing ingredient that Pacific needed. When dealing with one of these calls, Marcopulos tried to get off the phone as quickly as possible. But Olowokandi's decision to include the words *"I'm seven feet tall,"* in his opening pitch was enough to make Marcopulos put his sandwich down and keep this mystery caller on the line.

The two men chatted for a while and during the conversation, Marcopulos learned a lot about Olowokandi. He was born in Lagos, Nigeria and moved to London at the age of three, where he was now studying engineering at Brunel University. Olowokandi freely admitted that he had not played basketball before, instead telling Marcopulos that he grew up playing soccer and competing in track and field, excelling in both long jump and triple jump. He told Marcopulos that his ultimate goal was to one day play in the NBA.

A stunned Marcopulos could barely process all of the information that he was hearing and throughout the conversation, he kept interjecting with the same question- "How tall did you say you were again?" After sharing a condensed version of his life story, Olowokandi asked if Pacific was interested in having a seven-footer join their team. And while Marcopulos found the whole situation intriguing, he told Olowokandi that the school did not have any scholarships left, thinking that this would put an end to one of the weirdest conversations of his life. Instead, an unperturbed Olowokandi replied that this was not a problem, as he was happy to pay his own way. Marcopulos then informed Olowokandi that Pacific was one of the most expensive private universities in California. Olowokandi said that his father was a diplomat and that the cost, whatever it was, would not be an issue.

Marcopulos ended the call by telling Olowokandi that Pacific would be happy to have him, although he was careful not to offer any guarantees when it came to making the basketball team. A few months later, Olowokandi left England and flew over 5,000 miles to Northern California to pursue his hoop dreams.

When Michael Olowokandi first arrived at Pacific, the idea that he was just three years away from making his NBA debut was laughable. The good news was that Olowokandi hadn't exaggerated when it came to his height. He was a legitimate seven-footer. In fact, not only was Olowokandi tall, he also had huge hands, a 7'8" wingspan and the type of speed and athleticism more commonly associated with 6'4" guards. The bad news was that Olowokandi had also been brutally honest when discussing his previous exposure to the game of basketball.

Olowokandi's first American basketball experience was an individual workout with Marcopulos and it did not go well. Marcopulos started the session by saying, "Let's go down to the block and see what you can do." Olowokandi stared back at Marcopulos, like a deer caught in the headlights, and asked, "Where's the block?" If there were any doubts about the work that lay ahead for the coaches at Pacific, they were quickly evaporating. Olowokandi didn't know anything. He didn't know the difference between man-to-man and zone defense. He didn't know where the free throw line was. He didn't know how many fouls a player was allowed before they fouled out of a game. Olowokandi was a novice in the truest sense of the word.

Once Olowokandi started to practice with the rest of the team, he soon recognized just how far behind his peers he was. His initial how-hard-can-this-be bravado was replaced with a realization that it was going to take a lot of work just to crack into Pacific's rotation, much less play in the NBA. Olowokandi spent his first weeks in America learning the most basic of the basics, including how to catch the ball, how to pivot without travelling and how to make a lay-up. This was basketball kindergarten on a college campus.

Luckily for all concerned, Olowokandi was a fast learner with a good work ethic. He was always one of the first to arrive at practice and usually the last to leave. And his hard work was not just restricted to official training sessions. Ron Verlin, an assistant coach at Pacific, got used to receiving calls from Olowokandi at random times throughout the day. "Coach, are you ready?" Olowokandi would ask. "Meet me at the gym. It's time to go to work."

However, despite all of the effort being applied, Olowokandi's first college season was more like a Three Stooges movie than an installment of the Rocky series[169]. "Sometimes I wouldn't know if I was playing offense or defense," Olowokandi said. He would feign understanding when plays were being diagrammed in time-outs but he didn't have a clue what was going on. In one game, Olowokandi demonstrated his complete lack of awareness of the rules when he received an inbounds pass in the frontcourt and immediately threw the ball to a teammate, who was standing on the opposite side of the midcourt line. Another time, Olowokandi was fouled while making a basket. However, after missing the free throw attempt, he couldn't understand why the game resumed without him having his second shot. Olowokandi finished his first campaign with averages of just 4 points and 3.4 rebounds. Yet he remained steadfast in his belief that he was destined to play in the NBA.

During the summer of 1996, Olowokandi continued to work towards his lofty goal, attending the prestigious Pete Newell Big Man Camp and lifting weights twice a day. When he returned to campus at the start of the 1996-97 season, Olowokandi was ready to be a contributing member of

---

[169] Olowokandi's first season at Pacific was considered to be his sophomore year in terms of NCAA eligibility, due to the time he had already spent studying at Brunel.

the team. He was still a walk-on, but his vast improvement earned him a promotion into Pacific's starting line-up.

The first glimpse that Olowokandi might be headed for a career as a basketballer came in December, when Pacific travelled to Las Vegas to play against Georgetown. In the lead-up to the game, Olowokandi was more focused than usual, wanting to put in a good showing against one of the schools that he had cold-called two years earlier. Olowokandi finished with 16 points, 14 rebounds and 5 blocked shots, while holding future NBA player Jahidi White scoreless, as Pacific cruised to a 17 point win. Olowokandi averaged 10.9 points and 6.6 rebounds during his junior season and he helped Pacific qualify for the NCAA tournament for the first time in 18 years.

As Olowokandi prepared for his senior year, a future playing professional basketball seemed to be within reach- if not in the NBA, then possibly in one of the European leagues. Thomason decided to make Olowokandi the focal point of the Tigers' offense and he was able to use his expanding range of post moves to devastating effect. He finished the season with averages of 22.2 points, 11.2 rebounds and 2.9 blocks. Olowokandi's dramatic improvement was officially recognized when he won the Big West Player of the Year award.

Attention now turned to the upcoming NBA draft. And while the numbers from Olowokandi's senior year were certainly impressive, questions still remained about the quality of competition that he had faced. Bill Duffy, Olowokandi's newly employed agent, came up with a plan to cast his client in the best possible light. Olowokandi would be available for interviews and small group workouts only. No five-on-five scrimmaging and no appearances at any of the pre-draft camps. Duffy believed that this would accentuate his client's strengths and conceal many of his weaknesses. Duffy's other masterstroke was getting his hands on the list of physical tests and drills that each team liked to use when assessing potential draft picks.

Armed with this information, the Pacific coaching staff set about preparing Olowokandi for each of his pre-draft workouts like a college student cramming for an exam.

For the next few weeks, a well-prepared Olowokandi travelled across North America and put on a show wherever he went. In Vancouver, he dominated in the post against another potential draftee, at one stage scoring on ten consecutive possessions. In Denver, he wowed the Nuggets' coaching staff with an amazing show of force, dunking a 15 pound medicine ball 40 times in a row without pausing for a break[170]. However, there was perhaps no pre-draft performance that was as impressive as Olowokandi's workout with the Clippers. He was agile. He was fast. He was explosive. And by the time the session was over, Olowokandi had won over the Clippers' brains trust.

On June 24th 1998, Elgin Baylor made Michael Olowokandi the first overall selection of the 1998 draft, an inconceivable concept just three years earlier. For Olowokandi, this was a joyous moment and the ultimate payoff for his gamble to fly across the globe in pursuit of a dream. And the Clippers were equally pleased, believing that they had finally found a center who they could build a contending team around.

Contrary to the revisionist version of history that paints the drafting of Olowokandi as being viewed as an error at the time, most experts were full of praise for the selection. Respected Los Angeles Times basketball writer Mark Heisler called Olowokandi the best choice in the entire draft, labeling him "less than a blue-chip prospect, but more than a project." Stu Jackson, Vancouver's general manager, said the decision to take Olowokandi over Mike Bibby, who the Grizzlies selected with the second overall pick, was a "no-brainer." Meanwhile NBA veteran Andrew Lang, who played against

---

170 The Nuggets liked to use this drill to test the strength and stamina of their frontcourt players and Olowokandi's final tally set a new record. The previous best was 22 consecutive dunks by Dikembe Mutombo, a seven time All-Star who was considered to be one of the strongest players in the NBA.

Olowokandi at the Pete Newell Big Man camp, said that he was "going to be an All-Star for a long, long time."

On the day that Olowokandi shook David Stern's hand, he had played just 77 games of organized basketball, making him one of the least experienced first round draft picks in NBA history. If Olowokandi's professional career was going to get off to a good start, it was extremely important that he make the most of his first NBA training camp. Considering the Clippers' 20 year run of George Costanza-like misfortune, what happened next should come as no surprise.

A week after the draft, a labor dispute, which had been bubbling beneath the surface for the past few months, escalated to the point where the players were locked out by the owners. The lockout eventually lasted a total of 204 days, causing over 400 regular season games to be cancelled and millions of dollars of revenue to be lost. Perhaps no player's career was more adversely affected by all of this off-court chaos than Michael Olowokandi's.

At the time that Olowokandi was drafted, the NBA was the only major North American sporting league that had never cancelled a game as the result of an industrial dispute. The last collective bargaining agreement between the owners and players' union had been signed off on three years earlier and was supposed to last until 2001. However, this document contained a clause that allowed the owners to re-open discussions if the share of basketball-related income being paid to the players exceeded 51.8%. By the 1997-98 season, players' salaries accounted for 57% of basketball-related income, prompting the owners to call the players' union back to the negotiating table.

Discussions between the two parties took place over the next three months and during this time, a number of sticking points arose. The owners wanted to place limits on the amount that could be paid to individual players but the union naturally opposed this idea. Meanwhile the union was pushing for an increase in the minimum salary, which at the time was a little under $290,000. The two sides met a total of nine times in the lead-up to the 1998 draft. However, the negotiations went nowhere, prompting the owners to lock the players out.

The lockout meant that all official basketball-related activity ground to an immediate halt, which was obviously horrible news for the Clippers. Suddenly Olowokandi was not allowed to use the Clippers' practice facility or contact anyone connected with the franchise. This included members of the front office, trainers, team doctors and the coaching staff[171].

The dispute continued to drag on through August and September, causing training camps and the exhibition schedule to be postponed indefinitely. October arrived and with no resolution in sight, the league decided to cancel 99 regular season games- the first time in NBA history that such action had been taken. This decision meant a fifth month of Olowokandi being left to his own devices. However, while this lack of supervision was far from ideal, Olowokandi appeared to be working hard behind the scenes to ensure that he would be ready for the start of the season, whenever it occurred. He employed Kareem Abdul-Jabbar as a private coach and the two men began working out together three times a week. When Kareem was asked to assess his new protégé's progress, he was glowing, praising everything from his skill level, to his agility and strength, to his work ethic.

November turned to December and it was beginning to look increasingly likely that Olowokandi's NBA debut would not take place until the following season. Two days before Christmas, Stern delivered an ultimatum to the players' union- if there was no deal in place by January 7th, he was going to cancel the rest of the 1998-99 season.

---

171 This is a little misleading since the Clippers' coaching staff did not exist at this point in time. More on that soon.

It was around the time of Stern's announcement that Duffy informed his client of an intriguing offer that had come in from across the Atlantic Ocean. An Italian team, Kinder Bologna, wanted to sign Olowokandi for the remainder of the European season. This was an appealing proposition for a number of reasons. Firstly, the only way that Olowokandi was going to overcome his lack of basketball experience was by actually playing in some meaningful games. With the labor dispute preventing him from doing so in North America, it made sense for Olowokandi to look abroad for opportunities to continue his development. The second consideration that Olowokandi found tempting was the $1 million salary. He had only just left college and still hadn't signed his first professional contract. A million dollars for a few months of playing in Italy would have been a large enough carrot to entice many NBA veterans to head over to Europe, let alone a rookie still waiting to cash his first paycheck.

There was, however, one major problem with the Kinder Bologna offer. Italian rules stated that the last day that teams were allowed to sign new players was January 4th, which was three days *before* the deadline that Stern had given to the players' union. This meant that Olowokandi had to make a decision on whether to head over to Europe without knowing whether the NBA season was going ahead or not.

Olowokandi opted to sign with Kinder Bologna on January 4th.

Less than 48 hours later, the players' union voted in favor of accepting an offer from the owners, thus ending the lockout.

The final deal was viewed as a win for the owners, with the NBA placing limits on the salaries that individual players could earn[172]. A rookie pay scale was also introduced, where the amount paid to a rookie was automati-

---

172 Under the new agreement, players with one to five years' experience could earn up to $9 million per season, players with six to nine years' experience could now receive a maximum of $11 million and players with ten years' experience were eligible for a salary of $14 million.

cally determined by their draft position. However, the players' union did manage to win a few small concessions, such as a marginal increase in the minimum salary. The agreement meant that the 1998-99 season, which looked doomed at more than one stage, would finally go ahead, albeit in a heavily condensed format. Teams would play a 50 game schedule over a period of just 88 days[173].

The deal also meant that the Clippers would be opening their training camp on January 21st without the presence of their prized number one selection. However, Olowokandi would not be lost for the entire season, as his Italian contract contained a clause that allowed an early return to America if the NBA's labor dispute was resolved. The only problem was that the contract stated that Olowokandi would not be released before February 15th, meaning that he would miss training camp, all of the exhibition schedule and the opening five or six games of the regular season.

Amazingly, having Olowokandi stranded in Italy was not even at the top of the Clippers' list of concerns. With training camp due to start in a fortnight's time, the Clippers were yet to appoint a head coach for the upcoming season. Over the years, the franchise had earned a reputation for their parsimonious ways and this legacy continued during the lockout. Having fired Bill Fitch at the end of the 1997-98 season, the Clippers figured out a novel way to save themselves some cash. They decided to hold off on employing a new head coach or any assistants until it was confirmed that the 1998-99 season was actually going ahead. This allowed them to pocket whatever money they would have spent on the coaching staff's salaries across the duration of the lockout.

Obviously, this decision was good for the short term health of the organization's bank balance. However, while Donald Sterling sat back like Scrooge McDuck and counted the dollars that he was saving, many of the biggest names in the world of coaching were signing contracts with

---

173 Normally NBA teams play 82 games per season across approximately 170 days.

other teams. Rick Adelman inked a deal in Sacramento, Paul Westphal headed to Seattle to take over as the Sonic's coach, George Karl signed with Milwaukee and Kurt Rambis elected to stay on with the Lakers as an assistant.

By the time the lockout ended, the Clippers were like a single man in a bar with 15 minutes until closing time. The decision on who would be the franchise's next coach was now less a question of who was the best fit for the job and more a case of who was still available in their hour of need. With many of the most sought after coaching candidates already locked into positions with other teams, the Clippers appointed Chris Ford as the franchise's eleventh head coach. Ford, who had previous coaching experience in Boston and Milwaukee, was signed to a three year deal that paid around $1 million per season.

The team that Ford would be working with was fairly similar to the group that Fitch had coached in his last season in Los Angeles, with a few noticeable omissions. Loy Vaught, the franchise's all-time leader in both games played and total rebounds, signed a five year, $23 million deal with Detroit and Ike Austin signed a three year, $15 million deal with Orlando.

Halfway through training camp, the Clippers received some good news- Bologna had decided to release Olowokandi from his contract three weeks earlier than first expected. This meant that he would be able to participate in the final few days of pre-season workouts and play in the opening game of the regular season.

The exact reason behind Olowokandi's early return depended on who was telling the story. Duffy claimed that Bologna wanted Olowokandi to stay in Italy, even offering a $5 million deal to make this happen, and that they only decided to release him when they realized that he was planning on leaving as soon as he possibly could. Bologna, on the other hand, reported that the primary reason for their decision was that they were disappointed with Olowokandi's production. The raw numbers appear to support the Bologna version of events, with Olowokandi averaging just 7.7 points and 5.8 rebounds across the six games that he played. The good news was that Olowokandi was back. The bad news was that Olowokandi's recent form had many people questioning whether the Clippers would have been better off if he had stayed in Italy.

Season XXI: 1999

The Clippers opened the new season with a 9 point loss at home to Phoenix.

Two nights later, they lost again at the Sports Arena to a woeful, post-Michael Jordan Bulls team.

They then travelled to Canada, where they went down to the Grizzlies by 6.

Next stop was a rematch with the Suns, this time in Phoenix. The Clippers missed 10 of their 29 free throws in a 3 point overtime defeat.

The following night they were back in Los Angeles to play Minnesota, where they shot 37% from the field, 7% from three-point range and lost by 22.

Two nights later it took two overtime periods for the Grizzlies to claim their second victory of the season over the Clippers. Once again, poor free-throw shooting cost the Clippers, who were only able to convert 16 of 32 attempts.

Dallas came to town next and cruised to a 15 point win.

The Clippers then travelled to Utah, where they were once again on the wrong side of a 15 point margin.

Back home the following night, the Clippers looked like they might finally break through for their first win, until Bimbo Coles scored 8 points down the stretch to lead the Warriors to a come from behind victory.

The Clippers then played a home-and-home series against the Lakers which resulted in two losses and two injuries. In the first game, Maurice Taylor sprained his right knee in the third quarter. The following evening, Olowokandi went down with an ankle sprain that kept him sidelined for the next week and a half.

Atlanta travelled to California to take on the under-manned Clippers and the Hawks won in a blowout.

The Clippers then had to travel to Texas to play the Mavericks, Rockets and Spurs, which resulted in three defeats by a combined margin of 61 points.

Another home-and-home series with the Lakers saw yet another two losses added to the Clippers overall record[174].

After sitting around for three long months, waiting for the NBA season to commence, the Clippers managed to eliminate themselves from playoff contention in the space of just 33 days. They lost their first 17 games, tying Miami's 1988 record for the worst start to a new season[175]. Their first win did not occur until the middle of March, when they defeated Sacramento by 14 points at the Sports Arena. After securing his maiden victory as the Clippers' head coach, Chris Ford said, "Hopefully it's the beginning of something new for us."

It was not.

---

174 The Lakers must have felt that all of their Christmases had come at once. In the space of just two weeks, they played the Clippers four times, resulting in four victories by a combined margin of 54 points.

175 This was the same record that the Clippers had narrowly avoided just four seasons earlier.

In fact, the Clippers won just two of their next 15 games, bringing their overall record to an astonishingly bad 3-30. One of the major problems that confronted Ford was the dark shadow that looming free-agency cast over the team. In a set of circumstances that was eerily similar to what Larry Brown dealt with back in the 1992-93 season, nearly the entire Clipper roster was in the final year of their contracts[176]. This created all sorts of problems, with many players appearing to be primarily concerned with inflating their statistical output rather than playing the role that Ford was asking them to.

One of the few players who had a contract that extended beyond the current season was Olowokandi. And while there were times when the rookie center showed glimpses of being able to dominate around the basket, as he had done in his final season at Pacific, these were few and far between. Olowokandi's season averages of 8.9 points, 7.9 rebounds and 1.2 blocks were serviceable but well short of most people's expectations. The Clippers finished the lockout shortened season with a record of 9-41, the second worst in the entire league.

The Clippers had shared the city of Los Angeles with the Lakers for a total of 15 seasons and during this time, they had failed to make up any ground on their purple and gold rivals. But while the gap between the on-court performance of the Clippers and Lakers remained as wide as ever, the geographical distance between the two franchises was about to shrink to zero.

Season XXII: 1999-2000

The Clippers first moved to Southern California in 1978. Six years later, they began playing their home games at the Los Angeles Sports Arena, which was just seven miles from the Forum, the Lakers' home court at the time. At the start of the 1999-2000 season, both the Clippers and Lakers relocated to Staples Center, a $375 million state of the art arena located in

---

176 Seven of the Clippers top nine players were set to become free agents at the end of the season.

downtown Los Angeles. As a result of this simultaneous shift, the two franchises were no longer neighbors, they were now roommates.

From the Clippers' perspective, moving to Staples meant hosting games in an arena that also doubled as a shrine to the Lakers' legacy of success. From the statues of Magic, Kareem, West and Chick on the concourse, to the championship banners and retired jerseys hanging high on the walls, to the thousands of purple seats that surround the court like a swarm of violet locusts- this was clearly Lakers' territory. However, in spite of these unfavorable aesthetics, the Clippers were delighted to be playing in one of the league's premier arenas. Staples was a world class venue, allowing Clipper fans to watch games in an environment that seemed centuries removed from the relative squalor of the Sports Arena.

The Lakers secured a 25 year lease to play at Staples that included a number of conditions that the Clippers could only dream of obtaining. For example, the Lakers were set to receive approximately a quarter of the revenue that was generated from the sale of luxury suites and club seats, which was expected to amount to approximately $17 million per season. Conversely, the Clippers' lease stated that they were to receive none of the revenue from the sales of suites and a significantly smaller fee than the Lakers for any premium seats sold.

The Clippers and Lakers were also going to be sharing Staples with the NHL's Los Angeles Kings. This created a scheduling nightmare, the three teams all needing to host 41 games between the months of October and April. One only needs to perform some basic arithmetic to see that this was not going to leave very many spare dates and there was undoubtedly going to be plenty of backroom negotiation over which team received the most sought after slots.

When the schedules were finally released, it became abundantly clear that the Clippers were the venue's third priority. The Lakers and Kings were given first preference for many of the choice dates, leaving the Clippers with the leftovers. Games on Halloween, Sunday afternoon dates in the middle of the NFL season, 6:30pm tip-offs on New Year's Eve. Name a shitty date or timeslot and you can almost guarantee that it has been regularly used by the Clippers since moving to Staples. The popular view seemed to be that the Clippers should consider themselves lucky just to be allowed to play at the arena. Therefore, they had no reason to be complaining about the facility's color scheme, the dates of their games or anything else. Tim Leiweke, the president of Staples Center, summed up the prevailing mood when he said, "The Clippers have been given a gift. Our challenge to them is to make something of it."

The Clippers headed into their first season at Staples with a largely revamped roster, which meant that, once again, a number of familiar faces had departed during a busy off-season. Darrick Martin and Rodney Rogers both opted to sign elsewhere, while Elgin Baylor wisely decided not to renew Stojko Vrankovic's lavish contract[177]. Lorenzen Wright went to Atlanta in exchange for two first round draft picks and Lamond Murray was traded to Cleveland for Derek Anderson.

The final significant change to the roster was the drafting of a rookie who was so versatile, that he made the traditional notion of positions seem more outdated than the two-handed set shot. Lamar Odom was the type of player who made agents drool, fans cheer and coaches dream of championship glory. Standing at 6'10", he could post up and rebound like a center, while also possessing the ball handling and passing ability of a point guard. When David Stern announced Odom's name as the fourth overall pick in the 1999 draft, many experts believed that the Clippers had pulled off a major heist. Odom was widely regarded as the best player available and in the months leading up to the draft, it appeared to be a

---

[177] In the two seasons that Vrankovic spent with the Clippers, he scored a grand total of 80 field goals while being paid close to $8 million in salary, which equates to almost $100,000 for each successful basket.

fairly safe bet that he would be the first player selected. Or at least that was the case until a series of unfortunate events caused his draft stock to plummet.

Lamar Odom first catapulted into the spotlight when he scored 36 points as a high school sophomore and led Christ the King to New York's Catholic League City Championship. At the time, Odom was living with his grandmother. His mother had passed away from colon cancer when he was 12, while his father was reputedly battling heroin addiction and had not played an active role in his life for a number of years.

Odom's stellar performance in the championship game transformed him into an instant celebrity on the youth basketball circuit and this sudden rise to fame had a detrimental impact on some aspects of his life. There appeared to be an inverse relationship between the amount of attention lavished on Lamar Odom the basketballer and the amount of attention that Lamar Odom the high school student paid to his studies. In fact, by the time Odom was a senior, his poor grades looked like the only thing that stood between him and a scholarship at a Division One school of his choice.

In an attempt to improve his academic results, Odom transferred to Redemption Christian Academy early in his senior year. He lasted at Redemption for all of five months before moving again, this time to a school in Connecticut. This process of jumping from one school to another led to speculation that Odom was planning on bypassing college and heading straight to the NBA, a perception that was only further fueled when some colleges that had been recruiting him began to back away. But when the time came to make a decision, Odom surprised many of the so-called experts by announcing that he was going to be attending UNLV. It turned out that Odom's stay in Las Vegas would be very brief.

Not long after Odom arrived on campus, he claimed that he was visited in his room by a member of UNLV's basketball staff, who told him that it would be "better if you just leave." At the time, there were concerns beginning to surface about Odom's academic eligibility, after a Sports Illustrated article raised doubts the validity of his ACT college entrance exam results. Odom took the advice of this unnamed employee and departed UNLV without playing a single game[178].

After briefly considering offers to play in Europe, Odom decided to remain in America, where he enrolled at the University of Rhode Island. He was able to study but could not play for the Rams right away, due to an NCAA rule that requires players who transfer to sit out for a season. This meant that instead of showcasing his game for eager NBA scouts, Odom spent the 1997-98 season earning the academic credits that he needed to regain his athletic eligibility.

In November 1998, Odom finally made his college debut and while it came 12 months later than expected, it turned out to be well worth the wait. Odom fell one assist shy of recording a triple double and scored the game-winning basket, leading Rhode Island to an 87-85 victory over Texas Christian. This good form continued and he finished the season with averages of 17.6 points, 9.4 rebounds, 3.8 assists and 1.5 blocks. Odom had performed a wide variety of roles, from defending the opposition's best post player to serving as the Ram's primary ball handler, and it was this display of versatility that greatly impressed NBA scouts.

Odom's strong freshman season meant that he now had a big decision to make. He could elect to forgo the rest of his college eligibility and declare for the NBA draft, where he looked likely to be the first overall selection,

---

178 Years later, an NCAA investigation found that UNLV had committed numerous violations in the process of recruiting Odom. The charges stemmed from around $5,600 that Odom received in cash and other benefits from a Las Vegas dentist who was a close friend of UNLV coach Bill Bayno. As a result, the school was banned from post-season play for one year and was placed on a four year probation.

or he could return to play his sophomore year at Rhode Island. Odom hired an agent, informed the Rhode Island coaching staff that he was heading to the NBA and then flew to Vancouver for a pre-draft workout with the Grizzlies. He performed well in Vancouver and further workouts were scheduled with other teams. It appeared that Odom was well on the way to realizing his NBA dreams.

And then he began to have second thoughts about his decision to turn pro.

On the court, Odom felt at home and in control. But he was starting to realize that much of the action in the world of professional basketball occurs in boardrooms and lawyers' offices, places where he was like a fish out of water. The fact that Odom did not have confidence in the people who were providing him with guidance only added to the sense of fear that felt about the entire process.

While Odom was grappling with what his next move should be, he stopped showing up to the pre-draft workouts that had been organized. He was a no-show at sessions that were arranged by the Bulls and the Hornets, and he also missed the scouting combine in Chicago, a major event for any player hoping to be a lottery selection. From the outside, it appeared that Odom was deliberately burning all of the bridges that could transport him from the streets of Queens to the NBA. The reasoning behind his actions soon became apparent.

He had changed his mind.

Odom wanted to return to Rhode Island for another season.

There was just one problem with this new plan- Odom was no longer allowed to play for the Rams as he had forfeited his college eligibility on the day that he signed with an agent.

When Odom contacted the coaching staff at Rhode Island and told them about his change of heart, he was informed that re-joining the team was no longer a possibility. He pleaded with the school to try and get them to appeal to the NCAA on his behalf, arguing that since he had not received any money or services from his agent, he should be able to return to play his sophomore season. The school told Odom that they would not be lodging any sort of appeal.

This left Odom stranded. He had significantly damaged his draft prospects by failing to attend numerous workouts, and yet the option of returning to college for another season was now off the table. Clearly some drastic action needed to be taken.

Resigned to the fact that he was heading to the NBA, whether he liked it or not, Odom hired Jeff Schwartz as his new agent. With just a few days to spare before the draft, Schwartz arranged for Odom to work out in front of a number of NBA teams, including the Bulls and Clippers. Chicago owned the first overall selection and they obviously liked what they saw from Odom's workout. On the night before the draft, Odom was flown to Chicago for a meeting with the Bulls that lasted over five hours. But while the Bulls were clearly impressed with Odom's talent, they still had many reservations, some of which were in relation to the indecisive and erratic behavior that he had shown over the previous few weeks.

The following day, the Bulls opted to go with what they saw as the safe option, making Elton Brand the first selection of the 1999 draft. Vancouver picked Steve Francis at two and the Hornets used the third selection on Baron Davis. This left Elgin Baylor with one of the easiest draft day decisions he had ever made- selecting Lamar Odom with the fourth overall pick.

After Odom was drafted, he spoke of the various goals that he hoped to achieve during his professional career, including becoming one of the top

50 players of all-time, being inducted into the Hall of Fame and helping the Clippers to qualify for the postseason. It did not take long for Odom to realize that of all his lofty ambitions, helping the Clippers return to the playoffs might be the most difficult goal to turn into a reality.

For the fans of many NBA franchises, the idea of history repeating itself is seen as a welcome concept. The Celtics' run of Larry O'Brien Trophies in the 1980s brought back memories of their dominance of the 1960s. Detroit's 2004 championship winning squad was reminiscent of the "Bad Boy" teams of the late 1980s/early 1990s. Meanwhile, New York fans would love nothing more than to see their beloved Knicks transform themselves into a 21st century version of the Red Holzman-coached teams of the 1970s.

As the Clippers prepared to head into the 1999-2000 season, the makeup of their roster gave long-time supporters the same feeling you get when you are watching a familiar television show and are almost certain you have seen a particular episode. The similarities between the 1999-2000 Clippers' team and the 1989-90 model were uncanny. Both teams featured centers (Benoit Benjamin and Michael Olowokandi) who had showed a lot of promise in college and yet delivered very little once they arrived in the pros. Both teams had tall, athletic shooting guards (Ron Harper and Derek Anderson) who had been acquired from Cleveland via trade. And both teams' strength lay in a pair of young, versatile forwards. In 1989 it was Charles Smith and Danny Manning and in 1999, it would be Maurice Taylor and Lamar Odom.

The final similarity also doubled as a depressing wake-up call for anyone who was hoping that the move to Staples might signify the beginning of a new era. Like Harper, Manning and Smith had done many years earlier, Maurice Taylor headed into the 1999-2000 season openly declaring his intention to leave the Clippers at the first available opportunity. Taylor had emerged as one of the NBA's most promising young forwards during the previous season, leading the Clippers in scoring, with an average of 16.8 points per game. He still had one more year to run on his rookie deal but was hopeful that his impressive play would be enough to earn him a lucrative contract extension. Under the new collective bargaining agreement, he was eligible for a six year, $71 million deal, provided the Clippers felt he was worth it. They did not. Taylor took the front office's refusal to offer him an extension as a clear indication that his services were not valued, so he asked to be traded.

As the start of the season approached, Taylor had still not been moved and it was looking increasingly likely that he would have to play out the final season of his contract with the Clippers. Taylor chose to use media day as an opportunity to let everyone know exactly how he felt about being forced to remain a Clipper, saying, "I'm basically here to play the last year of my contract and then become a free agent."

When Chris Ford was asked about Taylor's comments, he said, "I've been around the game for 27 years and I've heard a lot of things said. Everything usually works itself out as far as contracts are concerned." This may have been the case in Boston or Milwaukee but Ford clearly did not know how these types of situations usually played out in Clipper-land.

A month later, with the regular season about to tip-off, Taylor again made his position crystal clear, saying, "Regardless of what happens, they know that I'm not coming back. This is like a farewell tour for us...basically to prove everything to Donald Sterling. We're going to go out and have a great year. We're going to win and then we're going to leave. It's as simple as that." The front office's decision not to offer a contract extension to Taylor was interpreted by many of the other players as a sign that Sterling had no intention of re-signing anyone else either. This created a sense amongst the players that, while they were officially playing for the Clippers, they were actually auditioning for a job with someone else.

The opening game of the Clippers' 1999-2000 campaign was not only the first NBA contest played at Staples Center, it also marked the official beginning of Lamar Odom's professional career. Odom immediately showed that he was a force to be reckoned with, finishing with 30 points, 12 rebounds, 3 assists, 2 blocks and 2 steals. Unfortunately, this remarkable debut mattered little, as the Clippers started the new season with a 12 point loss to Seattle.

This opening night defeat turned out to be a microcosm of the first month of the season. On a personal level, Odom played brilliantly, making fans in Chicago, Vancouver and Charlotte wonder why their teams had elected not to draft him when they had the chance. Odom was named the Rookie of the Month for November after compiling averages of 18.7 points, 7.8 rebounds, 3.6 assists, 1.4 steals and 1.2 blocks. However, despite Odom's individual brilliance, the Clippers achieved very little team success, winning just 4 of their first 14 games.

The middle of December saw the Clippers and Lakers play each other for the first time since the two franchises began sharing an arena. This was the first opportunity for the Clippers to show the basketball fans of Los Angeles that Staples was just as much their home court as it was the Lakers'. In the early stages of the game, the Clippers appeared to be putting up a good fight, trailing by one point with less than four minutes remaining in the first quarter. And then the Lakers awoke from their slumber and absolutely demoralized their opponents.

The Lakers closed out the first period with a 15-0 run, pushing their lead out to 32-16 at quarter time. During the second quarter, the game got uglier than a Dwight Howard-Shaquille O'Neal free throw shooting competition. The Clippers managed to hold the Lakers to just 17 points, which suggests that they were making their way back into the game. However, over the same 12 minute stretch, the Clippers scored a total of 3 points.

One field goal.

One free throw.

And that was it.

This was a remarkably horrendous stretch of basketball, even by the Clippers' lowly standards, and it resulted in an embarrassing half-time score of 49-19. The game looked more like a professional team playing against a squad of very average high school players, rather than a match-up between two NBA rosters[179]. It goes without saying that the Clippers eventually lost, with their final score of 68 points setting a new franchise mark for futility. The award for best post-game comment went to Maurice Taylor, who summed up the evening by saying, "Today, we played like we didn't even know how to play basketball[180]."

Three weeks later, the Staples Center co-tenants played each other on consecutive evenings and the Clippers lost both games by a combined margin of 41 points. These two defeats were part of a horrid run in which they lost 16 of 18 games, with an average losing margin of over 17 points. The 16th defeat, a humiliating 114-68 blowout in Phoenix, proved to be Chris Ford's final game as coach of the Clippers. Less than 24 hours after the 46 point thrashing, Ford was informed that he was being relieved of his duties. When Ford spoke with the media after his firing was announced, he did not sound like a man who had just lost a high-paying job in the field to which

---

179 Over the final 15 minutes and 50 seconds of the first half, the Clippers connected on just 1 of their 24 field goal attempts while also turning the ball over 11 times.
180 Taylor finished with a personal tally of 2 points and 2 rebounds.

he had devoted most of his life. Instead, he seemed more like someone who had been rescued from a near-death experience. "I'm very happy to be going home to be with my family." Indeed, who could blame him? At the time of this latest coaching change, the Clippers had won 11 of their 45 games, the second worst record in the entire league.

Ford was replaced with assistant coach Jim Todd, whose only previous head coaching experience was at Salem State, a Division Three school in Massachusetts. One of Todd's first moves was convincing the front office to hire Dennis Johnson as the team's new assistant coach. Johnson had an extremely impressive résumé from his playing days with Seattle, Phoenix and Boston. His list of achievements included three NBA championships, a finals MVP, five All-Star appearances, an All-NBA first team selection and six selections on the All-Defensive first team. After retiring, Johnson worked as an assistant coach in Boston, serving under both Ford and M.L. Carr. Alas, this change in faces and seating order on the bench did nothing to halt the slide that was occurring out on the court. In fact, it took three weeks and 11 defeats before Todd was able to celebrate his first victory.

Midway through this losing streak, the Clippers made another addition to their coaching staff, employing Kareem Abdul-Jabbar primarily to work with Michael Olowokandi. The Clippers front office had been hopeful that Olowokandi would show signs of improvement during his second professional season. However, with just 30 games remaining on the schedule, his output was almost identical to that of his rookie year.

Kareem's brief history of coaching Olowokandi during the lockout gave him reason to feel confident about his ability to reach the young center. Kareem admitted that he had not seen many of Olowokandi's NBA games since that time but he noted that the few he had caught had not been impressive. He went on to say that Olowokandi's career to date "hasn't been overwhelming." These opening comments would set the tone for a working relationship that was as acrimonious as it was short-lived.

Any rapport that had been established between the two giants evaporated almost instantaneously, only adding to the negative energy that was engulfing the team. Kareem was frustrated by Olowokandi's lethargic play and he believed that his attempts at constructive feedback were instead perceived as personal insults by his unwilling apprentice. At one stage, Olowokandi told Kareem that he would no longer accept any form of criticism in the presence of his peers. Considering that most of the opportunities to coach a player occur in front of their teammates, this request made it almost impossible for Kareem to do the job for which he had been hired.

It appeared that the same self-confidence which had served Olowokandi so well during his three years at college was now derailing his professional career. Having defied the odds by making it to the NBA, Olowokandi began to project an air that he had figured out the game of basketball. In short, he wanted to do things his way. There was a certain sense of irony to this, as it was Olowokandi's willingness to embrace feedback while at Pacific which had played perhaps the largest role in his meteoric rise.

Kareem's stint as a member of the Clippers' coaching staff failed to last beyond the 1999-2000 season. When asked to reflect on the experience of working with Olowokandi, Kareem was as blunt as a pair of preschooler's scissors, labeling him an "athletically gifted washout." And it wasn't just the coaching staff who noticed Olowokandi's reluctance to accept advice, with many of his teammates also left feeling frustrated and disappointed. "Kareem did what he could, everybody tried to help," Derek Anderson recalled. "But Olowokandi was just set in his own ways." Jim Todd's time as the Clippers' interim coach was also extremely short-lived. He was relieved of his duties at the end of the regular season, after winning just 4 of 37 games.

The 1999-2000 season may have started with much promise but it ended the same way that many previous campaigns had- with the Clippers finishing with the NBA's worst record. The last week of the regular season brought about one final humiliation, as the latest issue of Sports Illustrated hit the newsstands with a cover story that branded the Clippers as "the worst franchise in sports history[181]."

Season XXIII: 2000-01

The Clippers appointed Alvin Gentry to replace Jim Todd, making him the franchise's tenth head coach since 1989. Just a few weeks before accepting the Clippers' job, Gentry looked set to join San Antonio's coaching staff, where he had been hired as one of Greg Popovich's assistants. However, when Gentry was offered the Clippers' head coaching position, he thought it was an opportunity that was too good to pass up. One of the reasons for Gentry making the move from San Antonio to Los Angeles was the Clippers roster, which was now one of the most intriguing collection of players in the entire league, courtesy of a number of bold moves made by Elgin Baylor.

The Clippers entered the 2000 draft with an additional first round pick (18th overall), due to the Lorenzen Wright trade. Baylor then shrewdly took advantage of the fact that Orlando was desperately shedding as much payroll as possible in order to make a run at a number of high-profile free agents. He gave the Magic a future first round pick (2006) and in return received Corey Maggette, veteran power forward Derek Strong, an undisclosed amount of cash and yet another first round selection in the upcoming draft[182]. This deal was obviously a huge win for the Clippers and it meant that they now held the rights to three of the first 18 picks in the 2000 draft.

The Clippers used their own pick, the third overall selection, on Darius Miles, a skinny 6'9" forward from East St. Louis High who had a reputation for throwing down gravity-defying dunks. This was the first time that

---

[181] The accompanying photo could not have been more overt in its mocking of the organization. In it, three Clipper fans sat wearing paper bags over their heads, presumably to cover their faces in shame.

[182] The Clippers willingness to absorb Strong's $11 million contract was key to Orlando agreeing to this trade.

a top three pick had been used on a high school player and many experts labeled the drafting of Miles as a huge gamble[183]. However, the Clippers were confident that Miles' talent and phenomenal athleticism made it a risk worth taking. On the night that he was drafted, Miles demonstrated his awareness of the challenge that lay ahead, saying that the Clippers could not get any worse, as they were "already at the bottom." However, rather than feeling dismayed about joining the NBA's perennial cellar-dwellers, Miles seemed enthusiastic about being a part of yet another Clippers' rebuilding project.

One of the main reasons for Miles' decision to embrace his role as the Clippers' latest young savior was he knew that he would not be undertaking the task on his own. In fact, two of his closest friends, Maggette and Quentin Richardson, would be joining him. Miles, Maggette and Richardson had been teammates for much of their teenage years, playing for the same Chicago-based AAU team. Maggette was a 6'6" swingman with an uncanny ability to get to the free throw line. He had enjoyed a productive rookie season with Orlando, averaging 8.4 points and 3.9 rebounds while playing less than 18 minutes per night. Richardson, a lights out shooter with a proven ability to put points on the board, was drafted by the Clippers with the 18th overall selection. Rounding out the Clippers' impressive draft day haul was Keyon Dooling, a point guard who was drafted with the 10th selection that originally belonged to Orlando. The net effect of Baylor's wheeling and dealing was a total of four new faces joining the team- Miles, Dooling, Richardson and Maggette. Each was talented, athletic and yet to celebrate his 21st birthday.

These additions were partially off-set by the departures of Maurice Taylor and Derek Anderson, the Clippers' two leading scorers from the previous campaign. Taylor's decision to sign with the Rockets came as no

---

183 Prior to Miles' selection, the previous highest spot that a high school player had been drafted was fifth. This occurred on three different occasions- Darryl Dawkins in 1975, Kevin Garnett in 1995 and Jonathan Bender in 1999.

great surprise but most observers expected the Clippers to try and retain Anderson. At the conclusion of the 1999-2000 season, Anderson was a free agent who was hoping to receive a lucrative contract offer from the Clippers. He was just 26 years old and was coming off a career season, posting averages of 16.9 points, 4 rebounds and 3.4 assists per game. Instead of a multi-million dollar deal, Anderson got a brief voicemail left on his phone shortly after the final game of the season. "They just left a message saying, 'Thank you for coming and good luck to you,'" recalled Anderson. No negotiation, no contract offer, nothing more than an impersonal thank-you and the clear underlying message that he was no longer wanted. A shocked Anderson began exploring other options and a few weeks later, signed with San Antonio[184].

The loss of Taylor and Anderson left the Clippers with the second youngest roster in the league. Gentry decided that the best approach was to embrace the youth movement. So he named Lamar Odom as team captain, despite the fact that he was a 20 year old with a history of unpredictable behavior and a total of just 76 games of NBA experience.

It turned out to be a decision that backfired in a fairly major way.

By early March, the Clippers were once again stranded at the bottom of the league standings and it appeared to be a fairly safe bet that they were just a few weeks away from another early vacation. The last thing that Gentry expected over the closing stages of the regular season was for his young team to find themselves in the news headlines. However, that is precisely what occurred when Odom was suspended for violating the league's drug policy.

Odom was given a five game suspension after he tested positive for marijuana use and then failed to comply with the terms of his mandated

---

[184] Anderson went on to have another excellent year, playing a large role in San Antonio's league best 58-24 record. Along with Tim Duncan, he was the only Spur to start in all 82 games and he finished as the team's second leading scorer, with an average of 15.5 points per game.

after-care program. This news was obviously a huge blow for Gentry. Not only was his team struggling on the court, he now had to deal with the type of off-court drama that could easily fracture a young team. The Clippers won just one of the five games they played without Odom, dropping their overall record to 23-45.

When Odom resumed playing, he returned with a vengeance. In his first game back, he scored 25 points, leading the Clippers to a win over Philadelphia, the team with the league's best record at that point in time. The very next game, he had a triple double in a five point victory over Houston. Five nights later, the Clippers beat Detroit behind a 27 point, 16 rebound, 11 assist performance from Odom. When the Clippers beat Cleveland, Odom had his third triple double in the space of just ten days.

Odom's form in the final weeks of the season helped propel the Clippers to a strong finish and offered fans a glimpse of what the team was capable of. They won 10 of their last 12 home games and finished with a record of 31-51, more than doubling their win total from 12 months earlier.

A few weeks after the conclusion of the regular season, the NBA held its annual draft lottery and the Clippers got lucky, obtaining the rights to the second overall selection despite finishing the season with the league's eighth lowest winning percentage. This meant that for the fourth consecutive year, the Clippers entered the draft with a top four pick. And when the day of the draft finally arrived, Elgin Baylor made good use of this valuable asset, using it to obtain a 6'8", 265 pound power forward who would go on to become arguably the greatest player in franchise's history.

CHAPTER 13

Re-Branding Efforts

"What does the past have to do with us? This is Clippers 2001."

QUENTIN RICHARDSON

SEASON XXIV: 2001-02

As ELGIN BAYLOR PREPARED FOR the 2001 draft, he knew that he had a problem on his hands. The Clippers had the second overall selection and Baylor was determined to use it wisely. The consensus view was that there were three standout prospects in the draft- Kwame Brown, Tyson Chandler and Eddy Curry. All three were centers who were making the jump to the NBA straight from high school.

This is where things started to get tricky.

While the Clippers could certainly have used some help in the middle, the last thing they needed was another project player who was likely to take years to develop. Given the already inexperienced state of their roster, the Clippers wanted someone who was ready to contribute right away.

Meanwhile, over in the Eastern Conference, the Chicago Bulls were undertaking a rebuild of their own. They had played three seasons since the retirement of Michael Jordan and they had all been disasters on a

Clipper-esque scale, with the Bulls winning a combined total of just 45 games during this time. This was not a good result for any franchise but it was especially shocking for Chicago fans, who had grown accustomed to cracking the 45 win barrier each season by early March, during the Jordan-era.

The Bulls' front office executives were pinning their rebuilding plans on trying to inject their roster with as much youth as possible. Chicago owned the rights to the fourth overall selection in the draft and they were hoping to secure the rights to either Brown, Chandler or Curry. And then, they came up with a novel idea- what if they could find a way to get their hands on *two* of the high school stars? This would give them a nucleus that they could build around for the next decade. The only way that they could pull this off was to orchestrate a trade with the Wizards, Clippers or Hawks, the three teams with the top three draft picks. Luckily for Chicago general manager Jerry Krause, there was one player on the Bulls' roster whom the Clippers were very interested in.

Elton Brand was not your average 22 year old NBA player. He did not make regular appearances on SportsCenter for throwing down flashy dunks or swatting shots into the sixth row. Nor was he likely to be in the headlines for arguing with his coach or failing to turn up to practice or any other sort of indiscretion. Brand was an old school, blue collar power forward. The type of player you could rely on to get you 20 and 10 almost every night.

Born in Cortland, 45 miles north of New York City, Brand grew up in the Dunbar housing projects, where he was raised by his single mother. He started playing basketball at ten years of age and led Peekskill High School to two state championships. As a senior, he averaged 25.9 points, 16.2 rebounds and 6 blocks and was selected as a McDonald's All-American. Brand's high school career was so impressive that many pundits were predicting that he would be the latest in a growing list of players who skipped college altogether in order to head straight to the pros. He didn't. Instead, he signed with Duke, the most prestigious basketball program in the country.

By the end of Brand's sophomore season, he had blossomed into the best post player in the college game, winning both the Naismith and Wooden Player of the Year awards. He also lead Duke all the way to the national championship game, where they lost by 3 points to Connecticut. However, rather than return for his junior season to see if he could help the Blue Devils win another NCAA title, he decided to declare for the draft. Money was still a scarce commodity in the Brand household and he knew that the type of salary he could earn in the NBA would be life-changing for his family[185].

Chicago made Brand the first overall selection in the 1999 draft and he quickly went about establishing himself as someone the Bulls' fans could depend upon. During his first year as a Bull, he averaged 20.1 points and 10 rebounds per game, which was good enough to earn him the league's Rookie of the Year award. During his second season, he produced almost identical averages to his rookie campaign, solidifying his reputation as one of the league's best frontcourt players.

When the Clippers realized that the Bulls were interested in making a trade for one of the top three draft picks, they were curious. When they found out that Chicago was willing to part with Brand, their interest turned into action. From the Clippers' perspective, the acquisition of Brand, a known commodity, was a much better option than drafting an unproven teenager with no college experience.

---

[185] This was not a decision that was well received by the Duke faithful. Brand was the first player in the college's history to leave early in pursuit of a professional basketball career and some of the Blue Devil fans reacted by sending him hate mail.

There is no doubt that Chicago's front office would have preferred to retain Brand. However, at the time of the proposed trade, Krause was public enemy number one in Chicago, with the majority of Bulls' fans believing that he was responsible for the break-up of the Chicago teams of the 1990s. Thus, Krause was under considerable pressure to do something that would give the fan base a sense of hope for the future. And while trading away an emerging player who looked set to be an All-Star may seem counter-intuitive, it was a move that held a lot of appeal for Krause. One of the hidden benefits of choosing to rebuild around a pair of raw teenagers was that it would take years before the project could be declared a success or failure. By trading Brand, Krause was effectively hitting the re-set button on the post-Jordan era, thus turning down the intensity of the speculation about his future as Chicago's general manager.

However, despite both teams agreeing to the terms of the deal, there was still one last hurdle to clear. The Bulls only wanted to go ahead with the trade if they were able to draft Eddy Curry with the fourth overall pick. They believed that Curry could be utilized as a power forward, thus making Brand expendable. Hence, if they couldn't draft Curry, they did not want to trade Brand.

Washington selected first and opted to go with Kwame Brown. The Clippers were next and they took Chandler. They now faced a nervous few minutes, while they waited to see what Atlanta was going to do with the third overall pick. If the Hawks selected Curry, the trade with Chicago would be off and the Clippers would be stuck with Chandler[186]. Instead, the Hawks selected Pau Gasol and then traded him to Memphis. This left the path clear for the Bulls to select Curry and within minutes, the pre-planned trade was completed.

Brand was happy to be joining the Clippers, even passing up an opportunity to veto the trade. The Bulls had lost over 80% of their games in

---

186 Which would have been a pretty good consolation prize, given Chandler's solid career.

the two years since his arrival and Brand was looking forward to joining a team with legitimate playoff prospects[187]. With the addition of Brand, the Clippers now had six players between the ages of 20 and 22 and, amazingly, not a single one was a rookie. They planned to start Odom, Brand and Olowokandi up front, along with veterans Eric Piatkowski and Jeff McInnis in the backcourt. This line-up left the Clippers with a bench of Miles, Maggette, Richardson and Dooling- one of the most exciting collection of reserves in the league.

This impressive roster resulted in the hopes of Clipper fans soaring. Elgin Baylor left no room for doubt when he was asked about his goal for the coming season, saying, "Our goal is to make the playoffs." It seemed the only person who was interested in hosing down expectations was Alvin Gentry, who cautioned fans to be realistic and tried to remind everyone how difficult it was to secure a playoff berth in the ultra-competitive Western Conference[188].

When the regular season tipped off, Gentry's advice seemed to be spot on, as the Clippers lost their first three games. Unfortunately, this three game losing streak was not the worst piece of news to emerge from the opening week of the new campaign. In fact, it was not even close.

Lamar Odom was in tears. For the second time in eight months, he had been suspended for violating the league's drug policy. After his initial suspension, at the end of the 2000-01 season, Odom vowed that "this will definitely not happen again." And yet here he was, just one day removed from

---

187 Brand was also enthusiastic about being reunited with two of his former teammates. He had played AAU ball in New York with Lamar Odom, while Corey Maggette was a teammate from Brand's time at Duke.
188 The previous year had seen Houston win 45 games and still fail to qualify for the postseason, affirming the point that Gentry was trying to make.

his 22nd birthday, trying to explain his latest slip-up to the media. Odom denied that he had a problem with drugs, saying that this was simply a matter of him choosing to "experiment with marijuana."

There was no doubt that this latest indiscretion put the Clippers in a tight spot. They were already sitting at the bottom of the Pacific Division with a 0-3 record. Now, they would be forced to play their next eight games without the services of one of their most important players. Unless the Clippers were able to find a way to win some games in Odom's absence, they faced the prospect of falling out of the playoff race before the end of November[189]. Surprisingly, the Clippers managed to win five of the eight games that they played without Odom and nobody was more instrumental during this stretch than Brand, who averaged 21 points and 10.5 rebounds. Odom returned to active duty in late November but his comeback would prove to be very short-lived.

In the middle of December, Odom sprained his wrist, forcing him to sit out for a few games. When he returned to the line-up, it was clear that the injury was still bothering him. During a six game road trip in which the Clippers won only one game, Odom averaged just 13.3 points while shooting less than 37% from the field. He returned to Los Angeles and played one of his worst games of his short professional career, scoring just 5 points in a victory over the Cavs. This turned out to be his last game for the season.

With Odom's wrist showing little sign of improvement, the decision was made to place it in a cast, sending him back to the sidelines. Then, while still recovering from the wrist injury, Odom severely sprained his ankle,

---

189 In one of those it-could-only-happen-to-the-Clippers moments, "Lamar Odom Bobblehead Night" happened to fall right in the middle of the eight game suspension. So, while fans who attended the November 10th game against the Suns did not get the pleasure of watching Odom play, they were at least able to take home a plastic replica of him.

giving him a set of crutches to go with his cast[190]. These two injuries ultimately put a premature end to Odom's third NBA season.

Anyone who thought that the Clippers were going to roll over and die without the services of Lamar Odom was sorely mistaken. At the time that Odom played his last game for the season, the Clippers had a 20-20 record and were still very much in the hunt for a spot in the playoffs. And led by the inspired play of Elton Brand and Michael Olowokandi, they would remain in the race until the final days of the regular season. Brand's solid performance came as a surprise to no one and in February, he became the first Clipper to play in an All-Star game since Danny Manning was selected back in 1994.

The stellar play of Olowokandi, on the other hand, was not something that many people expected. In fact, over the first two months of the 2001-02 season, Olowokandi continued to churn out the same sort of mediocre numbers that Clipper fans had become accustomed to, averaging 6.2 points and 8.3 rebounds. However, when Odom went down with his wrist injury, Alvin Gentry began to play Olowokandi for extended minutes and he repaid this show of faith by producing the best form of his professional career.

In February, Olowokandi played 44 minutes and put up 27 points and 15 rebounds in a road game against the Celtics. A few weeks later, the Clippers travelled to Chicago and Olowokandi made sure that Brand got the win against his old team, finishing with 30 points, 16 rebounds and 3 blocks. Later that same month, the Clippers hosted the Spurs and Olowokandi outplayed David Robinson, tallying 26 points and 17 rebounds to Robinson's 19 and 5. Greg Popovich called Olowokandi's play "incredible," Bill Walton labeled his emergence "remarkable," while Gentry

---

190 In yet another it-could-only-happen-to-the-Clippers moment, this latest mishap occurred when Odom tripped on a loose basketball during an attempted dunk at a team shoot-around.

said that he "was as good a player as there was" over the last two months of the season[191].

In the middle of March, an unlikely playoff berth seemed to be within the Clippers' grasp, as they went on a four game winning streak that pushed their overall record to 34-31. They were now just half a game outside the Western Conference's top eight. Alas, this would be as close as they would get. Over the final four weeks of the season, the Clippers faced a fairly tough schedule and they were unable to win a single game against any of the playoff bound teams that they played. Their final tally was 39 victories, five games below Utah, the team that eventually claimed the West's eighth seed.

While it was natural for fans to be disappointed about once again failing to qualify for the post-season, they also had to be happy with the remarkable level of improvement shown by the team. After all, it was only two years earlier that the Clippers had won just 15 games across an entire season. And it was not just the on-court results that were impressive, it was the manner in which the team went about achieving them. The Clippers were young, brash and seemingly heading for bigger and better things.

The last home game of the 2001-02 season was an 8 point victory over Memphis and the post-game scenes are ones that long-suffering Clipper supporters will always hold dear. The players stayed out on the court long after the final buzzer sounded and literally gave fans the jerseys off their backs. They signed autographs and posed for pictures while mingling with the Clipper faithful. The gestures from the players seemed to be as much about acknowledging the support received during the franchise's horrid past, as it was about celebrating the better days that surely lay ahead. Even Lamar Odom, who was still injured at the time, hobbled up onto the press table to dance a jig.

---

191 During the months of March and April, Olowokandi averaged 16.5 points, 9.6 rebounds and 1.7 blocks per game.

While all of this was going on, Darius Miles walked the sidelines, handing out boxes upon boxes of shoes to the adoring fans. No one knew it at the time, but this was Miles' last appearance at Staples in a Clippers' uniform.

Season XXV: 2002-03

Despite failing to qualify for the playoffs, the Clippers headed into the summer of 2002 with a group of players who were the envy of many opposing teams. The centerpiece of their roster was undoubtedly their three forwards- Brand, Odom and Miles. Each had shown flashes of brilliance in their short NBA careers and considering that they were all 23 years of age or younger, it was likely that they had only just scratched the surface in terms of their ability. In the middle, the Clippers had Michael Olowokandi, whose form at the end of the previous season led to renewed hope that he might be on the verge of finally living up to his potential. At shooting guard, there were options galore, with Maggette, Richardson and Piatkowski each bringing something slightly different to the table. In fact, the only missing piece seemed to be at point guard. Or at least that *was* the case prior to Baylor pulling off another trade that had the rest of the NBA glancing nervously over their shoulders.

If Vegas was running a book on who would win Executive of the Year, Elgin Baylor would have been at pretty short odds. For the past four years, he had worked tirelessly to build a roster that could compete with the NBA's elite. Now, on the eve of the 2002-03 season, it appeared that the last piece Baylor needed to add was a point guard who was capable of bringing it all together. Twelve months earlier, New Jersey traded for Jason Kidd and his arrival had completely transformed the Nets, who went from winning just 26 games to playing in the NBA Finals in the space of one season. Baylor was optimistic that a similar metamorphosis could take place in Los Angeles, if only he could find a way to snare a blue ribbon point guard. A point guard like Andre Miller.

Baylor was able to acquire Miller via a trade that was made at the end of July and he appeared to be a perfect fit for the Clippers. Miller was just 26 years old, making him young enough to grow with the rest of the Clippers' collection of youthful stars but also experienced enough to provide the leadership that the team desperately needed. Miller had played three seasons in Cleveland since being drafted with the 8th overall pick in the 1999 draft. He was considered to be an exceptional playmaker, even leading the league in assists- with an average of 10.9 per game- during the 2001-02 season[192].

The addition of Miller should have been greeted with universal joy and acclaim, and yet it wasn't. In fact, many people within the Clippers organization were actually opposed to the trade. The reason for this surprising reaction can be explained in two simple words- Darius Miles. In order to land Miller, Baylor had to send Miles to Cleveland, effectively giving up on him before he reached legal drinking age[193].

Miles' transition from a high school star to an NBA newcomer had been anything but smooth sailing. There were moments where he showed flashes of the same brilliance that caused scouts to gush over him in the lead-up to the 2000 draft. But for every five star performance that Miles produced, there was a corresponding one star effort. However, despite this frustrating level of inconsistency, Miles was undoubtedly popular, both with fans and teammates. Richardson, in particular, was unhappy with the decision to trade Miles, as he had been close to him since they were teammates on the AAU circuit. During their time together with the Clippers, Miles and Richardson had been practically inseparable, supporting each other on the court and working together as the two primary subjects of a documentary

---

192 Miller was also a Los Angeles native, having grown up in Watts.
193 At the time of the trade, Miles was still two months short of his 21st birthday.

about the daily life of NBA players. Miles departed the Clippers with averages of 9.4 points and 4.7 rebounds.

Eric Piatkowski was worried. Very worried. No current player had been with the Clippers for longer than Piatkowski. In fact, he had played just four fewer games than Loy Vaught, the franchise's all-time leader in on-court appearances[194]. So, if anyone understood how things worked in Clipper-land, it was Piatkowski. On the eve of the 2002-03 season, Piatkowski could see that the front office had assembled enough talent to not only qualify for the playoffs, but perhaps even win a series for the first time in franchise history. On paper, the Clippers appeared to be a formidable opponent, with a starting line-up that featured Miller, Richardson, Odom, Brand and Olowokandi, and a bench of Maggette, Dooling, Piatkowski and Marko Jaric[195]. However, if there was one thing that Piatkowski was sure of, it was that NBA games are not won and lost on paper. He knew that in order for the Clippers to be successful, they needed more than just talent. They needed to find a way to develop into a cohesive group. And Piatkowski was beginning to sense that the current crop of Clippers might not be the most unified collection of players in NBA history.

The primary reason for Piatkowski's concern was a familiar problem- Donald Sterling's unwillingness to open his checkbook. Sterling had spent all summer talking about spending up big in order to keep the team together. When asked if he was willing to exceed the salary cap for the first time, his response was emphatic, saying that retaining the team's key players was his "number one objective in the universe[196]." When it came to the issue of signing Brand to an extension, Sterling even went into specifics, expressing

---

194 Vaught had played 558 games for the Clippers, while Piatkowski was sitting on 554.
195 Jaric, the Clippers' second round selection in the 2000 draft, initially elected to continue playing in Italy where he emerged as the best point guard in Europe. He led two different clubs to Italian league titles in consecutive seasons and also played a pivotal role in Serbia's 2002 World Championship gold medal.
196 He also added that this was not as issue because "money is no factor to me."

a preference to "sign him for six years." But while Sterling spoke about doing "whatever it takes" to hold on to the team's top young talent, not a single Clipper was able to secure a long-term deal by the start of the regular season.

Brand entered the 2002 off-season with one year remaining on his rookie deal. However, his agent, David Falk, was offering the Clippers the chance to extend his client's contract immediately, rather than wait until he became a free agent in 12 months' time. Falk was seeking a six year, $72 million deal. The Clippers' responded with an offer that covered the same length of time but paid $12 million less, which Brand turned down. This left Brand to play out the final year of his current contract and meant that he would become a restricted free agent at the conclusion of the upcoming season.

The next player whom the Clippers were unable to lock into a long-term deal was Michael Olowokandi. Unlike Brand, Olowokandi's rookie contract had already expired, therefore making him a free agent. Despite spending the majority of his four NBA seasons falling well short of expectations, Olowokandi entered contract negotiations hopeful that his recent good form would lead to a lucrative offer. At the end of the previous season, Baylor called Olowokandi "vital to the future of our franchise" and said that while the team had some tough calls to make, "losing our center can't be one of those decisions."

Olowokandi had heard all the talk of how important he was to the Clippers' future and so he audaciously asked for a seven year, $102 million deal. The Clippers countered with an offer for approximately half the money over the same period of time. As the two sides were unable to see eye to eye on an appropriate salary for any long-term deal, they eventually settled on a one year extension that paid $6.1 million.

Miller, Odom and Maggette were also eligible for contract extensions during the summer of 2002 but like Brand, did not sign anything. This meant that the Clippers were about to head into the new season with their best five players just a few months away from becoming free agents. This was unheard of, even in the Clippers' illustrious history.

Piatkowski knew that the uncertainty created by this situation was not going to be good for team harmony. "If we play together, we're going to be good," Piatkowski said. "If we don't, it's going to be a long and frustrating season." Piatkowski made it clear that he was not concerned about how looming free agency would affect Brand, saying, "Elton's going to play the right way," before adding, "There are a couple of other guys I'm worried about[197]." Unfortunately for the Clippers, Piatkowski's premonition proved to be spot on.

The 2002-03 season was a train wreck from the opening tip. The Clippers were forced to play the first two months without the services of Odom, who was still stuck on the sidelines with last season's ankle injury. However, given the Clippers' depth, this should not have been too great a concern. Maggette replaced Odom in the Clippers' starting lineup for the season opener, a home game against Darius Miles and the Cleveland Cavaliers. It was a game that the Clippers were expected to win easily but instead, they allowed the Cavs to come from behind and steal a two point victory[198]. This opening night defeat was a taste of things to come and after the first five weeks of the season, the Clippers had won just six of their 18 games.

By the time that Odom was ready to resume playing, it was the end of December and the team's record stood at 12-17. Odom's return, after 11 months on the sidelines, offered a glimmer of hope that a mid-season resurrection might still be possible. The Clippers finally had all the members

---

197 Gentry echoed Piatkowski's concerns, saying, "It will be tough to go into the season with our five starters each playing for a contract."
198 If you believe in bad omens, then the first few seconds of the Cavs' game told you all that you needed to know about the Clippers' 2002-03 campaign. The first basket of the new season was a dunk by Miles, who went on to play an instrumental role in the upset, finishing with 15 points, 5 rebounds, 3 assists and 2 steals.

of their starting line-up healthy at the same time and had over 50 games still to play. However, rather than make a charge towards the post-season, the team lost the first five games that they played with Odom back in the line-up. This latest losing streak effectively put an end to their playoff hopes before they had even reached the halfway mark of the season.

The primary reason behind the Clippers' inability to play up to their potential was not too difficult to figure out. With the bulk of the team on the verge of free agency, many players were clearly more concerned with their own individual agendas than the team's overall success. A meeting was held in early January in an attempt to get everybody back on the same page. However, instead of helping, it only seemed to make matters worse. One witness who was at the meeting later claimed that some players openly admitted that they were focusing on accumulating statistics to ensure a bigger pay day when they became free agents.

From here, things went from bad to worse. At the end of January, Olowokandi's season came to a premature end when he underwent arthroscopic surgery on his left knee, which had been giving him problems for the past few months. Then, in late February, the front office made a decision that was more predictable than the climax of a Van Damme movie, firing Alvin Gentry and replacing him with assistant coach Dennis Johnson. Baylor's explanation for firing yet another head coach was that Gentry was "probably too nice."

Under the direction of Johnson the Clippers won just eight of their final 24 games, giving the interim coach an almost identical winning percentage to the man who he replaced. The reality was that, due to a number of factors beyond both Gentry and Johnson's control, it was unfair to attribute the poor results of the 2002-03 season to either coach. Injuries played a part in derailing the Clippers' chances, with their starting unit of Miller, Richardson, Odom, Brand and Olowokandi able to play together on just seven occasions. But while most coaches have to deal with injuries, not many have to do it while also trying to overcome a plague of selfish play. Sterling's refusal to sign any of his key players to long-term contracts may have been successful as a money saving strategy, but it also played a significant role in the team's ultimate downfall.

The season ended with the Clippers sitting in last place in the Pacific Division with a 27-55 record, clearly a horrible result for such a talented collection of players. And with the team's top six scorers all about to become free agents, it appeared as if things were only going to get worse. All six would attempt to leave the franchise during the summer of 2003.

Only four were successful in escaping.

Season XXVI: 2003-04

Elton Brand wanted out. Brand's rookie contract had expired, thus making him a restricted free agent. This meant that he could sign an offer sheet with the team of his choice and the Clippers would have just 15 days to either match it or watch their star player walk out the door[199]. Unlike 12 months earlier, Brand's salary was now going to be determined by what the market thought he was worth, rather than what Donald Sterling was willing to pay him.

Utah was so keen to secure Brand's services that they were on the phone with Falk when the clock struck midnight on July 1st, the first day that teams were allowed to negotiate with free agents. Jazz general manager Kevin O'Connor offered Brand a six year, $82 million contract. Ten minutes later, the Clippers called with a five year deal that paid around

---

199 An offer sheet is the name given to the document that a restricted free agent signs with a new franchise. Under the collective bargaining agreement, the player's current team is then given the opportunity to match the offer and retain their player. If they do, the offer sheet is null and void and the player remains with their existing team. However, if the specified time period passes and there is no matching offer made by the player's current team, then the terms contained within the offer sheet automatically form the basis of a contract with the new franchise.

$65 million. Falk informed the surprised Clippers that he had already received a "max" offer and that his client would not consider signing for anything less.

Utah was not alone in offering Brand a "max" deal, with Miami making an $82 million pitch of their own. Brand considered both Utah and Miami to be desirable destinations, but he ultimately opted to sign with the Heat for two main reasons. First, playing for Miami meant playing for Hall of Fame coach Pat Riley, a proven winner who Brand was hoping could help him elevate his game to the next level. And secondly, Florida's lack of state taxes made Miami's offer a more fiscally appealing alternative. After announcing that his client had signed an offer sheet with the Heat, Falk used the rest of the press conference to try and dissuade the Clippers from matching the proposed deal. Falk said that the Clippers were well aware of Brand's intentions to leave if they could not offer a "max" contract. He also strongly implied that his client had been given an assurance by Sterling that the franchise would not stand in Brand's way. "Elton expects Donald to honor his word," Falk said.

Not surprisingly, Brand wasn't alone in his haste to depart. That very same day, Andre Miller and Corey Maggette both signed offer sheets of their own, with Denver and Utah respectively. And it appeared that the Heat, Nuggets and Jazz were going out of their way to discourage the Clippers from matching their bids. All three offer sheets included large, up-front cash payments that were designed to test Sterling's will to retain the trio of young stars. Under the proposed contracts, Miller, Brand and Maggette were set to receive a combined total of over $20 million before playing a single game for their prospective new teams.

Having signed an offer sheet with Miami, Brand was confident that his days as a Clipper were finally over. A quick glance at Sterling's track record when it came to spending large sums of money to retain players left Brand with the impression that it was unlikely that the Clippers would match the

Heat's offer. After four challenging NBA seasons, two in Chicago and two in Los Angeles, Brand was looking forward to a new beginning.

It took just three days for the Clippers to decide that Elton Brand was too good a player to lose. Sterling called Brand at the Mandarin Oriental Hotel in Miami, proclaimed his love for the All-Star power forward and informed him of the franchise's decision to match Miami's offer. In an instant, the Clippers went from being a shrinking image in Brand's rearview mirror to the team that he was going to be stuck playing with, *for the next six years*.

Not only did the Clippers retain Brand, they also went out and made a $60 million offer to Gilbert Arenas, an unheralded second round draft pick who had blossomed into one of the league's most promising young guards. At the end of the 2002-03 season, Arenas won the league's Most Improved Player award, posting averages of 18.3 points and 6.3 assists per game while playing for Golden State. The Clippers were not the only franchise that was interested in Arenas, with Washington putting in an almost identical offer. Arenas eventually elected to sign with the Wizards.

Having missed out on Arenas, the Clippers turned their attention to holding onto their existing players. One player whom they had no chance of retaining was Olowokandi, who signed with Minnesota on the first day that free agents were allowed to formalize contracts with new teams. Twelve months earlier, Olowokandi was optimistic of landing a lucrative deal on the free agent market, thus he turned down a five year, $45 million offer from the Clippers and instead signed a one year deal. He then set about showing the rest of the league that he was someone worthy of a large financial investment.

Olowokandi averaged 12.3 points, 9.1 rebounds and 2.2 blocks across the first three months of the 2002-03 season and it seemed like he was well on his way to securing a big pay day. However, after undergoing knee surgery in February, his stock plummeted. Not only did this procedure put a premature end to his season, it also caused many potential suitors to shy away amid concerns about whether he would fully regain his athletic gifts. Olowokandi eventually signed with the Timberwolves for $16.2 million over three years, which was a lot less than he was hoping to receive. Olowokandi's five years with the Clippers will be remembered by most fans as a catastrophic failure. However, this probably has more to do with the hopes that he carried as a number one draft pick than his actual on-court performance.

Clearly, Olowokandi never lived up to the lofty expectations that accompanied his arrival in Los Angeles. However, to label his Clipper career a bust is historically inaccurate. During the five seasons he played with the Clippers, Olowokandi was undoubtedly inconsistent, but he also showed that he was more than capable of being a solid starting center in the best league in the world. He played 323 games for the Clippers and averaged 9.9 points and 8.0 rebounds, a solid return during an era where productive centers were a scarce commodity. When you consider Olowokandi's late introduction to the game, this is a remarkable achievement. And while nobody can say for certain, it is quite likely that most observers would have a very different opinion of his professional career had he been selected a little later in the 1998 draft.

Ten days after the departure of Olowokandi, Eric Piatkowski also left, signing a three year, $8.5 million contract with Houston. Having lost Olowokandi and Piatkowski to Western Conference rivals, the Clippers' front office then had to decide whether to match the offer sheets that had been presented to Maggette and Miller. They waited until the final days of the two week deadline, before announcing that they were going to match Utah's $42 million offer and retain Maggette, but allow Miller to sign with Denver.

Attention now turned to Odom, the final key member of the roster whose future was still up in the air. The Clippers initially presented him with a low-ball offer of three years for $24 million, which Odom promptly rejected. The price for retaining the star forward then shot up dramatically when Miami inserted themselves into the negotiations. The Heat used some of the money that they had set aside for Elton Brand to sign Odom to a six year, $63 million offer sheet. Once again, Miami's front office was testing the Clippers' nerve, pushing a huge pile of chips into the middle of the table and then waiting to see how they would react. And whereas Brand relied on his agent to communicate the "I-want-out-of-LA" message, Odom took a more hands-on approach, speaking directly with the media and making it abundantly clear that he no longer wanted to play for the Clippers. Odom referred to himself a "disgruntled employee" and left no room for any doubt, saying that he wanted "to get as far away from the Clippers as possible." He cited a variety of factors behind his desire to leave, including the constant firing of head coaches and the lack of a regular practice facility.

Miami's bold move meant that the Clippers now had to confront the difficult question of just how much Lamar Odom was actually worth to them. He had undoubtedly shown flashes of brilliance during his short NBA career but he had also provided plenty of evidence for those who had reservations about him. In fact, there were red flags everywhere, including the two separate suspensions for contravening the league's drug policy, extended periods on the sidelines due to a range of injuries and the fact that his statistical output seemed to be trending in the wrong direction. In the end, this all added up to too great a risk as far as the Clippers were concerned. Citing "issues of character", they failed to match Miami's offer and allowed Odom to sign with the Heat.

The other significant off season move was the almost annual ritual of hiring a new head coach. After deciding that interim coach Dennis Johnson was not up to task, Mike Dunleavy was offered a four year, $10 million contract. Dunleavy was a former sixth round draft pick who had managed to scratch and claw his way to a nine year playing career with Philadelphia, Houston, San Antonio and Milwaukee. His playing days ended abruptly after he injured his back when the plane he was on jerked to a sudden stop while taxiing to the terminal. Dunleavy received a large compensation payout from the airline and momentarily left the NBA to become a Wall Street stockbroker. However, the world of high finance was not for him and he returned to the NBA in 1987 when an assistant coaching position opened up in Milwaukee.

His first head coaching job arrived in 1990, with Dunleavy taking the reins from Pat Riley at the Lakers. Dunleavy fell just three games short of winning an NBA championship in his first season, when the Lakers were defeated by Michael Jordan and the Bulls in the 1991 Finals. After two seasons in Los Angeles, he returned to Milwaukee, where he was not only employed as the Bucks' head coach, but also took on a role in the front office.

Dunleavy's next stop was Portland and in just his second season with the Blazers, he won the Coach of the Year award. In the 1999-2000 season, Dunleavy appeared to be on the verge of claiming the Larry O'Brien Trophy but the Blazers imploded, squandering a 15 point fourth quarter lead to the Lakers in Game 7 of the Western Conference finals. Dunleavy was subsequently fired by Portland at the end of the following season, after the Blazers were eliminated in the first round of the playoffs.

Dunleavy said he had "enough (people) to fill the building" trying to convince him not to take the Clipper job. He was eventually swayed to accept after receiving assurances that he would be consulted on player personnel matters. However, it didn't take long for Dunleavy to transition from "being consulted" to having the final say on trades, draft picks and free agent signings.

Not long after Dunleavy was hired, a meeting was scheduled at Donald Sterling's Beverly Hills office. Joining Dunleavy and Sterling was Elgin

Baylor and team president Andy Roeser. When the discussion shifted to the composition of the Clippers' roster, Dunleavy's optimistic approach and can-do attitude blew Sterling away. Here was a man who had taken two separate organizations to the cusp of winning NBA championships and he was now predicting that something similar could be achieved by the Clippers. Dunleavy's bold predictions were like music to Sterling's ears.

When the meeting concluded, Sterling pulled Dunleavy aside and said he was giving him the authority to make any transaction that he believed would benefit the franchise, regardless of whether Baylor agreed with the proposed move or not. The only problem was that Sterling didn't share this information with Baylor, setting up a front office where two different people sincerely believed that they were running the show.

In the lead-up to Dunleavy's first season there had been numerous changes made to the roster. Gone were the Clippers' starting point guard (Miller), best perimeter shooter (Piatkowski), starting center (Olowokandi) and most versatile player (Odom). Despite these departures, Dunleavy still had his fair share of talented, young players, with a projected starting line-up of Marko Jaric, Quentin Richardson, Maggette, Brand and Chris Kaman[200]. However, while their starting five appeared reasonably strong, the Clippers' bench had all the depth of an inflatable children's pool. If the Clippers were going to have any chance of securing an unexpected playoff berth, the one thing that they could not afford was for one of their star players to suffer a serious injury.

Elton Brand's foot was broken before the 2003-04 season even tipped off. At the time, the Clippers were in Saitama, Japan, where they were scheduled to launch their new campaign against Seattle. Brand was unsure of exactly when the injury took place, but he knew that it was sometime between

---

[200] Kaman was selected by the Clippers with the sixth overall pick in the 2003 draft.

Monday, when the team first arrived in Japan, and Thursday, when he took to the court for the first game of the season. "It was hurting," Brand said, "But not to the (point) that I thought it was broken." So, instead of sitting out, Brand lived up to his hard hat and lunch pail reputation and took his place in the starting line-up for the first game of the Mike Dunleavy-era. He played 37 minutes on a broken foot and finished with 21 points, 15 rebounds, 5 assists and 8 blocked shots. Unfortunately, this remarkable performance counted for little, as the Clippers meekly surrendered to a mediocre Sonics team. Afterwards, Brand was in so much pain that he could barely walk and a post-game MRI revealed a hairline fracture in his right foot.

Brand's injury kept him on the sidelines for five weeks and this injury was a fairly large factor in yet another season of unfulfilled expectations. By the time the All-Star break came around, the Clippers had won just 22 of their 51 games and were rapidly falling out of the playoff picture. Any slim hope of making a late run for the West's eighth seed evaporated over the last two months of the season, with the Clippers losing 25 of their final 31 games to finish with the Western Conference's worst record.

Amongst the gloom of another season filled with disappointments, Clipper fans were left to wonder what the franchise's next move would be. It turned out that the front office had an audacious plan that was very similar to what Irv Levin and Gene Shue had pulled off a quarter of a century earlier. The Clippers were going to go out and sign the biggest name in professional basketball.

CHAPTER 14

The Kobe Circus

"I could see myself playing for the Clippers."

KOBE BRYANT

DONALD STERLING STROLLED OUT OF the Four Seasons Hotel in Newport Beach feeling like a kid on Christmas morning. He had just finished meeting with Kobe Bryant and it appeared that the star guard was on the verge of signing a long term deal that would see him play the best years of his career in a Clipper uniform. Bryant hadn't gone so far as to give any concrete assurances and nothing had been formally put in writing, and yet Sterling still felt an overwhelming sense of anticipation. As he walked out into the warm air of a typically stunning Californian summer's evening, he realized that the championship parade that he had spent the past two decades dreaming about was almost within his grasp.

Kobe Bryant and Shaquille O'Neal were the NBA's version of "The Itchy & Scratchy Show." And by the end of the 2003-04 season, their relationship had become so toxic that they could no longer co-exist as teammates. Whether this meant that one or the other would be departing the Lakers was still uncertain. But it had become abundantly evident to the basketball fans of Los Angeles that both men would not be suiting up in the purple and gold for the upcoming season.

The imminent break-up of the Shaq and Kobe combination meant drawing the curtain on the most lethal duo in the history of the league. It could be argued that never before had two players with so much talent found themselves on the same team at the peak of their respective careers. Over the five season period from 1999-2000 to 2003-04, the Lakers made four appearances in the Finals, claiming the Larry O'Brien Trophy on three occasions. During this run of success, O'Neal averaged 27 points, 12 rebounds and 2.6 blocks, while Bryant posted averages of 26.2 points, 5.3 assists and 1.7 steals[201].

Over this five year period, there were two constants that Laker fans could rely on. The first was that their team would win around 75% of their regular season games before progressing deep into the playoffs. The second was that a feud would erupt between the team's best two players at some stage during the season. The reasons behind these disputes varied slightly over the years but they all centered around one consistent theme- who was the focal point of the team's offense.

Despite this seemingly constant bickering between O'Neal and Bryant, the Lakers dominated the early 2000s. The 2003-04 season was different. The Lakers still played well, advancing all the way to the NBA Finals before losing to Detroit. However, behind the scenes, the quarrelling between O'Neal and Bryant had progressed beyond that of

---

[201] Both players were also named on the All-NBA first team every year between 2002 and 2004, making them the first teammates to share this honor for three consecutive seasons in almost 40 years. The only other pairing of teammates to be named on the All-NBA first team for three successive years was another Laker duo- Elgin Baylor and Jerry West. Baylor and West were actually selected together for four years in a row between 1962 and 1965, however, this was back when the league consisted of only nine teams, thus making the All-NBA selection of teammates a more likely occurrence.

two teammates who were simply staking their claim for a bigger piece of the pie.

Their feud had now become personal.

In fact, the disagreement that would eventually prove to be the beginning of the end for the Shaq-Kobe dynasty had nothing whatsoever to do with the game of basketball. Instead, this final dispute was related to an alleged crime involving Bryant. A crime that could not only put an end to Bryant's career but could also see him sentenced to life in prison.

At approximately 10pm on June 30th, 2003, Kobe Bryant arrived at the Cordillera Lodge and Spa, an exclusive resort located around 90 miles from Denver. After another long and exhausting NBA season, Bryant was in Colorado to have an operation on his troublesome right knee. A few hours after checking-in, Bryant, who was married and had only just recently become a father for the first time, had sex with a 19 year old concierge who worked at the hotel. That much is not in dispute. What was less clear was whether the sex between Bryant and his alleged victim was consensual. He says it was. She says it wasn't.

This encounter resulted in Bryant being charged with sexual assault, a charge that he vigorously denied. He was willing to concede that he had been unfaithful to his wife but said that this was all he was guilty of. Bryant held a press conference where he proclaimed his innocence, stating the sex was consensual and that he was being falsely accused.

As the start of the 2003-04 NBA season approached, Bryant's unresolved legal troubles were clearly the most dominant storyline in the world of the NBA. Regardless of the outcome of the impending court case, the incident in Colorado had already put an end to Bryant's carefully cultivated image of a clean-cut star who could be relied upon to sell anything from shoes to hamburgers. It would also signal the end of what was, at the best of times, a strained relationship between Bryant and O'Neal.

The start of training camp is usually a relatively uninteresting portion of the NBA calendar. Players arrive in varying states of physical fitness and endure a few weeks of grueling practices to get their bodies ready for the eight months of intense competition that lies ahead. The Los Angeles Lakers' training camp of 2003 was anything but a mundane affair.

When Shaquille O'Neal flew to Hawaii for the first day of the preseason, he was not a happy man. Just a week earlier, O'Neal discovered that Bryant had made some serious allegations about him during an official police interview regarding the incident that took place in Colorado. At the end of a long and draining interrogation, Bryant told the officers that he should have done what O'Neal does in circumstances like these and paid off his accuser to avoid the legal penalties that he was now facing. The second that O'Neal was informed of Bryant's comments, any hope for a harmonious Laker season immediately vanished.

O'Neal chose to keep his knowledge of what Bryant had said to himself[202]. Instead, he used basketball-related issues to communicate the displeasure that he felt towards his teammate. When Bryant failed to attend the first day of training camp, O'Neal pointedly told the media that "the full team is here." A few weeks later, O'Neal offered his opinion that Bryant should focus on passing the ball more frequently. Bryant provided a quick rebuke, declaring that he did not need "advice on how to play (his) guard spot." O'Neal, never one to back away from a confrontation, responded by

---

[202] In fact, O'Neal did not publically address Bryant's comments until 12 months after they were made. When he finally did, he dismissed them as "ridiculous," saying that Bryant would have no idea about his personal life, as the two men had spent very little time together away from their official Laker-related commitments.

stating that he was not telling Bryant how to play his position but rather "telling him how to play team ball." He went on to say that it was the start of a new season and "shit's got to be done right." O'Neal finally added that he was going to continue voicing his opinion and if Bryant did not like it, he should opt out of his contract and leave at the end of the season.

O'Neal's comments prompted Phil Jackson to warn both players to knock it off, threatening to fine them if the public war of words continued. However, instead of retreating from the feud, Bryant called Jim Gray, an ESPN reporter, and told him exactly what he thought of his 7'1" teammate. Bryant made a number of inflammatory remarks, including calling out O'Neal for coming into training camp "fat and out of shape" and questioning his leadership[203].

If O'Neal was a simmering volcano that had been lying dormant for much of the summer, Bryant's unprecedented broadside was the event that triggered a violent eruption. The day after Bryant's comments surfaced in the media, the Lakers' center stormed into the team's practice facility with the intention of physically assaulting Bryant. Had it not been for the intervention of long-time teammate Brian Shaw, who was now working for the Lakers as a scout, the ensuing shouting match would most likely have escalated into something much more serious.

Instead, the two men traded insults rather than blows and emphatically aired a number of problems that had been bubbling beneath the surface over the past few years. The incident finished with Bryant and O'Neal agreeing on a truce that was sealed with a hug. But while this ceasefire may have been successful in stemming the flow of public comments, there was clearly still plenty of bad blood between them and this would eventually derail the Lakers' quest for a fourth title in five years.

---

203 Bryant told Gray that a real leader wouldn't "threaten not to play defense and not to rebound if (he) don't get the ball every time down the floor."

The regular season started off well enough, with the Lakers winning 18 of their first 21 games. This strong start came as no surprise because, despite the increased intensity of the Shaq-Kobe feud, the Lakers' front office had assembled one of the most impressive collections of talent in the history of the league. The off-season additions of Gary Payton and Karl Malone meant that their roster now featured no fewer than four future Hall of Famers. Unfortunately, their good form from the beginning of the season did not last beyond the month of December.

By the time the regular season concluded, the Lakers had stumbled to a 56-26 record, an impressive mark but significantly worse than most experts were predicting at the start of the year. Still, they managed to successfully navigate their way through the first three rounds of the playoffs, defeating Houston, San Antonio and Minnesota. This meant another trip to the NBA Finals, where they were scheduled to face-off against a seemingly over-matched Detroit team. The Lakers entered the Finals as strong favorites but the off-court chaos that had hovered over the team since the start of training camp finally caught up with them. The Pistons' roster may have been vastly inferior in terms of raw talent but they were clearly a more cohesive group. Detroit claimed the title with a 4-1 series win that ranks as one of the biggest upsets in NBA history, leaving Laker fans to shake their heads and wonder what went wrong.

June 18th 2004, is a day that is known as "Black Friday" amongst Lakers' insiders. In the space of just six hours, the organization was transformed from perennial championship contenders to the fringe of the Western Conference playoff picture. O'Neal demanded a trade, after the Lakers refused to offer him a contract extension that he viewed as commensurate with his unique abilities. Phil Jackson was informed that he would not be asked back for another season. And finally, Kobe Bryant opted out of the final year of his contract, thus making him an unrestricted free agent. For the legions of

Lakers' supporters located throughout the world, this sequence of events was the basketball equivalent of Armageddon.

By refusing to meet O'Neal's salary demands and effectively pushing Jackson out the door, the Lakers' intentions were clear- they were planning on building their next championship team around Bryant. The only problem was that Bryant had not made a similar commitment in return. In fact, he had done the exact opposite. Bryant's decision to opt out of his contract indicated that he was considering leaving the Lakers. And once it was clear that Bryant's time as a Laker might be coming to an end, it also became obvious that the Clippers were the frontrunners to secure his signature.

The Clippers had a number of strong selling points that they could pitch to the Bryant camp. Geographically, there was no other team which could offer Bryant the chance to leave the Lakers and not have to uproot his young family. Minimal disruption on the home-front was likely to be an important consideration, given the turmoil that the Bryant clan had recently endured. The Clippers also possessed a talented roster which would allow Bryant to immediately start competing for a fourth championship ring. If Bryant opted to sign with the Clippers, he would join forces with Elton Brand and again be half of one of the strongest duos in the league.

Your Skill Level is Off the Charts,
Your Athleticism is Exceptional and Your Energy is Remarkable, but We Can't Draft You

The Clippers' pursuit of Kobe Bryant during the summer of 2004 was not the first time that the franchise had the opportunity to secure his services. Back in 1996, when Bryant was just a teenager hoping to be selected in the upcoming draft, he visited the Sports Arena and worked out in front of Elgin Baylor and the Clippers'

coaching staff, which featured Bill Fitch, Jim Brewer and Barry Hecker. The Clippers had the seventh overall selection and were trying to figure out if they should use it on Bryant.

"We asked him to do the Mikan drill," Hecker recalled, "But instead of hooking the ball, he started dunking it- right hand, left hand, right hand, left hand." It was an astounding display of athleticism that left a lasting impression on those who were present, with Fitch labeling it "the best workout that anybody ever had."

Later that day, Baylor and Fitch took Bryant out to lunch, where he was told, "Your skill level is off the charts, your athleticism is exceptional and your energy and enthusiasm is remarkable." An excited Bryant momentarily thought this meant that he was heading to Los Angeles, before the Clippers' brains trust added, "But we can't draft you." A confused Bryant asked why they were not going to select him if his workout had been so impressive. He was told that the city of Los Angeles would not take the Clippers seriously if they were to use the seventh overall selection to draft a 17 year old kid straight out of high school.

And the rest, as they say, is history.

The Clippers instead drafted Lorenzen Wright, who played three largely disappointing seasons before he was traded to Atlanta. Meanwhile, Bryant was selected at number 13 by Charlotte and then traded to the Lakers two weeks later. He went on to win five championships, a league MVP trophy and is widely regarded as one of the greatest players in the history of the sport.

If there was one factor that was going to prevent Bryant from making a move to the Lakers' cross-town rivals, it was likely to be financial. In short, the Clippers were not known for their willingness to spend big money when trying to attract free agents. However, the Clippers knew that a player of Bryant's stature was only going to play for top dollar and so they quickly began to take steps to ensure that they could offer him the most lucrative contract allowed under the league's collective bargaining agreement.

The first attempt to clear salary off their books was a trade with Charlotte, handing the Bobcats the rights to the second overall pick in the upcoming draft in exchange for the fourth and 33rd selections. As part of this deal, Charlotte agreed to select Clippers' back-up center Predrag Drobnjak in the upcoming expansion draft. From the Clippers' perspective, getting rid of Drobnjak meant freeing up $5.3 million in salary over the next two seasons. Next, they allowed free agent Keyon Dooling to walk out the door, which cleared another $2.3 million in salary. Then, in the middle of July, the Clippers' front office made another trade with Charlotte, sending Eddie House and Melvin Ely to the Bobcats in exchange for a couple of second round draft picks. Under normal circumstances, swapping productive role players for second round picks would not have been considered to be a smart move. However, as this trade allowed another $2.5 million in salary to be wiped from the books, it was a deal that the Clippers happily consented to.

All of this wheeling and dealing meant that the Clippers now had enough room under the salary cap to offer Bryant a "max" contract, which was precisely what they did. Bryant met with key figures from the Clippers in early July and he was presented with the first nine figure contract offer in the franchise's history. The proposed deal was six years in length and worth a total of $106 million. Dunleavy and Baylor left the meeting with Bryant feeling upbeat about their chances of snaring the Lakers' star.

One of the positives that the Clippers tried to promote when talking with Bryant was their collection of young talent. They attempted to sell the idea that it was the Clippers, and not the Lakers, who offered the best chance of competing for more championships in the future. And there is no doubt that the Clippers' projected starting five looked very impressive once Bryant was added to the mix. Joining Bryant in the backcourt would be Shaun Livingston, who was selected with the fourth overall pick that was acquired from Charlotte. Livingston was the first point guard in NBA history to be drafted straight out of high school. He had excellent court vision and at 6'6", possessed the ability to see over defenders, allowing him to find open teammates with ease. The Clippers' forward pairing of Maggette and Brand were playing at an All-Star level, with both men posting 20 point averages during the previous season. And in the middle, the Clippers had Chris Kaman, who had impressed the coaching staff during his rookie season and looked to have a bright future ahead of him.

While the Clippers were busy talking up the merits of switching teams, the Lakers were doing all that they could to show Bryant that his best move was to make no move at all. Lakers' management attempted to show Bryant how important he was to the franchise's future plans by giving him a major say in the selection of the team's new coach. When Bryant made it known that he would like to play for Mike Krzyzewski, the Lakers went out and tried to get Mike Krzyzewski, offering him a deal that was reported to be in the vicinity of $8 million per season. Krzyzewski was flattered but he ultimately decided to remain at Duke.

The Lakers eventually hired Rudy Tomjanovich, who had proven himself as a more-than-capable NBA coach by winning two championships with Houston in the mid-1990s. One of the first things that Tomjanovich did after being appointed was reach out to Bryant to let him know how integral he was to the team's future plans. In order to illustrate the type of offensive structure that he was planning on implementing, Tomjanovich passed on a videotape to Bryant. The tape featured highlights of a number prominent guards like Clyde Drexler, Steve Francis and Sam Cassell, who had thrived while playing for Tomjanovich.

The Lakers had one other big selling point to highlight in their discussions with Bryant- money. Under the collective bargaining agreement, they were the only ones who could offer Bryant a seven year contract. All of the other NBA teams could only offer him a maximum of six years. In financial terms, this meant that the Lakers' proposed contract was worth in excess of $136 million, which was about $30 million more than what the Clippers were able to offer.

In the final days before making his decision, Bryant met once more with representatives from both teams. Dunleavy made one final attempt to convince Bryant that it was in his best interests to leave the Lakers, telling him that if he didn't, he would spend the rest of his career dealing with being the scapegoat for the break-up of one of the most talented teams in NBA history. Dunleavy told Bryant that the only way he could counteract the perception that the Lakers got rid of O'Neal and Jackson to appease him, was to start afresh with a new team. After speaking with the Clippers' contingent, Bryant was on the verge of doing the unthinkable. He was seriously considering leaving the Los Angeles Lakers in the prime of his career to play for the Clippers.

Before Bryant could make his final choice, there was one more person whom he needed to speak with- Lakers' owner Jerry Buss. Bryant had earlier assured Buss that he would be given the opportunity to make the final pitch before any decision was made. Buss called from Italy, where he was vacationing, and urged Bryant to "stay with the people who love you." He promised that he would immediately begin rebuilding the Lakers' roster to ensure that they would be back in the race for another championship as soon as possible.

Later that the evening, Bryant went for a walk with his wife Vanessa with the two options swirling around in his head. When he returned to his Newport Beach mansion, his mind was made up. His flirtation with the Clippers was over. Bryant was going to remain with the Lakers and attempt to lead them to a championship without the help of O'Neal.

The next morning, Baylor received the phone call that he had been dreading. As had happened so many times out on the court, the Clippers had again been defeated by the Lakers. Baylor said that they had done "every possible thing" to secure the signature of Bryant and called his decision to remain a Laker "disappointing." Dunleavy took a different view of the Clippers' runners-up finish in a race where there was a solitary prize up for grabs, labeling the entire experience as a "positive for us in many ways." Under Dunleavy's logic, the fact that a player of Bryant's caliber was so close to committing to the Clippers meant that the league-wide view of the franchise was beginning to shift.

No matter how the Clippers tried to spin it, their pursuit of Kobe Bryant ultimately came up short. And it turned out that Bryant wasn't the only high-profile shooting guard who choose not to play for the Clippers during the summer of 2004.

Season XXVII: 2004-05

While the Clippers were busy rolling out the red carpet for Kobe Bryant, Quentin Richardson was feeling underappreciated and had begun looking for a new team of his own. Richardson had just come off the best season of his professional career, finishing with averages of 17.2 points and 6.4 rebounds per game. At the start of the summer, Richardson's preference was to remain with the Clippers, while the franchise's top priority was to sign Bryant. And even though these two events were not mutually exclusive, for all practical purposes they may well have been.

At the same time as the Clippers were trying to wine and dine Bryant, Richardson received an intriguing offer of his own. The Phoenix Suns were planning on implementing a radical new game plan for the upcoming season, a kind of souped-up version of the Lakers' Showtime offense that had been so successful across the 1980s. Under new head coach Mike D'Antoni they were going to run and run, and then run some more. Phoenix had already signed up free agent point guard Steve Nash to be the general of D'Antoni's fast-paced offense, and now they needed a shooting guard. D'Antoni saw Richardson, an athletic player who could run the lanes and spread the floor with his ability to shoot threes in transition, as the perfect fit for his system.

The Suns were well aware that the Clippers were preoccupied with their pursuit of Bryant, so they swooped in and signed Richardson to a lucrative offer sheet that paid $45 million over six years. Richardson was sold on the idea of moving to Phoenix and playing in D'Antoni's up-tempo system. While Bryant was still hemming and hawing, Richardson made it clear that *his* decision was already made, telling reporters "it's time for me to move on and be a Phoenix Sun." When Bryant finally announced that he was sticking with the Lakers, many observers expected the Clippers to match Phoenix's offer and retain Richardson. Instead, they opted to save their money and allowed Richardson to leave.

The departure of Richardson opened up a window of opportunity for fellow Chicago native Bobby Simmons. Dunleavy decided that the best way to replace Richardson in the starting line-up was to move Corey Maggette over to shooting guard and start Simmons at small forward. Simmons made the most of his opportunity, tripling his career scoring average to 16.4 points per game, while contributing 5.9 rebounds, 2.7 assists and 1.4 steals. This rapid increase in production was recognized at the end of the season when Simmons was named the NBA's Most Improved Player, the first time a Clipper won a major award since Marques Johnson was named Comeback Player of the Year in 1986.

The Clippers may have claimed a second individual honor if Shaun Livingston had been able to remain healthy for his entire rookie season. Livingston's career got off to a relatively slow start, as he averaged just 5 points and 2.6 assists over his first 11 games as a professional. It was while preparing for his 12th appearance that Livingston landed awkwardly in practice and injured himself. The diagnosis was a dislocated right knee cap, not exactly good news but considering the possible alternatives, not entirely bad either[204].

Livingston spent almost three months on the sidelines and when he was finally able to resume playing, the Clippers were sitting on a 23-27 record, just three games behind the Lakers, who were clinging onto the West's eighth seed. Livingston played well in his first game back, finishing with 10 points and 9 assists in a narrow loss to the Raptors. However, in the very next game, Livingston dislocated his right shoulder and this injury kept him out of the line-up for another five weeks.

By the time Livingston was ready to return to action, it was late March and the Clippers were sitting seven games below .500 and out of the playoff race for another season. This left Livingston with 17 games to try and salvage something from an otherwise wretched rookie campaign. Dunleavy promoted him to the starting line-up in just his third game back and the move paid immediate dividends, with Livingston dishing out 11 assists in 25 minutes and leading the Clippers to a victory over Milwaukee. This turned out to be a preview of what was to come. Over the month of April, Livingston averaged 11 points, 7.4 assists and 4.4 rebounds, which was good enough to be given the nod as the Western Conference's Rookie of the Month.

The Clippers finished the 2004-05 season with a 37-45 record, which was a nine game improvement on the previous year. However, despite this progress, they still found themselves eight games short of qualifying for the playoffs. One consolation for Clipper fans was the fact that Kobe Bryant and the Lakers won even fewer games, finishing with a 34-48 record. This was just the third time in the 27 year history of the Clippers that they

---

204 After discovering the exact nature of the injury, Livingston said, "It's a tough break, but it could have been a lot worse. I feel God was looking out for me. You fall like that and you could tear something, but it's not an ACL or anything else." Years later, these comments sound like some sort of eerie premonition.

managed to win more regular season games than their purple and gold adversaries. On a personal level, Bryant enjoyed another impressive season, averaging 27.6 points and 6 assists per game but he had very little support around him. This left Clipper fans to ponder what might have been had Bryant made the switch nine months earlier and joined forces with Elton Brand [205].

Brand was now at the end of his sixth professional season and while he had been able to accumulate an impressive list of individual accomplishments, he was yet to taste any degree of team success. Since being drafted as the number one overall selection, Brand had failed to take any of his teams into the post-season. This was all about to change. In fact, not only was Brand about to lead his team into the playoffs for the first time in his career, he was about the carry them further than any Clipper team had ever been before.

---

[205] One piece of good news for Bryant was that the legal issues in relation to the sexual assault charge were resolved prior to the start of the 2004-05 season. Bryant's accuser filed a civil suit before the criminal case went to court. She then informed the prosecutors that she was no longer willing to testify in the criminal case, causing the charges against Bryant to be dismissed two months before the beginning of the new NBA season. A few days later, the two parties reached an undisclosed settlement in the civil matter, putting an end to the saga. While the terms of the civil settlement were never made public, Bryant did release a statement in which he apologized to the woman involved and acknowledged that, while he believed she had consented to their sexual encounter at the time it took place, he now realized she did not share this belief.

CHAPTER 15

Unchartered Waters

"History? Don't tell me anything about history because that's not what this is about. I've been in this game a long time and one thing I know is that yesterday doesn't matter."

SAM CASSELL

3.6 SECONDS.

That was all that stood between the Clippers heading back to Los Angeles with a 3-2 lead in their series against Phoenix, all but booking themselves a spot in the Western Conference finals. As the two teams headed to their respective benches for what would most likely be the game's final timeout, an eerie silence settled over the crowd at the U.S. Airways Center. It was almost as if the 18,422 people in attendance were collectively pondering how their mighty Phoenix Suns could possibly be eliminated from the playoffs by the *Los Angeles Clippers*.

While the fans were contemplating the home team's imminent demise, the Clippers had a solitary thought running through their minds- *one more stop*. In fact, given that they were holding onto a three point lead, they didn't even need to prevent the Suns from scoring. A lay-up. A fifteen footer. A couple of free throws. So long as they did not concede a three-pointer or foul somebody while they were converting a basket, they would walk off the floor on the cusp of achieving something that no other Clipper team had ever come close to. The two teams broke from their huddles and the noise from the crowd began to rise again.

3.6 seconds.

One defensive stand.

The referee handed the ball to Phoenix's Boris Diaw and Clipper history would never be the same again.

Season XXVIII: 2005-06

Yaroslav Korolev was not a name that was on the lips of many scouts or general managers in the lead-up to the 2005 draft. The 6'9" Russian forward was just 18 years of age and there was little about his brief career that suggested he was ready to make the jump to the NBA. Korolev spent the previous season playing for CSKA Moscow's junior team and while his production against other European teenagers was solid (15.9 points and 5.8 rebounds per game), it was hard to know what this meant in terms of his ability to match-up against the best players in the world. Korolev also represented Russia in the under-18 European championships and his form in this tournament (4.5 points and 3.1 rebounds per game, while shooting just 33% from the field) suggested that he was a fair ways off from being ready for the NBA. However, despite this questionable body of work, Korolev decided to declare for the draft to see if there was any interest from the world's premier league. It turned out that there was one NBA coach who was more than a little curious.

Mike Dunleavy had seen Korolev play while travelling through Europe and he was impressed by the lanky teenager. In fact, Dunleavy was so enthralled that he told Korolev's agent, Marc Fleisher, that the Clippers would use their first round selection in the upcoming draft on the lanky Russian[206]. Fleisher was happy to hear that his client was about to become an NBA player but he also happened to be a friend of Barry Hecker, the Clippers' director of player personnel. So Fleisher called Hecker to inform him of what was going on.

Hecker was livid. "I didn't even remember Korolev," he said. "I remembered players that could play and this kid couldn't fucking play." Hecker alerted Elgin Baylor to the fact that they were about to waste a first round pick and advised him to fire Dunleavy immediately. Hecker's recommendation to take such drastic action was not based solely on this one incident. Instead, it was due to Dunleavy's continued meddling in decisions that had traditionally been made by the front office.

Dunleavy first trod on Hecker's toes a year earlier, when he began contacting agents to discuss potential players for the Clippers' summer league team. Assembling the franchise's summer league entry was a task that Hecker was responsible for and thus he was more than a little annoyed when he discovered Dunleavy going over his head. "It was totally unprofessional, just bullshit," Hecker said. "Mike's making phone calls to agents to bring guys into the summer league, which was my job, and I don't even know about it." Hecker believed this interference was part of a Dunleavy plot to seize power. "I said to Elgin, 'Mike's going to end up with your job and my job before this is over. If you don't think he's acting like a general manager, you'd better take another look.'"

The next time that the front office's plans clashed with those of Mike Dunleavy was in the lead-up to the 2004 draft. The Clippers owned the rights to the fourth overall selection and were considering using the pick on either Devin Harris or Shaun Livingston. Hecker was leaning towards

---

[206] When Fleisher was asked whether anyone from the Clippers had given him a heads-up about drafting Korolev, he neither denied nor confirmed the allegation. Instead, he said, "If I had a deal with a player, I would never comment on it, privately or publically."

he was a freshman at Florida State, the Seminoles progressed all the way to the Sweet Sixteen, the school's deepest NCAA run in two decades. The following year, they went one better, qualifying for the Elite Eight. After two years at Florida State, Cassell declared for the NBA draft, where he was selected by Houston, a franchise that hadn't won a single championship in its 26 year history. Over the next two years, the Rockets claimed two Larry O'Brien Trophies, with Cassell playing a crucial role in both playoff campaigns.

After brief stints in Phoenix and Dallas, Cassell was traded to the Nets and his arrival in New Jersey coincided with a 17 win improvement in the team's record and a rare playoff appearance. He then moved on to Milwaukee, where the Bucks came within one win of qualifying for the 2001 NBA Finals. His final stop before becoming a Clipper was Minnesota, where he joined a Timberwolves team that had been eliminated in the first round of the playoffs for the past seven seasons. Cassell not only led Minnesota to their first ever playoff series win in his first season with the franchise, he helped take the Timberwolves all the way to the Western Conference finals[207]. During his time in Minnesota, Cassell was selected as an All-Star, named on the All-NBA second team and finished in the top ten in league MVP voting.

The Clippers acquired Cassell on the eve of the 2005-06 season, by shipping Marko Jaric to Minnesota[208]. The Clippers were hoping that Cassell would be able to fulfill two roles- provide immediate assistance to their on-court efforts and serve as a mentor to Shaun Livingston, the franchise's point guard of the future. Joining Cassell in the backcourt was Cuttino Mobley, a 6'4" two-guard who was renowned for his ability to shoot from long range. He signed with the Clippers after securing a five year deal

---

[207] Minnesota eventually lost to the Lakers in six games, despite holding home court advantage.
[208] The Clippers also picked up a future first round draft pick in the deal.

worth $42 million, the largest contract ever given to a free-agent from another team in the Clippers' 28 year history[209].

Initially, there was some suggestion that Dunleavy might elect to go with Livingston as the team's starting point guard. It only took one game for Cassell to put an end to this debate. The new campaign tipped off in Seattle, where the Clippers took on the Sonics without the services of Livingston and Maggette, who were both sidelined with injuries. As the game headed into the fourth quarter, the Clippers were trailing by 11 points and things were not looking promising. However, led by Cassell, they staged a dramatic comeback. Cassell scored 15 points in the final period and finished the game with 35 points and 11 assists. When the final buzzer sounded, the Clippers had managed to turn a predictable season-opening loss into an 8 point road victory. Afterwards, Cassell had a message for the rest of the NBA, telling reporters that "this is not going to be the old Clippers from the past." The Clippers used their win over the Sonics to launch the best opening month in franchise history and by the end of November, they sat atop of the Pacific Division standings with a 10-5 record[210].

While the Clippers front office was happy with the positive start, they also knew that they could not afford to rest on their laurels. They spent the next few months exploring ways to improve the roster and at one stage, came close to making a trade for Indiana's Metta World Peace[211]. The proposed deal was a straight swap of small forwards, with the Pacers receiving Corey Maggette and the Clippers getting World Peace. However, the trade fell apart after Indiana's medical team raised concerns when Maggette's left foot was placed in a cast to help a ligament injury heal.

---

209 The additions of Cassell and Mobley were partially off-set by the departure of Bobby Simmons, who was lured to Milwaukee via a lucrative five year deal worth over $47 million.
210 Elton Brand was also named the Western Conference's Player of the Month, the first time that a Clipper received this honor since Freeman Williams won the award back in December 1980.
211 At the time, World Peace was still known by his birth name of Ron Artest. He legally changed his name in 2011, saying that his decision to adopt a new moniker aimed to "inspire and bring youth together around the world."

Then, in the middle of February, the Clippers traded third year forward Chris Wilcox to Seattle in exchange for Vladimir Radmanovic, a 6'10" sharp shooting, power forward from Serbia. Dunleavy was hoping that Radmanovic's ability to hit from long-range would add a new dimension to the Clippers' offense.

The Clippers headed into the All-Star break with 30 wins in 51 games, which was good enough for the fourth spot in the Western Conference. One of the main reasons for this on-court turnaround was the impressive play of Elton Brand. He had worked hard during the off-season, adding a reliable mid-range jump shot to his repertoire of scoring options and shedding close to 20 pounds. With Brand now comfortable playing further away from the basket, there was more space down low for his teammates to operate in. Brand's offensive transformation was given a nod of recognition when he was selected as an All-Star for just the second time in his seven year career.

When play resumed after the All-Star festivities, the Clippers went right back to trying to win enough games to ensure they were able to host a playoff series. In early March, they received good news when Maggette's foot was given the all clear, allowing him to resume playing after sitting out a total of 43 games. Maggette's return triggered another burst of solid play, pushing the Clippers' overall record to 39-26. With just a month remaining in the regular season, they were on pace to win 50 games and looked set to be a legitimate title threat once the playoffs commenced.

And then, almost as if on cue, the Clippers started dropping crucial games to other teams in the playoff race, causing them to slide down the standings. However, unlike previous chapters of Clipper history, this time around, these losses were exactly the results that the franchise was hoping for.

As the Clippers headed into the final weeks of the regular season, they faced a choice that no team on the verge of qualifying for the playoffs should ever be confronted with. On the one hand, they could continue to put forth maximum effort and try to win as many games as possible. This would most likely result in a difficult first round match-up against either Dallas or San Antonio, played without the benefit of home-court advantage. Alternatively, they could deliberately lose some games, which should ensure home-court advantage for a series against Denver, a team that was vastly inferior to either of the two Texas options. If this sounds like a ridiculous scenario, that's because it was.

This ludicrous situation had arisen due to the league's decision to increase the number of divisions, from four to six, at the start of the 2004-05 season[212]. The rules at the time stated that the two teams who won their divisions in both the Eastern and Western Conferences were automatically seeded first and second, regardless of their win-loss record. When the divisional re-alignment took place in 2004, the league simply expanded this existing rule so that the top three seeds in each conference would now be granted to the three divisional winners.

While this may appear to be both reasonable and logical in theory, in practice it caused a number of problems. For example, the best two teams in the Western Conference during the 2005-06 season were undoubtedly San Antonio and Dallas, who both happened to play in the same division. At the conclusion of the regular season, the Spurs narrowly claimed the Midwest title, which meant that San Antonio entered the 2006 playoffs as the Western Conference's top seed. This was bad news for Dallas. With the second and third seeds reserved for the winners of the Pacific and Northwest Divisions, the Mavericks slid all the way down to fourth, an outcome that clearly made no sense at all. Dallas' 60 wins gave them the third best record

---

212 This change was brought about by the inclusion of the Charlotte Bobcats, which increased the total number of teams from 29 to 30. Switching to six divisions allowed the 30 teams to be broken into equal groups of five, rather than having four divisions with seven or eight teams in each.

in the entire league and yet they entered the playoffs as the West's *fourth* seed. Meanwhile, Denver was handed the third seed despite winning 16 fewer games than Dallas. Adding to the absurdity of the situation was the fact that the Spurs and Mavs were now scheduled to meet in the second round, assuming each team won its respective first round match-up.

It was not just the top of the Western Conference standings that was affected by the divisional re-alignment, it impacted the teams in the race for the bottom four playoff spots as well. As the regular season was winding down, it was clear to everyone that finishing in sixth or seventh position was going to be preferable to securing the fifth seed. With just a few weeks remaining before the playoffs began, the Clippers were on track to finish in the fifth or sixth spot, and thus were heading for a clash with either Dallas or Denver. Conventional wisdom suggested that the Clippers should aim to win as many games as they could in order to secure the best seeding possible. But, in this case, conventional wisdom was not going to lead to the optimal outcome for the Clippers. Finishing fifth locked in a match-up with Dallas, while dropping to sixth meant a first round series against Denver, a far less imposing mission. The Nuggets' option was made even more alluring by the fact that the Clippers would have the advantage of hosting the series, due to their superior regular season record[213].

The other team in contention for the fifth and sixth seeds was Memphis, who had spent the entire season lingering a couple games behind the Clippers in the standings. The question of whether the Clippers should take their foot off the accelerator, in order to drop below the Grizzlies, was put to Dunleavy in early March and he dismissed the idea. Dunleavy contended that the team's form heading into the playoffs was far more important than what seed they ended up with or who they played in the first round. And

---

213 Winning the Northwest Division meant that the Nuggets were given one of the top three seeds, but it did not guarantee them home court advantage. That benefit went to the team with the best record.

for a while, it appeared that Dunleavy was being sincere, with the Clippers winning six of their next seven games.

Then things started to get weird.

The Clippers travelled to Memphis in late March and suffered a ten point defeat, committing a season-high 24 turnovers along the way. This loss moved the Grizzlies to within half a game of the Clippers. Then, in early April, they lost three games in a row, their second longest losing streak of the season, bringing their overall record to equal that of Memphis with three games left to play for each club.

The Grizzlies played their 80th contest first and their 12 point win over Houston gave them a half game edge in the standings. The following evening, the Clippers hosted Seattle, a game that they were expected to win comfortably. However the Clippers, who were already playing without Corey Maggette (who was nursing a sore back), opted to give both Kaman and Mobley the night off to rest some nagging injuries of their own. In their place, Dunleavy went to the very end of his bench to give court time to some of the most marginal players on the roster. Even Yaroslav Korolev took to the floor for a little over 10 minutes of action, the first time in over a month that he had subbed into a game. With the Clippers electing to employ a second and third string line-up, the Sonics easily cruised to a comfortable victory.

The loss to Seattle put the Clippers in the driver's seat to secure the coveted sixth seed, placing them a full game behind the Grizzlies. After the game, Dunleavy tried to brush off any suggestion that his team's poor performance was by design. However, while Dunleavy remained coy about his team's true motives, the Clipper players were slightly more forthcoming. "All I know is that we get the home-court if we're sixth and we don't if we're fifth," Brand said. "I know something does not seem right about that, but that's just the way it is, and we're working under the rules." Meanwhile

Cassell made the whole mess seem incredibly easy to comprehend, saying, "You've got to be sixth to have the home-court, and we'd like to have the home-court, so then we need to be sixth. It's that simple."

The second to last date on the Clippers' schedule was another match-up with Memphis and it turned out to be one of the more farcical games in league history. The Clippers headed into the clash knowing that a loss would ensure that they finished the season as the West's sixth seed and they seemingly did everything in their power to make sure they were defeated. Maggette and Kaman were again given the night off and they were joined on the sidelines by Cassell and Radmanovic, leaving the Clippers without four of their top six scorers. The Grizzlies responded by sitting out Pau Gasol, the team's leader in points, rebounds, assists and blocks.

Once the game began, the Clippers got off to a horrible start and at the half, the score was 51-33 in favor of Memphis. By the middle of the third quarter, the Grizzlies' lead had climbed above 20 and it appeared that the Clippers had successfully secured home-court advantage for the first time in franchise history. All they had to do was keep the mediocre basketball going for another 18 minutes and they would have secured the sixth seed. However, while their plan seemed to be working to perfection, it soon became apparent that nobody had informed James Singleton about the team's true goal for the evening.

Singleton was a little known rookie who had spent much of the season buried at the end of the bench. However, with the Clippers in full tank mode, he was given a rare opportunity to start against Memphis and he was determined to take full advantage of it. In the third period, Singleton made three three-pointers, dragging the Clippers back to within 11 points of the Grizzlies. While Singleton continued to nail jumpers and almost single-handedly erase the deficit, Dunleavy frantically tried to find the "right" combination of players. At the end of the third quarter, Dunleavy pulled Brand and Livingston from the game and neither returned for the rest of the evening. Then, just a couple of minutes into the fourth, Mobley was subbed out, leaving the Clippers with a line-up of Daniel Ewing, Singleton, Quinton Ross, Walter McCarty and Zeljko Rebraca, all players with scoring averages of 4.7 points per game or lower.

Midway through the fourth quarter, Dunleavy subbed out Ross, the only player on the floor who was part of the team's regular rotation, and replaced him with Boniface M'Dong, another scarcely-used rookie. And yet the margin continued to dwindle. With a little over four minutes remaining, Ewing nailed a three pointer to cut the deficit to 6. When Singleton connected on another long-range bomb two minutes later, his fifth for the game, the Clippers had climbed to within four points of the Grizzlies[214]. With 29 seconds left, Ewing hit two free-throws to bring the Clippers to within three points of Memphis. They were now just one shot away from sending the game into overtime and potentially destroying their chances of securing home-court advantage for the first round of the playoffs.

Under normal circumstances, the Clippers would have played aggressively on the next possession to try and force a turnover. Instead, they served up a defensive effort that was so passive that even the Washington Generals would have been appalled. The Grizzlies effortlessly passed the ball around until it wound up in the hands of Mike Miller, who nailed an uncontested three-pointer to seal the win.

The result guaranteed that the Grizzlies would finish as the Western Conference's fifth seed, leaving the Clippers with the more desirable sixth slot. After the game, Memphis coach Mike Fratello pointedly told reporters that he was "very proud of (his) team and their professionalism," before adding that they had done "what you're supposed to do- win games." When Grizzlies' forward Shane Battier was asked to share his thoughts on the "contest" that had just taken place, he said, "It was a bizarre game, I'll leave

---

214 Singleton, who entered the game with a scoring average of 3.1 points per game, finished the Grizzlies' clash with a new career high of 23.

it at that." Having locked in the match-up that they wanted, the Clippers now had to try and achieve something that had never been done previously in the history of the franchise. They had to go out and win their first ever playoff series.

THE PLAYOFFS: ROUND 1 VS. DENVER

It had been 28 long years since the birth of the Clippers and not once in that time had the team progressed beyond the first round of the playoffs[215]. If the Clippers were going to put a stop to this run of misery, there was one person who would be crucial to their chances of success, and it was not Elton Brand or Sam Cassell or even coach Mike Dunleavy. It was Quinton Ross, who was about to be handed one of the most difficult missions in all of professional basketball- putting the clamps on Carmelo Anthony.

Both Anthony and Ross left their respective colleges at the end of the 2002-03 season to commence their professional careers, but this is where the similarities between the two players end. When Anthony departed Syracuse after his freshman season, he left as an all-conquering hero. In just one year, he led Syracuse to their first ever NCAA championship and was named an All-American, averaging 22.2 points and 10 rebounds. In contrast, Ross stayed at Southern Methodist University for the full four years and yet never played in a single NCAA tournament game. During this time, Ross enjoyed a solid, yet unspectacular college career, averaging 14.8 points and 5.5 rebounds per game.

Anthony went straight from Syracuse to the NBA when he was selected as the third overall pick in the 2003 draft. As a 19 year old, he led the Nuggets to the playoffs in his first professional season and finished runner-up to LeBron James in the voting for the Rookie of the Year award. Ross

---

[215] This represented the longest drought in NBA history for a franchise failing to win a playoff series. Just 12 months earlier, Washington, who was second on this list, put an end to their 22 year run without any playoff success when they defeated Chicago.

was also hopeful that the 2003 draft would launch his NBA career but he was not one of the 58 players who had their name called out during the evening. And while not being drafted was a setback, Ross was still determined to pursue his dream of playing in the NBA. Ross was invited to participate in the Clippers' 2003 training camp and came agonizingly close to securing a contract. However, he ultimately missed out, with the last spot on the roster going to a 7'2" project player named Josh Moore[216].

After being cut by the Clippers, Ross decided to launch his professional career in Europe. He played in Belgium, where he performed well, averaging 16.7 points and 4.8 rebounds per game. Towards the end of the 2003-04 season, Ross received a visit from Mike Dunleavy and Fabrizio Besnati, the Clippers' director of international scouting. They were there to ask if Ross was interested in returning to Los Angeles to play for the Clippers. Ross did not need much convincing and at the end of the European season, he signed a four year deal.

During the 2004-05 season, Ross provided the Clippers with solid minutes off the bench at both the two and three spots. When Maggette went down early in the 2005-06 season, Ross was given the chance to start and he grabbed the opportunity with both hands. His primary role was to defend the other team's best perimeter player and by the time the playoffs came around, he was a regular fixture in Dunleavy's starting line-up.

Matching-up on Anthony in a seven-game series represented the biggest challenge of Ross' short career. Anthony may have been just 21 years of age, but he had already made a name for himself as one of the NBA's most prolific scorers. He possessed the size and strength of a power forward and the shooting touch and scoring instincts of a two guard, making him a nightmare for opposing defenses to try and contain. As Dunleavy prepared for the upcoming match-up with Denver, he knew that if Ross was able to

---

216 Moore is also one of Shaquille O'Neal's cousins.

curtail Anthony's influence, it would go a long way towards ensuring a safe passage to the second round.

After the first three quarters of Game 1, it looked like Carmelo Anthony was going to have his way with Quinton Ross. The Nuggets' star entered the game's final period with a tally of 21 points, which was almost a third of his team's total output. However, the fourth quarter proved to be an entirely different story. Anthony missed all eight of his field goal attempts, including three in the final 45 seconds that would have sent the contest into overtime. Anthony's disappearing act allowed the Clippers to hold on for a two point victory. And while he still finished as the game's leading scorer, Anthony missed 17 of his 26 field goal attempts, indicating that he was finding it difficult to carry the offensive load against Ross' tenacious defense.

If Anthony was disappointed with his output from the series opener, Game 2 was even worse. He picked up two fouls in the game's first five minutes, forcing him to the bench for the remainder of the first period. Anthony returned at the start of the second quarter but lasted just 90 seconds before he was whistled for his third personal, putting a premature end to his first half. By the break, Anthony was scoreless, the Nuggets were trailing by 22 and the game was effectively over. Anthony had a more productive second half, finishing with 14 points on 5 of 15 shooting, but it was not enough to bridge the gap. The Clippers walked off their home floor with a convincing 98-87 victory, giving them a 2-0 series lead.

The Clippers arrived in Colorado expecting a desperate Nuggets team to throw everything they could at them and that's exactly what they got. Denver was able to overcome another poor shooting performance by crashing the offensive boards and forcing 24 Clipper turnovers. Anthony continued to struggle, missing 11 of his 17 field goal attempts but he was able to get to the free-throw line 19 times and still finished with a game-high of 24 points. The Clippers managed to keep the game close for much of the evening before the Nuggets pulled away for a 94-87 victory.

Game 4 was another evening that Anthony would prefer to forget. He fouled out in the middle of the fourth quarter, departing the game with 16 points on 29.4% shooting. With Anthony's inability to find any sort of offensive rhythm continuing for the fourth consecutive game, the Clippers stormed to a 14 point road victory, bringing them to within one win of the biggest accomplishment in the franchise's history. The Clippers were led by the inspired play of two of their reserves. Maggette led all scorers with 19 points, while Livingston's output of 16 points, 6 rebounds, 6 assists and 3 steals was labeled as "spectacular" by Dunleavy. After the win, Brand spoke about feeling a "sense of history" as the team prepared to head back to Los Angeles to try and close out the series.

Game 5 turned out to be less of a contest and more of a celebration for a franchise that had endured more than its fair share of hard times over the years. The Clippers comfortably booked their first ever trip to the second round of the playoffs with an 18 point victory and, once again, it was their two star reserves who led the way. Maggette finished with 23 points, while Livingston set a new Clipper playoff record with 14 assists. At the other end of the floor, Ross harassed and harangued Anthony into another sub-par performance, with the star forward connecting on just 8 of his 24 field goal attempts. Afterwards, Anthony paid tribute to Dunleavy's defensive schemes, saying that they had succeeded in preventing him from getting into any type of a rhythm[217]. The Clippers' four playoff wins in a ten day span equaled the franchise's combined total of post-season victories across the previous 28 years.

---

217 For the series, Anthony missed twice as many field goals as he made and his scoring average was 5.5 points less than his output from the regular season. Ross' defensive efforts against Anthony were even more noteworthy due to the fact that the young Clipper was playing with a herniated disk in his back.

The post-game talk coming out of the Clippers' camp was almost an equal split between proudly discussing their first playoff series victory and expressing a firmly held belief that the team had all of the necessary tools to progress a lot further than just the second round. Dunleavy articulated the prevailing mindset when he said that there wasn't "a team out there…that we don't think we can beat." The final word on this historic evening went to the Clippers' much-maligned owner, Donald Sterling, who summed up the internal mood of the franchise more succinctly than anyone else, saying, "We've come a long way. And we have a long way to go."

THE PLAYOFFS: ROUND 2 VS. PHOENIX

Just prior to the start of the Clippers-Suns series, Phoenix point guard Steve Nash was presented with his second consecutive MVP award. The list of players who have managed to win this award in back-to-back seasons is short and only includes the absolute cream of the crop in terms of exquisite basketball talent[218]. The odds of a 6'3" Canadian who grew up playing soccer joining this select group of players would have been so long, that you could have written your own ticket.

Amazingly, it wasn't until Nash's ninth year in the NBA that he established himself as one of the league's truly elite players. That was the 2004-05 season, when Nash signed with Phoenix as a free agent and Mike D'Antoni was about to embark on his first full season of coaching the team. And right from the start, the pairing of point guard and coach was a match made in heaven.

The mid-2000 Suns did not approach the game of basketball in the same manner as other teams around the world did. Their unique style of play was centered on the idea that the easiest way to get high percentage

---

[218] The players who have won consecutive MVP awards are: Bill Russell, Wilt Chamberlin, Kareem Abdul-Jabbar, Moses Malone, Larry Bird, Magic Johnson, Michael Jordan and Tim Duncan. Nash joined this elite group in 2006 and in the years since, only two other players have added their names to this list: LeBron James and Stephen Curry.

shots was to continually push the ball up the floor at breakneck speed. The mastermind behind this incredibly simple concept was D'Antoni and the person who made it work out on the floor was Nash.

In Nash and D'Antoni's first full season together, D'Antoni won the Coach of the Year award, Nash was named the league's MVP and the team more than doubled their win total from the previous season, jumping from 29 to 62 victories. Not only were the Suns winning, they were doing it by playing some of the most aesthetically pleasing basketball ever seen in the NBA. Phoenix averaged over 110 points per game, almost seven points ahead of the league's second highest scoring team. The Suns' wild ride finally came to an end when they were eliminated in the Western Conference finals by San Antonio. During the 2005-06 season, Phoenix was once again one of the league's top teams, despite playing nearly the entire campaign without the services of their leading scorer, Amar'e Stoudemire, who was sidelined with a knee injury. The Suns finished seven games ahead of the Clippers and qualified for the second round of the playoffs after surviving a grueling, seven-game series against Kobe Bryant and the Lakers.

The Clippers headed to Phoenix with one simple mission- win one of the first two games and steal home-court advantage. Brand certainly played his part in Game 1, producing the greatest individual playoff performance in Clipper history. He finished with 40 points, on better than 80% accuracy from the field, 9 rebounds, 4 blocks and 3 assists. Brand was ably supported by Cassell, who had 28 points, while Maggette (20 points) and Livingston (10 points, 9 assists) again provided a spark off the bench. As a team, the Clippers shot close to 60% from the floor and they finished with a total of 123 points.

They also lost the game.

Dunleavy quickly discovered that this series was not going to be decided by how much his team was able to score but by how many points they allowed their opposition to put up. In Game 1, the Suns scored often and easily, finishing with 130 points, including 74 in the second half. All of which added up to a seven point Phoenix victory and 1-0 series lead for the home team.

In Game 2, Phoenix's small frontline failed to mount any sort of meaningful resistance to the Clippers' big men, allowing the road team to cruise to a 25 point victory[219]. The Clippers won the rebounding battle by a margin of 57-26, had more than five times the amount of second chance points as the Suns (31-6) and scored a total of 58 points in the paint. Brand again led the way, with 27 points and 10 rebounds, while Cassell finished with 23 points and 6 assists. Having snatched home-court advantage, the Clippers headed back to Los Angeles knowing that they were just three wins away from their first trip to the conference finals.

In the lead-up to Game 3, D'Antoni decided to make two shrewd tactical adjustments. Tim Thomas, a 6'10" forward with a nice shooting touch, was inserted into the starting five to try and curb the influence of Brand, who was averaging 33.5 points on 73.7% shooting across the first two games of the series. This allowed versatile defensive specialist Shawn Marion, who had been the Suns' preferred option on Brand, to switch onto Cassell. Both moves paid immediate dividends. Brand was limited to 20 points at 41.2% in Game 3 while Marion used his four inch height advantage to harass Cassell into missing eight of his ten shots, holding the Clippers' floor general to just 6 points. The bigger Phoenix frontcourt was also extremely effective in narrowing the rebounding margin[220]. All of which made for a much tighter contest.

With just over 28 seconds remaining, the Suns had possession and were clinging to a one point lead. They decided to put the ball into Nash's hands

---

219 Phoenix's starting frontcourt of Shawn Marion, Boris Diaw and James Jones were all 6'8" or shorter.
220 In Game 2, the Clippers grabbed 31 more boards than the Suns but in Game 3, that difference was reduced to just a single rebound.

to force the Clippers to foul him. However, the Clippers elected not to send Nash, a 92.1% free throw shooter, to the free throw line. Instead, they allowed him to stand near half-court and use nearly the entire shot clock. With just a few seconds remaining, Nash drove hard to his left, stopped 14 feet away from the basket and threw up a tough step-back jump shot that hit nothing but the bottom of the net. This left the Clippers with one final chance to tie up the game. The ball ended up in Radmanovic's hands but his long-range shot was off-target. Phoenix's 94-91 victory not only gave them a 2-1 lead in the series, it also meant that they had regained the all-important home-court advantage.

The coaching battle was playing out like a chess match between two Grandmasters and in Game 4 it was Dunleavy's turn to make a bold move. He made two adjustments to the starting five, one for tactical purposes and the other out of necessity. Radmanovic replaced Kaman, who sat out with a shoulder injury, while Ross was benched in favor of Maggette. This new-look line-up caused plenty of headaches for the Suns' coaching staff. Previously, they asked Nash to defend Ross, whose lack of an offensive game allowed the star point guard to basically hide on defense. That would no longer be a possibility. If they wanted to continue to have Marion check Cassell, Nash would be forced to defend either Mobley, Maggette or Radmanovic, who were all considerably bigger and capable of scoring points in bunches.

The Clippers again lived off a steady diet of Brand post-ups and the big man played his role to perfection. Brand finished with 30 points, 9 rebounds and 8 assists but, amazingly, was not the Clipper who came closest to recording a triple double. That honor went to Cassell, who had 28 points, 11 rebounds and 9 assists. Late in the fourth quarter, the Clippers held a double digit lead but a 12-0 run by the Suns helped cut the margin to one point with a little over a minute remaining. The Clippers, hadn't scored in the last five minutes and they appeared to be freezing up at the most crucial juncture of the series. If they lost this game, they would be facing a 3-1 deficit, reducing their chances of progressing to the Western Conference finals to somewhere between extremely slim and zero. They needed someone to step up and make a play for them. Not one, but two Clippers would answer the call.

On the next possession, Brand caught the ball at the edge of the free-throw line and hit a 12-footer to extend the lead to three. Then, after a Tim Thomas miss at the other end, Cassell drained a three-pointer, widening the margin to six points and thus sealing the victory. The series was now tied at 2-2, setting-up a critical clash back in Phoenix.

Game 5 turned out to be a classic playoff battle that NBA fans would talk about for many years to come. Unfortunately, much of the discussion centered on a coaching decision and a miracle shot that saw the Clippers snatch defeat from the jaws of victory.

If Raja Bell's three-point attempt had missed, it is unlikely that anybody would have noticed Mike Dunleavy's decision to sub Daniel Ewing in for the final seconds of Game 5. If Bell's shot failed to find the bottom of the net, the Clippers would have been boarding a plane for Los Angeles safe in the knowledge that, with a 3-2 series lead, they were in the driver's seat to progress to the Western Conference finals. If Bell's three pointer had been off-line, the majority of the post-game talk would have focused on what a great job Dunleavy had done, transforming the Clippers into legitimate title contenders. But Bell's three pointer didn't miss. It went in, making Dunleavy's decision to play a little used rookie for the final seconds of a crucial playoff game one of the most talked about substitutions in the history of the NBA.

While there are many professions that receive an inordinate amount of scrutiny, perhaps no job is as over-analyzed as that of an NBA head coach.

Each and every game, coaches make literally hundreds of decisions that are out there for the public to discuss, dissect and debate. Coaches can get 99% of these decisions correct and find that not a single one of these wise tactical moves receives any coverage. However, if a coach happens to make an error, the harsh glare of the media spotlight is ready to swiftly engulf their world. In fact, the very nature of basketball means that in many cases, a coach can make the right call and still end up with an unfavorable result. Even in these circumstances, it is highly likely that the coach's actions will be called into question. Welcome to the world of Mike Dunleavy on May 16th 2006.

Daniel Ewing was a 6'3" guard who was selected by the Clippers in the second round of the 2005 draft. He earned his spot on the roster by impressing the coaching staff with his ability to play excellent defense. Ewing averaged a little over 14 minutes a game during the regular season but once the playoffs began, he found his court time drastically reduced. In fact, before being subbed in to play the final 3.6 seconds of overtime, Ewing had only made one other brief appearance in Game 5, playing the final 18 seconds of the first half. This meant that Ewing had been sitting on the bench for over an hour of real time when he was asked to remove his warm-ups for the most crucial possession in Clipper history.

Ewing's role in the playoffs was almost exclusively limited to exactly what he was called upon to do at the end of Game 5- check in at the end of quarters to defend for a single possession. It was a role that he had performed well. Ewing had been subbed in on three previous occasions in the Phoenix series and each time he was successful in preventing his opponent from scoring.

With the Clippers clinging to a three point lead with just 3.6 seconds remaining in overtime, Dunleavy decided that the best way to approach this final possession was to put his best five perimeter defenders on the floor. Not only was Ewing subbed in for this crucial defensive play, Ross and Walter McCarty were as well[221]. Dunleavy went with a line-up that featured five interchangeable perimeter players, who were instructed to switch on all screens to ensure that any three-point attempt from the Suns was a contested one. The Clippers also had one foul to give before they reached the bonus. However, Dunleavy was understandably worried about fouling a Phoenix player who was in the act of shooting a three and thus instructed his team to only foul if their opponent put the ball on the floor.

In the other huddle, D'Antoni decided to put the fate of Phoenix's season in the hands of Raja Bell. Bell shot over 44% from long-distance during the regular season and was on track to set a new playoff record for three pointers made in a seven game series, with 21 already across the first five games. As the Suns' coaching staff was deciding what play to run, Bell sat on the bench telling himself- *"If it comes to me, I know I'm going to make it."* The play drawn up by D'Antoni was remarkably simple. Bell would start in the low block and run towards the free-throw line to create the illusion that he was setting a backscreen, before cutting back towards the baseline, where he would receive a pass from Diaw and take the shot from the corner.

The action back on the court unfolded exactly like it had been drawn up on D'Antoni's whiteboard. However, Bell failed to shake free of Ewing and as he cut to corner, the Clipper guard was just inches away. Bell caught the pass directly in front of the visitor's bench and elevated to take the shot, with Ewing shadowing him. Ewing was now so close to Bell that his feet were touching the three point line. Conscious of not fouling, Ewing elected not to jump, but as Bell was releasing the ball, he got both of his hands up, forcing the Suns' sharp shooter to take a tough, contested shot.

It hit nothing but the bottom of the net.

The game was now tied and heading to a second overtime.

---

221 McCarty had not played a single second in Game 5 up until this point.

The Phoenix crowd broke into a wild celebration and the Suns never looked back. The second overtime period was close throughout but the Clippers were never able to take the lead. Phoenix eventually sealed a 125-118 win from the free-throw line.

Nearly all the post-game talk was predictably focused on Dunleavy's decision to put Ewing into the game at the end of the first overtime. Critics of this substitution made their case by pointing out three simple facts. One, Ewing was a rookie. Two, he had spent nearly the entire evening sitting on the bench. And three, Ewing was the player who was defending Bell when he launched the game-tying three. The common opinion was that these three pieces of information added up to a catastrophic coaching blunder that would surely cost the Clippers a Western Conference finals berth.

However, those who were quick to blame Dunleavy ignored one simple, yet important fact- Ewing had played nearly flawless defense on Bell. In fact, even Bell himself acknowledged how difficult his three-point attempt was, saying he "didn't have a clean look" and that he "just threw it up there." In reality, Bell had done what NBA players had been doing for years- converting a clutch shot despite the presence of some very good defense. It is hard to imagine that the outcome would have been any different if Cassell had been left in the game in order to guard Bell.

The other area the media decided to focus on concerned something that Dunleavy elected not to do, rather than something that he did. Many analysts believed that the Clippers had erred in even allowing Bell to get his three-point shot off, believing that he should have been fouled as soon as he caught the inbounds pass. The Clippers had a foul to give, meaning that Ewing could have made contact with Bell as soon as he had possession and forced Phoenix to take the ball out of bounds again. Even Cassell called out his coach, saying, "We've got a foul to give. We've got to put Raja Bell in the fifth row with the popcorn man." At first glance, this sounds like a fairly reasonable idea. However, when one actually considers how this change of tactics might have played out, it suddenly becomes a lot less attractive.

The number one priority for the Clippers was not to foul a Phoenix player in the act of shooting a three-pointer. If they did, they faced the prospect of giving up a four-point play and losing the game on the spot, without even having a chance to play the second overtime. Given that Bell moved into his shooting motion almost instantaneously after catching the ball, it is hard to find a moment where Ewing could have fouled him and not risked putting Bell on the line. At best, there may have been a split second opening but if the Clippers elected to foul, they were placing themselves at the mercy of the referees[222]. The best the Clippers could have hoped for if they had opted to foul was to force the Suns to take the ball out of bounds again, with 3.5 or 3.4 seconds remaining on the clock. Clearly, the possible risks involved in implementing this tactic did not justify the minuscule reward on offer.

After this heartbreaking defeat, Brand, who finished with 33 points, 15 rebounds, 5 assists and 5 blocks, said he was troubled to hear Dunleavy become the scapegoat. "I've heard some of the criticism about Coach, but those people are novices to Clippers' basketball. They haven't watched us all season," Brand said. "These are people who got on the bandwagon a little bit late. They missed those same scenarios that worked many times." Brand was referencing the fact that Dunleavy had successfully been using similar late-game substitutions throughout the season without much attention or fanfare from the media.

As far as Dunleavy was concerned, people could say what they wanted about his coaching philosophies. The opinions of the masses were not going to influence the way that he approached his job. And in the lead-up

---

[222] Had Bell heaved up a shot as he felt the contact, there is every chance that it would have been ruled a shooting foul, placing him on the line for either one extra attempt, in the case of a made three-pointer, or for three free throws if the initial shot missed. Either way, neither of these scenarios looks especially appealing.

to Game 6, he made another bold decision, removing Maggette from the starting line-up and re-inserting Ross. To most observers, this appeared to be a defensive-oriented move, aimed at ensuring that Nash did not get into an early groove. However, Ross not only did a good job of chasing Nash around on defense, he also put considerable pressure on the league's MVP at the opposite end of the floor. In fact, Ross played the best offensive half of his career, using his height advantage to post-up and basically have his way with Nash. Ross converted 8 of his 10 field goal attempts to finish the first half with 16 points, helping the Clippers to build a 62-50 lead.

The margin continued to hover around the 12 point mark for much of the second half, before the Clippers finally secured a 118-106 win, tying the series up at 3-all. Brand again played a leading role for the home team with 30 points, 12 rebounds and 5 blocks, while Maggette scored 25 points off the bench from just 8 field goal attempts. This victory meant that the entire season came down to one game. If the Clippers were going to achieve the unthinkable and progress to the Western Conference finals, they would have to complete one of the most difficult feats in all of professional basketball.

They needed to win Game 7, on the road.

The Suns were exhausted. This should come as no surprise considering the amount of time that their best players had spent on the court. Over a 26 day period, Phoenix had played 13 physically and mentally draining playoff games and while the whole team was tired, perhaps no one was quite as worn-out as Steve Nash. Nash had played at least 35 minutes in each of the Suns' post-season outings and he was averaging close to 41 minutes per game across the first six games of the current series. And, if you consider the style of play that had prevailed throughout the series, it is easy to see why Nash looked like a man who was in need of a holiday. Phoenix's entire game plan was built around playing at a frenetic pace, meaning that Nash was responsible for pushing the ball on nearly every offensive possession. At the defensive end, the Clippers had made it a point of emphasis to attack Nash whenever possible. With Dunleavy deliberately playing line-ups that forced Nash to defend bigger players, he was spending much of his evenings battling for position in the post and wrestling with opponents who had been instructed to crash the boards at every opportunity. It was clear that this combination of tactics was taking a physical toll on Nash.

Aside from Game 1, which he dominated with 31 points and 12 assists, Nash had struggled throughout the series. Over the past five contests, he was averaging just 13.6 points and shooting under 39% from the field, well below his regular season numbers of 18.8 points at 51.2 %. Even more troubling was his lack of accuracy from three-point range, where he had converted only 2 of his 18 attempts. Nash was carrying a variety of hamstring, back and ankle complaints and the one thing that he needed above all else was some time to rest his weary body. And, courtesy of a quirk in the schedule, that was exactly what he was about to get.

The dates of the first six games of the series had followed a predictable every-other-day pattern, giving teams one day to recuperate between each game. However, the NBA decided to schedule the Game 7s from each conference on the same day, to ensure that no team got any extra rest in the lead-up to the conference finals. This meant that instead of the usual one day off between games, the Clippers and Suns had three. This extended break clearly helped the Suns more than it did the Clippers[223].

When Game 7 finally got underway, one thing was immediately obvious- Steve Nash was well-rested and ready to play. He opened the Suns'

---

[223] Amazingly, Nash's average of 40 minutes and 58 seconds did not put him at the top of the Suns' list for minutes played. Marion was averaging over 42 minutes a night against the Clippers, while Bell was playing over 43 minutes. These huge numbers came as a result of D'Antoni's decision to basically go with a six man rotation of Nash, Bell, Marion, Thomas, Diaw and Barbosa, with James Jones still making the occasional cameo appearance.

scoring by draining a long three-pointer from the top of the key and then set up Marion and Thomas for triples of their own. The Clippers were also on target early, shooting 61% from the field and at the end of the first quarter, the score line was 32-28, in favor of Phoenix. By half-time, the Suns had increased their lead to eight and, had it not been for the stellar play of Brand, it is likely the Clippers would have been behind by even more. Brand was almost single-handedly keeping his team in the game, finishing the first half with 20 points on 10 for 15 shooting.

The Clippers managed to hang around for much of the third quarter, before things started to unravel in the final minutes. First, Mobley was whistled for a technical foul. This was followed by a 24 second violation on the Clippers' next possession and then, a few minutes later, Maggette threw the ball away twice in a row. Throughout all this Clipper chaos, the Suns continued to knock down open three-pointers. At the end of the third quarter, Phoenix was in front by 15 points. When Thomas and Jones each connected on triples in the opening minutes of the fourth quarter, the margin grew to 19 and the game, and the series, were effectively over. The final score was 127-107 and the difference maker was clearly Nash. The three days of rest and recovery served him well and he played Game 7 with a bounce in his step that had been absent for much of the series, contributing 29 points and 11 assists.

Despite being blown-out in the second half of Game 7, the Clippers had a lot that they could be proud of, including setting a new franchise record for most regular season victories (47) and progressing to the second round of the playoffs for the first time. Most observers were predicting that the team was only going to get better in the coming years and, given the make-up of their roster, it appeared that this optimism was well placed. Outside of Cassell and Mobley, all the members of the Clippers' regular rotation were 27 years of age or younger. And, with the emergence of Shaun Livingston in the playoffs, it seemed that the Clippers' future floor general was already in uniform. But amongst all the congratulatory back-slapping and high-fiving, one basketball sage was still skeptical about the idea that the Clippers had left their dark past behind them. "Getting to the Western Conference finals one time in 25 years doesn't mean you've turned the corner[224]," said Charles Barkley. "You haven't even gone halfway down the block."

---

224 Actually, the Clippers only made it as far as the Western Conference semi-finals.

CHAPTER 16

One Step Forward, Two Steps Back

"I went up for a lay-up and just kind of lost my balance coming down."

SHAUN LIVINGSTON

SEASON XXIX: 2006-07

IN THE WORLD OF SPORTS writing, the term "horrific" pops-up from time to time. It is sometimes used to describe a one-sided defeat, a poor performance by an individual player or a particularly bad refereeing display. However, in reality, it is rare that anything truly horrific actually happens within the confines of a sporting contest. Unfortunately for the Clippers, February 26th 2007 was one such occasion where the term "horrific" accurately describes what took place on the Staples Center floor.

Shaun Livingston was on top of the world. For the first time since the end of his rookie season, his job title was exactly as he had envisioned it would be. He was a starting point guard in the best basketball league in the world. This was what Dunleavy had in mind when he traded for Sam Cassell 18 months earlier. Cassell would play the starting role for the first season, providing on-court leadership while also mentoring Livingston. In season two, the team would be handed over to Livingston, allowing Cassell, who had recently turned 37, to reduce his minutes and remain fresh for another playoff run.

Livingston was making the most of his recent promotion. His scoring average had almost doubled from the previous season and he was also putting up career-best numbers in assists, steals, rebounds, blocks and field goal percentage. After battling through two injury-interrupted seasons, Livingston appeared poised to make the jump into the stratosphere of the NBA's elite point guards.

However, while things were going well for Livingston on an individual level, the same could not be said for the Clippers' team as a whole. After the first two thirds of the season, they were sitting four games below .500 and struggling to keep pace with the rest of the Western Conference playoff contenders. In late February, they scored a crucial home win over Golden State, another team in the race for a playoff spot and no player contributed more to the Clippers' cause than Livingston, who finished with 14 points and 14 assists. The Clippers' next game was also at Staples, against the lowly Charlotte Bobcats. If they were able to secure another win, they would move back inside the West's top eight, placing them in a good position to make a run over the final two months of the season.

The Bobcats' game was only a few minutes old when Cuttino Mobley poked the ball away from ex-Clipper Derek Anderson, causing it to spill free at the top of the key. Livingston pounced on the loose ball and charged down the court, with Raymond Felton in pursuit. When Livingston reached the other end, he elevated on the left side of the basket but was slightly off balance, causing him to miss his lay-up attempt. What happened next was so gruesome that the televised replays came with accompanying warnings about the graphic nature of the footage.

As Livingston landed, his left leg buckled underneath him, causing his knee to collapse at an angle in which it was clearly not meant to be. The cameras covering the game momentarily left Livingston crumpled on the baseline to follow the play, as Charlotte pushed the ball back down the opposite end. However, while Livingston might have been out of sight, his traumatized screams could be clearly heard as they echoed through a suddenly quiet Staples Center. It was immediately apparent that Livingston was badly hurt. Just how serious his injuries were would soon shock the basketball world.

Play was stopped and Clippers' team doctor Steven Shimoyama was one of the first people on the scene. When he looked at Livingston's knee, it reminded him of a pretzel. It was actually dislocated in *two* different places- the knee cap and a posterior lateral dislocation, which pushed the shin bone out to the side. Shimoyama instinctively put his elbow behind Livingston's knee and then tugged as hard as he could, trying to re-align both the lower leg and knee cap at the same time. Livingston was then rushed to Centinela Hospital. He tried to remain calm during the ambulance ride, reminding himself that he had already successfully recovered from a dislocated knee during his rookie season. If this was the only damage which he had sustained, Livingston knew that he was facing months of rehabilitation, but he drew strength from his previous experience with this type of injury, knowing that it was something that he could manage.

When he arrived at the hospital, Livingston soon discovered that his injury was much worse than he had imagined. Doctors told him they needed to take blood tests in order to determine whether the artery in the back of his leg had been damaged. A shocked Livingston was then informed that if the artery was in fact torn, there was a risk he would get gangrene, meaning he was facing the prospect of having his leg amputated.

Any thought of making a speedy recovery suddenly vanished.

Livingston was left to wonder whether he would retain all of his limbs, much less resume his basketball career.

It turned out that amputation was not necessary but simply reading a list of what had been damaged in Livingston's knee gave a pretty good indication of just how serious the situation was. On top of the dual dislocations, Livingston had torn his anterior cruciate ligament, posterior cruciate ligament and medial collateral ligament. He underwent immediate surgery and was informed that it might take several months of rehabilitation before he would be able to walk again. News like this would be imposing for any healthy 21 year old, but for a professional athlete who relies on their body to make a living, it was truly horrific.

While Livingston was left to ponder the prospect of spending an unspecified amount of time on the sidelines, the Clippers attempted to salvage something from what was quickly becoming another season to forget. Dunleavy initially turned to Cassell to fill the void created by Livingston's absence. The only problem was that Cassell had spent much of the season dealing with a variety of injuries of his own with his latest problem, a pulled abdominal muscle, still not fully healed. Cassell was briefly able to put any pain he was experiencing aside and turn back the clock. First, he led the shell-shocked Clippers to a 7 point win over the Bobcats on the same night that Livingston went down. He followed this up with a 16 point, 5 assist effort in a victory over Seattle. But any joy from the Sonics' win almost immediately dissipated when it was discovered that Cassell had sustained a groin injury in the final minutes of the game, forcing him to join Livingston on the sidelines.

This left the Clippers without a viable option at the point guard position, meaning Dunleavy had little choice but to start Daniel Ewing for the first time in over a year. However, it was immediately apparent that the second year player was not going to be a long-term solution for the team's point guard woes. Ewing, a marginal NBA talent at best, was clearly better suited to playing shooting guard and after just a few games, the Clippers' front office decided to enlist some outside help. Jason Hart, a 6'3" journeyman who had spent his entire professional career bouncing around from team to team, was signed as a free agent. At the time that Hart joined the team, the Clippers were sitting in the West's eighth position. If they were going to hold on to a playoff berth, they needed Hart to step in and provide solid play from day one, which is exactly what he did. Unfortunately, it was not enough to save the Clippers' ailing season.

Hart played 25 minutes off the bench in his Clipper debut and finished with 9 points, 4 assists and no turnovers. This was good enough to earn a promotion to the starting five, where he remained for the rest of the season. With Hart playing as well as could be expected and the return of a somewhat healthy Cassell, the Clippers won enough games to break away from the Hornets, Kings and Timberwolves, leaving Golden State as the only team left to challenge them for the West's final playoff spot. Over the closing weeks of the regular season, the Warriors had transformed themselves from underperforming also-rans to one of the hottest teams in the entire league.

Golden State's surprisingly good form left the Warriors and Clippers sitting on identical 39-40 records, with three games remaining on each team's schedule. The Warriors played the Timberwolves and got the win that everyone expected. On the same evening, the Clippers hosted Sacramento, a team with a 32-47 record and absolutely nothing to play for. In one of the most lackluster performances in the history of the franchise, the Clippers somehow found a way to blow the game. They fell behind by 19 points at the half and by midway through the third quarter, the margin had grown to 24. To an uninformed observer, it appeared as if the Clippers were the team that was already out of the playoff race rather than the Kings.

At some point in the third period the Clippers woke from their slumber, but it was a case of too little, too late. The Kings held on for a 105-100 win, pushing the Clippers to the brink of elimination. After the game, the normally tactful Brand spoke out about his team's lack of intensity, saying he felt "sick" and that perhaps some of his teammates would prefer to "go fishing and do other things" rather than extend their season by qualifying for the playoffs.

This loss meant that the Clippers could only make the playoffs if the Warriors dropped one of their final two games. Considering the Warriors were playing a dismal Portland team in their season finale, the Clippers' best chance for a Golden State loss seemed to be in their next game, which was against Dallas. The Mavericks were on their way to posting the league's best record, giving the Clippers hope that their playoff dream still had a pulse. However, as soon as the game between the Warriors and Mavs tipped off, it became immediately clear that Dallas had very little interest in securing the win. Having already locked up home court advantage for the entire playoffs, Dallas decided to rest three of their most important players, including Dirk Nowitzki, who was weeks away from winning the league's MVP award. Joining Nowitzki on the sidelines were Josh Howard and Jerry Stackhouse, while the Mavericks' regular starting backcourt of Devin Harris and Jason Terry played drastically reduced minutes. Given the weakened state of Dallas' line-up, it came as no great surprise when the Warriors ran away with an easy 29 point victory.

This Warriors' win rendered the Clippers' result from the same evening as almost meaningless, which was a shame, because they played one of their best games for the season. The Clippers won on the road against Phoenix, the only other team besides Dallas to crack the 60-win barrier.

It was a dejected Clippers team that flew back to Los Angeles. Golden State's final opponent was Portland, a team that was 17 games below .500, making a Warriors' loss highly unlikely. Golden State travelled to Portland and comfortably took care of business, winning by 22 points and booking their first post-season berth in 13 years. The Warriors' win over the Blazers was the final nail in the coffin for a Clippers' season that had been on life-support ever since Shaun Livingston's knee gave way. They were left to play out a meaningless home game against the Hornets, which they lost, giving them a final record of 40-42. In the space of twelve months, the Clippers had gone from falling one game short of qualifying for the Western Conference finals, to finishing with a losing record and missing out on the playoffs altogether.

The Clippers headed into the 2007 off-season facing a number of pressing questions. In fact, it seemed the only constant that they could depend on was Elton Brand, who had just finished another outstanding year. He shot a career high 53.3% from the field, while averaging 20.5 points, 9.3 rebounds and 2.2 blocks. Brand had now been playing for the Clippers for six years and throughout this time, he had been as solid as a screen set by Benoit Benjamin. If the Clippers had any hope of digging themselves out of this latest ditch, one thing was certain- they had better make sure that there was a shovel in the hands of Elton Brand.

Season XXX: 2007-08

The Clippers' 2007-08 season was over before it even had a chance to get started. It didn't end on the court of a Western Conference rival, after a dramatic seven-game series played in May. Nor did it end in the final days of the regular season, with the Clippers falling short in the race to secure a playoff spot. The Clippers' season ended in August of 2007, during an otherwise meaningless game of one-on-one played at the team's practice facility.

Elton Brand and Chris Kaman were coming to the end of an off-season workout when they decided to play a best-of-five series of one-on-one.

Brand won the first two games and could have completed a sweep if he had received a foul call as he attempted a potential series-winning shot in the third game. Instead, no call was made and Kaman came back to win, cutting the series deficit to 1-2. In the fourth game, Brand again raced out to an early lead and it appeared that he was just minutes away from finishing his workout and hitting the showers.

And then, disaster struck.

Brand had possession of the ball and was attempting to drive around Kaman when he heard a bang that sounded like a loud drum. An accompanying sharp pain in the back of his foot immediately let Brand know that the noise was the snapping of his left Achilles tendon, an injury that usually takes around nine months to fully heal.

With Brand joining a still-recovering Livingston on the sidelines, the Clippers were left to ponder the prospect of playing an entire season without the services of either their starting point guard or power forward. And while the Clippers had been hopeful that they might be able to cover the loss of Livingston, there was no way that they could do the same for a player of Brand's caliber. In the split second that it took for Brand to rupture his Achilles, the Clippers' chances of returning to the playoffs in 2008 were effectively reduced to zero. One would think that losing your star player to a serious injury before the season had even begun would be about as bad as it could get for most NBA franchises. Yet the Clippers somehow found a way to take this terrible situation and make it a whole lot worse.

Brand first hurt his Achilles six months earlier, while playing a game in Toronto during the previous season. However, rather than take some time off to recover, Brand stuck to his rule- *If he could run, he would keep playing.* So he kept playing. In fact, despite the pain in his left foot, Brand played a game-high 43 minutes against the Raptors, finishing with 21 points, 10 rebounds and 6 assists.

After the game, he had an MRI and the scan indicated that there was a problem in the Achilles region of Brand's left foot. However, as no one was 100% sure of the exact nature of the issue, and with the Clippers locked in a dog-fight for the final Western Conference playoff spot, Brand decided to continue playing. He was given a cortisone shot, which helped relieve some of the pain and he went on to play all but two of the Clippers' final 35 games.

When summer came around, Brand knew that his body needed time to rest and heal, so he made the difficult decision to give up his spot on the national team. While the U.S. team was in Las Vegas trying to qualify for the Beijing Olympics, Brand was back in Los Angeles rehabilitating. After a month of less strenuous skills work, he was given the all-clear to start participating in competitive scrimmages again, which led to him playing one-on-one with Kaman on that fateful August afternoon. And while hindsight suggests that Brand may have been given the green light to resume playing a little too early, surely this was not the time for finger pointing and accusations? The Clippers did not need to start looking for who to blame, they needed to band together and support Brand through his upcoming rehabilitation.

Or so one would have thought.

While most people viewed Brand's injury as a simple case of rotten luck, there was at least one unidentified person in the Clippers' organization who had another theory- performance enhancing drugs[225]. And rather than keep this baseless supposition to themselves, this person apparently decided that it would be a good idea to ask Brand about whether

---

225 There is some evidence suggesting that using muscle-building PEDs increases the likelihood of suffering a ruptured Achilles.

he was using PEDs and if they had played a role in his injury. Not surprisingly, Brand was not impressed by this line of questioning. He had played in pain during the previous season in an effort to help the franchise secure a rare playoff berth. He had given up his spot on the national team so that he could be in the best shape possible for the 2007-08 campaign. And the Clippers thought the best way to repay his efforts was to quiz him on whether he was using PEDs?

Brand took to the internet, where he used his blog to express his displeasure at the "Clipper brass." He said that it "was very disappointing" to face questions about whether he had used illegal substances that might have led to a weakening of his Achilles tendon. "When people use performance enhancing drugs it decreases the integrity of the tendons," Brand wrote. "But what we're talking about here is my integrity[226]."

A spokesperson from the Clippers tried to dismiss the episode as nothing more than a "misunderstanding," but it was obvious that somebody from the franchise had upset Brand. What remained unclear was whether these hurt feelings would come back to haunt the Clippers at the end of the season, when Brand was able to opt out of the last year of his contract and become a free agent. In the meantime, Brand's injury left the Clippers facing the grim prospect of playing an entire season without the services of their best player. One thing appeared to be certain, the Clippers were in serious trouble.

It only took 13 months for Mike Dunleavy to go from Donald Sterling's penthouse to the doghouse. In December of 2006, Sterling decided to make Dunleavy one of the league's highest paid coaches when he signed him to a four year, $22 million contract extension that more than doubled Dunleavy's annual pay rate. At the time, the Clippers were coming off their successful playoff run and Sterling viewed Dunleavy as some sort of basketball Medusa.

---

226 This blog post has long since been removed by its author.

On the day that Dunleavy's new deal was announced, the Clippers' head coach spoke about the role that the owner's support had played in the franchise's recent rise. "Mr. Sterling has been behind our staff the whole time," Dunleavy said, "and we're in this position because of him." However, it did not take long for the Sterling-Dunleavy relationship to deteriorate.

By the halfway mark of the 2007-08 season, the Clippers were once again struggling. Without Brand or Livingston, the team had won just 12 of their first 36 games, placing them at the bottom of the Pacific Division standings. Their next game was at home against Utah and when the Jazz scored an easy blow-out victory, it was more than Sterling could stand. "I'm not happy," said Sterling. "I want to make L.A. fans proud of this team, but if (Dunleavy and Baylor) can't make it happen, then I have no choice but to make changes." Sterling also added that rookie forward Al Thornton could be a special player if "he gets some coaching."

Dunleavy's response was both swift and emphatic. He acknowledged that it was Sterling's team and said "he can do whatever he likes" but added that firing another head coach in the middle of a season "would be the biggest mistake (Sterling) ever made." Dunleavy claimed that people who were "not in basketball operations" had put a halt on multiple player personnel moves that he wanted to make over the previous summer. He said that if he was going to be the man who bore the responsibility for the team's success or failure, he needed to be able to make decisions without interference[227].

If this public war of words was not embarrassing enough, the franchise's attempts to patch things up was even worse. A few days after the initial outbursts, Dunleavy told the media that a "good conversation" had taken place between himself and Sterling and said that they were now both on "the same page." This sounded like a positive resolution to a messy situation. The only problem was that the "good conversation" between the two

---

[227] Dunleavy also added that he "totally disagreed" with Sterling's assessment that some of his players needed more coaching.

Clipper powerbrokers never actually occurred. This fact was revealed when Sterling was asked about the discussion that was meant to have taken place and the owner made it abundantly clear that he was still yet to speak with Dunleavy. The next day, Dunleavy acknowledged that he had not spoken with Sterling and said that he had misled the public because team president Andy Roeser told him to make-up the story.

This feud continued to simmer over the next six weeks and during this time, Dunleavy was unable to get Sterling to take his calls. This was an extraordinary public falling-out between an owner and a coach, even by Clipper-standards. Had Dunleavy not been less than a quarter of the way through a $22 million contract, it seems likely that he would have received a pink slip, like so many other Clipper coaches before him. However, Dunleavy *was* contracted until the end of the 2010-11 season, which meant that if Sterling wanted a new head coach, he would be forced to pay-out over $16 million in order to make it happen. So, with his eight-figure contract acting as a protective shield, Dunleavy was able to hang onto his job.

In February, the collection of players at Dunleavy's disposal was depleted even further when the brief but entertaining Sam Cassell era came to an end. Cassell knew that the 2007-08 season was most likely his last as a player and with the Clippers wallowing at the bottom of the standings, he decided that he wanted out of Los Angeles. Cassell asked the Clippers' front office to buy out his contract so he could join a contending team for one final playoff run. After some back and forth about how much money he would have to forfeit, the two parties reached an agreement and Cassell left the Clippers to "chase another dream"[228].

---

228 Cassell agreed to forgo $850,000 in salary in order to be allowed to break his contract. Four days after his departure from the Clippers, Cassell signed with Boston, where he provided veteran leadership throughout the 2008 playoffs, which eventually finished with the Celtics claiming their 17th Larry O'Brien Trophy. This meant that Cassell finished his final professional season the same way as he capped off his rookie year, by being crowned an NBA champion.

Brand was eventually able to return for the final eight games on the Clippers' schedule and in his first game back, he led the team to a win over Seattle. However, this would be the only winning game in which Brand played, as the Clippers lost their final seven contests, finishing the season 36 games below .500.

It was clear that if the Clippers were to return to the playoffs, Brand was going to need some help. Luckily, the front office had a plan to provide him with the on-court assistance that he so desperately required. In fact, if this latest scheme was successful, it would result in the best inside-outside combination seen in Los Angeles since the days of Shaq and Kobe playing for the Lakers.

CHAPTER 17

Betrayal

"It was a disaster."

BARON DAVIS

Baron Davis was coming home. The Clippers had flirted with the idea of bringing Davis back to Los Angeles for a number of years and now, in the summer of 2008, they finally decided to make it a reality. The acquisition of Davis not only provided Elton Brand with an All-Star sidekick who was in the prime of his career, it also sent a message that the Clippers were serious about returning to the playoffs and working their way towards winning their first NBA championship.

Baron Davis was born in Los Angeles and raised by his grandparents in a modest two-bedroom home in South Central. At age three, his love affair with basketball began when his grandfather built a court in the family's backyard, as a Christmas present for his grandson. Davis loved the gift, spending countless hours playing against his older cousins and a variety of other local children.

Growing up in an underprivileged neighborhood meant that Davis was exposed to the harsh realities which many people who live in urban

America are forced to confront from an early age. In fact, had fate not intervened, it is quite possible that Davis' life might have headed in a very different direction. The fork in the road came when Davis graduated from elementary school- the time when a boy becomes a man in South Central. Davis was going to have to start catching the bus to middle school, which meant navigating his way through streets filled with danger, drugs and decay. However, an alternate path suddenly emerged when Davis was approached by Daryl Roper, the basketball coach at Crossroads, a prestigious school located in Santa Monica. Roper, who was also a product of South Central, encouraged Davis to interview for a place at Crossroads. Davis applied and he was not only offered a spot at the school, he was granted a full scholarship.

When Davis first arrived at Crossroads, he found the transition to this new world difficult. While his classmates, many of whom were the offspring of Hollywood's most famous movers and shakers, shared stories about their overseas holidays, the best Davis could offer were tales of playing dominoes in South Central with his uncles. After one year, Davis asked his grandmother, Madea Nicholson, to let him transfer to the local public school, so he could hang out with the kids he grew up with. Nicholson told Davis that the only way he would be leaving Crossroads was when he graduated and she urged him to focus on the academic side of his schooling. However, it was clear that Davis' passion was reserved for the basketball court.

Davis had big ambitions, telling anyone who would listen that he was going to play in the NBA. However, despite his obvious skills, he stood at just 5'5" as a sophomore, making a career as a professional basketballer seem extremely unlikely. However, a growth spurt in the lead-up to his senior year transformed Davis from an overconfident kid with unrealistic goals to a legitimate Division One prospect.

Davis led Crossroads to a state title in his senior year, averaging 25 points and 8 assists and by the time he was ready to move onto college, he had become something of a minor Los Angeles celebrity. Davis' decision to enroll at UCLA only added to his growing profile[229]. After two successful years in Westwood, he decided to declare for the 1999 NBA draft, where he was taken with the third overall pick by the Charlotte Hornets.

In Davis' first five seasons with the Hornets, the team qualified for the playoffs every year and his stellar play earned him two All-Star selections. However, by year six, the Davis-Hornets relationship had soured. With Davis struggling due to a back injury, the team got off to one of the worst starts in NBA history, winning just twice in their first 31 games. The Hornets' front office began actively shopping Davis around the league until they eventually found an interested party, the Golden State Warriors.

Davis arrived in the Bay Area in February 2005 and immediately set about rejuvenating the previously downtrodden Golden State franchise. At the time of the trade, the Warriors were 22 games below .500 but, led by their new point guard, they managed to go 14-4 over the final 18 games of the season, providing fans with some hope that better days lay ahead. The 2005-06 season was Davis' first full campaign with Golden State and for the first 50 games, the Warriors were in the thick of the playoff race. However, when Davis injured his ankle in early February, the Warriors tumbled down the standings and ultimately missed out on the playoffs for the 12th consecutive season.

If you had taken a poll three quarters of the way through the 2006-07 season, it's unlikely that many people would have predicted that it was going to turn out to be a career year for Davis. In early March, the Warriors were dead last in the Pacific Division and they appeared set for another early summer vacation. However, the team surprised everyone by reeling off 16 wins in their last 21 games to snatch the West's final playoff spot on the last day of the regular season.

---

229 The announcement of where Davis was attending college was even televised live during the half-time break in one of the Clippers' 1997 playoff games.

As the playoffs got under way, little was expected from Golden State, with most analysts predicting that they would be swiftly eliminated by Dallas, who had won 67 games that season. However, led by the inspired play of Davis, the Warriors caused one of the greatest upsets in league history, knocking the Mavericks out in six games[230]. For the series, Davis averaged 25 points, 6.2 rebounds and 5.7 assists, while shooting 54% from the field and 45% from three-point range. The Warriors' season eventually came to an end a few weeks later when they lost in the Western Conference semi-finals to Utah. The following year, Davis led Golden State to a 48-34 record which, amazingly, was not good enough to qualify for the playoffs in the ultra-competitive Western Conference.

Despite failing to led his team to a second consecutive post-season appearance, Davis felt optimistic that Golden State's front office was about to offer him a contract extension. He had played a pivotal role in transforming the Warriors from also-rans to one of the league's up-and-coming teams and along the way, captured the hearts and minds of the Bay Area's basketball fans. However, instead of receiving a lucrative long-term extension, Davis was presented with an offer which he later described as "very insulting." Davis took this low-ball offer as a clear signal that he should opt out of the final year of his contract and he immediately began searching for a new place to call home.

Davis did not have to wait very long for another team to submit an upgraded bid, with the Clippers presenting him with a five year, $65 million contract. Joining the Clippers intrigued Davis for a number of reasons. For starters, it would allow him to spend more time with his grandmother, who still lived in the same South Central home where she had raised her grandchildren. Davis had also recently started his own film production

---

230 Golden State became the first eighth seed to eliminate a number one seed in a seven-game series.

company, thus playing in close proximity to Hollywood was an especially appealing prospect[231].

The final reason why Davis ultimately chose to sign with the Clippers can be explained in two five-letter words: Elton Brand. In the days after Davis' new contract was announced, he said he couldn't wait to "play with one of the best big men in the game" and that the chance to team up with Brand was "a big reason" why he elected to join the Clippers. Davis believed that over the next three seasons, the inside-outside combination of himself and Brand would help transform the Clippers into legitimate championship contenders.

Once Davis accepted the Clippers' offer, all that remained was for the front office to re-sign Brand who, like Davis, had decided to opt out of the final year of his contract. Having your star player elect to become a free-agent is usually a sign of trouble, as it indicates that he is considering switching teams. In the case of the Clippers, a player opting out of the last year of their deal is almost always a sure sign of an imminent departure. However, the early sound bites coming from Brand's camp gave the Clippers reason to feel optimistic about retaining him. Prior to Davis' signing being announced, Brand said that his decision to opt out "definitely doesn't mean I'm leaving the Clippers," before adding, "My intention is to stay." His agent, David Falk, spoke about how Brand's decision to forgo the $16.4 million that he was due to be paid was actually his client's way of being helpful. This move would provide the Clippers with additional payroll flexibility and allow them to sign another elite player.

Brand also spoke about his belief that the Clippers were not too far off being able to "do some damage" in the playoffs and said that signing a quality point guard should be the franchise's highest priority. When

---

231 Davis' company, Verso Entertainment, was responsible for a number of projects, including the critically acclaimed documentary "Crips and Bloods: Made in America," which chronicles the history and the devastating impact of Los Angeles' gang culture.

the Clippers secured a commitment from Davis, they assumed that Brand would be pleased and quickly follow suit. There was a period of about a week between Davis first agreeing to play for the Clippers and the time when free-agents were officially allowed to sign a contract. It was during this relatively short window of time that things went horribly awry.

Exactly what went wrong in the contract negotiations between Elton Brand and the Los Angeles Clippers depends on who is telling the story. One thing that both sides can agree on is that the Clippers' front office offered Brand a five year deal worth a total of $70 million fairly early on in the negotiation process. This was well short of the $125 million maximum that Brand was eligible to receive but the Clippers believed it was a fair amount for a player who was coming back from a torn Achilles[232].

Falk informed Mike Dunleavy that $70 million was not going to be enough to retain his client and asked to speak directly with Donald Sterling so he could try and negotiate a better deal. Falk claims he was told that Sterling was not available to discuss the contract, and thus "this was the Clippers' best offer- take it or leave it." Given the Clippers' apparent reluctance to negotiate, Falk immediately began trying to leverage more money by shopping his client to other teams. However, unbeknownst to Falk, Brand continued to communicate directly with Dunleavy about a potential new deal.

It is at this point that the precise details of what occurred start to get a little murky. Based on their conversations, Dunleavy believed that Brand was happy with the terms of the Clippers' original proposal and thus planning on re-signing as soon as league rules permitted him to so. A few days later, news of a five year, $90 million offer being made to Brand by Golden

---

[232] At the end of the previous season, Brand played in 8 games and while his form had been good, his averages of 17.6 points and 8 rebounds were well below his career numbers.

State surfaced and the Clippers began to get a little nervous. It appeared that their sure thing of a few days earlier was crumbling before their eyes, so Dunleavy tried to reach out to confirm that Brand was still intending to sign with the Clippers. However, Brand was no longer answering his coach's calls. Dunleavy was surprised at his inability to get Brand on the phone, as they usually returned each other's calls promptly.

There was a good reason for Brand's sudden evasiveness- he was acting on the advice of his agent. Falk had discovered that his client had been communicating directly with the Clippers and he was not happy about it. His instructions to Brand were simple- "Turn your phone off, you're not talking to them anymore. I'm your agent. Let me do my job."

While the Clippers anxiously waited to find out what Brand was going to do, Falk continued to shop his client to any franchise with substantial salary cap room. The next team to put in a bid was Philadelphia, who tried to lure Brand with a five year, $82 million deal. And while the Sixers were offering less money than Golden State, they were able to highlight the franchise's history of success as a key selling point[233]. After Brand took a visit to Philadelphia and was impressed by what he saw, the Sixers became the new frontrunners to secure his services. The Clippers then tried to increase their offer to $81 million, however, they claim that Brand was never informed of this development due to Falk's failure to pass on the information.

Falk's timeline of events is slightly different.

Falk acknowledged that the Clippers did in fact up their proposed deal to $81 million, but said that this new pitch was only made *after* Brand had formally accepted Philadelphia's offer. Either way, the result of this messy back-and-forth was that Elton Brand had played his last game for the Clippers.

---

233 At the time, Philadelphia had won two NBA titles and had qualified for the playoffs in seven of the previous ten seasons.

When Dunleavy found out that Brand had signed with Philadelphia, he was devastated. In the days following the announcement, Dunleavy made his feelings on the matter crystal clear, saying, "I thought we had a deal with Elton." A day later Dunleavy upped the ante in the war of words, saying, "I don't know what poisoned Elton against us, but obviously something did."

Meanwhile, both Falk and Brand re-stated their belief that the initial offer from the Clippers of $70 million was presented as an ultimatum[234]. "You don't expect a team to give a franchise player an ultimatum," Falk said. "You wouldn't expect the Lakers to do that with Kobe Bryant. You wouldn't expect the Heat to do that with Dwyane Wade." When Brand was asked if he thought the Clippers' first offer was an ultimatum, he said, "That's exactly what it was." Dunleavy scoffed at the idea. "After I supposedly gave him a take-it-or-leave-it offer, we raised the offer to $75 million and $81 million," Dunleavy said. "They can spin this any way they want to try and spin it. The bottom line is, anything Elton ever wanted, I did for him. They stopped having communications with us about a week ago."

It is unlikely that anyone outside of the key players will ever truly know whether Brand made a verbal commitment to Dunleavy. However, comments made by the power forward at the time seem to indicate that he definitely gave some sort of assurance. When questioned on the matter, Brand said, "No matter what was said, David Falk, my registered agent, never agreed to any deal." Brand's choice of words seem to strongly imply that there was some sort of verbal agreement, only it wasn't made in the presence of his agent.

One thing was clear- when Baron Davis agreed to sign with the Clippers, he believed that Brand was going to be his teammate. And now, just a week later, Brand was leaving. When asked about this dramatic turn of events, a clearly disappointed Davis said, "I did think Elton was going to come and I talked to him and tried to say, 'This is the best place for you, we can do

---

234 As far as ultimatums go, this would have to be one of the better ones.

great things,' but obviously, he chose otherwise." Elton Brand departed Los Angeles as the most successful player in Clipper history. He was a crucial part of the first Clipper team to win a playoff series and was the franchise's all-time leader in both scoring and rebounding.

With the departure of Brand, the Clippers' signing of Davis suddenly seemed much less exciting. On the day that the agreement with the All-Star point guard was first announced, hope was building amongst Clipper fans that a Brand-Davis combination was about to lead the franchise into an era of prosperity. Now, just a week later, Brand was in Philadelphia and the Clippers were left wondering if they would ever be able to replace him.

On the same day that Brand signed with Philadelphia, the Clippers also lost their second most productive player. Corey Maggette began his off-season in the same manner that Brand had, electing to forgo the final year of his contract so he could explore his options on the free agent market. However, while the Clippers were desperate to retain Brand, they seemed far less stressed about the prospect of losing Maggette. In fact, Maggette claimed that after he received a five year, $50 million offer from Golden State, *he* had to call the Clippers to check if they were interested in putting in a counter offer. He was told that they were not going to match the Warriors' deal and so Maggette began making plans to move 400 miles up the coast to Oakland[235].

A third member of the 2006 playoff team also departed during that off-season, with Shaun Livingston deciding to leave the Clippers so that he could make a fresh start somewhere else. The fact that Livingston was ready to resume his basketball career was something of a minor miracle, given the severity of the knee injury that he suffered a year and a half earlier.

---

235 Maggette departed as the second leading scorer in Clipper history, just 501 points behind Elton Brand.

However, courtesy of countless hours of grueling rehabilitation, Livingston had been given the medical all-clear to return to the NBA and he signed a two year contract with Miami[236].

Season XXXI: 2008-09

The Baron Davis era got off to a horrendous start when the Clippers were on the wrong end of a 38 point blow-out against the Lakers in the season-opener. From here, things only went from bad to worse, with the team losing their next five games. During this miserable stretch, the Clippers' on-court problems were visible for all to see. A lack of outside shooting. Too many turnovers. An inability to rebound. However, less obvious to the viewing public were the internal conflicts playing out behind the scenes, the most concerning of which was a difference of opinion between Dunleavy and Davis about the team's style of play.

The dispute centered on Davis' opinion that Dunleavy was too controlling and not open to adapting his game plan. He hated Dunleavy's habit of calling plays from the bench and believed that the team's regimented system was stifling his creativity. Davis was not content to keep these opinions to himself, telling the media that Dunleavy had to "figure out how to relax his grip." Dunleavy tried to hose down speculation of a growing rift, saying that while he and Davis were working through some issues, "everything would be fine." A few days later, Davis backtracked from his initial comments and acknowledged that he threw his coach under the bus by going public with his frustrations. However, despite Davis and Dunleavy's best efforts to convince the world that they had kissed and made up, the tension between the two men continued to grow.

---

236 For the next six seasons, Livingston bounced the around the league, making stops in Miami, Oklahoma City, Washington, Charlotte, Milwaukee, Cleveland and Brooklyn. Livingston's big break finally came at the start of the 2014-15 season, when he signed a three year deal to play for Golden State. He played an important role off the bench for a Warriors team that would go on to claim the 2015 NBA championship.

In late November, the Clippers travelled to Philadelphia to take on the Sixers. This clash was the first time that Brand had crossed paths with his old team since the star forward's messy departure and while four months had passed, there was still plenty of lingering bad blood. In the lead-up, Dunleavy said he still did not understand the reasons behind Brand's decision to leave, while Davis said he wouldn't be engaging in any type of pre-game chat with Brand, as he had "nothing to say to him." The contest went down to the wire and it was Brand who made the decisive play in the game's final minute, converting a 15-foot jumper to give the Sixers an 89-88 victory. This loss dropped the Clippers overall record to 2-10.

With the team floundering at the bottom of the standings, the Clippers' front office pulled the trigger on a blockbuster trade, sending Cuttino Mobley and Tim Thomas to New York in exchange for Zach Randolph. From the Clippers' perspective, this trade achieved two objectives. First, sending Mobley to the Knicks freed up extra playing time for rookie shooting guard Eric Gordon, a dynamic scorer whom the Clippers' selected with the seventh pick of the 2008 draft. Gordon averaged over 20 points per game as a freshman at Indiana and was already showing flashes of brilliance since arriving in the NBA. Secondly, the trade once again gave the Clippers a low-post scoring threat. Like Brand, Randolph was an old school power forward who could get you 20 and 10 every night without ever popping up on the highlight reels. Over the preceding five seasons, Randolph averaged 19.7 points and 9.8 rebounds per game, almost identical to the numbers that Brand put up in his time with the Clippers.

While the on-court production from Randolph and Brand was almost identical, their off-court images were polar opposites. Brand was almost universally regarded as one of the league's good guys, Randolph arrived in Los Angeles with a past that was more colorful than Craig Sager's wardrobe. His rap sheet was both long and varied and included shoplifting, battery and two counts of receiving stolen guns. In 2006, he was sued by an exotic dancer for sexual assault, although no criminal charges were ever filed. Randolph also infamously fractured a teammate's eye socket during a practice session[237]. However, the Clippers decided that despite this extensive history of concerning incidents, Randolph's talent was such that he was worth taking a risk on.

On the day of the trade, Dunleavy spoke of the coaching staff's plan to bully their way back into playoff contention. Dunleavy's vision was to play different combinations of Randolph, Kaman and Marcus Camby[238] in the four and five spots for the majority of games, giving opposition big men no respite. It was a scheme that lasted all of 12 minutes. Randolph made his Clipper debut on November 26th against Denver. By the end of the first quarter, the Clippers were trailing by double digits and Kaman had sustained a foot injury that kept him out of action for the next three and half months. He would soon have plenty of company on the sidelines. A few weeks later, Randolph hurt his left knee in a one-sided loss against Toronto, an injury that resulted in him missing 19 games. Just nine days later, Davis was forced to sit out for 4 weeks due to a bruised tailbone.

This spate of injuries meant the Clippers had to play nearly the entire month of January without three members of their starting five, leaving second year forward Al Thornton and Eric Gordon to hold down the fort. Gordon made the most of this opportunity, averaging 21.9 points and 4.1 assists on his way to winning the Western Conference's Rookie of the Month award. However, Gordon's individual exploits counted for little in the overall scheme of things, as the Clippers lost 14 of the 16 games they played in January, giving them an overall record of 10-37. And then, just when it looked like things couldn't get any worse, they did.

---

[237] Randolph was playing for Portland when he hit Ruben Patterson, a player with whom he had a long history of feuding. The incident took place following an argument between Patterson and another teammate. Randolph interjected but instead of playing the role of peacemaker, he punched Patterson in the face.
[238] The Clippers had acquired Camby, a former Defensive Player of the Year, via trade at the start of the season.

Elton Brand was not the only high-profile Clipper to leave the franchise during the 2008 off-season. Elgin Baylor, the longest tenured general manager in the entire league, also ceased to be an employee of the Clippers, although the exact cause of his departure was more than a little unclear at the time. Baylor's exit was announced on the eve of the 2008-09 season via a confusing press release titled: *"Clippers Add General Manager Role to Head Coach Mike Dunleavy's Duties."* The statement made only passing mention of the fact that Baylor, who had been working as the franchise's general manager for the past 22 years, was the person who was being replaced by Dunleavy. But while the press release failed to make any reference to the circumstances that led to Baylor's departure, it soon become patently obvious that the parting was less than amicable.

Over the next few days, Baylor was contacted by the media and he clarified that there was a "dispute" between himself and his former employer. Beyond that revelation, Baylor, acting on advice from his lawyers, was unable to provide any additional details. The following day, one of Baylor's attorneys, Carl Douglas, spoke with the press and a clearer picture began to emerge[239]. Douglas confirmed that Baylor was unhappy with being "put out to pasture" and said that he was working on "trying to get the matter resolved informally."

Baylor was initially offered a $120,000 retirement package by Andy Roeser at a meeting that took place in August of 2008. Baylor thought that this proposal was "insulting" and thus promptly rejected it. In September, Baylor's attorneys asked the Clippers for a slightly more lavish payout, requesting $11 million to cover past economic loses, $11 million for future economic loses, $21,000 for stress and emotional therapy, $68,000 for legal fees and a "well-budgeted" retirement party[240]. Given the vast difference between what

---

239 Douglas had an extensive history of representing high profile clients including O.J. Simpson, Michael Jackson, Tupac Shakur, Jamie Foxx, Sean "P-Diddy" Combs and Todd Bridges.
240 In addition, Baylor's legal team also asked the NBA to employ their client as a goodwill ambassador at a price tag of $2 million per season.

Baylor was seeking and what the Clippers were offering, it came as no great surprise when Douglas held a press conference in early February to announce that the matter remained unresolved and was now headed for court.

Baylor's legal team filed a 22 page complaint that was filled with numerous allegations about Sterling, Roeser and the NBA. The most explosive of these claims was that Sterling had a "pervasive and ongoing racist attitude" which in turn influenced many of the basketball-related decisions that he was responsible for. One example provided was an incident that took place while Baylor and Sterling were trying to negotiate Danny Manning's first NBA contract. Baylor alleged that when Manning's agent requested a salary increase for his client, Sterling responded by saying he was already offering "a lot of money for a poor black kid[241]." This apparently resulted in an upset Manning storming out of the room[242].

The complaint also stated that Baylor was grossly underpaid, relative to other NBA executives who performed similar roles, and this was again linked back to the issue of race. The pay discrepancy between the Clippers' head coach and general manager was highlighted by Baylor's lawyers to illustrate this point. After leading the Clippers to within a game of the 2006 Western Conference finals, Dunleavy was rewarded with a four-year, $22 million contract extension. Meanwhile, Baylor's salary remained unchanged at the "comparatively paltry" rate of $350,000, despite being named the NBA's Executive of the Year during the same playoff run[243].

---

241 Baylor's legal team also stated that David Stern was present when this comment was made- an allegation which was quickly retracted. Any mention of Stern's presence at the meeting in question was deleted in an amended complaint, with Douglas labelling the initial accusation of the commissioner's involvement as nothing more than a typo.
242 When asked to comment on this story by the Los Angeles Times in February 2009, Manning sent a short reply via email that said: "I knew I wasn't wealthy, but I don't think I was poor either."
243 Most NBA franchises tend to pay head coaches around twice as much as their general managers, although this varies from team to team. According to Baylor's legal complaint, the ratio of Dunleavy's salary to his own was somewhere in the vicinity of 15:1.

It was this relatively meager salary that led to the inclusion of the NBA as one of the defendants in the lawsuit. Baylor's legal team believed that the league had a responsibility to intervene when they became aware of the "gross pay disparity" between their client and many of his peers, most of whom were white. Alvin Pittman, another of Baylor's lawyers, said that the NBA was "deaf, blind and mute" on the issue of employment discrimination within their executive ranks.

Baylor also provided a glimpse of what it was like to be employed by Sterling when he revealed that he had been working without a formal written agreement since 1993. He said that whenever he tried to ask Sterling about a contract, he was told he did not need one as he was a "lifer," who "would remain with the Clipper family until (he) decided to retire." Yet, rather than being treated like a member of the family, Baylor claimed that his final few years at the franchise were spent dealing with co-workers trying to force him into retirement by "repeatedly hassling him" and making "ageist comments." Baylor also said that many of his core duties had been secretly re-assigned to Dunleavy, which only further fueled his perception that the Clippers were trying to get rid of him.

Not surprisingly, the Clippers said that they would contest the lawsuit vigorously. Robert H. Platt, the franchise's lawyer, called Baylor's claims "ridiculous" and said the "decision to bring the suit was driven by publicity-seeking attorneys hoping to draw attention to themselves[244]." Baylor's lawyers sought to support their client's claims with suggestions that the alleged conduct was in keeping with some previous legal issues that Sterling had faced. Carl Douglas stated at the time, "I think it very interesting that this owner has had a history of questionable conduct in both his other business ventures. It lends credence and support to many of the allegations we are making in the lawsuit."

---

244 It should be noted that while Platt was happy to mock Baylor's accusations, he also admitted during the same press conference that he had not yet read the 22 page legal complaint.

The earlier situations that Douglas appears to refer to have been well documented. Three years earlier, Sterling was sued for housing discrimination by 19 of his tenants and the nonprofit Housing Rights Center. Sterling was accused of adopting a "no blacks, no Mexican Americans and no children" policy when screening for potential occupants. One witness recounted a time when she heard Sterling attribute a foul odor in one of his apartment complexes to "all the blacks in this building." It was also alleged that some of Sterling's employees deliberately made life difficult for black and Hispanic tenants, by refusing to do repairs and harassing them with surprise inspections.

Sterling eventually settled the case by agreeing to make a confidential payment to the plaintiffs. He was also ordered to reimburse their legal fees, which equated to nearly $5 million. In making this ruling, the judge accused Sterling's attorneys of using "scorched earth" tactics and labeled their conduct as "often unacceptable and sometimes outrageous." However, despite this settlement, Sterling made no admission regarding the allegations that had been made.

Unfortunately for Sterling, the end of the civil lawsuit was not the final chapter of this story, with the U.S. Department of Justice launching their own investigation, which eventually led to criminal charges being filed for housing discrimination. The Justice Department's case included plenty of new allegations, from security guards who only made black and Hispanic people sign in before entering the building, to tenants being asked to provide details about their nationality when asking for garage door openers. Witnesses gave evidence alleging that Sterling has made statements, including that Latinos "smoke, drink and just hang around the building," and blacks being less desirable tenants because they "smell and attract vermin."

However, perhaps the most damning accusation was that Sterling implemented a deliberate and well-coordinated plan to discriminate in favor of tenants with Korean backgrounds at one particular complex[245]. Numerous examples of questionable practices were provided to support this allegation, including changing the name of the building to "Korean World Towers," placing advertisements that specifically expressed a preference for Koreans and putting up Korean flags and signs written exclusively in Korean. Sterling eventually agreed to pay the Justice Department $2.75 million to settle the case, the largest settlement ever obtained in a housing discrimination lawsuit, although this hefty financial penalty once again came without any admission of guilt.

The conclusion of the 2008-09 season couldn't arrive fast enough for the Clippers. They ended their campaign in pretty much the same manner as they had started it, with a humiliating defeat on their home floor, losing by 41 points to Oklahoma City, a team that won just 23 games for the year. The Clippers finished with 19 wins and 63 losses, a hugely disappointing result for a team that had been optimistic about returning to the playoffs back when Baron Davis was first signed.

If the Clippers' season was classified as a failure from a team perspective, then Davis' individual performance could best be described as a complete nightmare. He spent a large chunk of the season battling injuries and never came close to re-capturing his best form. Davis finished the season with a scoring average of 14.9 points per game, his worst output since his second year in the league. Meanwhile, his field goal percentage of just 37% was not only a career low, it was also the least accurate shooting percentage in the *entire* league[246].

---

245 Sterling was said to favor Koreans because "they pay their rent on time and don't cause problems."
246 Of the 119 players who took enough shots to be eligible for the NBA's field goal percentage rankings for the 2008-09 season, Davis was 119th. For the year, he missed a staggering 604 of the 959 field goals that he attempted.

Dunleavy labeled the 2008-09 season as the worst he had ever been involved in, before adding, "It's not going to be that way next year, no matter what." Long-suffering Clipper fans could be forgiven for thinking that they had heard these kinds of wait-till-next-season promises before. This type of chatter was usually nothing more than talk in Clipper-land, talk that was rarely accompanied by any meaningful improvement. But there was one genuine reason for Clipper supporters to feel optimistic as they headed into the summer of 2009. For the third time in the past 21 years, the Clippers had secured the rights to the number one pick in the NBA draft and they were going to use it to select one of the most awe-inspiring players ever to lace up a pair of sneakers. Someone who would eventually play a pivotal role in transforming the Clippers from the league's longest running joke to one of the most feared opponents in all of the NBA.

CHAPTER 18

A New Hope

"All that stuff happened in the past...If I'm with the Clippers, it's going to be all about the future. No disrespect to anybody, but I could care less what happened 20 years ago."

BLAKE GRIFFIN

SEASON XXXII: 2009-10

THERE WAS NOTHING SUBTLE ABOUT Blake Griffin's arrival as an NBA player. In fact, Griffin accumulated more highlights in the seven exhibition games that he played during the fall of 2009 than most players manage to compile across their entire careers. Two-hand power dunks, spectacular alley-oops, tip jams- Griffin did it all. The NBA had not seen a big man capable of providing this type of constant stream of awe-inspiring dunks since Shawn Kemp played for Seattle.

While Griffin's impressive aerial assaults had the SportsCenter crowd drooling, it was the other facets of his game that drew rave reviews from the league's coaches and general managers. Lakers' general manager, Mitch Kupchak noted how mature Griffin was after watching him dominate in the summer league. San Antonio coach Gregg Popovich, someone not normally known for hyperbole, labeled Griffin a "monster" after he scored 23 points in 29 minutes against Tim Duncan. But if the Blake Griffin

Fan Club had a president, it would have been Mike Dunleavy. Dunleavy praised all aspects of Griffin's game, from his ball handling and passing to his work ethic and intelligence[247].

As the 2009 exhibition schedule drew to a close, Clipper fans could hardly contain their glee at the prospect of watching the NBA's latest bona fide star play for *their* team. In fact Griffin was so impressive, that he had many pundits predicting that the Clippers would make an immediate return to the playoffs.

The Clippers' final exhibition game was against New Orleans, and once again, the Blake Griffin Show was on display for all to see. With a little over four minutes remaining in the third quarter, the Hornets looked set to convert an uncontested lay-in when Griffin flew in from the weak side and swatted the shot away. Griffin then picked up the loose ball and threw an outlet pass to Sebastian Telfair, the Clippers' new back-up point guard. As Telfair pushed the ball up the left side of the court, Griffin sprinted in a straight line, taking the shortest possible route to the opposite basket. When Telfair reached the three point arc, he shoveled a look-away pass back to Griffin, who caught the ball as he crossed the free throw line, elevated off both feet and slammed home a stunning right-hand dunk.

The entire sequence lasted only six seconds, but it would have a profound impact on both Griffin's career and the Clippers' upcoming season. With most fans caught up in the excitement of what they had just witnessed, many people failed to notice Griffin's reaction to the play. As soon as he landed, Griffin winced and grabbed hold of his left knee. And while no one realized it at the time, the Clippers' latest great hope had just sustained an injury that would keep him out of action for his entire rookie season.

---

[247] Dunleavy described his new power forward as a cross between Charles Barkley and Duncan.

Before Blake Griffin became the NBA's most talked about newcomer, he was Taylor Griffin's kid brother. The two Griffin boys grew up not only as friends but, as is often the case with siblings, as fierce rivals. This competitiveness was made even more intense due to the fact that the two brothers were homeschooled by their mother for many of their formative years. This meant that Blake and Taylor, who were three years apart in age, spent the majority of their spare time playing with one another. And it seemed that no matter what they were doing, they could find a way to turn it into a competition. From footraces to basketball to whatever challenges the boys could dream up, everything was a chance for one brother to assert physical dominance over the other. And more often than not it was Taylor who would come out on top.

Blake and Taylor ceased being home-schooled and enrolled at Oklahoma Christian School when they were in the eighth and tenth grades respectively. Despite no longer being taught by their mother, they remained under the watchful eyes of a parent, as the head basketball coach at Oklahoma Christian was their father, Tommy Griffin. Blake and Taylor thrived in their new environment and, thanks largely to the input of the Griffin family, Oklahoma Christian won consecutive state titles in 2004 and 2005. At the end of the 2004-05 season, Taylor graduated and headed off to Oklahoma University, where he had earned a basketball scholarship.

The question of whether Oklahoma Christian could continue to compete for the state title was now largely dependent on whether Blake was able to step up and fill his older brother's shoes. Blake had spent years watching Taylor's meticulous approach to the game of basketball- the way he prepared for games, tackled his workouts and looked after his body. Now, Blake would do such a good job of emulating his brother that he almost made the student body at Oklahoma Christian forget that Taylor even existed. During Blake's junior season, Oklahoma Christian won 27 of their 28 games on their way to their third consecutive state crown. And there was no doubt as to who was the star of the show, with Blake winning the MVP award for the state tournament while averaging 21.7 points, 12.5 rebounds and 4.9 assists per game.

It was around this time that Blake began attracting serious interest from a number of prominent Division One schools, including Duke, Kansas and North Carolina. But, after a personal plea from Taylor to come and join him at Oklahoma, Blake committed to the Sooners. With the decision of where to attend college out of the way, Blake led Oklahoma Christian to their fourth consecutive state championship. He finished his senior year with averages of 26.8 points, 15.1 rebounds and 4.9 assists and was again named MVP of the state tournament.

When Blake and Taylor re-united on the campus of Oklahoma University for the 2007-08 season, it quickly became apparent that the younger Griffin had surpassed his older sibling in every facet of the game. Blake averaged 14.7 points and 9.1 rebounds as a freshman, compared to Taylor's output of 6.5 points and 4.9 rebounds. At the end of the season, most observers believed that Blake was going to join the growing trend of "one-and-done" players and declare for the 2008 NBA draft. He had been projected by many experts as a probable lottery pick, meaning millions of dollars in guaranteed salary, a financial carrot that most individuals would find hard to turn down. However, Blake surprised everyone when he elected to forgo the riches of the NBA so that he could play one final season with his big brother. It proved to be a wise decision.

Oklahoma finished the year with a 27-5 record, good enough for a second seed in the NCAA tournament and they progressed all the way to the South Regional final, before their season finally came to an end at the hands of North Carolina, the eventual national champions. Meanwhile, Blake led the Big 12 in both scoring (22.7 points per game) and rebounding (14.4) and also won every major national player of the year honor, including the Naismith College Player of the Year and the John Wooden Award. And whereas twelve months earlier Blake shocked the basketball world by deciding to return to Oklahoma to play his sophomore season, this year there would be no such surprise. After the Sooners were eliminated, Blake announced that he would forgo his final two years of college eligibility in order to declare for the draft.

As soon as the Clippers won the right to select first, there was never any doubt about whom they were going to choose[248]. Blake Griffin was announced as the number one overall pick of the 2009 draft on June 25th and he immediately set about trying to kick-start a new era of Clipper basketball[249]. From the moment Griffin arrived in Los Angeles, he made it clear that he didn't care about the long list of big names whose careers had faltered while playing for the Clippers. Instead, he consistently preached the same message- what happened in the past had no bearing on the franchise's future.

Just three weeks after drafting Griffin, the Clippers' front office sent a message of their own when they traded away Zach Randolph. Randolph had performed well since arriving in Los Angeles, averaging 20.9 points and 9.4 rebounds in his 39 games with the Clippers. However, despite this impressive output, Randolph was shipped off to Memphis so that the Clippers could free up front court minutes for their incoming rookie sensation[250].

Trading Randolph sent a clear signal to everybody connected with the team. The franchise was embarking on another rebuilding effort and the

---

248 The Clippers made no attempt to hide their intentions to draft Griffin. On the day that they won the lottery, Dunleavy said, "Clearly, we're taking Blake Griffin." By the very next day, Griffin's image was featured prominently on the Clippers' website, despite the fact that the actual draft itself was more than a month away.
249 On the night of the 2009 draft, the Griffin family had two reasons to celebrate. 47 picks after David Stern announced Blake's name, Taylor was selected by Phoenix. Taylor went on to appear in 8 games for the Suns during the 2009-10 season, finishing the year with totals of 10 points, 2 rebounds and 2 blocked shots. This brief stint would prove to be the end of his short-lived NBA career.
250 Randolph was sent to the Grizzlies in exchange for Quentin Richardson. The Clippers then traded Richardson for Sebastian Telfair and a couple of role players just a few weeks later.

centerpiece of this latest attempt to turn things around was Blake Griffin. And judging by Griffin's form in the lead-up to the regular season, he looked like he might just be up to the gargantuan task of transforming the Clippers from laughingstocks to legitimate contenders.

As the curtain was being drawn on the exhibition schedule, the Clippers looked capable of earning one of the Western Conference's eight playoff berths, provided that their key players were able to remain injury-free. While maintaining a healthy roster had historically proven to be a near impossible task for the franchise, this did not seem to faze Dunleavy. In fact, the Clippers coach decided to tempt fate by telling the media that it was nice to "get through the exhibition season relatively healthy."

In reality, nothing could have been further from the truth.

Unbeknownst to Dunleavy, Griffin had seriously hurt his knee during his spectacular end-to-end play in the Clippers' final exhibition game. Griffin felt some pain in his knee after his explosive dunk but continued to play. Experiencing some discomfort in this area was nothing out of the ordinary, as Griffin had been dealing with tendinitis in his left knee throughout the pre-season. It wasn't until after the game, when his knee started to swell, that the Clippers' medical staff began to get concerned.

It turned out that Griffin had suffered a stress fracture in his left knee cap, which was initially expected to keep him on the sidelines for the first six weeks the season. However, when the six week mark came and went, Griffin's knee was still not ready to resume playing on. In fact, it was not even close. It took nine weeks before Griffin was allowed to start running on a treadmill and 11 weeks before he was cleared to join in light shooting drills with the rest of the team.

While the rehabilitation process was progressing at a slower pace than initially predicted, Griffin still seemed to be on track for a comeback sometime during the second half of the season. The Clippers had managed to hover around the .500 mark in Griffin's absence, meaning that they were still very much in the hunt for a playoff berth. The best-case scenario was for a healthy Griffin to resume playing and provide a much needed boost over the final 35-40 games, helping to push the Clippers into the West's top eight.

However, any hopes of seeing a Hollywood-inspired ending to the season were officially put to bed in the middle of January, when the team announced that Griffin was going in for season-ending surgery. This decision was prompted by Griffin experiencing pain while doing jumping exercises in the pool, a clear sign that the stress fracture had still not properly healed.

Blake Griffin's rookie season was over before it had ever begun.

The news that Griffin would not play a single regular season game had even the most hardened skeptics wondering if there was some sort of cosmic force conspiring to prolong the Clippers' misery. It seemed that whenever the front office had assembled a team that looked promising, at least one of the Clippers' key players suffered a serious injury. It happened in the late 1970s and early 1980s with Bill Walton's seemingly constant stream of physical problems. It happened when Derek Smith, Norm Nixon and Marques Johnson were all injured at the same time in the mid-1980s. It happened when Danny Manning and Ron Harper both hurt their knees at the turn of the decade. It happened again when Stanley Roberts snapped both of his Achilles tendons, putting a serious dent in the franchise's playoff hopes for much of the 1990s. And more recently, it happened when Shaun Livingston and Elton Brand suffered major injuries.

At the press conference to announce Griffin's surgery, Dunleavy went for the glass half-full approach. Rather than harp on the immediate disappointment, Dunleavy chose to highlight the fact that Griffin was having the surgery early enough to give him "plenty of time" to rehabilitate and get ready for the start of the following season. Dunleavy's optimism turned out to be well-placed. When the 2010-11 season commenced, Griffin's knee was fully healed and he was ready to take his place in the Clippers' starting line-up. The only problem was that by the time that Griffin was healthy enough to launch his NBA career, Dunleavy had already lost his job. Twice.

When Mike Dunleavy was first employed by Donald Sterling, the Clippers had never won a playoff series in their 25 year history. Three years later, Dunleavy led the franchise to within one victory of the Western Conference finals and in the process, convinced Sterling that he was the modern day version of Red Auerbach. For the first time ever, Sterling was the owner of an NBA team that was a legitimate championship contender and he rewarded Dunleavy with a lavish four year contract extension.

However, any hope of building upon the success of the 2006 playoff campaign quickly evaporated when both Shaun Livingston and Elton Brand sustained career threatening injuries. Dunleavy's long-term plans were left in ruins. The Clippers quickly sank back to the bottom of the standings and Sterling began to publically speculate about Dunleavy's future with the franchise. The fact that the besieged head coach was ultimately able to hang onto his job probably had more to do with Sterling's desire to avoid a large payout than any indication that faith in Dunleavy had been restored.

Fast forward two years and Dunleavy was again facing questions about his job security. At the time when Griffin's season-ending knee surgery was announced, the Clippers were clinging to a 17-19 record. However, when the team's fortunes took a turn for the worse, speculation about whether Dunleavy would retain his job returned once again.

The final nail in Dunleavy's coffin was a game played in New Jersey against a team with a 3-40 record. The Nets had just returned from a road trip in which they lost all four games by a combined margin of 100 points. Making matters worse, New Jersey was forced to play the Clippers without either member of their starting backcourt, as both Devin Harris and Courtney Lee were injured. The undermanned Nets took the lead midway through the first quarter and never relinquished it, cruising to a 16 point victory.

When the team arrived back in Los Angeles a few days later, Dunleavy announced that he was stepping down from his position as head coach immediately, but that he would continue to work as the franchise's general manager. Dunleavy said that he thought a new coach might be able to get better results, as he believed that his message was no longer getting through to the players[251]. At the time of his resignation, Dunleavy was the third-longest tenured coach in the league, behind only Jerry Sloan and Greg Popovich. The 541 games that Dunleavy had spent on the Clippers' bench also placed him at the top of the franchise's list for most games coached, well ahead of Bill Fitch, who was in second place with 328. And while everyone connected with the Clippers was sticking to the script, by saying Dunleavy would have more time to focus on his general manager duties, it was hard to escape the feeling that this move away from the bench was not entirely voluntary.

Dunleavy handed the whiteboard over to Kim Hughes, a former NBA and ABA player who had been assisting him for the past six and a half seasons. Hughes spoke of his desire to play at a faster tempo and simplify the game plan by reducing the number of play calls from the bench. When Hughes was announced as interim coach, many players spoke positively

---

251 Al Thornton described the eight-game road swing that eventually cost Dunleavy his job as "a decent trip." He was asked to elaborate on what he meant by "decent" and Thornton responded by asking, "What was our record on this trip anyway?" When told that the team had won just 2 of the 8 games they played, Thornton laughed and said, "I guess not so decent then. My bad."

about him and the changes that he was planning to make. The team would run more, producing an aesthetically pleasing style of game that would lead to better on-court results. It sounded fantastic, until the Clippers actually had to take to the court and play another game.

Hughes' coaching debut was played at a frenetic pace but rather than lead to a slew of fast break dunks, it resulted in a huge spike in missed shots and turnovers. After one quarter, the Clippers had converted just four of their 19 field goal attempts and the score was 28-10 in favor of San Antonio. By half-time, the margin had grown to 22 and the Clippers had thrown the ball away a staggering 14 times. They eventually lost by 17, the first of five consecutive double digit defeats under Hughes' direction.

With Friends Like These...

Five years earlier, Kim Hughes was facing a very different sort of battle, as he learned that he had been diagnosed with prostate cancer. He was told that he needed surgery to have his prostate removed but was assured that this procedure could wait for a few months. Hughes was happy to put the surgery off as it was just a few weeks before the 2004 training camp was set to begin and he did not want to miss any of the upcoming season. However, when Hughes went to see another doctor for a second opinion, he was told that the surgery could be performed straight away. This seemed like an ideal solution as it would hopefully take care of the cancer and allow Hughes to return to the bench before the start of the 2004-05 campaign.

There was just one little problem. The Clippers would only cover the surgery if Hughes waited to have it done, as the second doctor he saw was outside of the network used by the team's insurance company. Hughes assumed that there would be some way around

> this but was informed that if he elected to have the surgery right away, he would be out of pocket for any expenses incurred. "(The Clippers) didn't talk to me directly about it," Hughes said. "They told... my agent that the reason they couldn't pay for the surgery is that if they paid for mine...the onus would be on them to pay for everybody else."
>
> Hughes elected to get the surgery done immediately, which proved to be a wise decision. The doctors discovered that the cancer was more aggressive than they initially thought and was now threatening to spread to other parts of his body. Dunleavy spoke to some of the players about Hughes' ordeal and a group that included Corey Maggette, Elton Brand, Marko Jaric and Chris Kaman, decided to chip in to pay the bill, which was somewhere in the order of $70,000. "Those guys saved my life," said Hughes. "They paid the whole medical bill...it wasn't cheap."
>
> The surgery was a success and Hughes was able to return to the bench for the Clippers, where he remained forever grateful for the support he received from a group of players who stepped up in his time of need. Hughes' feelings towards his employer were undoubtedly not as warm.

The All-Star break delivered a much-needed dose of good news, when Chris Kaman was informed that he would be participating in the league's marquee event. For Kaman, this honor was an official nod of recognition for what was clearly the best season of his seven year career. At the time of his All-Star selection, Kaman was averaging over 20 points and 9 rebounds a game and had been twice named the Western Conference's Player of the Week[252].

---

252 Kaman played a little over 10 minutes in the All-Star game and finished with 4 points and 3 rebounds.

In early March, the storm clouds returned.

The Clippers again found themselves in the headlines for all the wrong reasons, when they announced that Dunleavy no longer worked for the franchise. If you are wondering how an organization can fire the same person twice in the space of a month, the answer is not that complicated. The Clippers simply transformed the act of getting rid of Dunleavy into a two-part process. Stage one was completed back in February, when Dunleavy "resigned" from his coaching position. Stage two was a blindside that was so swift and ruthless, even Jeff Probst would be left shaking his head in amazement.

As is the case with most political assassinations, the victim, who in this case was Mike Dunleavy, was the last person to know when his time was up. In fact, Dunleavy first discovered that he had been fired from the general manager position when friends who had heard troubling rumors, called to find out what was going on. Dunleavy was unable to fill in the blanks because he "had no clue" that his employment with the Clippers had just been terminated.

Dunleavy had believed that his position in the front office was reasonably safe. He had a year and a half remaining on his contract and he felt confident that he was performing his general manager duties as well as could be expected. In the four weeks since he stepped down from the head coaching role, Dunleavy had made a number of shrewd off-court moves that gave the Clippers the necessary salary cap room to go after a prominent free agent in the upcoming off-season[253]. Just a few days before he was fired, Dunleavy had dinner with Sterling and nothing mentioned during this meal gave him any clue that his job was in jeopardy.

---

253 The list of players who were about to become free agents included LeBron James, Dwyane Wade and Amar'e Stoudamire.

The Clippers communicated this latest public relations disaster via a tersely worded press release that was sent out in the middle of one of their games. The statement said that the franchise had "severed ties" with Dunleavy but failed to explain the specifics that led to this stunning decision. Dunleavy was not even given a token "thank you" for his seven years of service. Instead, he was blamed for the team's failure to make "sufficient progress" and characterized as an obstacle that was standing in the way of a successful future. Dunleavy was replaced by Neil Olshey, a former actor who had worked in the Clippers' front office for the past six and a half seasons.

Predictably, Dunleavy's pay checks stopped coming on the day that he was fired. Dunleavy had wisely anticipated that a situation like this might arise when he signed his contract extension two and a half years earlier. Therefore, he made sure that his contract included a clause which stated that any dispute that arose between himself and the Clippers was to be settled by an independent arbitrator. This meant that Dunleavy could expect a resolution on his severance package without being dragged through the courts by the Donald Sterling.

A few weeks after Dunleavy was terminated, he filed for arbitration. The Clippers' responded by filing a lawsuit. They claimed that Dunleavy had defrauded the organization by signing a contract extension to coach the team when he had no intention of seeing out the full four years. Miles Clements, Dunleavy's lawyer, said the Clippers' allegations did not pass "the laugh test" and he labeled the lawsuit a simple "delay tactic." The outcome of this latest quarrel was unlikely to be known for quite a while, thus the dysfunction which continued to surround the Clippers would remain at the forefront of any discussion about the franchise.

One person who was able to stick around until the end of the 2009-10 season was Kim Hughes, but even he barely made it to the finish line. Hughes took charge for the final 33 games and was only able to add another eight wins to the team's total. After coaching the final game of the regular season, a surprising victory over the eventual champion Lakers, Hughes was planning on spending the next few days conducting exit interviews with the players. On the very next day, Hughes found himself sitting in an exit interview. His own. It seems that Olshey came to the conclusion that Hughes was not going to be the man to coach the team for the 2010-11 season and so he decided to relieve him of his duties right away. Olshey and Andy Roeser met with Hughes, whose contract ran until the end of June, and told him that his days with the Clippers were over.

As the Clippers looked toward the future, all their hopes seemed to rest on the shoulders of an unproven 21 year old who was recovering from a serious knee injury. Over the previous 32 years, the challenge of elevating the NBA's most downtrodden franchise had proven to be too great a burden for all who had attempted the task. Not only would Blake Griffin find a way to succeed where so many others had failed, he would do it in the most spectacular fashion imaginable.

Season XXXIII: 2010-11

Donald Sterling and Jerry Reinsdorf have a lot in common. Both are former lawyers who made millions of dollars in real estate and property development. Both used part of their fortunes to purchase NBA franchises, with Sterling buying the Clippers in 1981 and Reinsdorf acquiring the Bulls in 1985. Both transformed their teams from financially struggling enterprises into hugely profitable businesses that generate millions of dollars in revenue each and every year. And both have a reputation for being careful with their money, especially when it comes to spending on their respective sporting teams.

Given all of these similarities, it should come as no surprise to learn that the two basketball moguls had developed quite a close friendship over the years. In the summer of 2010, Sterling and Reinsdorf had one more thing that they could add to their list of similarities- they were both locked into contractual obligations that required them to pay millions of dollars to recently sacked coaches. In Sterling's case, he owed Dunleavy close to $7 million, while for Reinsdorf, the total due to Vinny Del Negro was a more modest $2.2 million.

Del Negro was a former second round draft pick who played over 700 games in an NBA career that spanned 12 seasons. At the peak of his career, he was a 14 point per game scorer on a Spurs team that won 59 games. After Del Negro retired from playing, he did some radio commentary for the Suns, before spending a couple years working in Phoenix's front office. Del Negro's big break came in the summer of 2008, when he was offered the position as Bulls' head coach, despite having no previous coaching experience. He spent two years in Chicago and during this time, he led the Bulls to consecutive playoff appearances. However, by the end of the 2009-10 season, the relationship between Del Negro and Bulls' vice president John Paxson had deteriorated to the point where the two men almost came to blows during an argument. So, it came as no great surprise when it was announced that Del Negro would no longer be coaching the team after the Bulls were eliminated in the first round of the 2010 playoffs.

The decision to fire Del Negro created a financial headache for Reinsdorf, as the departing coach still had one year remaining on his contract. This meant that, unless Del Negro was able to find another job, Reinsdorf was going to be stuck paying him over $2 million to effectively sit around and do nothing for the next 12 months. Conversely, if Del Negro secured a position with another team, the Bulls' liability would be reduced by whatever amount he was able to earn.

Reinsdorf placed a call to Sterling to ask if Del Negro was one of the candidates being considered for the Clippers' vacant head coaching position. When Sterling replied in the affirmative, Reinsdorf proceeded to outline all of Del Negro's most redeeming features. In late June, a dinner was organized at Montage, an exclusive five star hotel located in Beverly

Hills. At this meal, Del Negro won Sterling over with his upbeat outlook. However, while Sterling may have left the meal convinced that the search for a new coach was over, the Clippers' front office was leaning towards employing Dwane Casey. Casey had previous head coaching experience with the Timberwolves and was working as an assistant coach with the Mavericks at the time. How great an impact Reinsdorf's opinion actually had on the final decision is something that only Sterling will ever truly know, but when the announcement was made, it was Del Negro who was unveiled as the franchise's 17th head coach.

Del Negro was given a three year contract to try and turn around over three decades of ineptitude. On the day that the signing was announced, Del Negro said all of the right things, speaking about his belief that the organization was heading in a new direction. Clipper fans were accustomed to hearing this type of talk from incoming coaches and players. They knew that the test of whether their team was truly embarking on a new course would occur in late October, when on-court action replaced optimistic statements made at press conferences.

The good news for Del Negro was that Blake Griffin was back. Griffin took his place in the starting line-up for the Clippers' first game of the new season and he immediately demonstrated that he had not lost any of his explosiveness as a result of his injury. The new campaign was a little over three minutes old when Griffin scored his first NBA field goal- a spectacular alley-oop dunk. His second dunk, a left-handed tip jam, came just 90 seconds later. By the end of the night, Griffin had 20 points, 14 rebounds and 4 assists.

If this debut was not enough to convince observers that the league's next great power forward had arrived, Griffin's game against New York just three weeks later converted the remaining naysayers. Griffin finished the Knicks' clash with 44 points, 15 rebounds and 7 assists. Along the way, he produced an astounding play that looked like it belonged in a game of "NBA Jam" rather than on a real-life basketball court.

In the middle of the third quarter, Griffin was attempting a dunk when he was confronted in mid-air by 7'1" Knicks center Timofey Mozgov, who tried to stop his progress by crudely shoving him. Instead of ending up sprawled on the Staples Center floor, Griffin elevated even higher, so that his head was now level with the rim. But with Mozgov blocking his path, he was still about two feet away from the basket. In a feat that seemed to defy the laws of gravity, Griffin then reached forward and threw the ball *down* into the ring without his hands ever touching the hoop. With this spectacular basket, Griffin emphatically announced his arrival as the newest star in the NBA universe.

The only problem was that despite Griffin's stellar play, the Clippers were still pretty much the Clippers. Griffin's 44 point effort against New York was not enough to lead the home side to victory, as they trailed for the entire second half before losing by nine points. This was defeat number 13 in a season that was just 14 games old. Those looking for a scapegoat for this woeful start, did not need to look much further than the team's starting point guard.

After spending much of his first two seasons with the Clippers grumbling about the team's playing style under Mike Dunleavy, Baron Davis finally had a new coach who was keen to employ the up-tempo pace that he favored. In order to implement this game plan, Del Negro was hoping to see a fit and motivated Davis report to training camp. However, when Davis arrived at the Clippers' practice facility, the only shape he was in was rotund, causing his new coach to shake his head in dismay. Davis spouted all of the usual clichés about being fired up for the new season, but Del Negro showed his willingness to play the role of bad cop by calling him out. When asked about whether his point guard was physically prepared for the start of the new season, Del Negro said, "Talking about it and getting it done are two different things."

The negative impact of Davis' lack of conditioning soon became apparent. He lasted just three games before going down with a knee injury and, given the way that he was playing, the Clippers were almost happy to see him hobble off to the sidelines. At the time of the injury, Davis was averaging 10.3 points and 5.3 assists while shooting under 33% from the field and just 11% from three-point range. It was a far cry from the dynamic, All-Star point guard whom the front office thought they were getting when they gave Davis a $65 million contract back in 2008.

When Davis was healthy enough to resume playing, his performance actually got worse, which led to one of the more bizarre public feuds in Clipper history. Donald Sterling began heckling Davis from his courtside seats, calling him a variety of unflattering names including a "bastard." On one occasion, Davis approached the free throw line after the other team was called for a technical foul, only to have Sterling shout from his courtside seats that someone else should take the shot. "Why are you letting *him* shoot the free throw?" Sterling yelled. "He's awful! He's terrible! He's the worst free throw shooter *ever*![254]" As Sterling continued to publically demean his team's most senior and accomplished player, Blake Griffin, who was watching the unfolding spectacle out of the corner of his eye, felt embarrassed to be part of such a dysfunctional organization.

If Sterling was hoping to motivate Davis with his verbal tirades, he would have been disappointed with the results. Davis' scoring average dipped below 8 points per game and it was clear that he was losing his passion for basketball[255]. By All-Star weekend, Davis was reduced to being used as a prop in the slam dunk competition, joining a long list of gimmicks that included Reebok Pumps, blindfolds and Superman capes. At the peak of Davis' career he was a regular participant in the All-Star game but now,

---

254 At the time of this incident, Davis was coming off a season where he had converted over 82% of his free throw attempts.
255 Years later, Davis summed up his feelings towards Sterling and his approach to playing for the Clippers during this turbulent time by posing a simple question-"Why am I going to go out and give you my all when you hate me?"

his only official role for the weekend was throwing lob passes to Griffin, who went on to win the event.

The slam dunk title capped off a busy weekend for Griffin. On Friday night, he helped the rookie team to an 8 point win over the sophomores in the Rookie Challenge game. Saturday saw him jump over a Korean sedan and win the slam dunk competition[256]. Finally, on Sunday, Griffin became the first rookie to play in the All-Star game in eight years, scoring 8 points and helping the West to a 148-143 victory.

The first game after the All-Star break turned out to be Davis' last as a member of the Clippers. Having grown tired of watching the sluggish play of their point guard, Neil Olshey decided to pull the trigger on a risky trade that involved handing over a future first round draft pick to Cleveland. Davis was packaged with the Clippers' 2011 pick and shipped to the Cavs in exchange for Mo Williams. Williams was a former All-Star who was three years younger than Davis. He was capable of playing at either guard spot and it appeared that he would slot comfortably into the Clippers' backcourt, alongside Eric Gordon[257].

Having got rid of Davis, the Clippers now turned their attention towards putting an end to their legal disputes with Elgin Baylor and Mike Dunleavy.

More than two years passed between Baylor first filing his lawsuit and the case finally making it to trial. During this time, a number of interesting developments emerged from the hundreds of pages of legal documents that were generated. In his deposition, Baylor said that in all the time he

---

256 Griffin was only the second Clippers to win this event, joining Brent Barry, who won in 1996.
257 At the time of the deal, Williams was averaging 13.3 points and 7.1 assists per game.

was employed by the Clippers, he never used an agent when negotiating his salary because "Donald does not like to talk to agents." This lack of representation at least partly explained the relatively low salary that Baylor was paid. In 1986, when he was first employed by the franchise, Baylor's salary was less than $65,000 and over the next 22 years, it never exceeded $350,000.

Baylor also provided multiple examples of situations where he believed race played a role in Sterling's decisions. He claimed that Sterling tried to exclude him from contract negotiations with Michael Cage in 1988, on account of the fact that both Cage and Baylor were black. On another occasion, Sterling spoke out against drafting Joe Wolf, a Caucasian forward from North Carolina. "(Sterling) figured the white players break down too easily," Baylor said in his deposition. "He said that black players were more aggressive, bigger and stronger." Baylor said that numerous black players had approached him to complain about Sterling bringing female friends into the locker room after games. It was alleged that Sterling would make comments to these women like, "Look at those beautiful black bodies," while the players were showering or getting dressed.

Perhaps the most damning piece of evidence that Baylor presented was an incident that was alleged to have taken place in 1998. At the time, the Clippers were looking for a new head coach after firing Bill Fitch and one of the candidates was Jim Brewer, a former NBA player who had served as an assistant to Fitch for the previous four seasons. Brewer also happened to be black. Baylor gave the following account of a meeting between himself, Sterling and Brewer:

> *"I believe that (Sterling) was a little reluctant (to grant Brewer a meeting) at first but I said, 'We owe him that courtesy.' So we go there and we sit down and Brewer starts talking about his qualifications, that he believed he could do the job of head coach. And when he's finished, Donald said something that shocked me. He said, 'Personally, I would*

like to have a white Southern coach coaching poor black players.' And he looked at me and said, 'Do you think that's a racist statement?' I said, 'Absolutely, that's plantation mentality.'"

While Baylor's explosive claims regarding Sterling received plenty of media coverage, they ultimately had zero impact on the trial itself. The Clippers' legal team successfully had many of the statements attributed to Sterling excluded from the hearing, on the grounds that they were prejudicial or not relevant. This gave Baylor's lawyers little choice but to drop the racial element of their wrongful termination complaint, leaving them to focus on whether their client was discriminated against on the basis of his age[258].

At the trial, Baylor claimed that Roeser harassed him about his age by constantly asking him how much longer he planned to stay in the job. However, Robert Platt, the Clippers' lawyer, countered by playing a video of Baylor's pre-trial deposition in which he said that he was only asked how long he planned to continue working on one occasion. When challenged about this discrepancy, Baylor said that he initially remembered being subjected to this type of questioning once but had since recalled other times when it had occurred.

Baylor said he felt "crushed" when he discovered the franchise wanted him to retire, falling into a state of depression where he lost weight and had trouble sleeping. His attorney asked the jury to award nearly $2 million in lost wages and compensation for mental distress. Platt asserted that even though the Clippers had every right to dismiss Baylor, they instead offered him a "smooth landing" by giving him the opportunity to earn a six-figure salary as a consultant. He said that rather than take this option, Baylor chose to "lawyer-up to get some money."

When the time came for Sterling to testify, he said that it was unfair for Baylor to retrospectively complain about his earnings, as he was always

---

258 Baylor's legal team also dropped the NBA from its list of defendants on the eve of the trial.

paid the salary that he asked for. Sterling then proceeded to try and create the impression that the Clippers' poor results over the previous two decades had nothing to do with him and everything to do with Baylor. He said that Baylor was given autonomy when deciding who to draft, what to pay coaches and which free agents were worth pursuing. "The record speaks for itself," Sterling said. "Elgin Baylor is a good person but we lost seven out of 10 games with him. How can anyone feel good about that?"

While the Clippers were eager to portray Baylor as some sort of bumbling old fool who was solely responsible for the franchise's woes, the real story was far more complicated. Consider for a moment the list of factors that impacted Baylor's ability to perform his role which he had little or no influence on. A sustained run of serious injuries to the team's most important players. The constant firing of head coaches. The absence of a decent training facility[259]. And most importantly, an owner who scoffed at the idea of paying free agents according to the market-rate.

Baylor said that trying to build a winning team in this type of an environment was like "working with one hand behind (his) back." Over the years, Baylor had consistently drafted or traded for talented players who could have potentially formed the nucleus of a contending team. The Clippers' inability to take the next step and actually compete for a championship had a lot more to do with Sterling's unwillingness to spend the required money than anything related to the actions or inactions of the front office.

Unfortunately for Baylor, the jury in his case arrived at a different conclusion.

---

259 This lack of a regular practice venue meant that the Clippers were forced to hold training sessions at a variety of locations across Los Angeles for the entire time that Baylor was general manager. Former head coach Don Casey described the experience of never being sure from day-to-day where the next practice session was going to be held as like "coaching a whirlwind gypsy team."

The trial went for a little over three weeks but it took the jury less than four hours to return with a verdict. They unanimously rejected Baylor's wrongful termination suit, voting 12-0 in favor of Sterling and the Clippers. The jury's foreman said that they believed the Clippers' actions had more to do with the team's poor results than Baylor's age.

The conclusion of the trial signified a sad end to Elgin Baylor's storied NBA career, which began in 1958. Over the ensuing 50 years, Baylor competed as a player, coach and general manager in Minneapolis, Los Angeles and New Orleans. Baylor had hoped that the final chapter of his basketball narrative was going to take place on the Staples Center floor, with the Clippers team that he had assembled celebrating around him and the Larry O'Brien Trophy resting in his arms. Instead, on an otherwise unremarkable Wednesday afternoon, a dejected Baylor trudged out of the Los Angeles County Superior Court and did his best to put the 22 years he had spent working for Donald Sterling behind him.

The Clippers didn't have much time to celebrate their legal victory over Elgin Baylor. Just a few weeks later, the franchise was defending itself in *another* multi-million dollar dispute with *another* former employee. In the time since Mike Dunleavy first filed for arbitration, the Clippers had decided to drop their counter suit that alleged fraud on the part of their former coach. This meant that all that was left to be determined was whether Dunleavy was fired or if he quit voluntarily.

It took just a few weeks for the arbitrator to rule that Dunleavy's employment was in fact terminated by team management and the Clippers were instructed to pay a little over $13 million to their former coach. This figure took into account the $6.75 million that Dunleavy was owed at the time that he was canned plus interest and deferred compensation payments.

Miles Clement, Dunleavy's attorney, spoke on behalf of his client after the decision was announced, saying, "It's a good day."

This ruling was a crushing blow for the Clippers and it gave the franchise a 50% success rate in the legal department, which turned out to be a significantly better result than what they were able to achieve on the court during the 2010-11 season. The Clippers were able to recover from their 1-13 start to finish with a record of 32-50, which meant they fell 14 wins short of qualifying for the post-season. However, despite missing the playoffs for the 29th time in the franchise's 33 year history, it was not all doom and gloom in Clipper-land.

Griffin finished his rookie campaign with averages of 22.5 points, 12.1 rebounds and 3.8 assists, which was good enough to become just the third player to be unanimously voted the league's Rookie of the Year[260].

If Griffin appeared to be destined for stardom, then Eric Gordon looked set to join him. After three seasons in the NBA, Gordon had developed into a prolific scorer who could shoot from long-range and use his athleticism to attack the basket. Gordon also averaged over 22 points per game during the 2010-11 season, along with 4.4 assists. Not only were Griffin and Gordon talented, they were also both still just 22 years old, giving Clipper fans hope that the team had an inside-outside combination which they could build around for years to come.

One month after the regular season wrapped up, the league staged its annual draft lottery. This was something of a non-event for the Clippers, as they had already traded their first round selection to Cleveland, in order to get the Cavs to agree to add Baron Davis' huge salary to their payroll. The probability of Cleveland snaring the first overall selection with the Clippers'

---

260 Griffin received all 118 first place votes, joining David Robinson (1990) and Ralph Sampson (1984) as the only players to receive the highest possible vote tally in the award's 59 year history.

draft slot was just 2.8%, a figure so low it hardly seemed worth contemplating. But while the numbers said that Cleveland barely stood a chance, the Clippers' enduring history of misfortune gave Cavs' fans reason to be optimistic. When the time came to announce who had won the first selection, Cleveland was indeed the lucky team. Since the introduction of the lottery system back in 1985, this was just the second time that a franchise was able to select first in the draft using a pick that originally belonged to another team[261].

On the night of the actual draft, Clipper fans could only watch in horror as the Cavs used the first overall selection on Kyrie Irving, a 6'3" point guard who appeared to be destined for a long, productive career. In an alternate universe, Irving would have teamed up with Griffin and Gordon to form one of the most explosive young trios in NBA history. Instead, he headed to Cleveland, where he made an immediate impact, winning the 2012 Rookie of the Year award before becoming an All-Star midway through his second season.

The Clippers' front office came under considerable scrutiny for allowing Irving to slip through their fingers. However it did not take long for Neil Olshey to redeem himself. Just a few months after Irving was drafted, Olshey pulled off a trade that resulted in the Clippers obtaining the best point guard to play in Los Angeles since Magic Johnson.

---

261 Amazingly, the only other time that this occurred also resulted in the Cavs taking advantage of a pick that originally belonged to the Clippers. Cleveland selected Brad Daugherty with the first overall selection in the 1986 draft using the Clippers' first round selection, which they had traded away back in 1979 in exchange for Joe Bryant.

CHAPTER 19

Everybody Loves Chris

"There are a lot of places I can go where they've won...but building our own tradition and our own history would be huge."

CHRIS PAUL

KOBE BRYANT WAS LIFTING WEIGHTS at Equinox Fitness Club when his concentration was broken by the familiar sound of his cell phone's ringtone. Under normal circumstances Bryant would be reluctant to disrupt his workout but on this occasion, he stopped to take the call. The voice on the other end belonged to Chris Paul, the player widely regarded as the game's premier point guard. Paul was phoning to inform Bryant that he was about to be traded to the Lakers. This meant that the two former rivals were going to become teammates, thus forming arguably the strongest backcourt in the history of the NBA.

Bryant was familiar with Paul, with the pair teaming up in Team USA's backcourt during the 2008 Olympics, as well as playing together in three All-Star games, and he believed that their shared ultra-competitive approach to the game would make them ideal teammates. Paul was also excited, with the trade placing him in one of the league's largest markets and giving him the chance to play with one of the NBA's all-time great players.

The two men spent around 20 minutes talking on the phone, discussing how they were going to approach the upcoming season and speculating about how many championships they could win together. Feeling eager to start the next phase of his career, Paul hung up the phone and began making arrangements to fly to Los Angeles as soon as possible. Meanwhile, Bryant went right back to pumping iron.

Half an hour later, Bryant's workout was interrupted by another phone call. When he answered, he was greeted by a considerably less chirpy Paul. In fact, Paul sounded both angry and confused. He informed Bryant that the trade, which he had labeled a "done deal" during their previous conversation, was now dead. The story of how it collapsed involves an intervention by the NBA commissioner that was unprecedented, unpopular and is unlikely to be replicated ever again.

Chris Paul was always a strong-willed individual, dating back to his days growing up in Lewisville, North Carolina. If you were to ask a young Paul to do something that he thought was good use of his time, he would attack the task like an army of beavers. But try to get him to do something that he didn't want to and he would glare back like he was about to run you over. Paul was not only determined, he was also quite a talented athlete. He played quarterback and middle linebacker on his Pop Warner football team, leading them to the national championship game, and displayed a similar flair on the basketball court.

By the time Paul enrolled at West Forsyth High School, he was still only 5' tall and for the first time, his lack of height began to impact on his athletic endeavors. He tried out for the basketball team as a freshman and a sophomore but was unsuccessful on both occasions. Paul began to include a plea for additional inches in his nightly prayers and by the start of his junior year, he finally made the varsity team as a 5'10" point guard. Paul went on to play a large role in the Wolverines' run to the state semi-finals, averaging 25 points per game. Over the summer, he continued to impress the growing collection of college coaches who were keeping tabs on him, leading his AAU team to the national under-17 title and winning tournament MVP honors along the way.

On the eve of Paul's senior season, he signed a letter of intent to attend Wake Forest, a prominent Division One school that was located less than 15 miles from his home. Paul was happy to receive a scholarship to attend such a high profile school and he was especially pleased to share this news with his 61 year old grandfather, Nathaniel Jones. On the day that the announcement was made, there was nobody prouder of Paul than Jones, who stood behind his grandson as he told the awaiting media his plans. However, any lingering joy was snatched away the very next day, when Jones was beaten to death in his carport by a group of teenagers who were attempting to steal his wallet.

Two days later, West Forsyth played their first contest of the new season and Paul decided to turn the game into a tribute to his late grandfather by scoring 61 points, one for each year of Jones' life. Paul's final basket was a lay-in that he converted while being knocked to the floor by an opposition defender. As the ball passed through the net and the referee's whistle blew, an emotionally overwhelmed Paul lay on the court and looked up towards the ceiling of the gymnasium. He now had exactly 61 points, which meant that he needed just six more to break the state record. However, Paul was determined to make sure that his final tally did not exceed Jones' age. With his team comfortably in the lead and just a few minutes remaining on the clock, Paul purposely air-balled the ensuing free-throw and walked straight off the court, where he fell into his father's arms and cried.

This memorable game was part of a dominant senior year that made it clear to all observers that Chris Paul was the best high school player in North Carolina. And though West Forsyth fell short of its ultimate goal of winning a state title, Paul finished the year with averages of 30.8 points, 9.5 assists and 6 steals.

From here, Paul headed to Wake Forest, where he continued his impressive play. As a freshman, he led the Demon Deacons into the Sweet Sixteen of the NCAA tournament and was named the ACC's Rookie of the Year. The following year, Wake Forest appeared to be on track to claim a number one seed for the NCAA tournament, until Paul decided to punch an opponent in the testicles during the final game of the regular season. This literal and figurative low blow resulted in Paul being suspended for one game, forcing Wake Forest to play the opening round of the ACC tournament without their best player. Not surprisingly, the Demon Deacons lost and this defeat relegated them to a number two seed. Paul rejoined the team for the NCAA tournament but they were eliminated in the second round by a hot shooting West Virginia team, who put up 111 points. With the season over, Paul announced his intention to forgo his final two years of college eligibility and declare for the NBA draft. He left Wake Forest with career averages of 15 points and 6.3 assists per game.

Paul was eventually selected with the fourth overall pick by the New Orleans Hornets, which meant that for the first time in his young life, he would be living outside of North Carolina. The day after he was drafted, Paul travelled to New Orleans, where he spent the next few weeks familiarizing himself with his new home town. In late August, Paul and his older brother C.J. purchased a property located near a picturesque golf course, before returning to North Carolina to pack their belongings and say their goodbyes. Paul's plan was to be back in New Orleans by the start of September, which would give him a few weeks to settle in before Hornets' training camp was scheduled to begin.

On the morning of August 29th 2005, Paul was sleeping in the bedroom of his childhood home, when he was awoken by the sound of his mother's voice telling him to come and see what was happening on the television. A drowsy Paul stumbled out of bed and was confronted by some of the most shocking scenes he had ever seen in his life.

Hurricane Katrina hit New Orleans early that Monday morning and it left behind a trail of carnage that was unlike any natural disaster to strike inside the boundaries of the United States. The storm caused severe destruction along the Gulf Coast from Florida to Texas. However, nobody felt the effects of Katrina more than the people of New Orleans, where the levee system failed, resulting in mass flooding that persisted for weeks.

Michael Chertoff, the Homeland Security Secretary, described Katrina and its aftermath as "probably the worst catastrophe" in the country's history. A simple look at the raw numbers supports Chertoff's assessment. While the exact death toll resulting from Katrina is uncertain, the National Hurricane Center says that 1,836 fatalities can be attributed to the storm, with over 85% of these deaths occurring in Louisiana. Meanwhile the cost of repairing the damage caused to properties and infrastructure was estimated to exceed $100 billion.

In the aftermath of Katrina, it soon became apparent that the Hornets were going to have to look for an alternate venue to host their home games for the upcoming season. While the New Orleans Arena escaped the storm relatively unscathed, the surrounding area was practically uninhabitable due to severe flooding and a lack of electricity. The Hornets eventually settled on the Ford Center in Oklahoma City, where they would play the bulk of their home games for the next two seasons.

The Hornets were coming off a dismal 18-64 season and little was expected of them before Katrina, let alone now that they were being forced to play away from their home base. However, led by the inspired play of Paul, they won 38 games, falling just six wins short of securing an unexpected playoff berth. Paul averaged of 16.1 points and 7.8 assists and was an almost unanimous selection as the league's Rookie of the Year[262]. The following season, Paul played even better and while the team's overall record improved slightly, the Hornets once again failed to qualify for the playoffs.

The Hornets returned to New Orleans for the 2007-08 season and they set a new franchise record by winning 56 games. This meant that for the first time in four years, the Hornets were heading back to the playoffs. In the first round, New Orleans easily dispatched Dallas in five games, which set up a match-up with San Antonio, the league's defending champions. The Hornets raced to a 3-2 series lead before the Spurs stormed back to win the final two games and clinch the series. On an individual level, Paul put together arguably the best season of his professional career, averaging 21.1 points and a league best 11.6 assists per game. He was selected to play in his first All-Star game, was named on the All-NBA First team and finished runner-up to Kobe Bryant in the voting for the Most Valuable Player award.

As a key member of the franchise's on-court revival, Paul believed he had earned the right to be consulted about potential front office moves. New Orleans' general manager Jeff Bower was not of the same view. A year after the Hornets came within a game of qualifying for the conference finals, starting center Tyson Chandler was traded and back-up point guard Jannero Pargo, one of Paul's closest friends on the team, left via free agency. Paul's input was not sought in either case.

In the opening weeks of the 2009-10 season, head coach Bryon Scott was fired and replaced with Bower. And whereas Paul kept his cards close to his chest after the departures of Chandler and Pargo, he now chose to make his feelings known. Paul publically lamented the fact that no one from the Hornets' front office had reached out to him to discuss the coaching change, while reflecting on the pivotal role that Scott had played in his

---

262 Paul missed out on being a consensus pick by one vote, which went to Utah's Deron Williams.

development as a player. Under the guidance of Bower, the Hornets finished with a 37-45 record and missed the playoffs altogether[263].

Things only got more complicated at the start of the following season, when the franchise was sold to the league, the first time in the history of the NBA that this had occurred. This unusual state of affairs arose after George Shinn, the Hornets' previous owner, had difficulties finding a buyer when he was trying to sell the team. The league did not want Shinn selling for a bargain basement price, due to concerns about the impact that this might have on the value of their other franchises. So, the NBA's Board of Governors took the extraordinary step of purchasing the Hornets, meaning that the franchise was effectively owned by the league's other 29 teams.

Paul now had less than two seasons remaining on his contract and given the uncertainty surrounding the franchise's future, it was looking increasingly likely that he would sign elsewhere when his current deal expired. The Hornets returned to the playoffs in their first season under NBA ownership, where they were set to face the Lakers in the first round. In Game 1, Paul led New Orleans to an upset win at Staples, finishing with 33 points and 14 assists, before the Lakers won three of the next four encounters. This meant that the Hornets needed to win Game 6 in order to keep their season alive. However, with Paul limited to just 10 points, the Lakers cruised to an easy 98-80 victory. It turned out that this was the last game that Chris Paul ever played for the New Orleans Hornets.

In basketball terms, there was nothing normal about the December afternoon when news of the proposed Chris Paul to the Lakers trade first began to circulate. For a start, not a single NBA game was played on this day. In fact, it had been close to six months since any action had taken place on an

---

[263] At the end of the season, Bower and the Hornets "mutually" agreed to go their separate ways.

NBA court. This extended lay-off was the result of the owners' decision to lock out the players, after the two sides were unable to see eye to eye on the terms and conditions for a new collective bargaining agreement.

This was only the second time that the start of an NBA regular season had been disrupted due to an industrial dispute. And as was the case back in 1998, money was a central issue this time around. The owners were trying to reduce the players' share of basketball-related income and were also attempting to implement a number of new rules designed to stem the flow of superstar players heading towards the league's marquee franchises.

On the same day that the finishing touches were being put on the Paul-to-the-Lakers trade, the league's owners were congregated in New York City. They were there to ratify a new collective bargaining agreement, thus putting an end to the lockout. The ceasefire that had been negotiated called for each team to play an abbreviated 66 game schedule, with the shortened season set to tip off on Christmas Day. In order to end the dispute, the players accepted a much smaller slice of the league's revenue pie and the two parties also agreed on harsher penalties for teams who exceeded the salary cap[264].

This new agreement was sold to the fans as a win for the game of basketball. The message was that small market teams had a much better chance of retaining their best players under the new arrangements, thus creating greater competitive balance across the league. Those who were anxious to see how these new rules would work in practice did not have to wait very long for a test case.

A few days earlier, Chris Paul clearly signaled his intentions to leave New Orleans at the end of the 2011-12 season when he declined the offer of a one year contract extension. Paul's decision left the Hornets with two options. They could either trade Paul over the next few months or watch him

---

[264] Under the new agreement, the players' total share of basketball-related income dropped from 57% to between 49-51%.

walk out the door at the end of the upcoming season and receive nothing in return. The Hornets elected to go with the first alternative and negotiated a three-team trade with the Lakers and Rockets. Under the terms of the proposed deal, the Hornets would send Paul to the Lakers in exchange for a package that included Lamar Odom (from the Lakers) and Luis Scola, Kevin Martin, Goran Dragic and a first round draft pick (from the Rockets). Meanwhile, Houston would receive Lakers big man Pau Gasol.

When the first whispers of this trade began to leak out, it was nothing short of a public relations disaster for the NBA. The collective bargaining agreement was still yet to be ratified and one of the game's brightest young stars was already trying to force his way from a small market team to one of the league's most powerful franchises. This was clearly not a good look for a league that was trying to convince a jaded fan base that the disruption caused by the lockout would be worth it in the long-run.

News of this blockbuster trade not only annoyed fans, it infuriated many of the league's owners. Small market teams had grown tired of seeing talented players flock towards the bright lights of their big city competitors and they were hoping that the new collective bargaining agreement would put an end to this situation. However, reports of Paul playing in the same backcourt as Bryant left many owners wondering exactly what they had spent the past few months fighting for.

There was perhaps no one who was more outraged than Cleveland owner Dan Gilbert, who knew exactly what it felt like to lose a superstar player. It had only been a year since LeBron James infamously declared that he was "taking his talents" to Miami, thus turning his back on both Gilbert and the city of Cleveland. The idea of Paul forcing his way out of New Orleans struck a nerve with Gilbert and so he wrote a scathing letter to league commissioner, David Stern. In it, Gilbert labeled the proposed trade a "travesty," pointing out that not only were the Lakers getting one of the best players in the league, they were also saving themselves around $20 million in salary. He claimed that the vast majority of other owners shared his view, while also urging the league to take action to prevent the trade from occurring.

Under normal circumstances, the league would be powerless to block a trade that two or more of their franchises had agreed to. But, given the fact that the NBA owned one of the teams involved in the deal, this was far from a normal set of circumstances.

At the time when the NBA purchased the Hornets from Shinn, the plan was for Stern to act as the franchise's de-facto owner while the league negotiated its way through the lockout. Once the lockout was over, the team would be put back up for sale. And while this proposal had the broad support of the other owners, it also raised some interesting questions in terms of conflict of interest. When it came to trades, would Stern's decisions be made on the basis of what was in the Hornets' best interest or was he going to be guided by what he believed would be most beneficial for the league as a whole? It only took a few months for this question to transform from a fascinating hypothetical to a reality that Stern was forced to confront.

By the time the details of the Paul-to-the-Lakers trade were leaked to the wider community, the three teams involved shared the belief that they had reached an agreement. Jac Sperling, the Hornets' league-appointed trustee, approached Stern at the Board of Governors meeting in New York City and asked him to rubber stamp the deal. This was considered to be a mere formality. Up until this point in time, Stern had granted complete autonomy to the Hornets' front office, thus Sperling had no reason to think that there would be anything different about this particular deal. When Stern told Sperling that he would not be giving his approval to the trade, it came as a shock, not only to the Hornets but also the rest of the NBA universe.

Very few details about Stern's reasoning for this intervention have ever been made public. The league's initial attempt to hose down the brewing controversy, a short statement declaring that the trade was vetoed for "basketball reasons," was comically vague. The absence of anything resembling a clear explanation led to wide-spread speculation that a group of owners, led by Gilbert, had successfully lobbied Stern to veto the trade. The next day, Stern attempted to dismiss these allegations via a carefully worded press release. He claimed to have acted "free from the influence of other NBA owners" and justified his intervention by saying that New Orleans was "better served with Chris in a Hornets uniform than by the outcome of the terms of that trade."

The implication that the Hornets were not getting enough in exchange for Paul was not overly convincing. The package of Odom, Scola, Martin, Dragic and a first round draft pick seemed to be a fairly reasonable return, when you consider that Paul was just a few months away from becoming a free-agent[265].

The league's decision to block the trade may have appeased the Dan Gilberts of the world but it also led to howls of protest from fans across the league. Nowhere were these cries of foul play louder than in Los Angeles. The Lakers were coming off a disappointing season and news that Paul was about to join the team was greeted with much joy from fans of the franchise. However, this excitement proved to be extremely short-lived, with Stern's intervention coming just a few hours after media reports of the trade first surfaced. Stern's decision to veto the Hornets' first attempt at trading Paul was obviously horrible news for the Los Angeles Lakers. It also proved to be the single most important turning point in the history of the Los Angeles Clippers.

---

265 Odom was regarded as one of the most versatile players in the league and just a few months earlier, his unique skill set was officially recognized when he won the NBA's Sixth Man of the Year award. Meanwhile, Scola and Martin were two ready-made scorers (with the duo averaging a combined total of 41.8 points per game during the previous season) and Dragic was a talented, up-and-coming point guard.

The Lakers were not the only Los Angeles-based team looking to make a trade for Chris Paul on the eve of the 2011-12 season. In fact, the Clippers had been speaking with Hornets' general manger Dell Demps for months, trying to work out a way to get their hands on the star point guard. At the same time the Hornets were negotiating with the Lakers, the Clippers put in an offer of their own, albeit a fairly modest one- Chris Kaman, a future first round draft pick and Al-Farouq Aminu[266]. This was clearly not enough to grab the Hornets' attention, leading to a counter offer of Kaman, Aminu, Eric Gordon, DeAndre Jordan, Eric Bledsoe and a future first rounder, which was promptly rejected by the Clippers.

With the two sides miles apart, Neil Olshey asked for permission to speak directly with Paul, in order to gauge the likelihood of him re-signing with the Clippers if the two franchises were able to agree on a trade. Olshey and Paul spent close to two hours on the phone and during this time, the star point guard expressed a strong desire to team up with Blake Griffin and play for the Clippers. Paul also assured Olshey that he would exercise his player option for the 2012-13 season if the trade went ahead. This undertaking was crucial, as it meant that the Clippers would have at least two seasons to win Paul over before having to worry about losing him to free agency. Olshey then contacted the Hornets with the intent of submitting an upgraded offer, only to be informed that it was too late, as they were on the verge of accepting the Lakers-Rockets trade.

Thus when Stern killed off the Hornets' first attempt to trade Paul, there was no one happier than Olshey and he immediately resumed his discussions with Demps. Olshey had previously balked when Demps requested that Gordon be part of the deal, but he was now willing to include the promising third year guard. The only problem was that the Hornets were not satisfied with this fairly significant addition, they also wanted Bledsoe and another first round draft pick thrown in as well. While the Clippers

---

266 Aminu was a 6'9" forward who had just come off a fairly disappointing rookie campaign.

and Hornets went back and forth with different trade options, Olshey asked Paul to rank the small forwards who were available on the free agent market. Paul listed Caron Butler as his preferred teammate and Olshey showed that he meant business by immediately signing Butler to a three year, $24 million deal.

However, while Paul may have been impressed by the Clippers' aggressive attempts to upgrade their roster, it seemed that it would all be for naught. After working all weekend to try and make a trade for Paul work, Olshey woke up Monday morning and announced that the franchise had decided to head in a different direction, saying that the Hornets' asking price was simply too high.

Having seemingly exited the race for Chris Paul, the Clippers quickly set about ensuring that they would have the strongest possible roster when the season commenced on Christmas Day. On Monday afternoon, they signed former Finals MVP Chauncey Billups and retained promising young center DeAndre Jordan by matching a four year, $43 million offer from Golden State. These moves not only improved the Clippers roster, they also sent a clear message to the Hornets' front office that he was not bluffing when he said he was prepared to walk away from their negotiations. This left Demps to ponder the prospect of losing Paul at the end of the season without any compensation.

On Tuesday morning, Olshey was with Billups at an orthopedic doctor appointment when Demps called to re-open trade talks. The two general managers spent much of that afternoon discussing various offers and counter-proposals and by Wednesday, they had agreed on a deal. Paul was sent to the Clippers along with a second round draft pick and in return, the Hornets received Gordon, Kaman, Aminu and a first round draft selection. This time around, there were no last minute interventions from Stern or anyone else from the league's head office. Chris Paul was leaving the Hornets.

A week after the last minute collapse of the Lakers' trade, Paul boarded a private jet in the wee hours of the morning. He was finally heading to Los Angeles- only to play for the Clippers. As the plane took off, an exhausted Paul rested his head against the window and gazed out at the city of New Orleans. With tears slowly dripping down his cheeks, the memories from the past six years came flooding back to him. Paul was about to embark on the next phase of his career, where he hoped to lead the Clippers to the type of team success that he had been unable to achieve with the Hornets. If he was going to turn this vision into a reality, he would have to find a way to steer around the hazards and pitfalls that had sabotaged every other Clipper team over the previous 33 seasons. Chris Paul was about to discover just how formidable a challenge this would prove to be.

Season XXXIV: 2011-12

The addition of Chris Paul caused a dramatic surge in expectations for the Clippers' 2011-12 season. Olshey had assembled a roster that featured five All-Stars (Paul, Blake Griffin, Caron Butler, Chauncey Billups and Mo Williams), and a number of promising young players, including DeAndre Jordan and Eric Bledsoe. The Clippers were now viewed as a team that should comfortably qualify for the playoffs and by the end of January, they appeared to be on track, having won 12 of their first 18 games.

The Clippers' final game for the month was their best performance yet, a 12 point victory over Oklahoma City, the team with the league's best record. This win sent a clear signal to the rest of the league that the Clippers were now legitimate championship contenders. To the outside world, it seemed as if Paul had achieved the unthinkable, breaking a cycle of over three decades of misfortune in the space of just a few weeks. The Clippers were gracing the covers of national magazines, monopolizing the nightly highlight reels and ascending to the top of the Western Conference standings at a rapid pace. However, this period of smooth sailing would prove to be fleeting.

By February, a familiar mixture of bad luck and self-inflicted wounds resurfaced, with the first cracks appearing during an otherwise meaningless game in Orlando. Midway through the fourth quarter, everything appeared to be going well, with the Clippers holding an eight point advantage and seemingly on their way to another win. Nobody was playing better for the visitors than Billups, who had already scored 11 points in the fourth quarter, including a perfect 3 from 3 from behind the arc. With a little over six minutes remaining, Billups threw up another long-range attempt, only this time he was off-line. Rather than back-pedal to get into position to play defense, Billups moved towards the basket at which he had just shot in order to chase the ensuing rebound. But as he pushed off to pursue the loose ball, his left foot gave way, causing him to crumple to the floor. A post-game examination confirmed that Billups had ruptured his Achilles tendon, meaning that he would be unavailable for the remainder of the season.

Two nights later, things went from bad to worse.

After suffering another loss, this time to a mediocre Cleveland team, Mo Williams decided it was a good time to let the world know how unhappy he was with the state of affairs in Clipper-land. First on his list of complaints was the fact that he was not the player who was chosen to replace Billups in the starting line-up, with Del Negro electing to go with Randy Foye as the team's new starting two guard. Williams also questioned the front office's decision not to offer him the new contract that he was seeking. Stressing that it "had nothing to do with money", Williams compared his situation to being in a relationship with a girlfriend who doesn't tell you that she loves you every day. When asked to clarify what he meant, he said that the way the Clippers' could show that they loved him was to sign him to a contract extension

The end of February brought a brief reprieve from the doom and gloom, when Paul and Griffin were selected to play in the All-Star game, the first time that two Clippers had been given this honor during the same season[267]. Both played well, with Griffin scoring 22 points and Paul passing for a game-high 12 assists, helping the West secure a 152-149 victory.

When regular season play resumed, the problems continued, with the focus shifting from the players to the man calling the shots from the sideline. Vinny Del Negro entered the season as the league's most maligned coach, with analysts questioning everything from his substitution patterns to his ability to implement offensive and defensive schemes. By the middle of March, the Clippers had lost 12 of their last 19 games and the chorus of people calling for Del Negro's head was reaching a crescendo.

The low point came in late March, when the Clippers travelled to New Orleans to take on the Hornets, the team with the Western Conference's worst record. This was Chris Paul's first appearance back at the New Orleans Arena since December's trade and most people expected a triumphant homecoming for Paul. Instead, the Clippers played one of their worst games of the season and lost. This result only added to the growing speculation about Del Negro's job status.

In the locker room after the game, the players were very clear in stating that they still supported Del Negro but the same could not be said for the Clippers' front office. When Olshey was asked to comment on the rumors that Del Negro's job was in jeopardy, he elected to remain silent, failing to offer any words of support for his embattled coach. The team returned home knowing that they desperately needed a win to silence Del Negro's critics. Fortunately for Del Negro, they were able to deliver, securing a 101-85 victory over Memphis.

---

267 Both players were also voted into the West's starting line-up. The only other occasion when a Clipper started in an All-Star game was back in 1980, when World B. Free joined Magic Johnson in the backcourt of the West team.

The speculation over the Clippers' coaching position was finally put to bed a few days later, when Donald Sterling publically declared his support for Del Negro. Sterling said that he didn't know "where all these stories (were) coming from" before adding that he believed Del Negro would succeed as the Clippers coach, provided people were patient. On the same evening that Sterling backed Del Negro, Olshey also addressed the issue, although his support was less emphatic. Olshey admitted that the team's recent poor play had led to thoughts of replacing Del Negro. However, he said that this was not going to happen because "the good outweighs the bad with Vinny."

The confirmation that Del Negro was going to keep his job triggered another burst of strong performances, with the team reeling off 14 wins over their final 19 games to finish the abbreviated season with a 40-26 record. And while this winning percentage of just over 60% set a new franchise record, it was not enough to secure home-court advantage, with the Clippers falling just one win short of fourth-placed Memphis, the team that they were set to face in the first round.

A series against the Grizzlies meant a match-up with Zach Randolph, the player the Clippers traded away just three years earlier in order to make room for Blake Griffin. Randolph had since recast himself, becoming an All-Star and forging a reputation as a clutch playoff performer[268]. The Clippers were set to face the Grizzlies without the benefit of home-court advantage, which meant that they needed to win at least one game on the road in order to progress past the first round. With the series set to tip-off in Memphis just three days after the regular season concluded, the Clippers would not have to wait very long for their first opportunity to secure a road win.

---

268 Twelve months earlier, Randolph led the Grizzlies to a first round upset of Tim Duncan and the Spurs, as Memphis became just the second eighth seed in NBA history to eliminate a number one seed in a seven-game series.

The Playoffs: Round 1 vs. Memphis

The Clippers' first playoff appearance in six years couldn't have started off any worse. They fell behind by 20 points in the first quarter of Game 1 and went into the half-time break facing a 58-39 deficit. In the third period, things went further downhill when Caron Butler fractured his left hand and the Grizzlies' lead ballooned out to 27 points.

With eight minutes remaining in the fourth quarter, the game was effectively over. The Grizzlies held a commanding 95-71 lead and the thoughts of almost everyone in the stadium began to shift towards Game 2. Even the Clippers coaching staff were ready to throw in the towel, with Del Negro attempting to substitute Paul out of the game. However, Paul might have been the one person in the building who still believed that the visiting team had a chance to steal the win and he managed to convince Del Negro to leave him in for a few more minutes.

Paul immediately rewarded his coach's faith by triggering an 11-0 run that reduced the margin to 13 points. While this was definitely a more manageable deficit, it really only shifted the prospect of a Clipper comeback from beyond the realms of possibilities to extremely unlikely. Over the next few minutes, both teams struggled to score and with 2:57 remaining in the game, the Grizzlies held a 12 point lead that seemed to be very safe.

Ten seconds later, Clippers back-up shooting guard Nick Young hit his first three-pointer of the evening and the margin dropped to nine. On the very next possession, Paul found Young open on the opposite side of the arc and he again connected, reducing the lead to six. All of a sudden, the unthinkable had become possible, prompting the Memphis fans to rise to their feet in an attempt to inspire their beloved Grizzlies to hold on for just two more minutes. When Young converted his third consecutive long-range attempt on the next trip down the floor, a stunned silence descended over the FedEx Forum.

The Memphis lead that was once 27 was now down to just three. And there was still 1:47 remaining in the game.

Grizzlies coach Lionel Hollins called a timeout, hoping to settle his frazzled players but the Clipper onslaught continued when the game resumed. The first play after the timeout saw the ball in the hands of Memphis center Marc Gasol, who immediately turned it over. Griffin then drew a foul and hit both free throws, reducing the deficit to a solitary point. The next Grizzlies' possession finished with an air-ball from Randolph, which was immediately followed by a successful lay-in by Clipper big man Reggie Evans. The visiting team had done what seemed to be close to impossible just a few minutes earlier. After a 26-1 run, the Clippers were now in front by 1 point with just 50 seconds left to play.

The loss of the lead seemed to momentarily spur the Grizzlies back into action. A turnaround jumper from Rudy Gay put the home team back on top with 28 seconds remaining. The next Clipper possession resulted in Paul drawing a foul and he calmly converted the ensuing pair of free throws. The score was now 99-98 in favor of the Clippers, with just under 24 seconds remaining.

This gave Memphis the final possession and the Grizzlies' decided that Gay, their leading scorer, was going to take the last shot. Gay drove hard towards the basket, before pulling up at the edge of the free throw line and launching a contested jumper. As the ball sailed towards the hoop, the crowd collectively held their breath. If Gay's attempt was successful, the Grizzlies would escape Game 1 with a victory and 1-0 lead in the series. If he missed, the Clippers would have completed one of the greatest comebacks in the history of the NBA.

Gay's shot was on line.

But it fell a couple of inches short.

The ball bounced harmlessly off the front of the rim and into the hands of Griffin as the final buzzer sounded. The reaction from the Clippers was an equal mixture of shock and the type of unbridled joy that is usually seen at the end of championship-clinching games. As the Clippers embraced each other, the Grizzlies retreated from the scene in a state of disbelief.

Game 2 was a lot less eventful. The Clippers were forced to play without the services of Butler, who was expected to be sidelined for anywhere between four and six weeks. The Grizzlies took full advantage of Butler's absence, cruising to a 105-97 victory and tying the series at 1-1.

The biggest surprise to emerge from Game 3 was the sight of Caron Butler walking out for the game's opening tip. Butler's decision to play with a broken left hand undoubtedly gave his teammates an emotional lift but he was unable to provide much help on the floor, finishing with just 4 points and 3 rebounds.

If Game 3 had been decided solely on the basis of which team could shoot most accurately from the free throw line, the Clippers would have struggled to beat the Cal Tech Beavers, much less the Memphis Grizzlies. As a team, the Clippers missed 17 of their 30 shots from the charity stripe and not surprisingly, their inaccuracy almost ended up costing them the game. With 23 seconds remaining, the Clippers were in front by six and seemed to be on the verge of another hard-fought victory. However, a pair of successful three-pointers from Gay and five missed free throws from the Clippers over the ensuing 15 seconds set the scene for another nail-biting finish.

The Grizzlies were now facing a one point deficit with eight seconds still on the clock. As was the case in the series opener, this game would be decided by a last second attempt by Gay. Using a screen set by Randolph, Gay managed to momentarily shake free from his defender and launch a three-pointer. However, he was once again off-target and the Clippers held on for the 87-86 victory.

Two nights later, the game again went down to the wire and was decided by its final possession. This time around, it was the Clippers who had the ball and it came as a shock to no one that they decided to place their fate in the hands of Chris Paul. With the score tied at 87-all, Paul stood just inside the half-court stripe, calmly dribbling the ball as the clock raced towards zero. However, when the time came to make his move, Paul drove straight into a double team, losing both his footing and the ball. The buzzer sounded without the Clippers attempting a shot, sending the game into overtime. The extra period provided Paul with an opportunity for immediate redemption and he grabbed it with both hands. Paul finished overtime with 8 points on 4 for 5 shooting, leading the Clippers to a 101-97 win and a 3-1 series lead. The Clippers headed to Memphis hoping to close out the series.

If the first half of Game 5 was bad for the Clippers, then the third quarter was a complete disaster. They entered the half-time break facing a 15 point deficit and by the middle of the third period the margin had grown to over 20. As if things weren't going bad enough, Griffin suffered a sprained left knee late in the third quarter when he landed awkwardly after a hard foul by Gasol. The fourth quarter saw the Clippers rally, pulling to within six points with a little over six minutes remaining. However, any thoughts of a second miraculous comeback were put to bed when Paul hurt his hip, causing him to be pulled from the game.

In the lead-up to Game 6, the Clippers received some good news when Paul and Griffin were both cleared to play. However, they were far from fully fit, leading to a dramatic drop in their production. Paul finished with a series low of 11 points while Griffin had 17 points and just 5 rebounds. Despite the fact that their two star players were significantly hobbled, the Clippers somehow found a way to keep the game close and almost pull off an unlikely win. The score was tied at 66 at the start of the fourth quarter, when the Clippers went on a 10-2 run. For a brief moment it appeared that the battered and bruised home team might be on their way to victory. But the composed Grizzlies continued to pound the ball inside and eventually seized control of the game, winning 90-88 and sending the series back to Memphis for Game 7.

As Del Negro prepared for the second Game 7 of his young coaching career, he knew that not only was the Clippers' season on the line, his position as head coach also hinged on the result. If the Clippers were eliminated, they would have fallen well short of expectations and this would almost certainly cost Del Negro his job. This put Del Negro in a tough spot, as the odds were clearly stacked against him and his team.

In order for the Clippers to advance, they needed to win Game 7 as the visiting team, which has traditionally proven to be one of the most difficult challenges in the NBA. In the preceding 30 years, there had been 59 Game 7s played and in 49 of these contests, the home team had prevailed. The Clippers were also set to play the series decider with their top three scorers (Griffin, Paul and Butler) all operating at well below their best, due to injuries. Finally, there was the weight of a Clipper history littered with failure resting on the shoulders of the team as they flew to Memphis for their date with destiny.

While the rest of America seemed fairly sure that the Grizzlies were about to advance, the inner sanctum of the Clippers maintained a quiet confidence in their ability. In fact, the Clippers were so sure that they were going to win Game 7 that they packed extra clothing so that they would be ready to fly straight to San Antonio for the start of the Western Conference semi-finals.

After the first three quarters of Game 7, the score was 56-55 in favor of the Grizzlies, meaning that the series was still up for grabs. However, as Del Negro walked to the huddle to address the players at the start of the final period, he knew that he had a major problem on his hands. While he was happy that his team was still in the game, he was also acutely aware that his starting five simply were not playing very well. Griffin, the Clippers' leading scorer during the regular season, was clearly troubled by his injured knee and had thus far posted meager totals of 8 points and 4 rebounds. Butler had missed 9 of the 12 shots he had attempted, Randy Foye's contribution of 6 points came on 33% shooting and DeAndre Jordan's tally of 0 points and 2 rebounds was nothing short of embarrassing. Even Chris Paul was not his usual self. He had managed to fight through the pain from his sore hip to score 17 points, but he had also had as many turnovers as he did assists[269].

Knowing that he was likely to be just 12 minutes away from the unemployment line, Del Negro made the boldest decision of his coaching career- sitting all five starters for the most important quarter of the Clippers' season. In their place, Del Negro went with a line-up of Eric Bledsoe, Mo Williams, Nick Young, Kenyon Martin and Reggie Evans.

As the fourth quarter got underway, the Clipper reserves immediately began building an unlikely lead. A corner three from Young, a kamikaze coast-to-coast drive by Bledsoe and a two-handed dunk from Martin all helped the visitors transform a one point deficit into an eight point advantage. When Williams nailed a three a few minutes later, the Clippers lead grew to double digits and this proved to be enough of a cushion to hold on for a 82-72 victory.

This was just the second time in the Clippers' 34 year history that the team had made it past the first round of the playoffs and the players celebrated accordingly. Nearly all of the post-game discussion centered on the remarkable performances delivered by the Clipper reserves who scored 25 of their team's 27 points in the fourth quarter[270]. Having defeated both

---

269 4 of each.
270 The only contribution to the Clippers' fourth quarter total by a starter came from a pair of meaningless free-throws shot by Chris Paul in the game's final seconds.

Memphis and the odds, the Clippers boarded a plane for San Antonio armed with a healthy dose of self-confidence. They were now just four wins away from booking a spot in the Western Conference finals and becoming the most successful team in franchise history.

THE PLAYOFFS: ROUND 2 VS. SAN ANTONIO

It took the San Antonio Spurs just six days to eliminate the Los Angeles Clippers from the 2012 playoffs. And the manner in which San Antonio disposed of their Western Conference rivals was so decisive, that it left no doubt in anyone's mind about who was the better team. Game 1 was like a clinic, with the Spurs seemingly able to score at will, as they cruised to a 16 point victory. Afterwards, Paul said there was a simple solution to the Clippers' woes- they just had to "play better."

Whether or not the visitors played any better in Game 2 was debatable but either way, it was becoming obvious that this hobbled version of the Clippers was simply no match for the Spurs. San Antonio jumped out to a 15 point lead in the first quarter and controlled the game for the rest of the evening, eventually winning 105-88. The Clippers were again forced to play with their two star players at well below full health. Griffin did manage to crack the 20 point barrier for the first time since injuring his knee but he also finished the game with just 1 rebound- a new career low. Paul also set a new career mark by throwing the ball away eight times.

Despite being down 0-2, the Clippers took some comfort from the fact that they were heading home to play the next two games. And for one quarter, it looked like Staples Center was the answer to all of the Clippers' woes. The home team bolted out of the gates and took a 33-11 advantage into the quarter time break. The two players leading the charge were none other than Griffin and Paul. Griffin finished the first period with 14 points and 5 rebounds while Paul passed for 7 assists. The Spurs were able to cut into the deficit during the second quarter but the Clippers still entered the main break with a double digit advantage.

The home fans' spirits were high as the third period got underway. Not only was their beloved team in control of the game but their best two players appeared to be finally over their injury woes.

By the end of the third quarter, the Clippers' season was effectively over.

For a little over eight agonizing minutes, the home team was unable to score a single basket. They remained stranded on 57 points while San Antonio used a 24-0 run to push their score from 45 to 69, transforming a 12 point deficit into a 12 point advantage. From here, the Spurs maintained their lead and eventually secured a 96-86 victory. San Antonio still needed to win one more game to advance but for all intents and purposes, the series was finished.

Rather than meekly surrendering in Game 4, the Clippers turned in their best performance of the series. Unfortunately, this was still not enough to secure the victory which was needed to keep their season alive. The game was close throughout and with five minutes remaining, San Antonio trailed by 5 points. The prospect of dropping a playoff game to the Clippers seemed to shift the Spurs into high gear and they scored on their next six possessions, taking a 100-97 lead with 90 seconds remaining. A couple of free throws by Paul brought the margin back to a single point, setting the stage for a dramatic finish. As per usual, with the game on the line, Del Negro elected to put the ball in the hands of Paul. Unfortunately, Paul failed to save the Clippers' season not once, but twice.

On the first occasion, he drove into the heart of the Spurs' defense and threw a wild pass that was easily picked off by Manu Ginobili. Having lost possession of the ball with less than 12 seconds remaining, the Clippers were forced to foul. When Spurs' guard Danny Green missed one of his two free throws, the home team was given another chance. The Clippers could tie the game with a two-pointer or win it with a three. The ball went right back to Paul and he again elected to drive. This time around, Paul stumbled as he got into the paint and threw up an awkward looking runner that fell short. The Spurs controlled the rebound and progressed to the Western Conference finals for the first time in four years.

After the game, Paul took full responsibility for the defeat, although given that he was carrying an injury throughout the series, it seemed he was being unduly hard on himself. In fact, Paul was so tormented by his below-average performance that he made late-night phone calls to both Del Negro and Olshey to assure them that "this wasn't going to happen again." And it was hard not to agree with the sentiment of Paul's statements. This was a Clippers roster that appeared to be on their way to achieving something pretty special. In the space of just three seasons, the franchise had transformed itself from a cellar-dwelling, basket-case that couldn't crack the 20-win barrier, to one of the league's elite teams.

In the aftermath of being swept out of the playoffs, Paul knew that the Clippers could not afford to rest on their laurels. He acknowledged that the team had enjoyed a relatively good season but was quick to add that they needed to improve in order to compete with the league's best. Expectations were clearly rising. Now all the Clippers needed to do was make sure that their on and off court growth was able to keep pace.

Season XXXV: 2012-13

Vinny Del Negro entered the 2012 off-season unsure if he would get another opportunity to work with his emerging team. He had a one year option remaining on the original contract that he signed when he first joined the Clippers, but whether or not this clause was exercised was solely at the team's discretion. In this situation, most organizations will either offer a new contract for two or more seasons, in order to create a stable environment around the team, or decline the extension option altogether and employ a brand new coach. The Clippers chose to do neither. Instead, they took up the original 12 month extension option but failed to offer Del Negro any additional job security beyond the upcoming season. Thus for the second year in a row, Del Negro approached the new season as the ready-made fall guy.

While Del Negro was not overjoyed at his personal lack of long-term job security, at least he had a contract, which is more than could be said for Neil Olshey. Since taking over from Mike Dunleavy in the middle of the 2009-10 season, Olshey had built a reputation as one of the league's shrewdest wheelers and dealers. He was responsible for acquiring Paul, drafting Bledsoe and bringing in many other key players including Billups, Butler and Young. In the middle of the 2012 playoffs, Olshey's impressive overhauling of the Clippers' roster was recognized when he finished third in the voting for the Executive of the Year award[271]. However, what many people didn't know was that Olshey had been working throughout the 2011-12 season without a guaranteed contract. Instead, he was employed by the Clippers on a month-to-month basis.

As the 2012 off-season approached, Olshey's exploits were beginning to attract the attention of other owners from around the league. It was becoming clear that the Clippers would need to make a commitment longer than 31 days if they wanted to retain his services, so they offered him a one-year contract worth around $750,000. This represented a significant upgrade in terms of salary and on a Friday afternoon in early June, the Clippers announced that they had reached an agreement in principle with Olshey.

That weekend, Olshey met with Paul Allen, the owner of the Portland Trailblazers, a team that had been keeping a watchful eye on the Clippers' general manager. With Olshey on the verge of signing a new deal, Allen knew that he had to act decisively. Olshey was presented with a three year $3.6 million contract which came with one fairly significant catch- he was informed that the offer was only valid for that particular meeting. Olshey was not going to be given the opportunity to go back to his frugal employers to see if they were willing to match or beat the Blazers' terms. He had to either accept Portland's proposal on the spot or watch it vanish forever. With a difference in salary that was close to $3 million, he decided to sign with

---

271 Olshey finished just one vote behind the Spurs' R.C. Buford and 33 votes short of the eventual winner of the award, Indiana's Larry Bird.

Portland. On Tuesday June 5th, Neil Olshey was introduced as the Blazers' new general manager, just four days after the Clippers publically announced that he was staying in Los Angeles.

After Olshey's rapid departure, the Clippers turned over responsibility for player personnel decisions to a committee of three that included Del Negro, Andy Roeser and director of player personnel, Gary Sacks. Despite predictions that this arrangement would lead to more of the chaos that had typically been associated with the franchise, the trio surprised everyone by functioning extremely well together. In fact, the summer of 2012 was one of the most productive off-seasons in Clipper history. The Del Negro/Roeser/Sacks team was able to add two of the past three winners of the Sixth Man of the Year award by signing free agent guard Jamal Crawford and trading for Lamar Odom. Crawford was expected to provide a scoring punch for the second unit, while Odom was returning to the team where his career had begun to play a back-up role behind Griffin and Jordan. The Clippers also re-signed Chauncey Billups and rounded out their bench by picking up Grant Hill, Matt Barnes and Willie Green[272].

There was no doubt that this re-modelling of the roster was an exciting development; however everyone knew that re-signing Blake Griffin was the most important item that the Clippers' front office needed to take care of during the summer of 2012. Griffin had one year remaining on his rookie deal but the Clippers were hopeful that they could get him to agree to an extension, with many observers viewing this as an important test case for the franchise.

On the first day of the free agency period, Griffin was presented with a five year contract extension that allowed him to earn up to $95 million if all of the various incentive clauses were met. After taking close to two weeks to weigh his options, Griffin accepted the deal. This decision was seen as a

---

[272] Making way for this influx of new players was Mo Williams, Randy Foye, Nick Young, Kenyon Martin and Reggie Evans, who all departed for other NBA destinations.

massive tick of approval for a franchise with a long history of players walking out at the first available opportunity.

The Clippers headed into the 2012-13 season with a formidable line-up. Their starting five of Paul, Billups, Butler, Griffin and Jordan featured four All-Stars, while their bench unit of Crawford, Odom, Bledsoe, Barnes, Hill and Green looked to be one of the strongest in the league. The challenge now was to make sure that all of this talent was able to achieve the type of on court success that Clipper fans had been patiently waiting to see for over three decades.

Perfection is hard to attain in any field, and this is especially true in athletic endeavors. However, for the month of December 2012, the Los Angeles Clippers were about as close to perfect as a sporting team can be. The month started with a 35 point thrashing of the hapless Sacramento Kings and finished with an 11 point win over the Utah Jazz. In between, the Clippers played another 14 games and won them all, thus giving them a return of 16 in 16 games. This was just the third time in NBA history that a team had managed to play an entire calendar month and not lose a single game[273]. As a result of this remarkable run, the Clippers headed into 2013 with a league-leading 25-6 record[274].

The Clippers finally came back down to earth on the first day of the New Year. They missed 24 of their 29 three-point attempts, converted less than 45% of their free throws and suffered a 14 point loss in Denver, their

---

273 At the time, the only other NBA teams to go undefeated for a whole month were the 1995-96 San Antonio Spurs and the 1971-72 Los Angeles Lakers. The Spurs went 16-0 in March 1996, while the Lakers won every game that they played in both November *and* December of 1971 as part of an eventual 33 game winning streak.
274 This team success resulted in some key individuals also being acknowledged, with Paul being named Player of the Month for December and Del Negro winning his first Coach of the Month award.

first defeat in 35 days. However, this result did not prove to be a bad omen for what was to come in 2013. In February, Paul and Griffin were once again voted as starters for the All-Star game and the duo played a huge role in the Western Conference's 143-138 victory[275]. March was a slow month, with the team winning just half of their 14 games, but April brought about another extended winning streak, as the Clippers won their final seven games of the season.

The end of the regular season provided a brief opportunity for reflection. For the first time in franchise history, the team cracked the 50-win barrier, finishing with a final tally of 56 victories and claiming their first Pacific Division title. The Clippers had two players who led the NBA in statistical categories, with Paul topping the steals list with 2.4 per game and Jordan converting a league-best 64.3% of his field goal attempts. They also completed a 4-0 regular season sweep over the Lakers, the first time in 35 years that this had occurred. The Clippers entered the playoffs as the Western Conference's fourth seed and waiting for them in the first round was Memphis, setting up what promised to be a fiery re-match of last year's dramatic seven-game series.

THE PLAYOFFS: ROUND 1 VS. MEMPHIS

It was all smiles in Clipper-land after the first two games of their 2013 playoff campaign. Game 1 was close for much of the first three quarters and at the start of the final period, the Clippers were clinging to a six point lead. Then along came Eric Bledsoe. Bledsoe finished with a fourth quarter stat line of 13 points (on 6 for 6 shooting), 6 rebounds, 4 assists and 0 turnovers and this performance helped propel the Clippers to a comfortable 112-91 victory.

Game 2 was a lot closer. The Clippers' second unit played a pivotal role in building a handy 12 point lead but, unlike Game 1, the Grizzlies refused

---

[275] Griffin finished with 19 points on 81.8% shooting, while Paul was named the game's MVP with a stat line of 20 points, 15 assists and 4 steals.

to go away. Led by point guard Mike Conley, Memphis came storming back and with less than 2 minutes remaining, the game was tied at 89-all. On the Clippers' next possession, Paul connected on a tough step-back jumper to reinstate the lead, before a Marc Gasol dunk once again evened the score. This set the stage for another round of Chris Paul heroics.

With eight seconds remaining, Paul tried to drive to the basket but was unable to get into the paint, due to the exceptional defensive effort of Tony Allen. Instead, he dribbled down the edge of the key with Allen draped all over him. For a split second, it looked like Paul might not be able to get a shot off but he somehow managed to create enough separation to launch an awkward, one-handed runner. The ball kissed off the backboard and then settled into the bottom of the net as time expired.

This last gasp victory meant that the Clippers were heading to Memphis with a 2-0 series lead. They had now beaten the Grizzlies in six of their past seven encounters and everyone connected with the Clippers seemed extremely confident that they were just a few days away from finishing off the series. As Chris Paul and his teammates walked off the court at the conclusion of Game 2, few people would have predicted that the Clippers had just won their last game for the season.

The Clippers didn't just lose Games 3 and 4, they got "punked," or at least that was Matt Barnes' description. In Game 3, the Clippers were horrible, shooting an abysmal 38.8% from the field while turning the ball over 18 times on their way to a 12 point defeat. Two nights later, they played even worse. The Grizzlies evened the series with a 104-83 victory that was fueled by a complete domination of the paint. Marc Gasol finished with 24 points and 13 rebound, while his Clipper counterpart, DeAndre Jordan, had just 2 points and 2 rebounds[276]. Despite the one-sided nature of these

---

[276] Even more depressing was the fact that Jordan actually outscored two other members of the Clippers' starting five, with both Billups and Butler going scoreless, while shooting a combined 0 for 10 from the field.

two defeats, the Clippers returned to Los Angeles hopeful that a change of scenery would also lead to a change in their fortunes.

The greatest season in Clipper history ended the same way that many others had- with an unfortunate injury to one of the team's best players, killing off any chance of success. Blake Griffin sprained his ankle when he accidently stepped on Lamar Odom's foot during a light practice session on the eve of Game 5. The sprain was so severe that it initially appeared doubtful that Griffin would play again in the Memphis series. However, after receiving round the clock treatment and a healthy dose of painkillers, Griffin was able to take his spot in the starting line-up for Game 5.

Griffin started strongly enough, contributing 4 points, 3 rebounds and 2 assists during the game's first nine minutes. During the quarter time break, Griffin went back to the locker room to receive some treatment and when he returned, he looked very much like a player with a serious injury. Over the next two quarters, a clearly hobbled Griffin failed to score a single basket and he was eventually pulled from the game for good, with a little over five minutes remaining in the third period. At the time of Griffin's departure, the Grizzlies held a nine point advantage. The fact that the Clippers still had a chance to steal the win was attributable to one person- Chris Paul, who finished the game with a new playoff-high of 35 points. However, the Grizzlies managed to keep their noses in front for the entire second half before eventually pulling away for a 103-93 victory.

The post-game commentary from the Clippers' locker room was filled with the usual bluster about the series being far from over. But the reality that faced the team was fairly grim. With Griffin injured and less than 72 hours between Game 5 and Game 6, the probability of a Clipper win in Memphis seemed extremely unlikely.

The good news was that Griffin was cleared to play in Game 6, after scans confirmed that there was no structural damage to his ankle. However, while Griffin was able to take to the court, he was clearly a shadow of his former self, finishing with 9 points, 4 turnovers and 3 rebounds. Without the usual production from their All-Star forward, the Clippers were in serious need of someone to step up and support Chris Paul. The most likely candidate appeared to be Jamal Crawford, a player who had built a reputation as one of the league's most prolific scorers. The only problem was that on this particular evening, Crawford was having trouble finding his range. He missed all five of his first half field goal attempts and at half-time, the score was 58-53 in favor of the Grizzlies.

The Clippers opened the second half with a line-up of Jordan, Odom, Butler, Billups and Paul. After four minutes, Del Negro subbed in Griffin. A minute later, Barnes checked-in. Halfway through the third period, Del Negro went all the way to the end of his bench and inserted Willie Green and Grant Hill, who hadn't played a single second in the first five games of the series. As Del Negro continued to pull different players off the bench, a shocked Crawford sat and wondered when he was going to get his chance to get back into the game.

It turned out the answer would be never.

In one of the most bizarre decisions of Del Negro's coaching career, he elected to leave Crawford on the bench for the entire second half. This was the same Jamal Crawford who was the team's third leading scorer, averaging 16.5 points per game during the regular season. The same Jamal Crawford who finished a close second in the NBA's Sixth Man of the Year award[277]. The same Jamal Crawford whose fourth quarter scoring average was the third highest in the entire league, behind only Kevin Durant and Kobe Bryant.

---

277 Crawford finished runner-up to New York's J.R. Smith.

At the start of the fourth quarter, Del Negro inserted Eric Bledsoe into the action, the tenth Clipper to take to the court in the second half who was not named Jamal Crawford. This left Crawford to watch from the bench as the game, and the series, slowly slipped away. Paul once again played exceptionally well, finishing with 28 points and 8 assists, but his individual brilliance was not enough to get the Clippers over the top, with the Grizzlies securing a 118-105 victory.

When Del Negro was quizzed after the game about leaving Crawford stranded on the bench for the entire second half, the best explanation he could offer was that there was "no real reason" for his decision. Rather than provide an offensive spark to cover for the reduced production from Griffin, Crawford played a season low of less than 13 minutes and turned in his only scoreless game for the year. Crawford's frustration was clear for all to see when he responded to a question about his failure to score by asking, "What do you want me to do? I can't score much in 12 minutes."

While the Grizzlies moved on to face Oklahoma City, the Clippers quickly turned their attention to the most important off-season in franchise history. It had now been two seasons since Chris Paul's arrival in Los Angeles and in that time he had played a pivotal role in the transformation of the franchise. Under Paul's leadership, the Clippers had gone from being professional sport's longest running joke to one of the NBA's elite teams in the space of just 17 months. However, the conclusion of the 2013 play-off campaign also signaled the end of Paul's current contract, meaning the Clippers had arrived at a fork in the road.

Chris Paul was about to become an unrestricted free agent who could choose to play with whichever team he liked. If Paul decided to re-sign with the Clippers, the franchise was well positioned to continue its ascent toward claiming that elusive first championship. However, if he opted to play elsewhere, the Clippers were just one Blake Griffin trade demand away from returning to dark days of the mid-1980s.

As the Clippers entered the 2013 off-season, the focus of the entire organization was locked in on one goal- convincing Chris Paul to sign a long-term deal. It seemed that everyone connected with the franchise understood the overwhelming importance of ensuring that Paul elected to remain a Clipper when the time came for him to make his decision.

Everyone, that is, but one man.

Donald T. Sterling.

CHAPTER 20

The Fish Rots from the Head

"When ignorant folks want to advertise their ignorance you don't really have to do anything, you just let them talk."

BARACK OBAMA

VINNY DEL NEGRO WAS NO longer the coach of the Los Angeles Clippers and it was all Chris Paul's fault. Or at least, this was what Donald Sterling strongly implied after it was announced that Del Negro's contract was not going to be renewed for another season.

When news that the Clippers were once again searching for a new head coach first broke, it was widely interpreted as an indication that Del Negro did not have the full support of Paul. Given Paul's status as an unrestricted free agent and his standing as one of the best players in the league, it was highly likely that he would have been consulted before any changes were made in the coaching department. The idea was to keep Paul happy in order to retain his services.

Only it seemed that somebody forgot to fill Donald Sterling in on this plan.

On the same day that Del Negro's termination was announced, Sterling spoke with T.J. Simers from the Los Angeles Times and all but confirmed

Paul's involvement in the decision. When asked if axing Del Negro was done simply to hang onto Paul, Sterling replied, "I always want to be honest and not say anything that is not true. So I'd rather not say anything." It was an astoundingly candid response. Simers then asked if the players were calling the shots and Sterling said, "This is a player's league and, unfortunately, if you want to win, you have to make the players happy."

If Sterling was hoping to "make the players happy" then he missed the mark in a fairly major way. Within days of Sterling's frank comments, reports that Paul was "angry" with the Clippers began to surface. "Chris is a man of principle and if he feels you have gone against his principles, it will affect how he feels about you," said one source who was reportedly close to the situation. "He's very agitated that his name has been put out there as the reason for Vinny's firing. He had nothing to do with it."

This was the worst possible turn of events for the Clippers, who were just weeks away from either re-signing Paul to a long-term deal or losing him to free agency. Up until this point, Paul had successfully cultivated and maintained a fairly clean-cut image, which he used to help land a number of lucrative endorsement deals. Being cast as a coach-killer in the latest tale of Clipper dysfunction was not a role that Paul was keen on embracing.

It was clear that Paul was feeling alienated by the franchise's handling of Del Negro's termination so Gary Sacks, the vice president of basketball operations, was sent out to try and calm the situation. Sacks did his best to appease Paul, telling the press that the decision to change coaches was made by the front office and "had nothing whatsoever to do with the players."

There was now exactly one month until July 1st, the date that Paul was free to sign a new contract with whichever team he pleased. And while the chances of retaining Paul were not helped by the star guard being blamed for Del Negro's demise, there was one factor that was still working in the Clippers' favor- money. Paul was eligible to receive a maximum offer of $107.3 million over five years from the Clippers. However, if he opted to leave and sign with one of the NBA's other 29 teams, he would only be able to sign a four year, $79.7 million contract.

The Clippers' front office knew that while this sizable financial difference was going to be helpful, they could not rely on it to seal the deal. If they were going to give themselves the best chance of re-signing Paul, they needed to prove that they were serious about competing for a championship. And the best way to do this was to make sure that their new head coach was someone with impeccable credentials. Fortunately, the Clippers had just the person in mind- a former Coach of the Year who was one of only four active coaches to lead a team to an NBA championship. Even more importantly, this was someone who actually wanted to take on the challenge of coaching the Clippers.

There was just one small problem.

The person whom the Clippers' front office had their hearts set on was already under contract to coach another team.

The Boston Celtics had just been eliminated from the first round of the 2013 playoffs and Doc Rivers was already thinking about next season. Unfortunately for Danny Ainge, Boston's president of basketball operations, Rivers was not planning the next stage of the Celtics' rebuild. Instead, he was contemplating leaving Boston. Rivers was deciding between a return to the broadcasting booth, travelling or spending time with his family down in Florida. At some stage, Rivers also began to ponder a move to California, where he would become the new head coach of the Los Angeles Clippers.

Two years earlier, Rivers signed a five year, $35 million contract extension that tied him to the Celtics until the end of the 2015-16 season. At the time of this deal, Ainge was so confident about the stability of the

Rivers-Celtics partnership, he began speculating that Red Auerbach's franchise record of 795 coaching victories might one day be broken[278].

Over the next two years, Boston went from being one the league's elite squads to a team that barely qualified for the playoffs and when the Knicks secured an 88-80 Game 6 victory in early May, it brought an abrupt end to the Celtics' 2012-13 season. In the immediate aftermath of this defeat, Rivers began thanking members of the Celtics' inner circle. To the untrained eye, it may have appeared that Rivers was simply expressing his gratitude for the efforts of the players and coaches during a particularly emotionally draining season. However, those who knew him well could sense that something else was going on. Rivers was beginning to say goodbye to the organization that had been his home for the past nine years.

Five days later, Rivers and Ainge got together for a discussion about the future of the Celtics. "I was curious as to which way was he leaning," Ainge said. "He was uncertain still at that time but (he) wondered what his options might be." While Rivers was initially considering taking some time off or returning to broadcasting, Ainge was beginning to hear from other general managers who were interested in hiring the Celtics' coach. Representatives from the Nets and Nuggets made preliminary queries to ascertain the likelihood of Rivers being released from his contract but both of these advances were quickly rebuffed by Ainge. Rivers asked if there was any truth to the rumors that teams were contacting the Celtics to inquire about his availability and Ainge confirmed that this was the case. Ainge then asked Rivers if he would be interested in coaching the Clippers.

There were many reasons why the Clippers appeared to be an excellent fit for Rivers. They had assembled a very strong roster that was filled with players who were approaching the prime of their careers. Yet, despite this obvious talent, the Clippers had thus far been unable to achieve any sort of

---

278 On the day that the extension was signed, Rivers had won 336 regular season games as Boston's head coach.

meaningful success, winning just six of their 17 playoff games under the direction of Del Negro. The Clippers front office believed that hiring the right coach was the key to unlocking the team's championship potential and by the summer of 2013, Rivers was regarded as one of the league's top coaches. He had already proven that he was capable of leading a team to a championship by coaching the Celtics to the 2008 title and he was also immensely popular with players from across the league[279].

The good news for Boston fans was that Rivers' contract contained a non-compete clause, which meant that he could only pursue another coaching job with the Celtics' blessing. When Rivers let Ainge know that coaching the Clippers was an opportunity that interested him, the two men decided to explore the situation further. They agreed that they would try to negotiate a mutually beneficial deal but in the event that this was not possible, Rivers would return to coach the Celtics for the 2013-14 season.

From this point, things progressed in pretty much the same manner as most deals involving the Clippers. The negotiations were long, messy and, at more than one stage, appeared destined to go nowhere. Boston initially hoped to secure a compensation package that included DeAndre Jordan, Eric Bledsoe and two future first round draft picks. In exchange, Ainge was prepared to release Rivers, trade Kevin Garnett and buyout the final year of Paul Pierce's current deal, thus giving the Clippers a potential starting line-up of Paul, Chauncey Billups, Pierce, Blake Griffin and Garnett. However, the Clippers did not want to include Bledsoe in the trade, as they planned to use him in a subsequent deal.

With Bledsoe off the table, the talks between the two front offices began to stall. The Clippers did their best to show the Celtics that they were serious about walking away from the negotiations by scheduling

---

279 A 2012 survey asked NBA players to name the coach whom they would most like to play for and Rivers received the highest tally of votes, ahead of Mike D'Antoni and Gregg Popovich.

interviews with a range of other head coaching candidates[280]. The next proposal that was discussed was a slight variation on the initial trade- Rivers and Garnett in exchange for Jordan and two first round draft selections. The Clippers balked once again, believing that two first round picks was too steep a price to pay.

While the two franchises continued to go back and forth in an attempt to come up with a deal they could both agree on, another substantial roadblock emerged. On June 20th, commissioner David Stern revealed that the different trade scenarios being investigated by the Clippers and Celtics were not actually permitted under NBA rules. "The teams are aware that the collective bargaining agreement doesn't authorize trades involving coach's contracts," Stern said. "The only consideration that can be done here in player transactions is other players, draft picks and a very limited amount of cash."

It seems that the Clippers and Celtics had been informed of this inconvenient rule but were hoping to get around it by breaking the trade up into two separate transactions. For example, one deal could involve Garnett's rights being dealt for Jordan and a first round draft pick, with the Clippers subsequently handing over another first round selection in exchange for Rivers being released from his contract. When presented with this type of scenario, Stern's response was unequivocal, saying that the rules could not be circumvented by completing the trade in two distinct stages. "If you think those are separate transactions," Stern said, "I have a bridge that I would very much enjoy selling to you."

Three days after Stern's comments, Rivers was ready to give up on the idea of coaching the Clippers. He called Ainge from the parking lot of a gym and told him that he was ready to return to Boston. "I thought the Clippers' deal was (dead)," Rivers said, "and I had no problems with that. I

---

280 This list of coaches that the Clippers spoke with included Brian Shaw, Byron Scott, Alvin Gentry, Nate McMillan and Lionel Hollins.

said, 'Hey listen, I have decided I am not going to take a year off. I'm going to come back and we're going to start this rebuilding phase.'" As far as Rivers was concerned, this conversation signaled the end of his brief flirtation with the Clippers. He climbed out of his car, switched off his phone and made his way inside to watch his youngest son play.

When the game finished, Rivers turned his phone back on and immediately realized that something fairly major must have occurred, due to the unusually large number of missed calls that appeared on his home screen. The first call that he returned was to his agent, Lonnie Cooper, who informed Rivers that the Celtics and Clippers had somehow managed to agree on a deal in the two hours that had just passed. All that remained was for Rivers to confirm that he still wanted to coach the Clippers, which he told Cooper he did.

Three days later, Doc Rivers was introduced as the new head coach and senior vice president of basketball operations for the Los Angeles Clippers. It had been over six weeks since Ainge and Rivers first discussed the option of making a deal with the Clippers and yet, despite this prolonged time period, the agreement between the two franchises was extremely straightforward. The Celtics released Rivers from the final three years of his contract and were given the Clippers' 2015 first round draft pick as compensation[281]. Rivers became the first former Clipper player to be appointed as the franchise's head coach.

When asked about the factors that made a move to the Clippers seem especially appealing, Rivers said that being offered a front office role and thus having greater influence on player personnel matters played a crucial role in his final decision. "I can go somewhere and not only be coaching,

---

[281] While deals between two NBA teams for a coach are rare, they are not unprecedented. In 1995, Pat Riley left New York to coach Miami, forcing the Heat to send $4 million and a first round draft pick to the Knicks as compensation. And in 2007, Stan Van Gundy was released from his contract by Miami and became Orlando's new head coach, after the Magic agreed to compensate the Heat with a second round draft pick.

but doing something else that I've never done and have a voice," Rivers said. "Most coaches don't ever have that opportunity." Rivers was now part of a three person operation, joining Gary Sacks and Andy Roeser in the front office.

The trio's first job was re-signing Paul and, in sharp contrast to the luring of Rivers, this transaction was completed very swiftly. On July 1st, the first day of free agency, Paul made his intention to stay in Los Angeles clear, sending out a two word, one hashtag tweet that read- "I'M IN!!! #CLIPPERNATION". Paul's willingness to commit to the Clippers without attending a single formal meeting with any opposition coach, general manager or owner was interpreted by most observers as a strong endorsement of the decision to employ Rivers.

Having secured a commitment from their point guard, the Clippers now looked to upgrade the other half of their backcourt. On the same day that Paul announced he was re-signing, Rivers shared a meal with J.J. Redick, a 6'4" guard with a deadly outside shot. Redick was on the verge of leaving Milwaukee and signing with Minnesota, thus Rivers spent much of the evening outlining the virtues of playing for the Clippers instead. Redick was told that they would be able to pay an almost identical salary to what the Timberwolves were offering, while also giving him the opportunity to play a major role for a championship contender. Redick liked what he heard and told Rivers that if the Clippers were able to find a way to financially match Minnesota's offer, he was ready to make the move to California.

Over the next 48 hours, Rivers negotiated a three team deal in which Milwaukee signed Redick to a four year, $27 million contract and then traded him to the Clippers. The Clippers would send Bledsoe and Caron Butler to Phoenix in exchange for Jared Dudley, a 6'7" small forward. Finally, the Bucks were set to receive two second round draft selections, one from the Clippers and one from the Suns.

This seemed like a good deal, one that benefitted all of the teams who were involved. In exchange for Redick, Milwaukee ended up with two second round picks, a good return for a role player whom they were about to lose to free agency. Phoenix received a potential future All-Star in Bledsoe and a former All-Star in Butler. Meanwhile, Rivers was especially happy with the trade, believing Redick and Dudley were precisely the type of complimentary players that the Clippers needed. Both were excellent shooters who were bound to get plenty of good looks playing alongside Griffin and Paul. All that remained was to wait until July 10, the first day that trades and new player contracts were able to be formally processed[282].

In Los Angeles, the pending trade was almost universally hailed as a shrewd deal and, for a brief moment, it seemed that the Clippers were finally putting an end to their long running tale of chaos. In the space of just one week, they had successfully lured Doc Rivers from Boston, re-signed Chris Paul to a long-term contract and negotiated a trade that brought in two new starters. The Clippers appeared to be making all of the right moves to put themselves in a position to compete for an NBA championship.

And then, late one evening, Doc Rivers received a phone call from Andy Roeser. "We've got a problem," Roeser said. "Donald's changed his mind."

The terms of the proposed Bledsoe and Butler for Redick and Dudley trade were first presented to Donald Sterling on July 1st and he initially gave the deal his blessing. However, over the next few days Sterling, who was

---

[282] Trades were not allowed to be completed during the moratorium period, which runs from July 1 to July 10, in order to allow time for a financial audit of the previous season to be completed. The information gained from this audit is used to set the salary cap for the following season.

holidaying in the Hamptons at the time, reconsidered and on July 3rd, he told Roeser that he was withdrawing his approval. Without the green light from Sterling, the trade was essentially dead.

Sterling's backflip was especially problematic for J.J. Redick. A day earlier, Redick's agent, Arn Tellem, had called Minnesota and informed them that his client was about to be traded to the Clippers and thus would not be signing with the Timberwolves. With Redick off the market, Minnesota offered a four year, $27 million contract to Kevin Martin, which he quickly accepted. This was bad news for Redick, as the Clippers and the Timberwolves were the only two franchises that had been prepared to offer him the type of long term deal that he was seeking.

On July 4th, as Redick was getting ready to go out for dinner with some friends, he received a call from Doc Rivers. When Rivers opened the conversation by saying, "You'd better play for me, motherfucker," Redick immediately sensed that there was a problem. A confused Redick responded, "That's the plan. We figured this out two days ago, right?" And despite the conversation continuing for another ten minutes, Rivers failed to outline the exact nature of the issue that was causing him to doubt whether he would get the chance to coach Redick.

The first words that Redick said to his wife after hanging up the phone was, "Something's going on." And indeed, something was. Rivers was working at a frantic pace behind the scenes to try and save the trade. And it was not just the trade that Rivers was fighting to resurrect, it was also his reputation as a man whose word meant something.

Rivers had sold Redick on the idea that the Clippers were embarking on a new era of professionalism, something worlds away from the franchise's embarrassing history. Now, the very first trade that Rivers tried to execute was about to blow up in his face, due to the indecisiveness of Sterling.

Rivers knew that he had to either take a stand now or face the same sort of interference from Sterling in the future. He called Sterling from the parking lot of the Orlando Airport and spent an hour on the phone, engaged in what he would later characterize as a "screaming match." Rivers was trying to convince Sterling that they had to proceed with the trade, whether the Clippers owner was in favor of the deal or not. They had given their word to all of the involved parties and this was not something that Rivers was prepared to go back on.

At some stage in this heated conversation, Rivers delivered a stunning ultimatum to Sterling- either the Clippers followed through with the proposed trade or he was going to resign and walk away from his three year, $21 million contract. "I knew if I walked, with Sterling, it would have been three years with me out of the league. There's no way that he would have allowed me to coach (another team)," Rivers said when reflecting on the incident years later. "I was going to have to take a three year break and I was going to do it."

The next morning, Roeser called Rivers and told him that Sterling had changed his mind once more, thus the trade was back on again.

On July 6th, Redick received a call from Tellem, who filled his client in on the events from the past few days and informed him that the deal was now proceeding. When Redick discovered that the Clippers had almost backed out of the trade, he was left to shake his head and wonder just what sort of an organization he was about to join.

Season XXXVI: 2013-14

The Clippers launched their new campaign by holding a press conference to show off the fruits of a very busy off-season. Rivers, Paul, Redick and Dudley were presented to the media along with Darren Collison, who was brought in as a free agent to fill the back-up point guard slot. Rivers spoke glowingly about the new additions, labeling them "great fits" and saying that their willingness to "stay in their lane" and play team basketball would be crucial to the Clippers' fortunes.

But while Rivers sung the praises of those on stage with him, he knew that the one player who was most vital to the Clippers' success was the team's longest serving member- DeAndre Jordan. Since being selected in the second round of the 2008 draft, Jordan had played five seasons with the Clippers and during this time, he had developed from a scarcely used bench player to a serviceable starting center. In the 2012-13 season, he averaged 8.8 points and 7.2 rebounds, while connecting on a league-best 64.3% of his field goal attempts. However, while Jordan was extremely efficient when it came to converting pick and roll dunks and put-backs, he was a poor mid-range shooter, had almost no low-post moves and was woeful when it came to hitting free throws. Jordan made just 38.6% of his free throw attempts during the 2012-13 regular season and this lack of accuracy from the charity stripe meant that he frequently found himself watching the fourth quarters of close games from the bench, a situation that he was not overly pleased with

Rivers knew that in order for the Clippers to become serious championship contenders, they had to find a way to harness Jordan's strengths. This meant that Jordan needed to pay less attention to his offensive output and instead focus on the defensive side of the game. Rivers' first chance for a serious conversation with Jordan came when they met at a Japanese restaurant in West Hollywood. Over a meal of albacore tuna and yellowtail sushi, Rivers reeled off a list of names for Jordan to consider- Dennis Rodman, Tyson Chandler, Ben Wallace. None were prolific scorers. All were key contributors on championship-winning teams. Rivers told Jordan that he could join this group of highly acclaimed big men and win a championship ring of his own if he was prepared to embrace a similar role. Jordan had been waiting for a coach who made him feel valued and from the moment he first sat down with Rivers, he was sold. If Rivers wanted him to focus solely on defense, then Jordan would do his very best to become a modern day version of Bill Russell.

At media day, Rivers shared his vision with the rest of the world, boldly declaring that Jordan would be a candidate for the Defensive Player of the Year award. It was clear from Jordan's comments that, after years of angling for a larger offensive role, the young center was on the same page as his new coach. "My thing is mainly defense," Jordan said. "That's my only focus this year. Defense is my first, second and third priority."

When the regular season finally got underway, Jordan's play made it clear that he was committed to backing up the off-court proclamations with on-court results. In the middle of November, Jordan demonstrated his ability to dominate a game without being an offensive focal point, putting up just three field goal attempts while grabbing 16 rebounds and blocking 5 shots in a victory over Brooklyn. Later that month, he came agonizingly close to recording the first triple double of his career when he tallied 10 points, 15 rebounds and 9 blocks in a win against Sacramento. A week before Christmas, the Clippers hosted Antony Davis and the New Orleans Pelicans and Jordan produced the best game of his career. He finished with 14 points, 20 rebounds and 5 blocked shots, helping propel the Clippers to a 13 point victory.

On Christmas Day, the Clippers played the Warriors, the second meeting of the season between the two franchises. The first match-up was played back in October and won by the Clippers. It was also a clash that was marred by a number of ugly incidents, including Jordan getting into a shoving match with Golden State center Andrew Bogut and Griffin exchanging words with Warriors' coach Mark Jackson. Any idea that the festive mood of a holiday might lead to a calmer contest on December 25th went out the window in the third quarter, when Golden State forward Draymond Green threw his forearm into Griffin's throat. Green was ejected but his absence did little to quell the rising tensions. At the start of the fourth period, Griffin was also given his marching orders after he and Bogut got into a wrestling match under the basket. The loss of Griffin proved to be too much for the Clippers to overcome and they eventually lost by two points. Afterwards, Griffin made his feelings about the tactics used against him abundantly clear when he accused the Warriors of playing "cowardly basketball."

The teams met twice more over the second half of the regular season. In late January, the Warriors secured a 19 point win over a Clippers team that was playing without Chris Paul, who was sidelined with a shoulder injury. Six weeks later, the two teams met again in another game that was tarnished by a number of spiteful incidents, the most notable of which was a Green tackle on Griffin that looked to be more at home on an NFL field. The Clippers managed to overcome this questionable use of force to secure a 111-98 victory. However, on this occasion even the final buzzer was not enough to put an end to the hostilities, with Warriors' center Jermaine O'Neal and Griffin getting into a heated argument outside of the Clippers' locker room.

The Clippers eventually set a new franchise record for most wins in a season (57) and a big reason for this success was the outstanding play of DeAndre Jordan. He led the league in field goal percentage (67.6%) and rebounds (13.6), and also finished third in blocked shots (2.5). Jordan's improved play was not enough for him to achieve his pre-season goal of being named Defensive Player of the Year, although he did finish with the third most votes[283]. The Clippers entered the 2014 playoffs as the Western Conference's third seed, which meant a first round grudge match with the sixth-seeded Golden State Warriors.

---

283 Jordan finished behind Joakim Noah and Roy Hibbert, which was a remarkable effort considering that he had never tallied a single vote for Defensive Player of the Year across his previous five NBA seasons.

The Playoffs: Round 1 vs. Golden State

As the Clippers and Warriors prepared for their first round playoff series, it was clear that they shared a healthy dislike for one another. On the eve of Game 1, Golden State guard Klay Thompson added more fuel to the fire when he told a local radio station that Blake Griffin was a "flopper." If Thompson was hoping to subtly influence the referees, he would have been very happy with the manner in which the series opener was officiated. Griffin was whistled for fouls early and often, forcing him to spend extended periods of time on the bench. He ended up playing less than 20 minutes and was eventually called for his sixth foul with 48 seconds remaining and the score knotted at 105. With Griffin watching from the bench, the Clippers next three possessions ended with two turnovers and a pair of missed free throws, allowing the Warriors to snatch home court advantage with a 109-105 victory.

The Clippers didn't just win Game 2, they sent an emphatic statement, crushing the Warriors by 40 points. They were led by Griffin, who managed to stay out of foul trouble and score 35 points on just 17 field goal attempts.

The series now shifted to Oracle Arena in Oakland, where the Clippers had lost 15 of their past 17 games. However, with just 11 seconds remaining, the Clippers had both a one point lead *and* possession of the ball. The Warriors were forced to foul Chris Paul, who was only able to convert one of two free throws, leaving the door ajar for Golden State to steal the win. However, Paul made amends on the next possession, playing exceptional defense on Stephen Curry and forcing the Warriors' sharp shooter to air-ball his last second three point attempt. The final score was 98-96 and the Clippers were once again led in the scoring department by Griffin, who had 32 points. Griffin received plenty of support from Jordan, who produced the best all-round playoff game of his career, with 14 points, 22 rebounds and 5 blocks.

This result gave the Clippers a 2-1 series lead and put them back on track to qualify for the Western Conference semi-finals. The aftermath of this victory should have been a happy time for an organization that had endured more than its fair share of misery over the previous 36 years. Instead, this win will always be remembered as the game that immediately preceded the biggest scandal in NBA history.

The demise of Donald Sterling began in a similar manner to the downfall of many prominent public figures- with a decision to commence a relationship with a woman who was not his wife. The exact nature of the association between Sterling and V. Stiviano remains somewhat ambiguous, however it seemed to have all of the key characteristics of a rich, old man and a much younger mistress.

Sterling first met Stiviano during 2010 at a Super Bowl party in Miami. She was 27 years old. He was 75. They immediately hit it off and, not long after the New Orleans Saints claimed their first Vince Lombardi Trophy, Stiviano was employed as Sterling's personal assistant. Stiviano never had a written employment agreement and rather than receiving a regular pay check, she was compensated with a combination of cash and lavish gifts. Sterling bought Stiviano a Ferrari, two Bentleys and a Range Rover as well as an assortment of other presents including jewellery and designer clothes. He also took her on vacations to exotic destinations like Dubai, Paris and Thailand and purchased her a Spanish-style duplex valued at $1.8 million. Sterling and Stiviano were often seen together in public and yet nobody seemed to think that anything out of the ordinary was taking place.

Donald had been married to Shelly Sterling since 1955 and during this time, he developed a reputation for both having extra-marital affairs and not being overly discreet about them. In 1996, he was sued for sexual harassment by a former employee named Christine Jaksy. She claimed Sterling touched her in ways that made her feel uncomfortable, offered to buy her clothes in return for sexual favors and asked her to locate a massage therapist who could service him sexually. This case eventually disappeared from the public eye when the two parties reached a confidential, out of court settlement.

Sterling's bedroom affairs were next dragged into the limelight in 2003, when *he* filed a lawsuit against Alexandra Castro, a woman with whom he shared an intimate relationship between 1999 and 2002. During this time, Castro received many generous gifts from Sterling, including a $1 million home that was located on South Rodeo Drive. However, when Castro tried to sever ties with Sterling, he sued her for embezzlement, claiming that Castro had used underhanded tactics to gain ownership of the property.

When questioned under oath, Sterling initially denied having a personal relationship with Castro. However, after he was confronted with a series of photos and love letters that clearly contradicted his version of events, Sterling changed tact and instead tried to portray his association with Castro as that of a prostitute and a client. Sterling proceeded to outline graphic details of his sexual encounters with Castro, while also labeling her a "piece of trash" and "a total freak." As with the Jaksy case, this lawsuit was resolved with another confidential, out of court settlement.

In 2005, Sterling was again sued over sexual harassment and this time the case actually made it to trial. Sumner Davenport was employed by Sterling as a property supervisor. She claimed that he tried to kiss her, touch her breast and, on one occasion when she visited Sterling's home, he appeared at the door wearing nothing but a towel. Sterling responded by stating that Davenport was nothing more than a disgruntled former employee who was "vindictively hatching a scheme to discredit, harass and embarrass" him. The trial lasted nine weeks and the jury eventually cleared Sterling.

By the start of 2014, Donald Sterling and V. Stiviano had known each other for four years and during this time, Shelly began to suspect their relationship had progressed beyond that of a boss and a personal assistant. Shelly had seen Stiviano blowing kisses at her husband during Clipper games and she instinctively knew that something was not right. However, unprepared to confront the idea that Donald was being unfaithful in such a public manner, Shelly tried to push these doubts to the back of her mind.

In early March, Shelly decided that she could no longer bury her head in the sand and so she did what Sterlings do best- she filed a lawsuit against Stiviano. In it, Shelly asked for over $2 million worth of "community property" to be returned, claiming that Donald had given it to Stiviano without her knowledge or consent.

Stiviano initially tried to get Donald to convince his wife to drop the lawsuit but to no avail. And then, a month later, Stiviano received a text message which made it abundantly clear that her relationship with Donald had changed for good. That evening, the Clippers were hosting Oklahoma City and Stiviano was planning on watching the contest from a luxury suite, using tickets that Donald had given her. However, in the hours leading up to the game, Stiviano was informed via a text message from a team employee that the luxury suite passes were being sold to someone else. Stiviano wrote back, stating that she had been able to procure an alternate set of tickets, and thus would still be in attendance. The employee responded: "Mr. Sterling said to let me know if you need anything. We don't want any issues at the game." Stiviano replied: "No tell Mr. Sterling that I don't need anything nor do I want anything…But thanks for asking. LET THE GAMES BEGAN (sic)."

A couple of minutes later, the employee received another text message with an attached audio file. This set in motion a chain of events that would eventually lead to the Sterling family doing something that Donald swore he would never do- selling the Los Angeles Clippers.

The recording in question was of a private conversation between Donald Sterling and V. Stiviano that had taken place six months earlier. Sterling was upset because Stiviano had posted photographs of herself posing with African-American males on social media and as he made his displeasure known, she pressed record on her iPhone. Sterling questioned why Stiviano was taking pictures with minorities and she asked him, "What's wrong with black people? What's wrong with Hispanics?" Sterling sarcastically responded, "There's nothing wrong with minorities. They're fabulous. *Fabulous.*" Stiviano then asked if it mattered whether the people in her photographs were "white or blue or yellow?" Sterling replied, "Maybe you're stupid. Maybe you don't know what people think of you. It does matter, yeah. It matters." Less than a minute later, Sterling said, "It bothers me a lot that you want to broadcast that you're associating with black people. Do you have to?"

When the discussion turned to Magic Johnson, one of the "black people" whom Stiviano had allowed herself to be photographed with, Sterling said, "I know (Magic) well and he should be admired." However, he followed this up by yelling, "During your entire fucking life, your whole life, admire him. Bring him here, fed him, fuck him, I don't care. You can do anything. But don't put him on Instagram for the world to have to see, so they have to call me. And don't bring him to my games."

These musings on race were clearly out of touch with prevailing community attitudes and were especially jarring given that they were coming from the owner of an NBA team, a league where over three quarters of the players were African-American. The Clippers employee who first received a copy of the recording passed it on to Andy Roeser, who informed Sterling of its existence. However, after Sterling and Roeser spoke, the employee was asked to delete the audio file and all other messages that had been exchanged with Stiviano. It seemed Sterling's plan of attack was to simply refuse to acknowledge that the problem existed. Unfortunately for him, Stiviano was not going to quietly fade into the background.

On April 23rd, the Clippers received a phone call from TMZ, a celebrity gossip website that had managed to obtain a copy of the offending recording. They were planning on releasing the audio and the reporter wanted to know if the franchise had any comment to make before it went online. The Clippers declined to say anything and the tape was uploaded to the TMZ website two days later.

The condemnation that followed was swift and almost unanimous, with everyone from Snoop Dogg to President Obama expressing their disgust at Sterling's remarks. Meanwhile, the initial response from Sterling was predictably tone-deaf. Rather than take responsibility for his comments, Sterling instead chose to question the authenticity of the recording, via a statement released by Roeser. On top of suggesting that the tape might have been "altered" in some way, Roeser also attempted to link the release of the audio file to the ongoing legal dispute between the Sterling family and Stiviano. Finally, Roeser said that he believed that Stiviano was responsible for giving the audio file to TMZ, a claim that she strongly denied.

The NBA's first official response came from Adam Silver, the league's new commissioner. However, Silver's initial remarks gave little comfort to the growing number of people who were calling for decisive action to be taken against Sterling. Silver announced that an investigation into the matter was under way but also spoke about Sterling being part of the "NBA family" and refused to speculate on what sanctions could be imposed.

On the same night that Silver made his first statement on the Sterling tape, another NBA heavyweight also publically addressed the issue. LeBron James was widely regarded as the league's best player and his comments left no doubt about how he felt. He said that there was "no room for Donald Sterling in our league," called on Silver to be "aggressive" in resolving the issue and even broached the idea of the Clippers refusing to play in some or all of their remaining playoffs games. It turned out that a boycott was an idea that was gathering momentum behind the scenes.

On Saturday morning, the day after the tape was first released, the Clippers held a team meeting at the hotel where they were staying. The players had been receiving calls and messages from other NBA players, offering words of support and a common piece of advice- they should refuse to participate in Game 4. Players from across the league were offended by Sterling's comments and wondered exactly what type of penalty the Clippers' owner would receive. Given Sterling's extensive history of escaping sanctions when accused of wrongdoing, many players were concerned that he might get off with nothing more than a slap on the wrist. This was not an outcome that they were prepared to stand by and allow to happen.

At the Clippers' team meeting, a variety of opinions were expressed, from those who favored boycotting Game 4 to those who believed that to do so would only serve to impose a penalty on themselves. One of the players who spoke against a walk-off was Blake Griffin, who had recently seen "42," a film which detailed the struggles experienced by Jackie Robinson as he attempted to become the first African American to play Major League Baseball. Griffin was inspired by the way that Robinson continued playing, despite all the adversity that was thrown his way and he wanted the Clippers to take a similar approach to their current situation.

The Clippers eventually agreed to play Game 4 and it was left to Doc Rivers to explain this decision. "This is a situation where we're trying to go after something very important for us- something we all dreamed about since our childhoods," Rivers said. "Donald, or anyone else, has nothing to do with that dream and we're not going to let anything get in the way of those dreams."

The following day, an extended version of the audio file was released to the public and this contained more of Sterling's commentary on race in America. At one point in the recording, Sterling says to Stiviano, "Don't come to my games. Don't bring black people and don't come." When Stiviano informs Sterling that he is being racist, he responds, "There's no racism here. If you don't want to be walking into a basketball game with a certain person, is that racist?" Stiviano also asked if Sterling was aware that he has a "whole team that's black that plays for (him)?" Sterling replied, "Do I know? I support them and give them food, and clothes, and cars, and houses." Sterling then rhetorically asks, "Who makes the game? Do I make the game or do they make the game?"

A few hours after this second part of the recording was released, the Clippers assembled in the locker room of Oracle Arena to get ready for Game 4. While preparing, they came up with a plan that would allow them to make a statement about Sterling's remarks, without having to boycott the game. After running out on court for the pre-game warm-ups, the Clippers' players huddled together at the center circle, removed their warm-up shirts and symbolically dumped them in a pile near the halfway line. Underneath, they were all wearing their red shooting shirts inside-out, so that the Clippers' logo was not on display. The message was clear.

The Clippers wanted nothing to do with Donald Sterling.

They were now playing for themselves.

When Game 4 finally got underway, the biggest statement was made by a member of the Golden State Warriors. Stephen Curry converted five three-pointers in the first quarter, helping the Warriors to build an early 20 point lead that the Clippers never came close to making up. Curry finished with a game-high 33 points, as Golden State cruised to a 118-97 victory over a flat Clippers team that appeared to be distracted by the ongoing off-court drama.

The series was now tied at two games apiece and Rivers knew that in order to progress to the second round, he had to bring his team's focus back to the game of basketball. Let the rest of the world debate race, freedom of speech and what type of punishment should be imposed on Donald Sterling. Rivers was employed to coach. The Clippers returned to Los Angeles on Sunday evening and Rivers decided to give the players Monday off, sensing that rest would be more beneficial than a morning spent at the team's practice facility.

While the Clippers were trying to re-group and work out how to win two of the next three games, Adam Silver was busy trying to build a case against Sterling. Silver had only taken over from his predecessor, David Stern, on February 1st and now, after less than three months in the job, he was being called upon to resolve arguably the biggest crisis that the NBA had ever faced.

Within hours of the scandal breaking, Silver employed David Anders, an attorney who specialized in internal corporate investigations. Anders was asked to find out how the recording was made, whose voices could be heard and whether the audio file in question had been altered or edited in any way before being given to the media. On Monday, Anders met with Stiviano and she verified that it was hers and Sterling's voices on the tape. Stiviano said the conversation took place in September 2013 and that Sterling knew she was recording on the day in question, as this was something she often did in an attempt to help coach him on his image. Anders also spoke with Sterling and he too confirmed that it was his voice on the tape, although he claimed that the file had been tampered with.

While Anders was gathering evidence, the pressure on Silver to take some sort of action against Sterling continued to grow. Mark Jackson called on fans to make a statement by not going to Staples to watch Game 5, saying that as an African-American man who knows right from wrong, he "would not come to the game." And it seemed that some of the Clippers' biggest corporate backers agreed with Jackson's sentiments, with a number of companies, including Sprint, State Farm, Samsung, Kia and Adidas, deciding to either suspend or terminate their sponsorship agreements with the franchise.

Meanwhile, players from a variety of NBA teams were seriously considering boycotting their upcoming games, thus threatening to throw the remainder of the 2014 playoffs into complete chaos. In fact, Golden State had not only discussed the idea, they had gone so far as to iron out specific details of what a boycott might look like. The Warriors planned to participate in all of the regular pre-game rituals, including the warm-ups, national anthem and introduction of the starting line-ups. Curry, Thompson, Andre Iguodala, David Lee and Green would then head to the center circle for the opening tip, as if everything was normal. But, as soon as the referee lofted the ball into the air, they were going to walk off the court and exit the stadium, with Golden State's bench following close behind[284]. The Warriors were hoping the other five teams that were scheduled to play on Tuesday would join them in their boycott[285].

If Silver hadn't already recognized the need to address the Sterling scandal as quickly as possible, the prospect of multiple playoff games being disrupted due to player boycotts made this abundantly clear. On Monday afternoon, the league's head office released a statement announcing that there was going to be a press conference the following morning.

At 10am on Tuesday April 29th, the Clippers assembled at the team's practice facility for their regular game day shoot around. Midway through the session, a team employee gave Rivers a handwritten note from Andy Roeser. It was a summary of what Silver was about to announce to the waiting media. Rivers opened the note, read it and then placed it back into his pocket. Practice would go on. As far as Rivers was concerned, today

---

284 Curry later explained the motives behind this plan, saying, "It would have been our only chance to make a statement in front of the biggest audience."
285 The other teams who had games that evening were the Clippers, Wizards, Bulls, Thunder and Grizzlies.

was about Game 5 and his job was to make sure that the Clippers were as focussed on this contest as possible.

Two and a half thousand miles away, in New York City, Adam Silver walked purposefully to a podium in the ballroom of the Hilton hotel. After apologizing for running slightly behind schedule, he made the following statement:

> *"Effective immediately, I am banning Mr. Sterling for life from any association with the Clippers organization or the NBA. Mr. Sterling may not attend any NBA games or practices. He may not be present at any Clippers facility and he may not participate in any business or player personnel decisions involving the team. He will also be barred from attending NBA Board of Governors meetings or participating in any other league activity."*

Not only was Sterling banned for life, he was also fined $2.5 million and a plan was announced to force him to sell the team. Silver explained that a forced sale was permitted under the NBA's constitution, so long as three quarters of the league's owners voted to support this action. Silver said he would "do everything in (his) power" to ensure that this occurred.

These were the harshest penalties in NBA history and they received widespread support, from both the general public and league insiders. The Clippers players were informed of the sanctions during the team's post-practice film session and when Rivers relayed the news, it was met with stunned silence.

Donald Sterling was exiled.

However, the team would not have much time to process this latest shocking development as the severity of the penalties imposed on Sterling meant that the proposed boycott of Game 5 would no longer go ahead. In less than eight hours, the Clippers would be back on court at Staples Center, playing one of the biggest games in the franchise's history.

───────

It had been four days since TMZ released the now infamous audio of Donald Sterling's and V. Stiviano's conversation and during this time, Chris Paul and his teammates had become central characters in a drama in which none of them wanted to be involved. They were basketball players attempting to achieve a lifelong goal- winning the NBA championship. And yet, their lives had become consumed by the racist remarks of the man who paid their salaries. However, with Silver announcing a lifetime ban for Sterling, Paul was beginning to see some light at the end of a very long tunnel.

Game 5 was important, and not just in the context of the Clippers' current playoff campaign. It also offered an opportunity for the players and coaches to put the events from the past four days behind them and bring their focus back onto the game of basketball. As Paul prepared to run out for the pre-game warm-ups, he was unsure of what to expect. This was the Clippers first home game since the scandal broke and no one knew how the fans were going to react.

As the Clippers exited the players' tunnel, the Staples Center crowd rose to their feet and gave them a standing ovation. The message was clear. The players and coaches were not responsible for the mess that they had been forced to endure. The fans recognized this and would continue to support the team, no matter what the next few days, weeks or months had in store. As Paul looked around and saw the support from the people of Los Angeles, he almost broke down and cried. The previous four days had been emotionally draining and now, Paul had to find a way to channel his remaining energy towards securing a Game 5 victory.

When the on-court action finally got underway, the Clippers played as if a huge burden had been lifted from their shoulders, rushing out of the gates and quickly building a double digit lead. However, the Warriors were too good a team to be dismissed by this early onslaught and over the next two quarters, they slowly clawed their way back. With a little under two minutes remaining in the third period, Curry drained a three from the top of the key to put Golden State in front for the first time since the game's opening minutes.

Having surrendered their lead, the Clippers desperately needed someone to steady the ship and it was Paul who answered the call. He connected on two long range shots in the last 90 seconds of the quarter, allowing the home team to head into the final break with a five point buffer. From here, the Clippers maintained their advantage and eventually secured a 10 point victory, giving them a 3-2 edge in the series.

Game 6 was back at Oracle Arena and it presented an opportunity for the Clippers to win a playoff series for just the third time in the franchise's 36 year history. However, with Griffin and Paul combining to miss 22 of their 33 field goal attempts, the visitors were unable to capitalize on some sloppy play from Golden State. The final score was Warriors 100- Clippers 99, with Curry's 24 points leading all scorers.

It seemed only fitting that a series filled with such drama, both on and off the court, was going to go the full distance. In the lead-up to Game 7, Jamal Crawford said that home-court advantage placed the Clippers in a good position to progress to the second round. However, while Crawford spoke confidently about his team's chances, many observers couldn't help but wonder whether the Clippers would have anything left in the tank for the series decider.

As soon as Game 7 began, it was clear that the Clippers had a serious problem on their hands. During the 2013-14 regular season, Golden State earned a reputation as one of the best outside shooting teams of all-time. Curry led the league in three-pointers, connecting on 261 at an accuracy rate of better than 42%, while the NBA's second most prolific marksman was Thompson, who made 223 threes at 41.7%[286]. As a team, the Warriors connected on 774 threes, the 11th highest total in NBA history. So when Golden State nailed consecutive three-pointers on their first two possessions of Game 7, most Clipper fans realized that this was a bad omen.

They were right to be worried.

At the end of the first quarter, the Warriors were shooting 80% from behind the arc and had a 10 point lead. By half-time, they had nailed 9 of their 13 three-point attempts and the score was 64-56 in favor of the visitors.

If the Clippers were going to have any chance of making a comeback, they needed to find a way to clamp down on Golden State's outside shooting. In the third quarter, this is exactly what occurred. The Warriors were restricted to a solitary three-pointer and scored just 20 points, allowing the Clippers to take an 87-84 lead into the final period. The stage was set for a dramatic conclusion to the series and the person who wound up playing the role of the hero was not one of the usual suspects. Exactly 12 months earlier, DeAndre Jordan sat on the bench for the entire fourth quarter and watched as the Clippers were eliminated by Memphis. A year later, Jordan would not only be on the court for the final minutes of the game, he would play a crucial role in deciding its outcome.

With less than four minutes remaining, Jordan converted an alley-oop to give the Clippers a one point lead. A few possessions later, Curry was

---

286 Curry and Thompson were the first teammates to finish as the NBA's top two three-point shooters. Their combined total of 484 three-point conversions was 79 more than that of the entire Memphis Grizzlies team.

racing towards the basket for a seemingly uncontested lay-in, when Jordan blocked his shot from behind, triggering a fast break that finished with a Griffin dunk. On the Clippers' next possession, Jordan tipped in a miss from Paul, extending the lead to five points with just over a minute left on the clock. He then threw down a two-handed dunk with 22 seconds remaining that effectively brought an end to the series. Jordan finished with 15 points, 18 rebounds and 3 blocked shots, while the Warriors were again led by Curry, who had 33 points and 9 assists.

As the final seconds ticked off the clock, an emotional Doc Rivers slapped high fives with fans and pumped his fist towards the crowd. The Clippers had somehow managed to persevere amid enormous off-court distractions and win a tense, seven game series against one of the best young teams in the NBA. After the game, Rivers reflected on the events from the past nine days and said that he was "very proud" of his players.

The Clippers would not have much time to celebrate their inspiring series victory. Less than 24 hours after the conclusion of Game 7, they were back on the team plane. Waiting for them in Oklahoma City was Kevin Durant, who was just a few days away from being recognized as the NBA's Most Valuable Player.

The Playoffs: Round 2 vs. Oklahoma City

Chris Paul was exhausted. On the court, he had spent the past two weeks chasing Stephen Curry around, while battling a hamstring injury and a sprained right thumb. Off the court, his role as president of the NBA Players' Association meant a much greater level of involvement with the Sterling scandal than any of his teammates.

Not long after arriving in Oklahoma City, the Clippers assembled to watch some film on their second round opponents. Assistant coach Tyronn Lue was highlighting the individual tendencies of the different Thunder players, when he noticed that Paul had fallen asleep. Lue scanned the rest of the room and quickly realized Paul was not the only one who looked fatigued. It was clear that what the Clippers needed at that moment was rest, so Lue cut the film session short and sent the players back to their rooms. The series opener was scheduled for the following evening and the fact that the team's captain was struggling to keep his eyes open during an important meeting was obviously not a good sign. When Game 1 began, Oklahoma City got off to a fast start and midway through the first quarter, the score was 16-10 in favor of the Thunder.

With a little over six minutes remaining in the opening period, Paul dribbled the ball up court and casually hit a three-pointer.

Two minutes later, Paul used a pick from Griffin to create some space and converted another three.

On the Clippers' next possession, Paul hit a triple from the left wing, this time over the out-stretched hands of Durant.

With 1:59 on the clock, Griffin took a pass in the high post, drew a double team and immediately threw the ball back out to Paul, who was behind the three-point line. Paul's shot hit nothing but the bottom of the net.

Then, with less than three seconds remaining in the period, Paul hit a step-back three in front of the Clippers' bench, giving the visitors a 39-25 lead.

In the final 6:21 of the first quarter, Paul scored 17 points, on perfect 5 for 5 shooting from behind the arc. From here, the Clippers coasted to an easy victory, leading by as many as 29 before settling for a 122-105 win. Paul finished the game with 32 points and 10 assists, converting 12 of his 14 field goal attempts and 8 of 9 from three-point range.

The following day, the focus once again shifted away from the on-court action, when the NBA announced that Andy Roeser was taking an indefinite leave of absence. Roeser was the second longest serving employee of the franchise, having first started working for the Clippers when the team moved to Los Angeles in 1984[287]. He was initially employed as an executive vice president and two years later was promoted to the position of team president, a title which he held for the next 28 years. During this time, Roeser developed a reputation as Sterling's closest confidant. He was also known as someone who would use any available leverage to drive down the salary of whomever he was negotiating with.

The likelihood of Roeser keeping his job was greatly reduced in the first 48 hours of the Sterling scandal, when he allowed quotes questioning the authenticity of the audio file to be attributed to him in a press release. This angered many Clipper employees. Once league investigators were able to confirm that the recording obtained by TMZ was legitimate, it was clear that Roeser's days with the franchise were numbered. NBA spokesperson Mike Bass explained the removal of Roeser, saying that it would create a "clean slate" for whoever took over as the franchise's new CEO.

Over the next three days, the Clippers' 1-0 series lead transformed into a 1-2 deficit. Game 2 began with Kevin Durant being presented with the MVP trophy and finished with him falling one assist shy of a triple double. Durant's stat line of 32 points, 12 rebounds and 9 assists was remarkably similar to that of Russell Westbrook, who finished with 31 points, 10 rebounds and 10 assists, as Oklahoma City evened the series with a comfortable 11 point victory. The Thunder then travelled to Los Angeles and snatched back the all-important home-court advantage with a 118-112 win in Game 3. Durant was the high scorer once again, this time with 36 points.

---

287 Ralph Lawler has worked as a Clippers broadcaster since 1978.

Game 4 got off to a bad start for the Clippers, when Thunder big man Serge Ibaka accidently hit Griffin in the testicles in the first minute of action. From here, things rapidly went downhill. Oklahoma City scored 13 unanswered points to open up an early double digit lead and then followed this with a 12-0 run, giving them a 29-7 advantage late in the first quarter.

The Clippers managed to reduce the margin to 10 points in the third quarter, before Griffin was forced to take a seat on the bench due to foul trouble. This allowed the Thunder to steady themselves and with nine minutes remaining in the game, the margin stood at a seemingly insurmountable 16 points.

Rivers knew that a bold coaching move was required if his team was going to have any chance of staging a comeback. So, he threw caution to the wind and played a small line-up that featured Paul, Crawford and back-up point guard Darren Collison. With the Thunder fielding three traditional front court players, this meant that one of the Clipper guards had to defend a much taller opponent. Rivers asked Paul to guard Durant and it was this unconventional tactic that ultimately turned the game in the Clippers' favor.

Chris Paul stood 6'0" tall, while Kevin Durant was 6'9" and renowned as one of the best outside shooters to ever play in the NBA. Clearly, Paul's distinct height disadvantage was going to make it difficult for him to contest Durant's shots. Instead, he focused on using his quick hands to pressure and harass Durant and this worked well, with Paul able to repeatedly force turnovers. Meanwhile, on offense, the speed of the two Clipper point guards was causing all sorts of problems for Oklahoma City, with Collison and Paul combining to score 20 points in the fourth quarter.

The Clippers didn't take their first lead until the final 90 seconds of the game, when Crawford converted a three-pointer to cap a 31-13 run. From here, the Clippers were able to hang on for a 101-99 victory. Paul finished with 23 points and 10 assists, while Collison and Crawford both scored 18 points off the bench. This stirring comeback was one of the greatest wins in Clipper history, although the team's time in the spotlight would be cut short the very next day.

Donald Sterling had one simple objective for granting an interview to CNN's Anderson Cooper- to apologize for his controversial statements on the recording made by V. Stiviano. At the time, he believed that there was still some chance of retaining ownership of the Clippers and he was hoping that this interview would be the first step towards achieving this goal.

The first ten minutes of the interview went reasonably well. Sterling repeatedly apologized, saying that he had made a "terrible, terrible mistake." He said that his comments were fueled by jealousy rather than racism, asking Cooper, who is openly gay, "Did you ever like a girl or were you ever jealous of her a little bit if she was with other guys?" Sterling also claimed that he had no knowledge of the fact that he was being recorded while speaking with Stiviano and said he did not know how TMZ managed to get their hands on the tape. When asked by Cooper if he and Stiviano had been in an intimate relationship, Sterling declined to answer, saying that a gentleman did not discuss these types of matters.

Things took a turn for the worse when the topic shifted to Magic Johnson, who had recently said that he would not attend another Clipper game as long as Sterling was the team's owner. Sterling accused Johnson of trying to manipulate him into not making any public comments in the first few days after the tape was released, alleging that this was part of a plot by Johnson to try and purchase the franchise. Sterling then sarcastically mocked Johnson, saying, "Big Magic Johnson, what has he done? He's got AIDS." After Cooper pointed out that Johnson actually had HIV, Sterling rhetorically asked, "What kind of guy goes to every city, has sex with every girl and then catches HIV? Is that someone we want to respect and tell our kids about? I think he should be ashamed of himself."

When Cooper said that Johnson had done a lot for the inner-city communities of Los Angeles, Sterling switched his focus to what he perceived was the difference between African-Americans and the Jewish community. "Jews, when they get successful, they will help their people. And some of the African-Americans, maybe I'll get in trouble again, they don't want to help anybody." It was a stunning statement, especially considering that Sterling had spent the first half of the interview trying to convince the audience that he was not a racist.

Any miniscule chance of a shift in public opinion towards Sterling evaporated with the airing of this interview. Magic Johnson was not only one of the most successful and popular athletes in all of America, he had also founded a charity that had given away over $15 million to support a variety of projects, including programs designed to raise awareness about HIV/AIDS and scholarships for minority students.

The following day, Adam Silver issued an apology to Johnson on behalf of the NBA, saying that he didn't deserve to be "dragged into this situation and be degraded by such a malicious and personal attack." Johnson also chose to address Sterling's comments in an interview of his own with Anderson Cooper. He said that Sterling was "living in the Stone Ages" and labeled him "delusional." Johnson also had some unsolicited advice for Sterling, saying that he should abandon his fight to retain ownership of the Clippers and instead use whatever money he was able to get from the sale of the franchise to "go and enjoy (his) life."

Amid the fallout from Donald Sterling's latest public relations disaster, the Clippers did their best to block out the surrounding chaos and focus on the task that lay in front of them- winning Game 5 in Oklahoma City.

For the first 47 minutes of Game 5, the Clippers played exceptionally well. With just over a minute remaining, Blake Griffin drew a foul and headed to the free-throw line to try and add to the Clippers' four point lead. Griffin hit the first free throw but his second attempt fell short. However, this miss proved to be fortuitous when back-up forward Glen Davis secured the offensive rebound. The ball was passed to Paul, who allowed valuable seconds to tick off the clock before calmly converting a mid-range jumper.

The score was now 104-97 with just 49 seconds remaining, placing the Clippers on the cusp of returning to Los Angeles with a 3-2 series lead.

Oklahoma City coach Scott Brooks called a timeout to diagram a play and when the two teams returned to the floor, Kevin Durant came off a screen and hit a three-pointer.

104-100.

43 seconds left to play.

On the next possession, the Clippers again tried to run the clock down, before Jamal Crawford missed a fairly easy lay-in.

22 seconds remaining.

Russell Westbrook fired an outlet pass to Durant, who caught the ball as he was crossing the halfway line, took two dribbles and dropped in a right-handed finger roll.

104-102.

17 seconds left on the clock.

Barnes inbounded the ball to Paul and the Clippers' fortunes seemed to be in safe hands. Given that there was less than 24 seconds remaining, it appeared that the Thunder would have to foul Paul, who was an 85% free-throw shooter.

As Paul dribbled the ball up the right sideline, he had an idea- what if he heaved up a shot from the backcourt at the exact same time as he was fouled? If the referees judged that Paul was in his shooting motion when the contact occurred, he would be awarded three free-throw attempts rather than two. So, as Westbrook came charging towards him to foul, Paul picked up his dribble and tried to throw the ball to the hoop at the opposite end. However, as Paul attempted to launch this 75 foot shot, Westbrook reached in with his right hand and knocked the ball free, without committing a foul[288].

Thunder guard Reggie Jackson swooped in, scooped up the ball and charged towards the basket. The only person standing between Jackson and an uncontested lay-in was Barnes, who was still underneath the hoop after inbounding the ball just seconds earlier. Barnes tried to knock the ball loose and it sailed out of bounds.

It was initially ruled that the ball was last touched by Barnes and possession was awarded to Oklahoma City. However, when the referees elected to look at a video review of the play, it seemed that the call would be reversed. While Barnes appeared to hit Jackson on the wrist, it was clear that the ball had been deflected out of bounds by the Thunder. The rules stated that the referees were not allowed to retrospectively call a foul on Barnes, after watching the replay. The only decision that they could change was in relation to who knocked the ball out of court.

While the referees were huddled around a courtside monitor, Doc Rivers was watching the same footage on the giant screen located above the court and he was certain that the call was about to be overturned. In fact, he was

---

288 Paul later referred to this failed attempt to draw a shooting foul as "the dumbest play I've probably ever made."

so confident that he grabbed a whiteboard and started drawing up a play to allow the Clippers to get the ball inbounded safely. It turned out that this was not necessary because, despite the video showing that Jackson was the last player to touch the ball, the referees opted to stick with their original call. As an irate Rivers howled in protest from the sidelines, possession was handed to the Thunder with 11 seconds still to play.

The ball was inbounded to Westbrook and he launched a three-pointer that fell well short, barely grazing the bottom of the backboard. But before the Clippers could grab the rebound, the sound of a referee's whistle halted play. Paul had fouled Westbrook as he was shooting, hitting him on his right forearm. Westbrook walked to the line and calmly converted all three attempts to give the Thunder a one point lead.

104-105.

6.4 seconds remaining.

Rivers called a time-out and chose to place the ball in Paul's hands, giving his All-Star point guard a chance at immediate redemption. However, when Paul drove into the lane he bobbled the ball, causing it to spill free as the final buzzer sounded.

Clippers 104-Thunder 105.

As the Oklahoma City players celebrated around him, Rivers stormed onto the court to complain about the out of bounds call made with 11 seconds left on the clock. And he continued complaining for most of his post-game press conference, saying, "We got robbed because of that call."

Game 6 was back at Staples and the Clippers got off to a good start, restricting Durant to just 1 for 7 shooting and building a 30-16 quarter time lead. In the second period, Durant began to find his range, connecting on three consecutive three-point attempts and helping the Thunder to trim the deficit to eight points by half-time. In the third quarter, Durant's hot shooting continued, scoring 14 points for the period without missing a single field goal. As the fourth quarter began, the game was tied at 72-all.

The fourth quarter belonged to the Thunder. They seized control with a 10-0 run midway through the period and were able to withstand a late surge from the Clippers to record a 104-98 victory. Durant again demonstrated that he was a worthy recipient of the MVP award, overcoming his slow start to finish with 39 points, 16 rebounds and 5 assists.

After the game, the Clippers reflected on the role that the Sterling scandal played during their post-season campaign. Some players attempted to downplay the impact of the affair but Crawford acknowledged how mentally and physically draining it had been. "When everything first happened, I was tired but I couldn't go to sleep," Crawford said. "There were so many emotions…You got so many texts and emails, people saying this and that, everybody having an opinion." Rivers agreed saying, "The playoffs are hard enough without any of this stuff." With the Clippers' season over, attention shifted to whether Adam Silver was going to be able to force Donald Sterling to sell the franchise.

On May 13th, two days before the Clippers were eliminated from the playoffs, Shelly Sterling attended a meeting with Adam Silver in New York City. For the past 33 years, Shelly shared ownership of the Clippers with her husband through a family trust. She had hoped to one day leave the franchise to her children, however this was beginning to seem unlikely. When the NBA filed formal charges against Donald, they also made it clear that they wanted an entirely new ownership group to purchase the team. In other words, as far as the NBA was concerned, Shelly Sterling retaining any share of the franchise was not an acceptable outcome.

Silver told Shelly that he wanted to avoid a legal fight and this mirrored her view. Shelly feared that a prolonged legal battle might lead to the dismantling of the Clippers' current roster. In this scenario, even if the Sterlings were able to prevail in court and maintain ownership of the franchise, they would be left with a shell of a team that no one wanted to play for. Given these concerns, Shelly was coming around to the idea that cooperating with Silver and helping to facilitate the sale of the Clippers might be the best option.

Three days later, Donald Sterling was driven to Cedars-Sinai Medical Center by a friend named Lawrence, where he underwent CT and PET scans to determine if he had dementia. The idea that Donald might be suffering from dementia was first raised by Shelly, who had noticed troubling warning signs over the previous year, such as out-of-character mood swings and worrisome bouts of forgetfulness. After watching her husband's interview on Anderson Cooper's show, Shelly became convinced that something was wrong. This man making inflammatory statements about Magic Johnson was not the same person who she married 59 years earlier. So when Shelly returned to Los Angeles after meeting with Silver, she asked Donald to get himself checked-out and he agreed.

Donald was examined by Dr. Meril Sue Platzer. She put him through a standard mental status exam, which included tasks such as being able to spell the word "world" backwards and count backwards from 100 by increments of seven. Donald was unable to complete either task. He was also unaware of what season it was and had difficulty drawing a clock, an activity that most third graders can complete with relative ease. Platzer concluded that Donald had Alzheimer's disease, the most common form of dementia.

On Thursday May 22nd, the Sterlings got a second opinion from Dr. James Spar, a professor specializing in geriatric psychiatry at UCLA. During this assessment, Donald got so frustrated while trying to complete a seemingly simple connect-the-dots task that he threw his pen down and stormed out of the room. Spar concluded that Donald was "substantially unable to manage his finances and resist fraud and undue influence." He confirmed Platzer's diagnosis, saying that Donald was "no longer competent to act as trustee of his trust."

On that same day, Donald and Shelly decided it was time to sell the Clippers. Douglas Walton, the couple's longtime personal attorney, sent a letter to the NBA that read, in part: "Mr. Sterling agrees to the sale of his interest in the Los Angeles Clippers." The letter also authorized Shelly to negotiate the sale on behalf of the family trust. If it meant avoiding a messy legal battle, the league was prepared to work with Shelly to sell the team and she was provided with a list of potential buyers.

Two days later, Shelly was awoken at 7am by the sound of a ringing phone. When she picked up the receiver, she was greeted by a boisterous, booming voice that belonged to the man who was about to become the new owner of the Los Angeles Clippers.

Steve Ballmer was just 24 years old when he made a decision that would change his life forever. At the time, he was studying at Stanford Business School when a friend approached with a job offer to be the business manager of a new software company. The salary was $50,000 and Ballmer would also receive 10% of all profits that he generated. The friend's name was Bill Gates and the software company was Microsoft. Ballmer dropped out of Stanford, moved to Seattle and began working for Microsoft in 1980.

Over the next few years, computers went from being a boutique item to a standard device used in homes and workplaces everywhere. This rapid increase in computer ownership helped to transform Microsoft from a relatively small tech company to one of the largest and most powerful corporations in the world. And as Microsoft's profits increased exponentially, so did the size of Ballmer's bank balance. Ballmer eventually agreed to cancel the profit-sharing clause in his contract in exchange for becoming an 8% owner of Microsoft and by 2000, he had risen all the way to the position of CEO, a title that he held for the next 14 years. During this time, revenues and profits continued to soar and with Ballmer wisely deciding to hang onto the bulk of his shares, he soon became one of the wealthiest men on the planet. In the mid-2000s, Ballmer began to explore ways in which he could use some of his fortune to purchase an NBA team.

Ballmer's love affair with hoops dated back to his time as a teenager, when he was a student at Detroit County Day School. Lacking the necessary skills to play for the school's varsity squad, Ballmer signed on as team manager, looking after equipment and cheering on from the bench. As an undergraduate student at Harvard, he moonlighted as a statistician for the school's basketball team and he was also well known for his love of early morning scrimmages while working at Microsoft.

Ballmer's first serious run at becoming an NBA owner came in March 2008. Amid fears that the Seattle Supersonics were about to be relocated to Oklahoma City, Ballmer led a group of local investors who pledged $150 million towards a proposed $300 million renovation of the Sonics' home court, KeyArena. This was part of a failed plan to purchase the Sonics and keep them playing in Seattle[289]. Four years later, Ballmer was involved in another ownership bid, joining forces with hedge fund manager Chris Hansen in an attempt to purchase the Sacramento Kings and move them to Seattle. However, this also fell through.

By early 2014, Ballmer was in his final days at Microsoft, after announcing his retirement as CEO a few months earlier. While Microsoft was extremely profitable during Ballmer's reign, the company also received

---

289 At the end of the 2007-08 NBA season, the Sonics were re-branded as the Thunder and moved to Oklahoma City.

plenty of criticism for missing the boat on important technology trends, including failing to capture the market in areas such as mobile devices and the internet. Ballmer's imminent departure from Microsoft only strengthened his desire to get involved in the NBA. He briefly considered purchasing the Milwaukee Bucks and possibly moving the franchise to Seattle, before fate, in the form of the Sterling scandal, intervened.

It was Ballmer's son, Peter, who first planted the seed in relation to purchasing the Clippers. The morning after the Sterling-Stiviano audio was released, Peter called his dad and predicted that the Clippers were about to enter the marketplace. Ballmer initially had his doubts, wondering what Sterling could possibly have said that would trigger such an unlikely chain of events. Peter assured his father that the Clippers longtime owner was in serious trouble and urged him to listen to the tape for himself. Ballmer did and yet he remained unconvinced.

Still, Ballmer suspected that some sort of severe penalty was coming Sterling's way. He contacted other NBA owners that he knew for advice, including Portland's Paul Allen and Dallas' Mark Cuban, and was told to "get (his) face out there." So, on the day that Sterling's lifetime ban was announced, Ballmer flew to Los Angeles and attended his first ever Clippers game. After watching the Clippers secure an emotional Game 5 victory over the Warriors, he was convinced that he *had* to find a way to buy the team.

Ballmer next spoke with Adam Silver, who recommended that he contact Donald or Shelly directly. June 3rd was the date that had been set aside for the rest of the league to vote on the motion to terminate the Sterlings' ownership. Up until this day, Donald and Shelly remained the franchise's legal owners and thus they were free to negotiate a sale in the same manner as any of the NBA's 29 other owners.

Ballmer called Shelly on the morning of May 24th and immediately showed off his enthusiastic and exuberant nature, offering to fly down from

Seattle to speak with her immediately. Instead, they agreed to meet up the following day, at Shelly's Malibu beachfront mansion. When they sat down to talk, one of the first questions Shelly asked was about the likelihood of Ballmer trying to move the Clippers to Seattle. It was a reasonable query, given that Ballmer's previous NBA ownership bids centered on having the teams in question based in Seattle. He assured Shelly that relocating the Clippers was not part of his future plans, as it would result in a significant decrease in the franchise's value.

Ballmer then tried to steer the conversation away from financial matters, speaking instead about his passion for basketball and his desire to see the Clippers bring a championship to the city of Los Angeles. He managed to make a good first impression and the discussion continued into the evening, with the two sharing dinner at Nobu, an upscale sushi restaurant. By the end of the evening, Ballmer had formed the view that purchasing the Clippers was now a distinct possibility. Shelly's legal team was fronted by Pierce O'Donnell and he told all interested parties that bids had to be submitted by May 28th, giving Ballmer just three days to put something together. With this in mind, Ballmer decided not to fly back to Seattle. Instead, he extended his stay at the Peninsula Hotel in Beverly Hills and set about putting a competitive bid together.

O'Donnell received three formal bids- $1.2 billion from a consortium that included former NBA All-Star Grant Hill, $1.6 billion from another group which was fronted by entertainment mogul David Geffen and Ballmer's which was somewhere around the $1.9 billion mark. Just a few weeks earlier, the Milwaukee Bucks sold for $550 million, setting a new NBA record for the sales price of a franchise. Therefore, most observers believed that Ballmer's offer was extremely generous and likely to be the successful bid.

However, Shelly's legal team was not blown away. In fact, they suspected that Ballmer was prepared to pay even more and over the next 24 hours, they continued to push for additional money. Shelly pitched it as a once in a lifetime deal, telling Ballmer that he probably wouldn't get another opportunity to own an NBA team in a market the size of Los Angeles. She also reminded him of just how good the Clippers' playing roster was.

Ballmer eventually caved, increasing his offer to $2 billion and granting Shelly a number of concessions, including two floor seats for all Clipper home games and the official title of "owner emeritus." It was also agreed that if the Clippers ever won an NBA championship, Shelly would receive three championship rings. It seemed that Shelly had managed to negotiate a great deal. The sales price of $2 billion was almost four times what the Bucks had just sold for and around 160 times the original price the Sterlings had paid for the Clippers back in 1981[290].

On May 29th, Shelly and her legal team went to B.J.'s Restaurant & Brewhouse in Century City for dinner. They were set to meet Ballmer later that evening to sign some paperwork and the mood at the table was one of relief. It had been a long few weeks but the saga appeared to be reaching a conclusion. After the meal, they returned to O'Donnell's office and shortly before midnight, Ballmer arrived. He greeted Shelly with a hug and assured her that he would take good care of the team. Both parties then signed a term sheet that was sent off to NBA head office for approval. Ballmer had already organized for a deposit of $300 million to be placed in escrow and it seemed that he was on the verge of becoming the new owner of the Los Angeles Clippers.

There was just one small problem.

Donald Sterling had changed his mind.

---

290 While $2 billion seems like an astronomically high amount to pay for an NBA franchise, it was less than 10% of Ballmer's estimated $22.5 billion fortune.

And he was not going to leave the NBA without putting up one hell of a fight.

———

Donald Sterling broadcasted his intention to retain ownership of the Clippers by suing the NBA for $1 billion. His attorney, Max Blecher, said that the lawsuit attempted to address a number of issues, including "invasion of constitutional rights, violation of anti-trust laws, breach of fiduciary duty and breach of contract[291]." However, while Donald wanted to fight the NBA, Shelly remained steadfast in her view that acquiescing to a sale was the family's best option. It turned out that Shelly's take on the matter was even more important than that of her husband.

Donald Sterling may have been the person who was known as the owner of the Los Angeles Clippers but the franchise actually belonged to the Sterling family trust, of which Donald and Shelly were co-trustees. In December 2013, the trust was modified to include a provision outlining protocols to deal with a co-trustee who was suffering from mental incapacity. The new passage stipulated that a co-trustee could be removed from their position if they were unable to conduct their business affairs in a reasonable and normal manner, as determined by two independent doctors.

When Donald made it known that he was no longer cooperating with the sale of the franchise, Shelly sent a letter informing him that she would be taking control of the family trust. She had already obtained two medical reports stating that Donald was suffering from cognitive impairment and Shelly's legal team believed that this gave her the power to sell the Clippers without her husband's approval[292].

---

291 Blecher was the same anti-trust specialist whose services had been retained by Donald Sterling 30 years earlier, when the Clippers moved from San Diego to Los Angeles without the NBA's permission.
292 Donald was still entitled to his share of the proceeds of any sale.

Meanwhile, the league responded to Donald's latest lawsuit by labeling it "entirely baseless." The reason behind this dismissive attitude could be traced to a couple of sentences hidden away in the terms of sale document, in which Shelly had agreed to indemnify the league against future litigation by her husband. This meant that if Donald decided to proceed with his legal action, he would essentially be suing himself, as any money won would be paid out of the family trust.

A few days later, there was another plot twist when one of Donald's attorneys announced that his client had changed his mind. For a brief moment, it seemed that Donald was prepared to sell the Clippers and drop the billion dollar lawsuit. However, when Adam Silver responded by saying there was "absolutely no possibility" that Donald's lifetime ban would be lifted or his $2.5 million fine reduced, this conciliatory tone quickly vanished.

June 9th was a busy day for Donald Sterling. He wrote a letter stating that he was revoking the family trust, left abusive voicemails for both doctors who performed mental examinations on him and allegedly threatened Pierce O'Donnell's life[293]. The next day, Donald released a statement calling the NBA "despicable monsters" and "a band of hypocrites and bullies."

Within 48 hours, Shelly launched a counter-attack. She filed papers seeking an expedited hearing in the Los Angeles Superior Court, hoping to get a legal determination on whether she had followed the correct procedure when Donald was removed as a co-trustee. A ruling in Shelly's favor would validate her position as sole trustee and free the way for the sale of the Clippers to proceed. What started as a fight between Donald Sterling

---

293 O'Donnell claimed that Donald made a death threat during a phone conversation, purportedly saying that he was "going to take (O'Donnell) out." On that same day, Donald also called Dr. Platzer and told her she was a fraud, liar, cheat and a horrible woman and left a message for Dr. Spar, in which he yelled, "I'm not incompetent, you're fucking incompetent, you stupid fucking doctor."

and the NBA had now morphed into a battle between the Clippers' owner and his wife.

When the trial began, Donald continued to showcase the same erratic behavior that had been on display from the moment the scandal first broke. On day one, he failed to turn up at the courthouse, despite being subpoenaed to give evidence. During the trial's second day, he spent an hour on the witness stand and it was like watching John McEnroe interact with a chair umpire after a series of questionable line calls. Donald called Shelly's lawyer a "smartass" and at one stage told him to "stand up and be a man." When it was suggested that his attempts to retain ownership of the Clippers were more about appeasing his ego, Donald replied, "You're wrong, just like you've been wrong on every question you've asked today." Donald also alleged that the two doctors who declared him mentally incompetent were hired guns who had been directed to reach that conclusion and even accused Dr. Platzer of being intoxicated on the day that she examined him.

In amongst this antagonistic and combative performance, Donald managed to address his indecisiveness when it came to the issue of whether he should sell the team. He confirmed that he had consented to the sale at one point, but said this was only because he thought Shelly was going to retain a share of the franchise. He backed out of the deal once it became clear that Ballmer was purchasing a 100% stake of the Clippers. When Donald spoke about his wife, he cried and said she was "beautiful, wonderful and intelligent."

On day three of the trial, Donald called Shelly a "pig." The remark came after she testified about organizing for her husband to undergo tests to determine if he was suffering from dementia. Donald said he had been deceived by his wife and proclaimed that he would "never, ever sell (the) team."

When Dick Parsons, the Clippers interim CEO, took to the stand, he painted a very bleak picture of the franchise's future if Donald was able to maintain ownership, saying the organization would enter into a "death spiral". "If none of your sponsors want to sponsor you and your coach doesn't want to coach for you and your players don't want to play for you, what do you have?" Parsons asked rhetorically. Sponsors and players wanting to head for the hills was hardly considered news, but the idea that Doc Rivers might also walk away from his $7 million a year coaching job grabbed people's attention. "(Rivers) has told me that if Mr. Sterling continues to own the team," Parsons said, "he doesn't think he wants to continue as coach."

In the final days of the trial, Donald Sterling called Steve Ballmer and asked him to come to Los Angeles so they could sit down for a face-to-face meeting. Ballmer was unsure of what Donald wanted to discuss but keen to broker some peace and finalize the sale, he flew to California the next day. They met at Donald's Beverly Hills home and spent over an hour talking. During that time, Ballmer attempted to sell his vision for the future, with him as the Clippers' owner. However, Donald remained steadfast that he would not sell the team and Ballmer flew back to Seattle, no closer to finding a resolution.

On July 28th, Judge Michael Levanas handed down his decision, ruling that Shelly had acted within the terms set out in the family trust when she organized for her husband to undergo cognitive testing. This was an emphatic victory for the plaintiffs and it cleared the way for the sale of the Clippers to proceed. The NBA praised the verdict, releasing a statement that said, "We are pleased that the court has affirmed Shelly Sterling's right to sell the Los Angeles Clippers to Steve Ballmer. We look forward to the transaction closing as soon as possible."

Ballmer was vacationing in Montana on the morning that Levanas issued his final order. He had already been given the thumbs up to become the new owner of the Clippers by the NBA's board of governors, who voted 29-0 in favor of the former Microsoft CEO. This meant that there was just one more step required to complete the purchase. At 8:40am, while strolling past a picturesque lake, Ballmer gave orders over the phone for the remaining $1.7 billion to be transferred to the Sterling family trust. In a matter of minutes, the money was gone from his account and he officially became just the third person to own the Clippers. Ballmer said he felt "humbled and honored" and promised to do whatever was necessary to bring out the team's best.

However, while most people assumed that the fight for the Clippers was now over, Donald Sterling was determined to go down swinging. On the same day that Ballmer's purchase of the franchise was announced, Donald petitioned California's 2nd Court of Appeal to either prevent or overturn the transaction. This latest attempt to disrupt the sale was described by Pierce O'Donnell as "patently frivolous" and "not even a good Hail Mary pass." It took less than 24 hours for the appeal to be rejected, with the ruling stating that the sale of the Clippers had closed and therefore "there is nothing for this court to say."

This swift dismissal from the appeals court brought an end to Donald Sterling's 33 years as the owner of the Clippers[294]. During this time, the franchise had experienced a run of consistent failure that was unlike anything else seen in the history of professional sports. Under Sterling's stewardship, the Clippers qualified for the post-season on just seven occasions, won three playoff series and were never able to progress past the second round. Meanwhile, there were 22 different seasons where the team managed to lose 50 games or more[295].

---

[294] It took nearly two years for Donald's other major lawsuit in relation to the sale of the Clippers to be resolved and this case also ended with a humbling defeat. In May 2014, Donald sued the NBA for violating anti-trust laws, asking for $1 billion in damages and in March 2016, a federal judge dismissed these claims, saying that he was "skeptical Sterling suffered any injury at all, let alone an anti-trust injury."

[295] And that is not counting the lockout-shortened 1999 season in which the team suffered 41 defeats in just 50 contests.

Monday August 18th was the beginning of another working week for employees from across America. However, for the 130 people who worked behind the scenes for the Los Angeles Clippers, this was a special morning. The past few months had been rough for everyone who was connected with the franchise. But while the plight of the players and coaches had received plenty of attention, the impact of the Sterling scandal on the people who sold season tickets, worked with the media and chased down potential sponsors had gone practically undetected. Every day for the past four months, these men and women continued to do their jobs. And every day, they were confronted with a slightly different version of the same question from friends, family and strangers- *"How can you work for a man like Donald Sterling?"*

When Steve Ballmer walked into Clipper headquarters, it was clear that this was the first day of a new beginning. He delivered the kind of bombastic speech that made him a YouTube legend while working at Microsoft, enthusiastically raising his voice as he told the assembled employees to approach their jobs with passion. The start of the next NBA season was still ten weeks away and yet, it was hard not to feel excited by this display of raw emotion, especially after so many years of working for Donald Sterling. "I didn't buy this team to be mediocre," Ballmer proclaimed. "It's show time."

CHAPTER 21

There Are No Hollywood Endings Here

"Everybody wants this story to end with the guys who had to live through it succeeding."

STEVE BALLMER

GAME 7 OF THE CLIPPERS first round playoff series was less than ten minutes old when disaster struck. With the score 22-20 in favor of San Antonio, Chris Paul stole the ball from Boris Diaw, after the Spurs big man carelessly dribbled into a double team. Paul then charged up the right sideline, stopped outside the arc and buried a three-point shot to give the Clippers a one point lead. The Staples Center crowd was so busy cheering Paul's dramatic end-to-end play that few people inside the arena noticed him clutching his left hamstring just seconds before hitting the three-pointer.

At the next stoppage, Paul was substituted out of the game and as he slumped down on the sidelines with his head in his hands, it was clear that something was wrong. Less than a minute later, he slowly made his way from the bench to the locker room in order to have his injured leg assessed in private. Without Chris Paul, a Game 7 victory over the Spurs seemed extremely unlikely, leaving long-suffering Clipper fans to wonder whether their beloved team was ever going to catch a break.

Season XXXVII: 2014-15

Steve Ballmer's first major decision as the new owner of the Los Angeles Clippers was to appoint Doc Rivers as the franchise's president of basketball operations, while also signing him to a five year, $50 million contract extension. This placed Rivers in a rare position of power, as he was one of just two NBA head coaches who also had the final say on player personnel matters[296]. However, rather than take advantage of this newly acquired authority, Rivers chose to make minimal changes to the roster. Therefore the Clippers headed into the 2014-15 season with an almost identical collection of players as the group that had fallen short during the previous campaign.

It wasn't until January that Doc Rivers made his first significant trade and it was a deal that raised more than a few eyebrows around the league. Doc created the first father-son, coach-player combination in NBA history when he traded away Reggie Bullock and Chris Douglas-Roberts in order to acquire Austin Rivers from the Boston Celtics.

Two and a half years earlier, Austin appeared destined for a long and productive NBA career when he was taken with the tenth overall selection by New Orleans in the 2012 draft. He was a former high school All-American who had played well during the one season that he spent at Duke, averaging 15.5 points per game. However, once Austin arrived in New Orleans, he struggled, averaging 6.9 points per game while shooting just 39% from the field. Given his mediocre form, many observers openly questioned Doc Rivers' motives for making the trade, wondering whether his judgement

---

296 The other was Stan Van Gundy, who had been hired as Detroit's head coach and president of basketball operations just a few months earlier.

had been clouded by family loyalties. All of which only served to place more pressure on the young shoulders of Austin Rivers.

By the time the league paused for All-Star weekend, the Clippers had accumulated a 35-19 record. Blake Griffin and Chris Paul were again selected as All-Stars, the fourth consecutive year that the teammates had been invited to participate in the league's showcase event. Unfortunately, Griffin was unable to play due to a staph infection in his right elbow. In his absence, Paul was pivotal in the West's 163-158 victory, finishing with a game-high of 15 assists.

Griffin eventually needed to have surgery on his elbow and was unable to resume playing until the middle of March. Griffin's return to the lineup triggered the Clippers' best stretch of the regular season, as they won 14 of their final 15 games to finish with a 56-26 record. This was a one game decline from a year earlier but still good enough to secure the Western Conference's third seed. The good news was that the Clippers were heading into the playoffs with home-court advantage for the third consecutive season. The bad news was that their first round opponent was the San Antonio Spurs.

The Playoffs: Round 1 vs. San Antonio

In the lead-up to Game 1, each player from the Clippers was given a piece of paper that was filled with cut-and-pasted media predictions for their upcoming series against the Spurs. A total of 45 analysts from a variety of media outlets had been asked their opinion on who would progress to the second round. Forty-four picked San Antonio. One was backing the Clippers[297]. And while this document was a source of additional motivation for some of the Clippers players, there were plenty of good reasons why so many people were expecting that they would be knocked out in the first round.

---

297 The lone expert to predict a Clippers victory was Tas Melas from NBA TV's "The Starters."

Ever since Michael Jordan retired from playing for the Chicago Bulls, the San Antonio Spurs have been the standard by which all other NBA teams are measured. During the 16 year period between 1999 and 2014, the Spurs made nine trips to the Western Conference finals, six appearances in the NBA Finals and claimed five Larry O'Brien Trophies. Amazingly, they also won at least 50 games in each and every season throughout this run, with the exception of the lockout-shortened 1999 season[298]. The two constants that fueled this period of sustained excellence were Gregg Popovich and Tim Duncan. Never before in the history of the NBA had a head coach and star player been able to achieve so much success together across such a long period of time[299].

From the Clippers perspective, the Spurs were perhaps the least desirable first round opponent. San Antonio entered the playoffs as the NBA's defending champions, having easily defeated Miami in the previous year's Finals. During the 2014-15 regular season, there had been a slight drop in the Spurs' form but they still managed to compile a 55-27 record. The Clippers had firsthand knowledge of just how formidable a playoff opponent San Antonio could be, having been brushed aside in an embarrassing 4-0 series sweep in 2012.

In Game 1, the Clippers ensured that they would not be the victim of another sweep, securing a 107-92 win in front of a boisterous home crowd. The Clippers were led by Griffin, who almost singlehandedly turned a close contest into a blowout during the third period. Griffin terrorized San Antonio's back-up center Aron Baynes, dunking over him on three separate occasions and blocking his shot twice, all in the final six minutes of the quarter. During this time, the Clippers' four point lead mushroomed into a 15 point margin. Griffin eventually finished with 26 points, 12 rebounds

---

[298] During the 1999 campaign, the Spurs played a *total* of just 50 games, winning 37 of them before eventually claiming their first NBA title. San Antonio even managed to win 50 games during the 2011-12 season, despite playing a 66 game schedule due to the second NBA lockout.
[299] The closest comparison would be Red Auerbach and Bill Russell, who won eight championships in nine years.

and 6 assists and was ably supported by Chris Paul (32 points) and DeAndre Jordan (14 rebounds and 4 blocks).

In Game 2, the Clippers let an excellent opportunity to build a 2-0 series lead slip through their fingers. With just 32 seconds remaining, the Clippers had both the ball and a two point advantage. However, Griffin's sloppy ball handling resulted in a turnover that triggered a fast break opportunity for the Spurs. Patty Mills was eventually fouled in the act of shooting and he calmly converted both free throws, sending the game into overtime. In the extra period, the Spurs put on a clinic, scoring on all but two of their ten possessions and running away with a 111-107 victory. San Antonio was led by Duncan, who scored 28 points, while for the Clippers, Griffin recorded a rare playoff triple double (29 points, 12 rebounds and 11 assists).

Game 3 was a blowout. The Spurs turned up the defensive pressure in the third period, forcing the Clippers to miss 16 of their 20 field goal attempts and limiting them to just 11 points. At one stage in the fourth quarter, the score was 92-55 in favor of San Antonio, before the Clippers staged a late rally to reduce the final margin to 27 points. Kawhi Leonard, who received the NBA's Defensive Player of the Year award prior to the game, showed off his offensive ability, leading all scorers with 32 points. Meanwhile, no one from the Clippers was able to score more than 14 points.

Doc Rivers had less than 40 hours to prepare for Game 4 and he chose to spend two and half of these precious hours reviewing the tape of Game 3 with the rest of the team. As he sat watching the lackluster effort from the previous evening, Rivers spoke openly about what he felt was preventing the Clippers from playing up to their potential. On top of highlighting what they had done poorly in Game 3, Rivers also tried to impart one crucial message- it was up to the players to seize the initiative if the Clippers were ever going to achieve success in the playoffs. It was a message that the team took to heart.

Chris Paul typified the Clippers' approach to Game 4 when he appeared on the floor of the AT&T Center for a shoot-around over three hours prior to tip-off. And when the game finally got underway, it was clear that this was not the same Clippers team that had surrendered so meekly in the second half of Game 3. The Clippers played with poise and purpose, pulling away for a 114-105 victory that evened the series at two-all. As had been the case for the entire season, the Clippers were led by their dynamic duo of Paul (34 points and 7 assists) and Griffin (20 points, 19 rebounds and 7 assists). However, perhaps the least likely hero of this crucial road victory was Austin Rivers, who contributed 16 points off the bench, on 7 for 8 shooting from the field.

Game 5 was decided by a referee's whistle that came in the final moments of the contest. With just 6.9 seconds remaining, Griffin caught an inbounds pass and lofted a right-handed floater over the out-stretched arms of Tim Duncan. The ball bounced softly on the rim and for a split second, it seemed as if the basketball gods were deciding whether they should allow it to fall into the net or not. However, this decision was quickly taken away from any cosmic force, when DeAndre Jordan appeared on the opposite side of the lane and tipped the ball through the hoop.

The Clippers had a one point lead.

Or at least this would have been the case, had the referees not waved the basket away after calling offensive goaltending on Jordan. From here the Clippers were forced to foul and the Spurs converted 3 of 4 free throws, resulting in a final score of 111-107.

After the game, there was much speculation about whether Griffin's shot would have gone in had Jordan not interfered. One person who believed this to be the case was San Antonio veteran Manu Ginobili, who called his side's win "lucky." Meanwhile, Jordan, who finished the game with 21 points and 14 rebounds, attempted to shoulder the blame for the defeat, labeling his last second tip-in a "dumb play."

After 37 years, the Clippers had somehow stumbled across yet another way to lose a game and the majority of the Staples Center crowd left the arena feeling a mixture of shock and disappointment. With San Antonio now holding a 3-2 series lead and Game 6 scheduled to be played at the AT&T Center, there was an overwhelming sense that the Clippers were about to be eliminated from the 2015 playoffs.

Gregg Popovich and Tim Duncan had been involved in 13 different playoff series in which they entered Game 6 with a 3-2 series lead. On 12 of these occasions, San Antonio won the next game and ended the series[300]. On top of this daunting statistic was the fact that the Spurs had won their past seven close-out games at home, in a streak that dated back to 2006. Given the magnitude of the challenge that the Clippers were facing, Doc Rivers tried to get his players to focus on staying in the moment in the lead-up to the Game 6. "Don't use the word 'elimination'," Rivers told his team. "The 'E' we use is 'execution'."

Unfortunately for the Clippers, in the early stages of Game 6, Blake Griffin and Chris Paul were both having trouble executing. They missed a combined total of 12 of their first 15 field goal attempts and yet at half-time, the score was knotted at 51-all. In the third period, Griffin finally found his niche, scoring 10 points and helping the Clippers build a 66-58 lead.

Griffin's strong effort continued into the fourth quarter, where he added another 8 points, 4 rebounds and 3 assists. Behind the excellent play of Griffin, the Clippers maintained a buffer of between four and seven points for the majority of the final period. And when Jamal Crawford converted a mid-range jumper, increasing the margin to six points with less than 90

---

300 And had it not been for a miraculous three-pointer from Ray Allen with five seconds remaining in Game 6 of the 2013 NBA Finals, it would have been a perfect 13 for 13.

seconds remaining, it looked like the Clippers had secured arguably the biggest win in the history of the franchise.

However, the Spurs were not prepared to concede defeat just yet.

On San Antonio's next possession, Marco Belinelli hit an open three-pointer to cut the deficit in half. Paul responded with a tough floater but this was followed by another long-range bomb from Belinelli, his seventh three for the game. The score was now 98-96, with 15 seconds still to play.

The ball was inbounded to Crawford and as he struggled to regain his balance, he clearly committed a travelling violation. However, the referees failed to call this obvious infraction, forcing Belinelli to foul the Clippers' best free throw shooter. Crawford calmly converted both free throws, increasing the margin to four and putting the game beyond the Spurs' reach. The final score was 102-96.

After the game, the Clippers reflected on what it meant to win a potential elimination game on the road, against a first class franchise like San Antonio. "This is a great team, great organization," Paul said. "A lot of us on our team have been watching these guys since we were kids." However, after allowing himself this brief moment of nostalgia, the Clippers point guard brought his attention back to the task at hand. Paul knocked on the table for extra emphasis, as he summed up the situation that now confronted his team in one simple sentence.

"It all comes down to Game 7."

Clipper history is not filled with many positive memories. However, one area where the franchise has excelled during recent years is winning Game 7s, even when the team has faced great adversity. In 2012, the Clippers played Game 7 on the road, with their three top-scorers all nursing injuries[301]. And yet, they somehow found a way to beat Memphis and progress to the second round. Two years later, the Clippers first round series was again stretched to a decisive Game 7. This time, they stormed back from a double digit deficit to eliminate a very talented Golden State team, while also dealing with the ongoing fall-out from the Donald Sterling scandal.

So when Chris Paul strained his left hamstring in Game 7 of the Clippers 2015 series against San Antonio, his teammates knew that all hope was not lost. Paul was forced to exit the game with a little under two minutes remaining in the first quarter and the Clippers clinging to a 23-22 lead. Over the next seven minutes, Jamal Crawford made sure that the Spurs would not pull away in Paul's absence, as he either scored or assisted on 14 of the Clippers' next 15 points.

Midway through the second period, Paul re-joined his teammates on the bench and a minute later, he checked back into the game with the score 39-38 in favor of the Spurs. It was immediately clear that Paul's injury was going to have an adverse impact on his lateral movement and explosiveness. Yet despite being somewhat hobbled, he still found a way to have a positive impact on the game. In the third quarter, Paul hit three three-pointers, including a dramatic 37 foot bank shot in the waning seconds of the period that gave the Clippers a 79-78 lead.

All of this drama set the stage for a fourth quarter that was a fitting final act for one of the most entertaining first round playoff series of all-time. The final period featured an astounding 12 lead changes, as the Spurs and Clippers traded blows like prizefighters in the fifteenth round of a heavyweight title fight. In the end, it came down to the final 30 seconds of action.

---

301 Paul, Griffin and Caron Butler.

With the game tied at 107, Doc Rivers elected to put the ball in the hands of Paul, who used an on-ball screen to force a switch and subsequently draw a foul from Tim Duncan. With 13.3 seconds on the clock, Paul converted both free throws, giving the Clippers a 109-107 advantage.

On the next play, Belinelli took a hand-off from Duncan and drove towards the middle of the lane, before elevating for an 18 foot jump shot. However, when DeAndre Jordan did an excellent job of switching off Duncan and contesting the shot, Belinelli made a split second decision to pass the ball. He found Duncan, who drew a foul and calmly made his two free throws, tying the game up at 109-all.

The ball now went back to the Clippers with 8.8 seconds to play. This time Paul, who had barely ventured into the key since hurting his hamstring, drove hard down the right side of the lane. As Duncan came across to help, Paul launched an extremely difficult runner with his body floating *away* from the basket. Paul's shot was almost blocked but the ball sailed less than an inch above Duncan's fingertips, hit the backboard and dropped into the bottom of the net.

The Clippers led by two points with just one second remaining.

Gregg Popovich called a timeout and diagrammed an extremely simple play that was designed to send the game into overtime. Kawhi Leonard made it appear as if he was about to set a screen at the free throw line, before changing direction and cutting back towards the basket. Meanwhile, Boris Diaw threw what appeared to be a perfect inbounds pass. As Diaw's lob pass sailed above the heads of the Clipper defenders, it momentarily looked like Leonard was going to catch the ball in the air and lay it in from point blank range[302]. However, at the same moment that the ball was

---

[302] Some Clipper fans may have felt a little sick as they watch Boris Diaw throw this lob pass to Leonard. Nine years earlier, it was Diaw who threw the inbounds pass that led to Raja Bell's last second three-pointer in Game 5 of the Clippers-Suns series.

leaving Diaw's hands, Matt Barnes was drifting away from Belinelli, who was stationed outside the three-point line on the opposite side of the court. Leonard, who was now right in front of the rim, jumped to catch the ball but Barnes came flying in from the weak side and emphatically knocked the pass away.

The final buzzer sounded.

The Clippers had won Game 7.

Perhaps nobody described the scenes that unfolded next better than Jamal Crawford, who said, "If you wrote a script for a movie, I think that's how the ending would be." As "Celebration" by Kool and the Gang blared from the overhead speakers, Steve Ballmer yelled excitedly, Doc Rivers pumped his fists and the players hugged each other out on the court. Meanwhile, Chris Paul fought to hold back tears after producing arguably the greatest playoff game of his career. Paul finished with 27 points, including 18 in the second half from just 9 field goal attempts. Given the severity of his hamstring injury, this was a truly remarkable performance. He received plenty of support from Griffin, who recorded his second triple double of the series with 24 points, 13 rebounds and 10 assists.

Having eliminated the defending champion San Antonio Spurs, it momentarily appeared as if the Clippers' first post-Donald Sterling season was going to be remembered as a triumphant one. But the NBA playoffs are not designed to play out like the conclusion of a Hollywood blockbuster. Getting past the Spurs simply meant that the Clippers had a second round series to play against the Houston Rockets. For the Clippers, this provided yet another opportunity to progress to the Western Conference finals for the first time in franchise history.

It also presented another opportunity for things to go horribly wrong.

The Playoffs: Round 2 vs. Houston

When it was announced that Chris Paul would not be playing in Game 1, due to his injured hamstring, few people gave the Clippers a chance to win the opening contest of their second round series. The Clippers fell behind by 13 points midway through the second quarter and it appeared to be a foregone conclusion that the Rockets were about to draw first blood. However, the Clippers caught fire in the third quarter, shooting a perfect 6 for 6 from outside the arc. This hot shooting continued in the final period, with 5 more three-point baskets, allowing the Clippers to pull away for an unlikely 117-101 road victory. Blake Griffin compiled his second consecutive triple double with 26 points, 14 rebounds and a new career-high of 13 assists, while Austin Rivers, with 17 points and 4 steals, did an excellent job of filling in for Paul.

In Game 2, Houston struck back with a 115-109 win against a Clippers team that was once again forced to play without their starting point guard. The Rockets were led by their bearded assassin, James Harden, who had just finished second in league MVP voting[303]. Harden bounced back from a below par performance in Game 1 to score 32 points and pass for 7 assists.

When the series shifted back to Los Angeles, the Clippers completely blew the Rockets away, winning their two home games by a combined margin of 58 points. In Game 3, Paul returned to the starting line-up and scored 12 points in 23 minutes. However, it was Rivers who put the game beyond Houston's reach in the third quarter. Rivers scored 16 points in a decisive 23-0 run, helping the Clippers to cruise to a 124-99 victory.

Game 4 was also decided in the third period, as the Clippers outscored the Rockets 43-25, transforming a six point half-time advantage into a

---

303 Steph Curry won the 2015 MVP award with 1198 votes, Harden had 936 votes and LeBron James placed third with 552 votes.

103-79 lead. The final margin of 33 points was the second largest playoff win in Clipper history[304]. DeAndre Jordan led all scorers with 26 points, while Paul showed signs that his injured hamstring was continuing to improve, finishing with 15 points and 12 assists. The Clippers travelled to Houston knowing that, with a 3-1 series lead, they had the Rockets on the ropes. They now needed to win just one of the next three games to book a spot in Western Conference finals.

The knockout punch would not be delivered during Game 5. The Rockets dominated almost every single statistical category, jumping out to an early lead before eventually securing a 21 point victory. In the aftermath of this one-sided defeat, the Clippers were quick to shift their focus to Game 6, which was scheduled to be played in Los Angeles in two days' time. "We still have two more chances," said J.J. Redick. "I'm disappointed about (Game 5) but I expect us to play harder and better on Thursday."

Houston Rockets coach Kevin McHale was waving the white flag. With just over a minute remaining in third quarter of Game 6 and his team trailing by 17 points, McHale substituted James Harden out of the game. This was the basketball equivalent of a political concession speech as without Harden, the Rockets appeared to have no chance of mounting a comeback. Over the next six minutes, McHale chose to keep Harden on the bench and not surprisingly, Houston failed to make any significant inroads into the deficit.

With less than eight minutes to play in the fourth quarter, the Clippers had a double digit lead, prompting the Staples Center crowd to stand and cheer. It was clear that the Clipper faithful were celebrating more than just this one playoff victory. After 37 years of enduring misfortune, they were

---

304 The Clippers beat Golden State by 40 points in Game 2 of their 2014 first round series.

about to witness the Clippers qualifying for the Western Conference finals for the first time in franchise history.

30 seconds later, Houston forward Josh Smith converted a three-pointer.

For Clipper fans, this was hardly cause for alarm. In fact, when Smith made an outside shot it was usually a good sign for opposition teams, as there are two undeniable facts about Josh Smith. One- he liked to shoot three-pointers. And two- he was a terrible three-point shooter.

During Smith's first nine NBA seasons, he attempted 942 three-pointers while playing for Atlanta, of which he missed a total of 675[305]. By the summer of 2013, Smith was a free agent and he signed with Detroit, where he was given a four year, $54 million deal. In his first season with the Pistons, Smith put up a career-high of 265 three-pointers and made less than 27% of them. At the start of the 2014-15 season, Stan Van Gundy was hired as Detroit's new coach and after watching Smith's three-point conversion rate drop below 25% over the first 28 games, Van Gundy decided to release him.

Smith was now free to go wherever he liked and he chose to sign with the Rockets for the remainder of the season. When Smith arrived in Houston, he continued to fire up three-pointers at a frantic pace and he continued to miss considerably more than he made. So Clipper fans were not overly concerned about Josh Smith suddenly getting hot when he hit a wide open three-pointer with seven minutes to play in the fourth quarter of Game 6.

On the Rockets next possession, Smith launched another three from directly in front of the Clippers bench.

It hit nothing but the bottom of the net.

---

305 This equates to a conversion rate of less than 29%.

All of a sudden, the margin was down to just five points and the same people who had been celebrating just a few minutes earlier began nervously glancing at the scoreboard.

A minute later, Smith took advantage of the fact that Blake Griffin was now coming out to the three-point line to guard him, blowing by the Clipper big man for a left-handed lay-in that cut the deficit to three.

The next Houston field goal came after Smith pulled down a defensive rebound, dribbled the length of the floor and threw a beautiful bounce pass to Corey Brewer, who slammed home a two-handed dunk.

The Clippers lead, which was as large as 19 in the late stages of the third quarter, had now been completely erased and the score was tied at 102-all with a little over four minutes to play. Rather than enjoy a comfortable victory, it appeared the Clippers were going to have to scratch and claw to get the win that they needed to end the series.

What happened next was demoralizing, even by Clipper standards.

The Rockets scored on each of their next five possessions while the Clippers missed six shots in a row, turning what looked set to be a tight finish into a humiliating, one-sided defeat. The nail in the coffin came when Smith hit a step-back three-pointer over DeAndre Jordan, increasing Houston's lead to nine points with less than two minutes to play. The margin would grow to 15, before the Rockets settled for a 119-107 win.

In the aftermath of this stunning defeat, Clipper players, coaches and fans all struggled to make sense of what had just occurred. "What could have gone wrong went wrong," said Doc Rivers and it was hard to argue with this summation. The Clippers, who were outscored 40-15 in the final period, went almost seven minutes without converting a single field goal, while the Rockets hit 7 out of their 11 fourth quarter three-point attempts.

Josh Smith was undoubtedly the star of the show, scoring 14 points in an eight minute stretch, including three of four from outside the arc. What made this comeback even more remarkable was the fact that it was done without James Harden, who was neither injured nor in foul trouble and yet spent the entire fourth quarter watching from the bench.

The Clippers did not have long to dwell on this heartbreaking collapse. They did their best to appear confident in the lead-up to Game 7, packing not only for an overnight stay in Houston but also for a subsequent trip to Oakland, where they hoped to be battling it out with Golden State for a spot in the NBA Finals. However, the momentum of the series had clearly shifted and the Clippers were unable to mount any sort of serious challenge to the Rockets during the decisive contest.

The Clippers' first Game 7 possession ended when Matt Barnes caught a pass and immediately stepped out of bounds. On their final possession, Austin Rivers heaved up a three-pointer from 28 feet that hit the wire above the shot clock. In between these two sloppy plays, the Rockets never found themselves trailing, leading by as much as 20 before securing a 113-100 victory. As confetti and streamers poured onto the floor of the Toyota Center, the Clippers trudged back to their locker room, knowing that they had just become the ninth team in NBA history to lose a seven-game series after building a 3-1 lead.

It was a humiliating end to an otherwise promising season.

One year earlier, Clipper fans rejoiced when Steve Ballmer purchased the franchise. Many had believed that their team's continuing bad luck was some form of karmic payback for the sins of their previous owner. However, given the disappointing conclusion to the first post-Donald Sterling season, it was beginning to appear as if the negative aura that surrounded the franchise was bigger than any individual person.

EPILOGUE

Some Things Change and Some Stay the Same

"At the end of the day, until we do something, I guess we are the Clippers."

Doc Rivers

THE 2015-16 SEASON WAS ARGUABLY the most difficult of Blake Griffin's career.

On July 3rd, DeAndre Jordan, Griffin's best friend on the team, decided to leave the Clippers. Jordan, who led the league in both rebounding (15 per game) and field goal percentage (71%) during the previous season, agreed to sign a four year, $80 million contract with the Dallas Mavericks[306]. Then three days later, in one of those it-could-only-happen-to-the-Clippers moments, Jordan had a change of heart, leading to one of the most farcical situations in the history of NBA free agency.

The NBA's moratorium period did not end until July 9th, meaning that while Jordan had given Dallas owner Mark Cuban a verbal assurance that

---

306 Jordan became only the second player in NBA history to shoot above 70% from the field across a whole season, joining Wilt Chamberlin, who shot 72.7% in his final professional season.

he was going to play for the Mavericks, no paperwork had been signed as of yet. Jordan called Griffin on July 6th and told him that he was having second thoughts about leaving Los Angeles. Two days later, a delegation that included Griffin, Chris Paul, J.J. Redick, Doc Rivers and Steve Ballmer, descended on Jordan's Houston home to try and convince their straying center to reverse his decision and stick with the Clippers. By the middle of the afternoon, they had achieved their objective, with Jordan accepting a four year, $88 million offer from Ballmer. However, this was not the end of the saga.

Having already witnessed Jordan go back on his word once, the Clipper contingent decided to remain in his home until he was able to sign the contract and make his commitment to the franchise official. Some watched summer league games on television, some played cards, some ate chicken and some smoked cigars. All were waiting for the stroke of 11pm local time, when the moratorium would end, allowing Jordan to finally put pen to paper. Throughout this time, Cuban, who had also flown to Houston in hope of speaking with Jordan, was given the cold shoulder. Jordan refused to answer Cuban's text messages or calls, much less allow him into the house for a meeting.

Midway through the evening, Griffin decided to make light of the fact that Jordan had effectively barricaded himself in his own home, uploading an image of a chair blocking a door to his Twitter feed. This was one of many attempts to find humor in the situation on social media. Dallas forward Chandler Parsons, who had played an instrumental role in recruiting Jordan, got the ball rolling by tweeting an emoji of a plane, seemingly indicating that he too was flying to Houston. When the Clippers caught wind of Parsons' tweet, they decided to play along. Redick tweeted an emoji of a car. Griffin created the impression that his journey to Houston was a lot more complicated, sending out images of a plane, a helicopter and a car. Paul, who had cut short his Caribbean vacation with LeBron James, Carmelo Anthony and Dwyane Wade in order to fly to Houston, tweeted a banana and a boat[307]. Not to be outdone in the comedy stakes, Paul Pierce, who was about to sign a contract to join the Clippers, sent out a picture of a rocket ship. Even assistant coach Mike Woodson got in on the act, tweeting an emoji of somebody swimming.

At 11:01pm, the circus finally came to an end when Jordan officially re-signed with the Clippers. It was immediately clear that both his indecisiveness and unwillingness to meet with Mark Cuban had rubbed the Dallas Mavericks up the wrong way. Parsons labelled Jordan's actions "unethical" and "disrespectful," while Cuban said, "Never in a million years did I think I'd have to quarantine the guy."

Even with Jordan back in the line-up, the Clippers got off to a slow start, losing 13 of their first 29 games. On Christmas Day, the team received another blow when Griffin tore his left quadriceps in a blowout victory over the Lakers. The initial prognosis was that he would be out of action for at least two weeks. However, it turned out that Griffin's time on the sidelines would be a lot longer than this.

In late January, Griffin was still not ready to resume playing, although he was traveling with the team. The Clippers were in Toronto as part of a five game road trip and on the eve of their match-up with the Raptors, Griffin went out for dinner with Jordan and Matias Testi, the team's assistant equipment manager. Testi and Griffin were close friends but at some point in the evening the discussion at the table became heated, resulting in a physical altercation. Testi ended up with a swollen face. And Blake Griffin ended up with a broken hand.

Griffin was suspended for four games by the Clippers, although given the seriousness of his injured hand, this news was more of a footnote than the headline story. Griffin fractured the fourth metacarpal in his right

---

[307] This was in response to a picture that had surfaced on the internet which showed Paul, James and Wade together in a banana boat.

hand in the fracas with Testi and it would be another two months before he was given medical clearance to resume playing. And when Griffin was ready to return, he then had to serve his suspension, meaning four additional games on the sidelines. He ended up missing a total of 47 games and the Clippers finished the regular season with 53 wins and 29 losses, the team's worst record since Griffin's rookie season.

In the first round of the playoffs, the Clippers faced Portland, a team that they were expected to handle easily, with many experts believing the Blazers had overachieved just by qualifying for the post-season. When the Clippers comfortably won two of the first three games, they looked to be well on their way to a second round match-up with Golden State, who loomed as a much tougher opponent. The Warriors were not only the league's defending champions, they had also set a new NBA record by winning 73 games during the 2015-16 regular season, making them the overwhelming favorites to claim a second consecutive Larry O'Brien Trophy.

On April 24th, the Clippers finally caught a break.

Golden State was playing Houston in their own first round series and like the Clippers, they held a 2-1 edge and seemed to be on the verge of progressing to the next round. However, with just one second remaining in the first half of Game 4, Steph Curry, the league's MVP, slipped on a wet spot and injured his knee. The next day, the Warriors announced that Curry had sprained his right knee and would be forced to spend the next two weeks on the sidelines.

When news of Curry's injury reached the Clippers, it was like Christmas had come eight months early. If they could quickly finish off the Blazers, they faced the prospect of playing a depleted Golden State team, transforming an extremely tough second round series into one that was undoubtedly winnable.

It was a confident Clippers team that walked out onto the floor of Portland's Moda Center for Game 4 of their series against the Blazers. They had endured a challenging season but now, with a path to the Western Conference finals opening up, they were beginning to anticipate a deep playoff run. For once, it seemed that luck was on their side.

With a little over six minutes remaining in the third quarter of Game 4, Portland guard Gerald Henderson drove past Chris Paul and elevated on the right-hand side of the basket. But before Henderson could complete the lay-up, Paul reached in from behind and slapped the ball free. Paul then pounced on the loose ball and charged up the court, shoveling a pass to a wide open J.J. Redick, who was stationed outside the three-point line. As soon as the ball left Paul's hands, it was clear that something was seriously wrong. Rather than move into position for an offensive rebound, Paul grimaced and looked down at his hand.

Twenty seconds later, Paul was pulled from the action and he took no further part in the game. A few minutes after this, Blake Griffin also headed to the bench after aggravating his left quadriceps injury. Without their best two players, the Clippers were defeated by 14 points, meaning that the series was now tied at two games apiece. After the game, a somber Rivers told the media that the prognosis for Paul and Griffin did not look very good and it wasn't long before his worst fears were confirmed.

Paul had broken the third metacarpal in his right hand.

Griffin had re-injured his left quadriceps.

Both would be out for the remainder of the 2016 playoffs.

By now Clipper fans had become accustomed to their players getting injured in the same way that the Boston Celtic faithful are used to watching banner ceremonies. But losing two All-Stars to season-ending injuries in the same playoff game was almost unfathomable. It seemed all that remained was for the Blazers to put the Clippers out of their misery.

Game 5 was back in Los Angeles but even with the home crowd spurring them on, the undermanned Clippers were unable to hold off a Blazers team which clearly smelled blood in the water. Damian Lillard led Portland to a 108-98 victory with 22 points, including 16 in the fourth quarter.

Game 6 started badly, when Austin Rivers, who had been inserted into the starting line-up to replace Paul, received an inadvertent elbow from Blazers forward Al-Farouq Aminu. This left Rivers bleeding profusely from two separate cuts, one above and one below his left eye. He returned to the locker room, where he was inspected by the Clippers medical staff, who quickly decided that he was not going to be able to play for the rest of in the game. However, Rivers was desperate to help his already undermanned teammates, so after pleading his case, he was given 11 stitches and sent back into the game to see how he felt. Rivers was able to play but the swelling around his eye was so bad that he could barely see out of it.

At half-time, it appeared as if the Clippers were facing insurmountable odds. Not only were they playing an elimination game on the road, without the services of their best two players, but now Rivers would be forced to play the second half looking like he had just gone 15 rounds with Mike Tyson. Many Clipper fans had given up hope of securing the victory that was needed to force a Game 7. Defeat was surely coming, the only question that remained was by how wide a margin. And then Austin Rivers produced one of the grittiest playoff performances in recent memory.

At the start of the third quarter, Rivers converted a right-handed runner.

A minute later, he stole the ball from Aminu and passed to Luc Mbah a Moute, who laid it in, drew a foul and made the ensuing free throw.

On the Clippers' next possession, Rivers set Redick up for a three-pointer.

A minute later, Rivers made another runner, this time over the outstretched hands of Portland center Mason Plumlee.

A pair of free throws.

An assist for DeAndre Jordan.

A lay-up.

A finger roll.

A step-back three-pointer in front of Portland's bench.

And a drive and kick to Jamal Crawford, who knocked in a wide open 14 foot jump shot.

The third quarter ended with the Clippers holding a two point advantage and there was no question as to who was responsible for this unlikely turn of events, with Rivers contributing 14 points and 4 assists for the period. Rather than cruise to an easy victory, Portland suddenly found themselves in a dogfight.

The fourth quarter went a little better for the Blazers and with 1:37 remaining in the game, they held a 6 point lead. Once again, the Clippers looked dead and buried but they refused to throw in the towel. They scored on their next three possessions, tying the game up at 103-all with just 32 seconds to play.

On the next trip down the floor, Blazers guard C.J. McCollum failed to convert a point blank shot but in the ensuing battle for the rebound, Clippers forward Jeff Green was whistled for a foul. The Blazers were in the bonus and Plumlee made both free throws, giving Portland a two point buffer with 17 seconds remaining. Jamal Crawford then missed a contested runner and a quick foul once again put Plumlee on the line, where he made one out of two.

Portland now led by three with just 1.5 seconds to play, meaning that the Clippers had one final chance to save the game and their season. The ball was inbounded to Rivers, who caught the pass in front of the scorer's table, took one dribble and heaved up a shot from 42 feet away.

As the ball reached its apex, the buzzer sounded to signal the end of the game.

The crowd at the Moda Center froze to watch as the ball descend towards the basket.

The shot was online.

But it fell a few inches short, grazing harmlessly against the net, before falling to the floor.

The Clippers season was over.

Austin Rivers walked into the post-game press conference wearing a black t-shirt, a choice of color that matched his demeanor. Rivers' body language was reminiscent of somebody who was attending a funeral. He barely made eye contact, constantly shook his head in disbelief and fought back tears as he tried to explain the abrupt ending to the Clippers' season. For supporters of the team, this bleak media session perfectly summed up their feelings at the end of yet another season that promised so much and delivered so little.

Over the past 38 years, Clipper fans have clearly received a raw deal. From Bill Walton's feet to Benoit Benjamin's diet to Michael Olowokandi's attitude to DeAndre Jordan's free throws, bad news has almost always been followed by more bad news. Yet hope for a successful future still burns brightly amongst the Clipper faithful. And with a nucleus of Chris Paul, Blake Griffin and DeAndre Jordan playing under the direction of Doc Rivers, it is easy to see where this unwavering optimism comes from.

If the Clippers are going to finally break through and win the franchise's first NBA championship, they will have to overcome not just the San Antonio Spurs, the Golden State Warriors or the Cleveland Cavaliers, they will also have to stare down the ghosts of Clipper past. And when they do, you can be sure that Clipper supporters from around the world will celebrate like no other NBA fans before them.

After all, it's a party they have been looking forward to for almost four decades.

ACKNOWLEDGEMENTS

Firstly, I would like to thank everyone who took time out of their busy schedules to speak with me. Due to the nature of the book, I was often asking people to discuss some of the darkest times of their careers and yet, it never ceased to amaze me how open and honest people were during their interviews. So, a sincere thank you to Derek Anderson, Pete Babcock, Don Casey, Harvey Catchings, Don Chaney, Lester Conner, Lanard Copeland, Terry Cummings, Earl Cureton, James Donaldson, Johnny Doyle, Mark Eaton, James Edwards, Matt Fish, Tremaine Fowlkes, World B. Free, Barry Hecker, Mark Heisler, Bo Kimble, Tom Liegler, Randy Livingston, Bob Martin, John McBride, Swen Nater, Kurt Nimphius, Norm Nixon, John Olive, Olden Polynice, Pooh Richardson, Larry Roberts, Stanley Roberts, Paul Silas, Gene Shue, Bob Staak, Ron Verlin, Kermit Washington, Bob Weiss, Freeman Williams and Joe Wolf. Your input enriched this project beyond measure.

A special thank you to Jim Lynam, who was not only extremely generous in sharing his memories of what it was like to coach the Clippers during the chaotic years when Donald Sterling first purchased the franchise, he also agreed to write the foreword for the book. I couldn't think of a better storyteller to introduce *The Curse* and I hope you had as much fun reading Jim's words as I did interviewing him.

I would also like to thank those people who spoke to me for the book but asked that their names not be included in the acknowledgements. You know who you are and you know the sizable contributions you have made.

The following books were extremely useful: *Boys Among Men* by Jonathon Abrams, *Fab Five* by Mitch Albom, *The Selling of the Green* by Harvey Araton and Filip Bondy, *Elgin Baylor* by Bijan C. Bayne, *Laker Girl* by Jeanie Buss and Steve Springer, *Rebound!* by Michael Connelly, *The Inside Game* by Wayne Embry and Mary Schmitt Boyer, *Dr. J: The Autobiography* by Julius Erving and Karl Taro Greenfeld, *The Bald Truth* by David Falk, *The Punch* by John Feinstein, *A Season on the Inside* by John Feinstein, *The Breaks of the Game* by David Halberstam, *Obsession* by Bill Heller, *Madman's Ball* by Mark Heisler, *Eleven Rings* by Phil Jackson, *The Last Season* by Phil Jackson, *Ain't No Tomorrow* by Elizabeth Kaye, *24 Seconds to Shoot* by Leonard Koppett, *The Life* by Roland Lazenby, *Mad Game* by Roland Lazenby, *The Show* by Roland Lazenby, *The Big Three* by Peter May, *The Last Banner* by Peter May, *Seven Seconds or Less* by Jack McCallum, *Unfinished Business* by Jack McCallum, *Cavs: From Fitch to Fratello* by Joe Menzer and Burt Graeff, *Manute* by Leigh Montville, *Shaq Uncut* by Shaquille O'Neal, *Showtime* by Jeff Pearlman, *Loose Balls* by Terry Pluto, *Tall Tales* by Terry Pluto, *The Short Season* by John Powers, *The Whore of Akron* by Scott Raab, *Those Who Love The Game* by Doc Rivers and Bruce Brooks, *Perfectly Awful* by Charley Rosen, *Forty-Eight Minutes* by Bob Ryan and Terry Pluto, *Bill Walton* by Jack Scott, *Evergreen* by Dan Shaughnessy, *Kobe Bryant: The Game of His Life* by Jeffrey Scott Shapiro and Jennifer Stevens, *The Book of Basketball* by Bill Simmons, *The Jordan Rules* by Sam Smith, *Second Coming* by Sam Smith, *The Rivalry* by John Taylor, *Nothing But Net* by Bill Walton, *Back From The Dead* by Bill Walton, *Buffalo: Home of the Braves* by Tim Wendel, *Unguarded* by Lenny Wilkens and Terry Pluto and finally *Bad Sports* by Dave Zirin. Thank you to each and every one of these authors for their work.

Acknowledgements | 537

Extensive use was made of a variety of publications and websites, including: ABC News, Above the Rim blog, AOL News, Associated Press, Bloomberg Businessweek, Business Lexington, CBS Sports.com, The Chicago Tribune, Clippers.com, Deadspin, The Denver Post, ESPN The Magazine, ESPN.com, Esquire, Forbes, Grantland, GQ, Green Street blog, Hoops Hype, JeffPearlman.com, The Journal of San Diego History, The Journal Times, LA Weekly, The Los Angeles Daily News, Los Angeles Magazine, The Los Angeles Times, MassLive.com, The Miami Herald, NCAA News, The New York Daily News, The New York Post, The New York Times, NJ.com, The OC Register, The Orlando Sentinel, The Philadelphia Inquirer, The Plain Dealer, The Players' Tribune, The Riverfront Times, The San Diego Union Tribune, The San Jose Mercury News, Slam Magazine, Slate.com, The Sporting News, Sports Illustrated, SportsMedia101.com, Spurs Nation blog, The State, The Sun-Sentinel, The Times-Picayune, Tulsa World, USA Today, The Wall Street Journal, The Washington Post and Yahoo Sports. The following podcasts were also very helpful: The BS Report, The Moment and The Vertical with Adrian Wojnarowski. A special mention goes to the Basketball Reference website, which is quite frankly amazing.

Without the frontline work of the following group of writers and reporters over the past 38 years, this book would not have been possible: Alan Abrahamson, Jonathan Abrams, J.A. Adande, Sam Alipour, Sam Amick, George Anders, Dave Anderson, Kelli Anderson, Kevin Armstrong, Michael Arkush, Kevin Arnovitz, Chris Baker, Chris Ballard, Zack Baron, Kevin Baxter, Jeff Benedict, Ken Berger, Ira Berkow, Ben Bolch, Steven Bondy, Thomas Bonk, Robert H. Boyle, John Branch, Mike Bresnahan, Chris Broussard, Clifton Brown, Tim Brown, Marty Burns, Scott Cacciola, Matt Calkins, Nick Canepa, Matt Caputo, Andrea Chang, John Cherwa, Kim Christensen, Chris Cobbs, Everett Cook, Steve Coomes, Antony Cotton, Jerry Crowe, Seth Davis, Travis Degheri, Linda Deutsch, Sean Deveney, Lisa Dillman, Dave Distel, Tracy Dodds, George Dohrmann, Steve Dolan, Mike Downey, Josh Dubrow, Chris Dufresne, Kelly Dwyer, Bill Dwyre,

Helen Elliot, Nathan Fenno, Mike Fish, Chris Forsberg, Chris Foster, David Friedman, Tom Friend, Jim Furlong, Neal Gabler, Sam Goldaper, Ben Golliver, Michael Granberry, Blake Griffin, Tim Griffin, Isreal Gutierrez, Paul Gutierrez, Bill Haisten, Randy Harvey, Mark Heisler, Steve Henson, Greg Hernandez, Hank Hersch, James Hill, Baxter Holmes, Curt Holbreich, Scott Howard-Cooper, Adam Howes, Tiffany Hsu, Maryann Hudson, James Hughes, Roger Jackson, Scoop Jackson, Lee Jenkins, Greg Johnson, Grahame L Jones, Jim Kaplan, Jesse Kass, Tim Kawakami, Peter Keating, Victoria Kim, Jay King, Curry Kirkpatrick, Gary Klein, Jim Kleinpeter, Tony Kornheisler, Mike Kupper, Monica Langley, Ralph Lawler, Mitch Lawrence, Mark Lelinwalla, David Leon Moore, Stephen Moore, Josh Levin, Franz Lidz, Mike Littwin, Jere Longman, Rich Lorenz, Bill Lubinger, Tim MacMahon, Jackie MacMullen, Rick Maese, Rob Mahoney, Allan Malamud, Kevin Manahan, Chris Mannix, Arash Markazi, Douglas Martin, Peter May, Jack McCallum, Michael McCann, Barry McDermott, Range McDonald, Dave McKenna, Sam McManis, Mark Medina, Fred Mitchell, Jon Mooallem, Matt Moore, Jim Murray, Skip Myslenski, Bruce Newman, Bob Nightengale, Robyn Norwood, Peter O'Boyle III, Scott Ostler, Chris Palmer, Javier Panzar, John Papanek, Eric Patten, Alan Paul, Jeff Pearlman, Jim Peltz, Mike Penner, Charles P. Pierce, Bill Plaschke, S.L. Price, Lance Pugmire, James Rainey, Kenneth Reich, Jason Reid, William C. Rhoden, Ron Reid, Rick Reilly, Danny Robbins, Liz Robbins, Ben Rohrbach, Kurt Rosenberg, Mark Rowland, Chris Ryan, Harriet Ryan, Richard Sandomir, Brian Schmitz, Steve Serby, Andrew Sharp, Ramona Shelburne, Eric Shepard, Alan Siegel, T.J. Simers, Bill Simmons, Kevin Simpson, Sam Smith, Eric Sondheimer, Marc J. Spears, Steve Springer, Marc Stein, Matt Stevens, Larry Stewart, Kurt Streeter, Ethan Strauss, Phil Taylor, Elliot Teaford, Pete Thomas, Chris Tomasson, Marcus Thompson, Ian Thomsen, Rob Trucks, Broderick Turner, Ashlee Vance, Peter Vecsey, Duane Watson, Tom Weir, Mike Wells, L. Jon Wertheim, David Wharton, Lang Whitaker, Lonnie White, Michael Wilbon, Jon Wilner, Ira Winderman, Mike Wise, Billy Witz, Gery Woelfel, Dan Woike, Adrian Wojnarowski and Alexander Wolff.

Thanks to David Sornig, whose advice throughout the project was always extremely helpful. Matthew Minas spent hours transcribing interviews and for this I am eternally grateful. Pat Lucas, Adrian Holdsworth, Simon Hughes and James Minas all read and provided invaluable feedback on some of the earlier drafts of the book and Chris Brock was a fantastic sounding board throughout the project. A sincere thanks to each and every one of you for your input. I would also like to thank Andrew Ryan, for his assistance in tracking down Clipper games and Adam Ryan (no relation) for helping me to organize some of the interviews. Andrew Watt provided legal advice that went above and beyond what we had agreed to and along the way, even became somewhat of a Clippers fan. Thank you also to Greg Korn, whose attention to detail when editing the manuscript was exceptional.

Thanks to everyone who has been a part of the Moonee Ponds Mavericks over the past 25 years, especially the ten Mavs who made the trip to California back in 2008. Had we not been at Staples Center to watch the Clippers lose to the Lakers by 38 points, this book would never have been written. A special thanks to Hrvoje Deak, whose shared fascination for the weird and wonderful world of the Clippers eventually led to the idea to write this book. The feedback you provided on the early drafts of the manuscript helped shape the book. I'm looking forward to when we watch our next Clipper game together.

My mum has supported me throughout my life and this book was certainly no exception. Thanks for your tireless work proof-reading the various drafts of the manuscript and for everything else you have done over the years. Jae Scoleri, thanks for sharing your room. It all went fairly smoothly except for the day you decided that it would be a good idea to hide the articles I was using. Lyn Scoleri, thanks for all of the help you have given to our family. To my dad, who taught me that I could do whatever I wanted to do. I grew up in a household as one of four brothers and we each shared a love for the game of basketball. So to John, Jimmy and Andrew, thanks for all the memories we shared. I am pretty sure we are the only family to ever catch a tram from Ascot Vale to Nunawading just to play a domestic basketball game.

However, the unsung hero of this project is undoubtedly Carla Scoleri. Your support and encouragement throughout the past five and a half years has been nothing short of amazing. I'm not a good enough writer to translate my feelings into words that will properly convey just how grateful I am for everything you have done for me and our boys. So instead, I will keep it simple and say thank-you. And it's finally over!

ABOUT THE AUTHORS

Mick Minas has over two decades experience as a basketball coach and his writing has been published by New Matilda and Prime Number. He graduated from the University of Melbourne in 1998 and currently lives with his wife and two children in Melbourne, Australia. *The Curse* is his first book.

Jim Lynam was the first head coach hired by Donald Sterling, coaching the Clippers from 1983 to 1985. He also coached the Philadelphia 76ers and Washington Bullets as part of a decorated career that spanned five decades. He currently lives in Philadelphia, where he provides pre and postgame analysis for the 76ers on Comcast SportsNet.

Printed in Great Britain
by Amazon